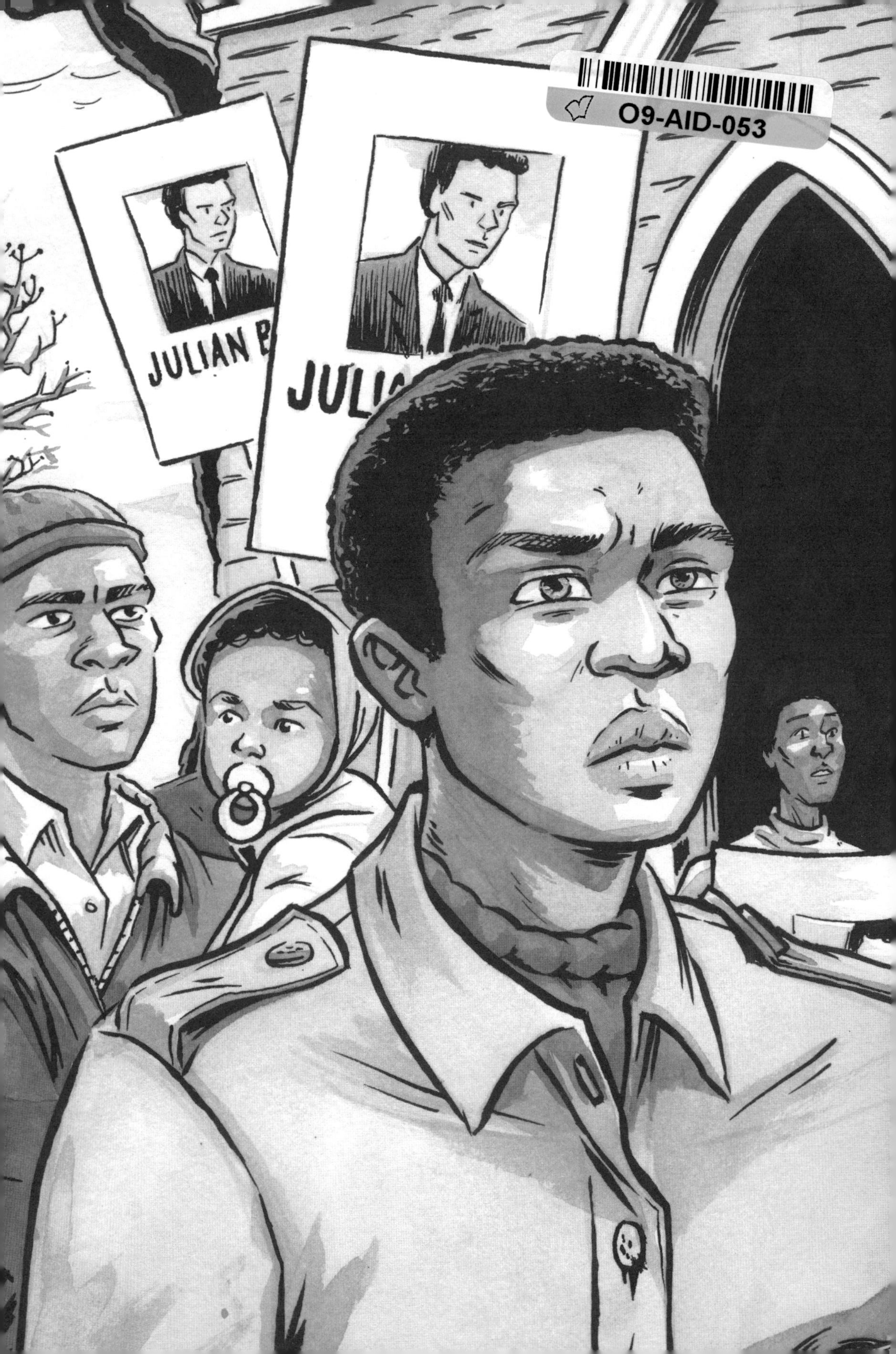
JULIAN B
JULI

RUN

ABRAMS COMICARTS • NEW YORK

GOOD TROUBLE
PRODUCTIONS

To the preachers of hope.

In March 2016, not long after finishing *March: Book Three,* John Lewis began work on *Run* with his co-writer Andrew Aydin. Together they finished the script and worked closely with artists Nate Powell and L. Fury to create this book, reviewing thumbnails, pencils, and inked pages. When Lewis passed in July 2020, the majority of the finished pages had been completed and reviewed.

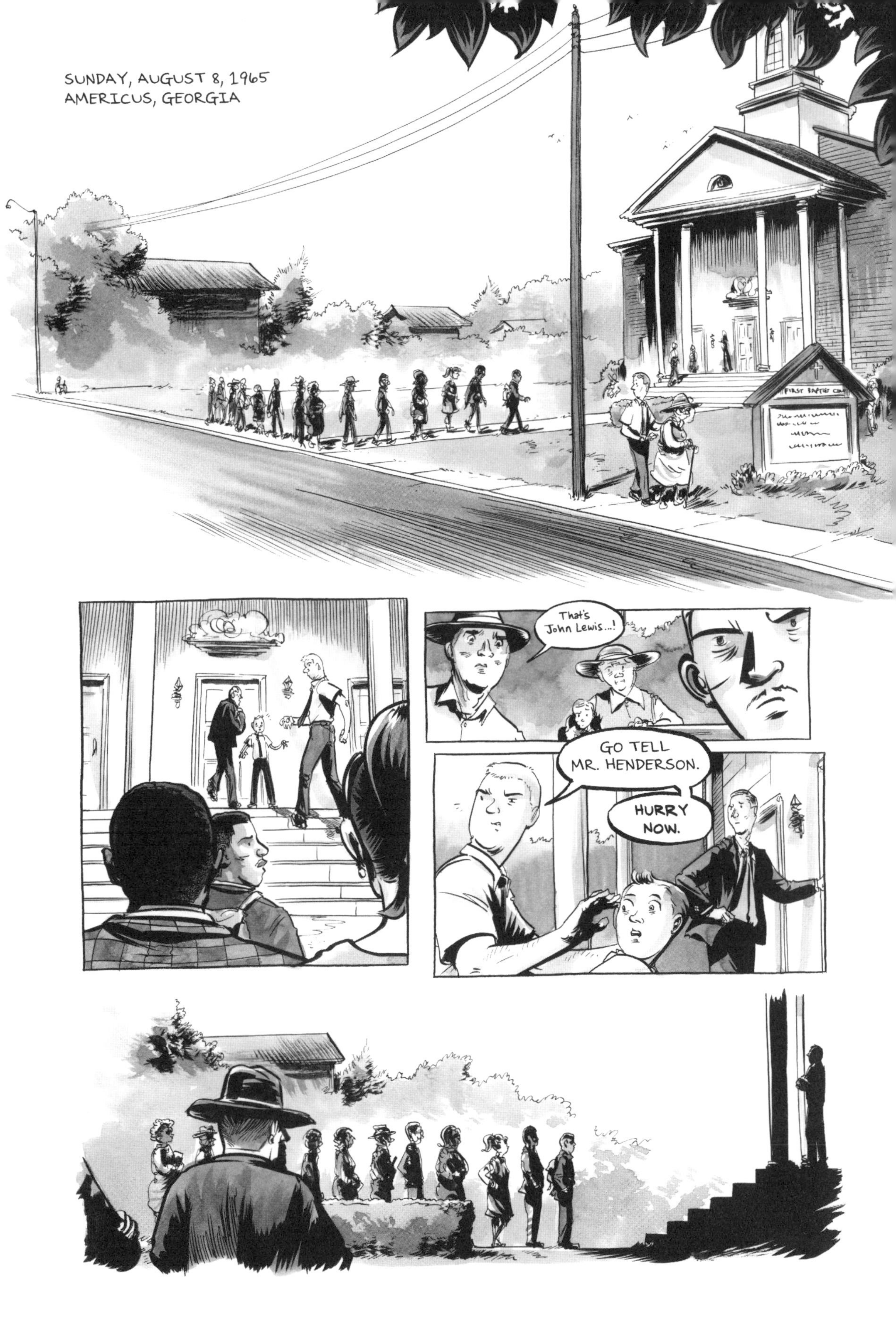
SUNDAY, AUGUST 8, 1965
AMERICUS, GEORGIA
FIRST BAPTIST CH
That's John Lewis...!
GO TELL MR. HENDERSON.
HURRY NOW.

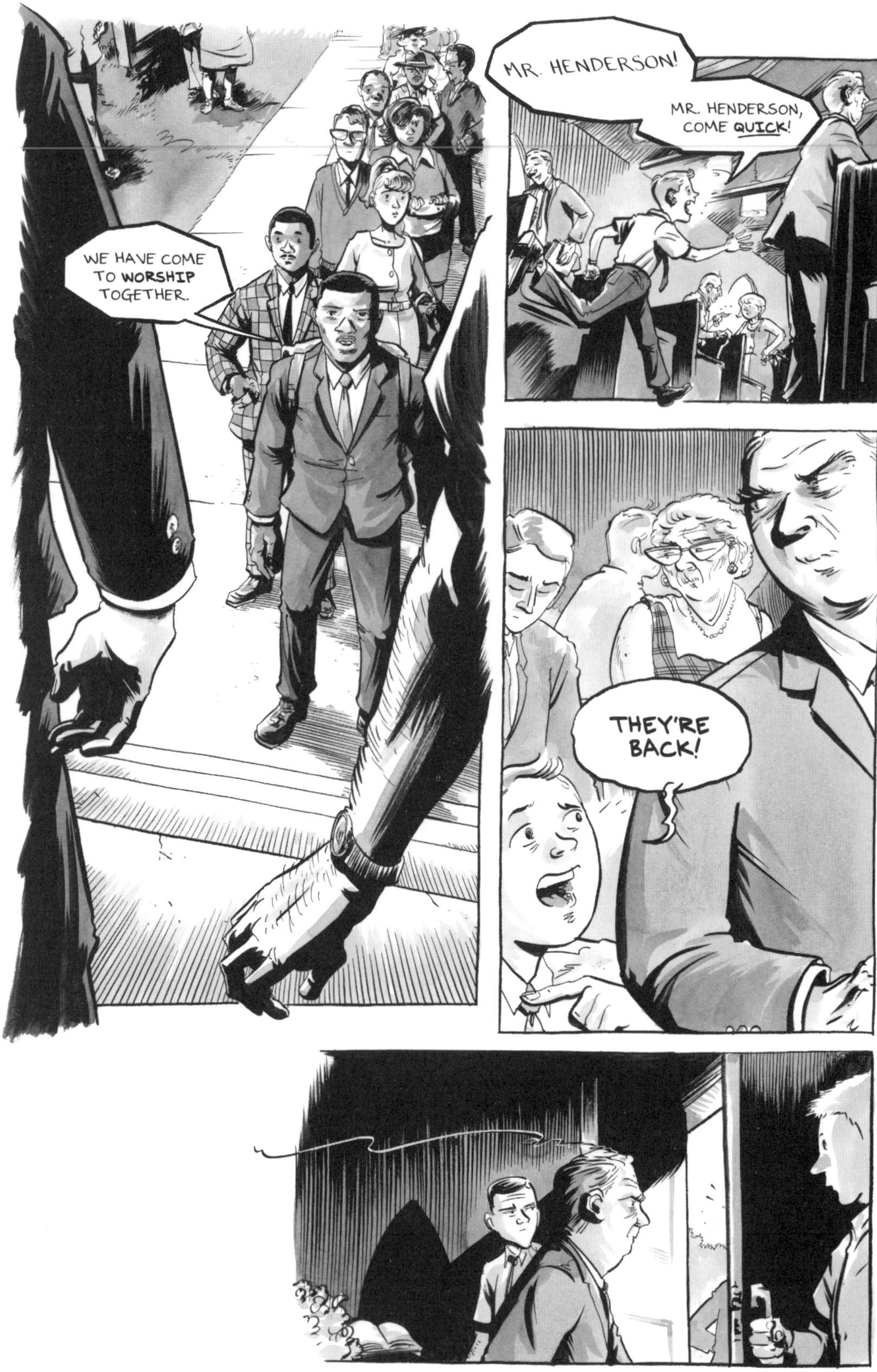
WE HAVE COME TO WORSHIP TOGETHER.
MR. HENDERSON!
MR. HENDERSON, COME QUICK!
THEY'RE BACK!

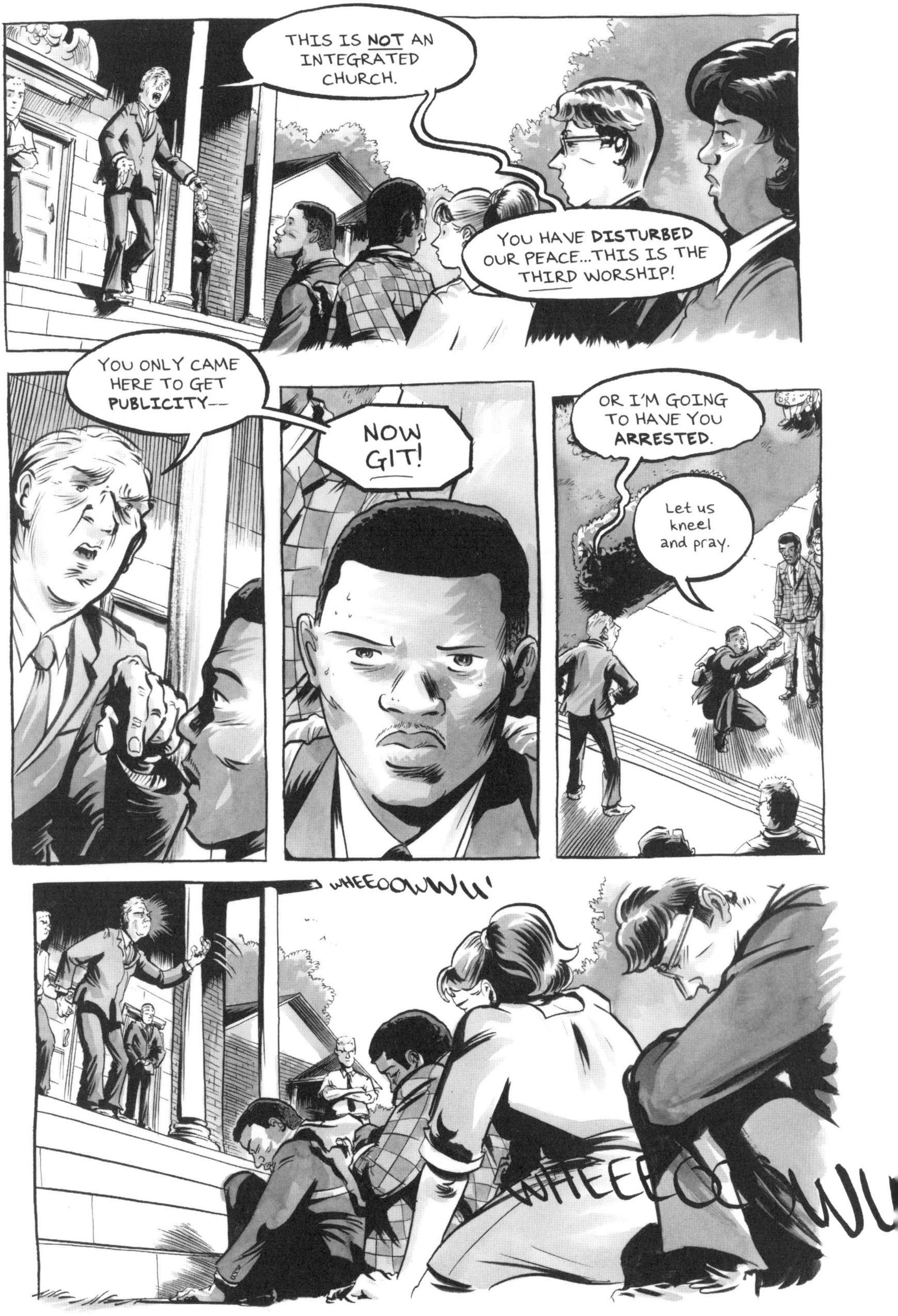
THIS IS NOT AN INTEGRATED CHURCH.
YOU HAVE DISTURBED OUR PEACE...THIS IS THE THIRD WORSHIP!
YOU ONLY CAME HERE TO GET PUBLICITY--
NOW GIT!
OR I'M GOING TO HAVE YOU ARRESTED.
Let us kneel and pray.
WHEEOOWWU'
WHEEEOOOWWU

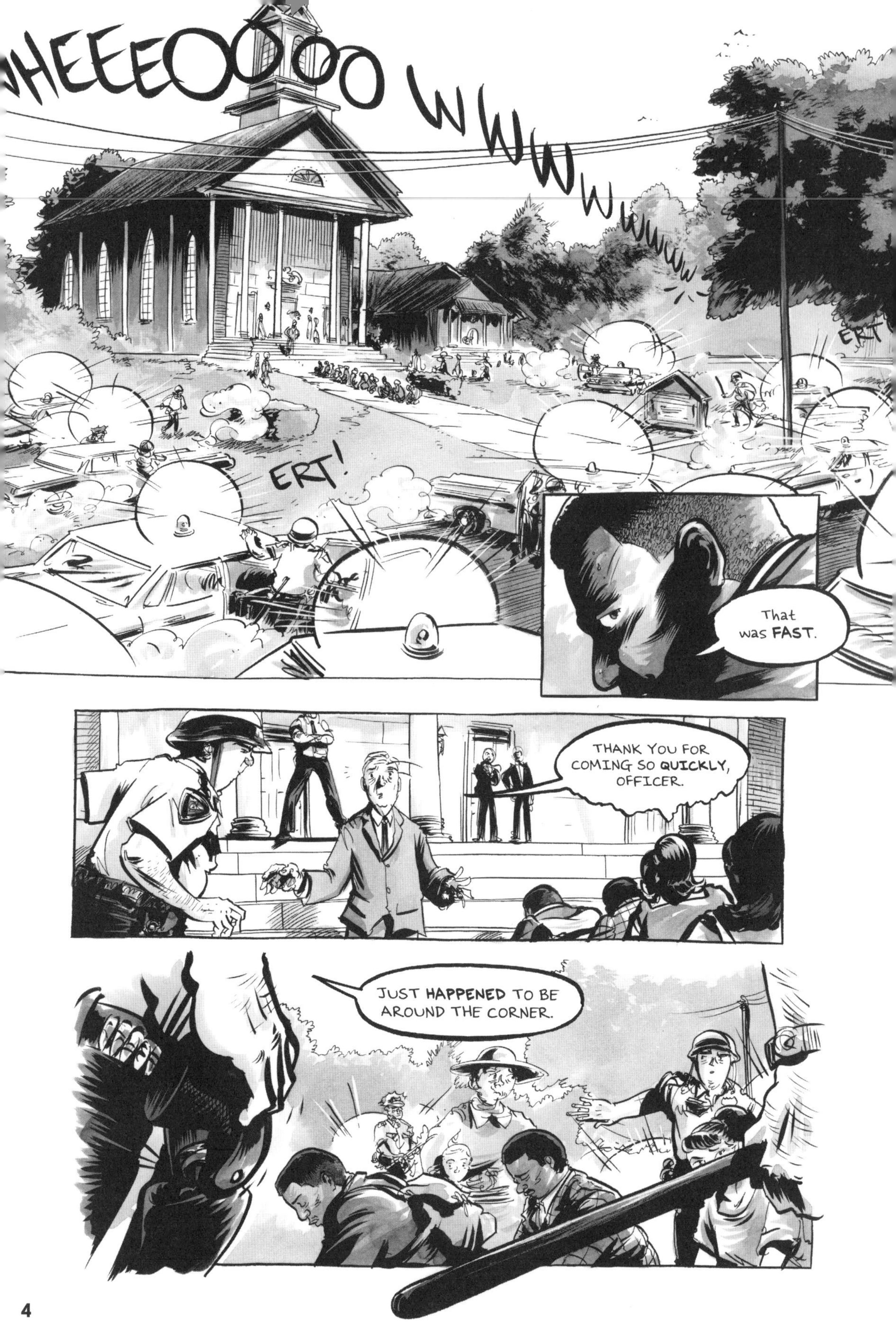
WHEEEOOOO WWWWWWWWW
ERT
ERT!
That was FAST.
THANK YOU FOR COMING SO QUICKLY, OFFICER.
JUST HAPPENED TO BE AROUND THE CORNER.

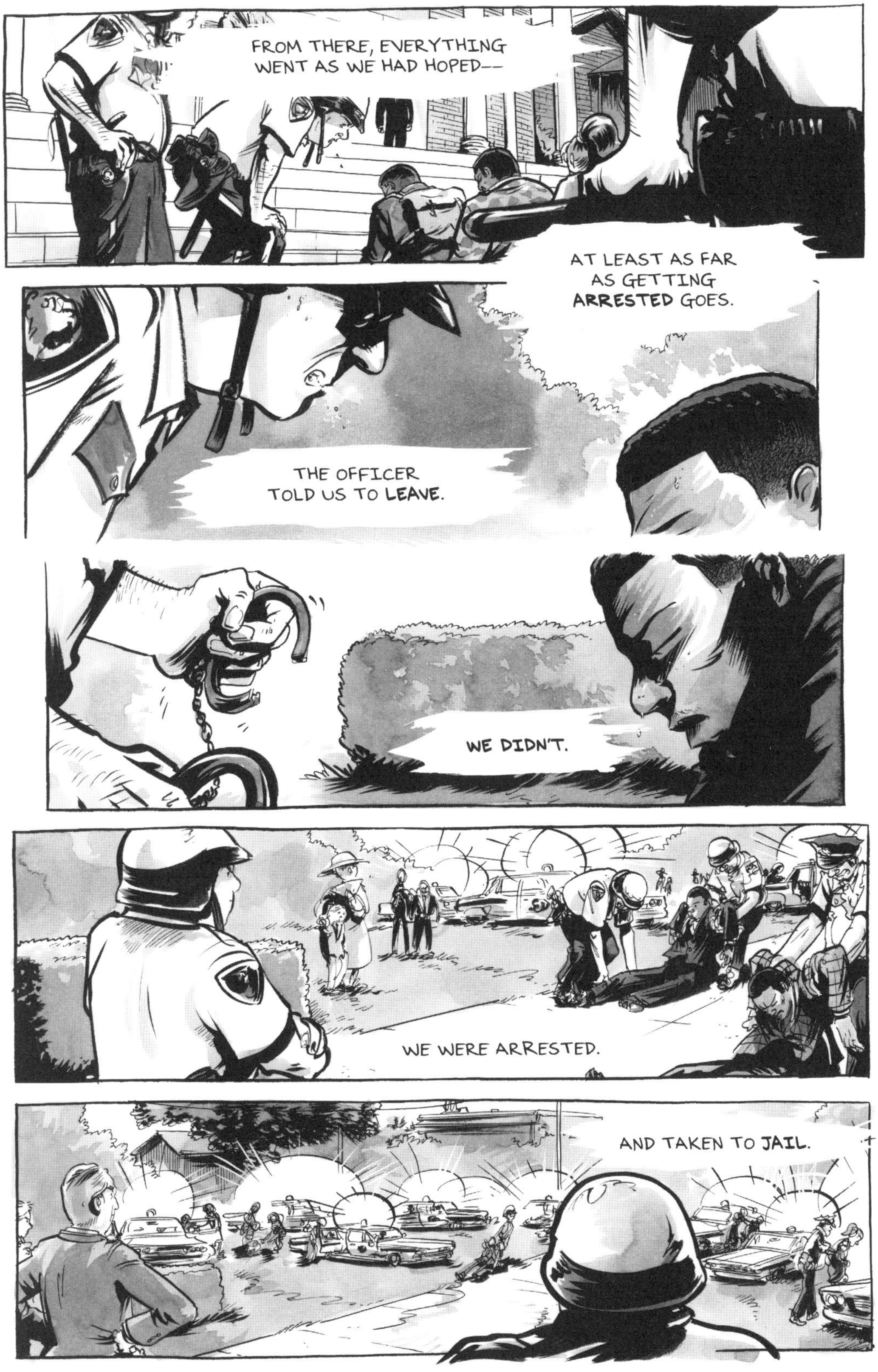
FROM THERE, EVERYTHING WENT AS WE HAD HOPED--
AT LEAST AS FAR AS GETTING **ARRESTED** GOES.
THE OFFICER TOLD US TO **LEAVE**.
WE DIDN'T.
WE WERE ARRESTED.
AND TAKEN TO **JAIL**.

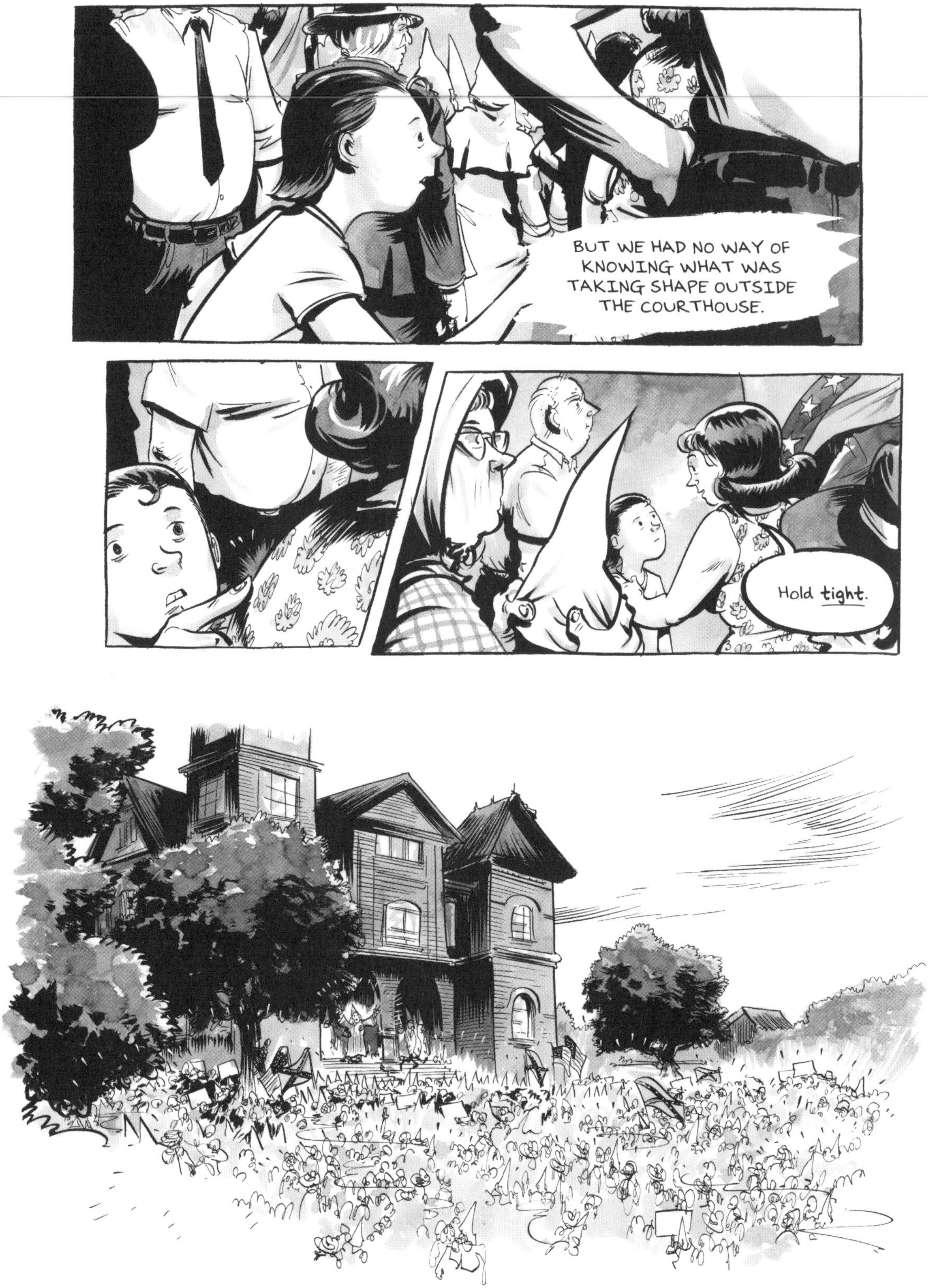

BUT WE HAD NO WAY OF KNOWING WHAT WAS TAKING SHAPE OUTSIDE THE COURTHOUSE.
Hold tight.

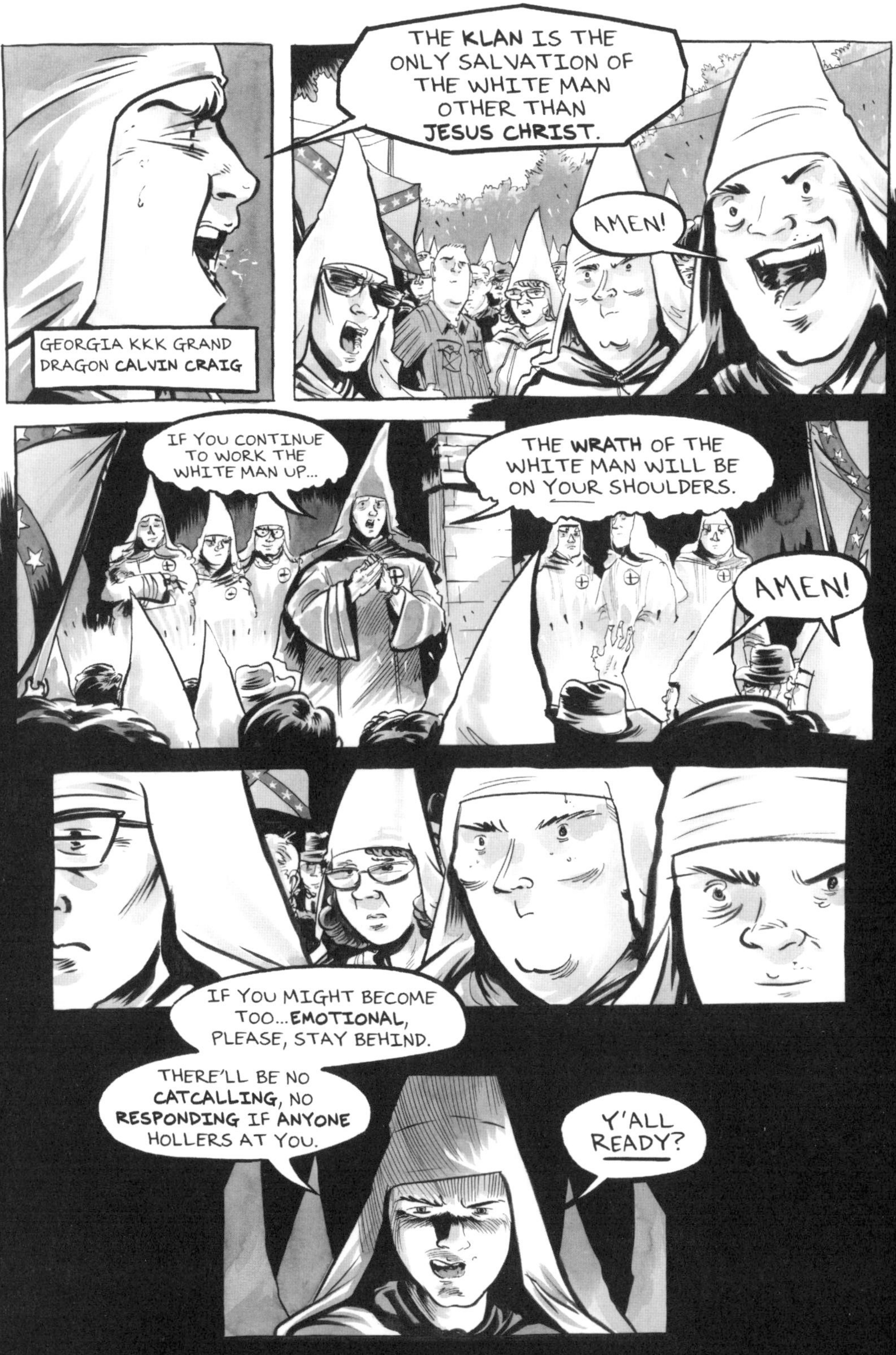
THE **KLAN** IS THE ONLY SALVATION OF THE WHITE MAN OTHER THAN **JESUS CHRIST**.
GEORGIA KKK GRAND DRAGON **CALVIN CRAIG**
AMEN!
IF YOU CONTINUE TO WORK THE WHITE MAN UP...
THE **WRATH** OF THE WHITE MAN WILL BE ON YOUR SHOULDERS.
AMEN!
IF YOU MIGHT BECOME TOO... **EMOTIONAL**, PLEASE, STAY BEHIND.
THERE'LL BE NO **CATCALLING**, NO **RESPONDING** IF **ANYONE** HOLLERS AT YOU.
Y'ALL READY?

THE INK WAS **BARELY** DRY ON THE VOTING RIGHTS ACT, BUT ALREADY FORCES WERE GATHERING TO FIGHT BACK, USING OUR **OWN** TACTICS.

AND AMERICA'S CITIES WERE **READY TO EXPLODE**...

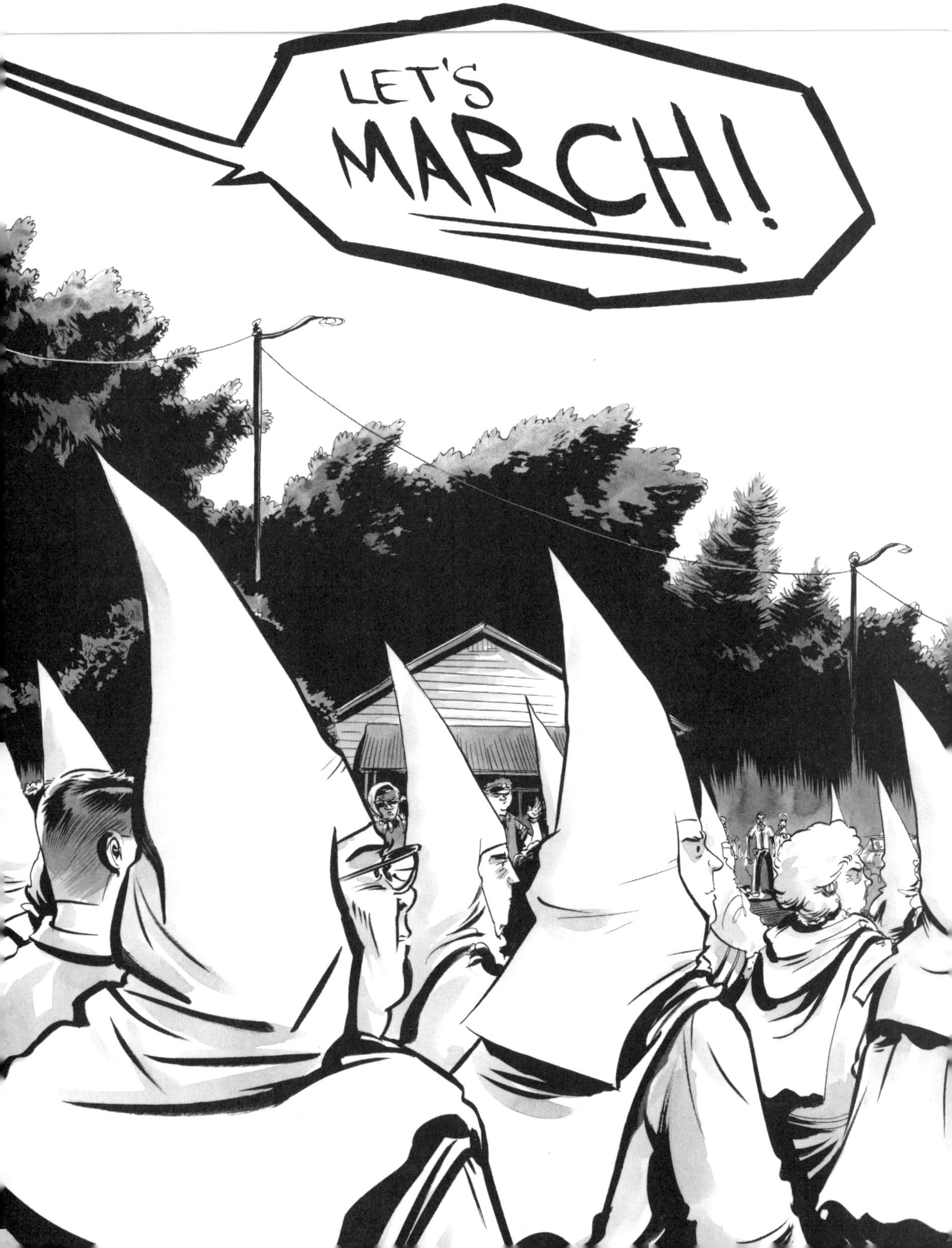
LET'S MARCH!

RUN

BOOK ONE

WRITTEN BY JOHN LEWIS
AND ANDREW AYDIN
ART BY L. FURY WITH NATE POWELL

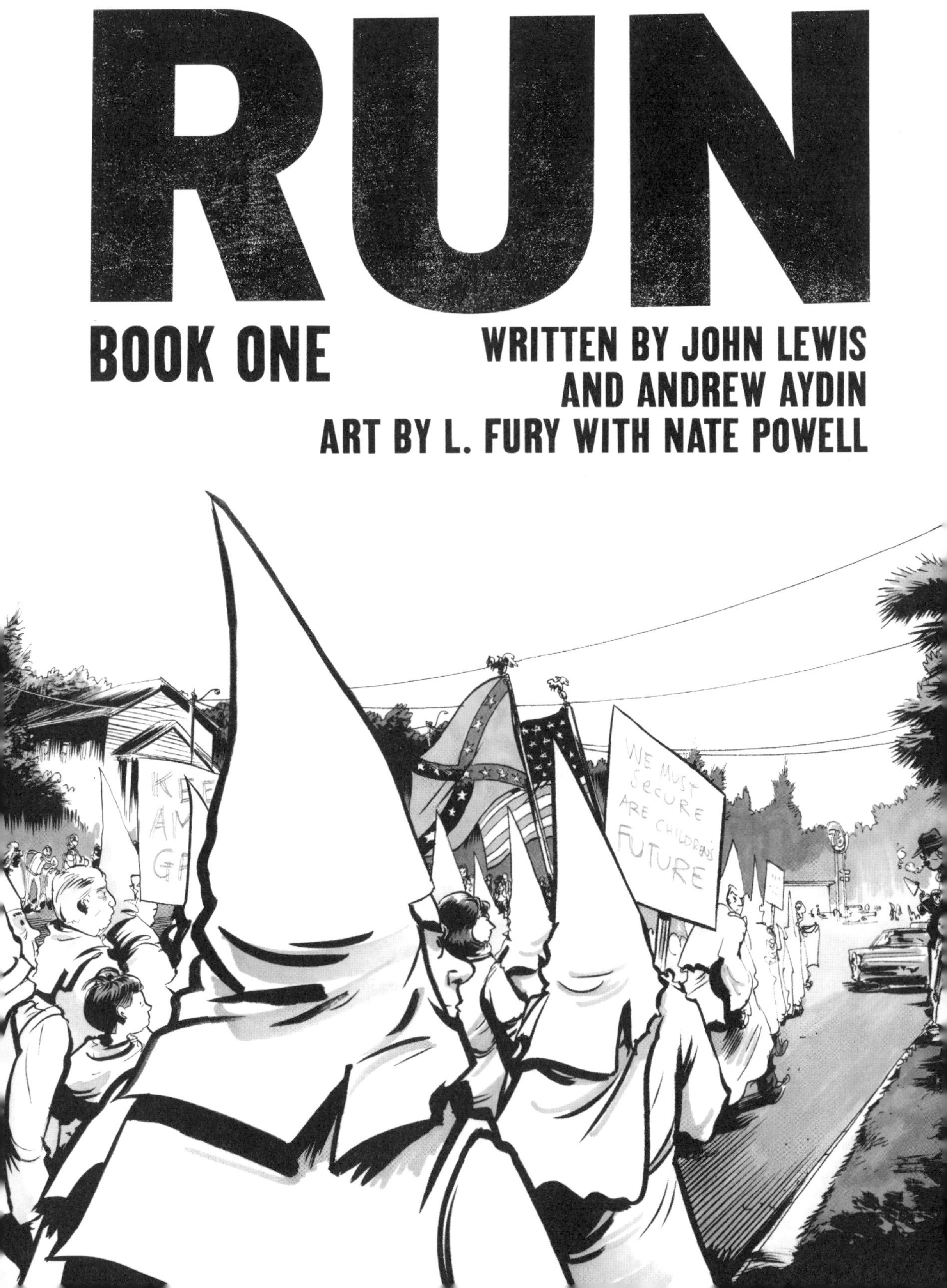
WE MUST
Secure
ARE CHILDREN'S
FUTURE

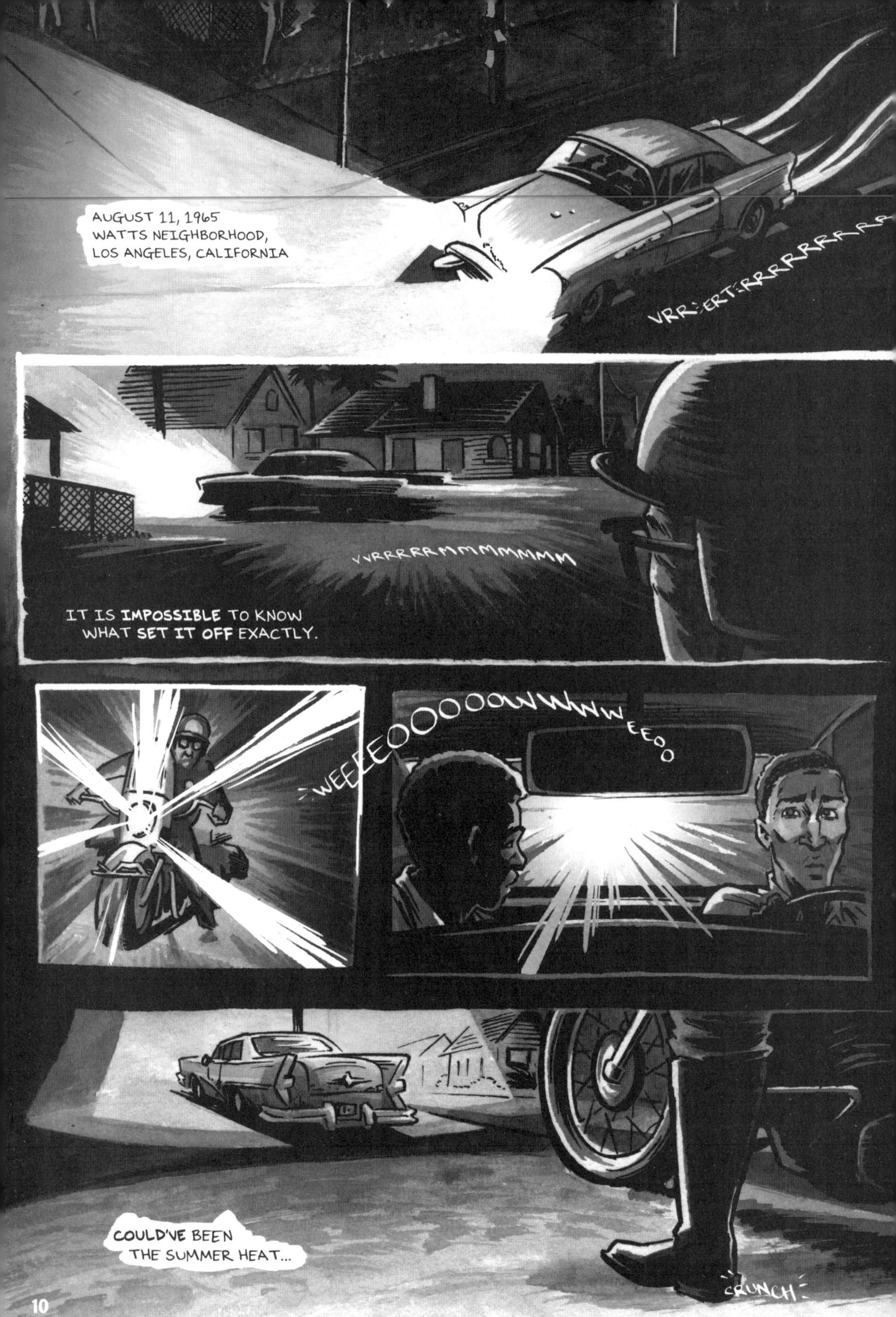

AUGUST 11, 1965
WATTS NEIGHBORHOOD,
LOS ANGELES, CALIFORNIA
VRR ERT RRRRRRRRRRR
VVRRRRRMMMMMMM
IT IS IMPOSSIBLE TO KNOW WHAT SET IT OFF EXACTLY.
WEEEEOOOOOOWWWWWEEOO
COULD'VE BEEN THE SUMMER HEAT...
CRUNCH

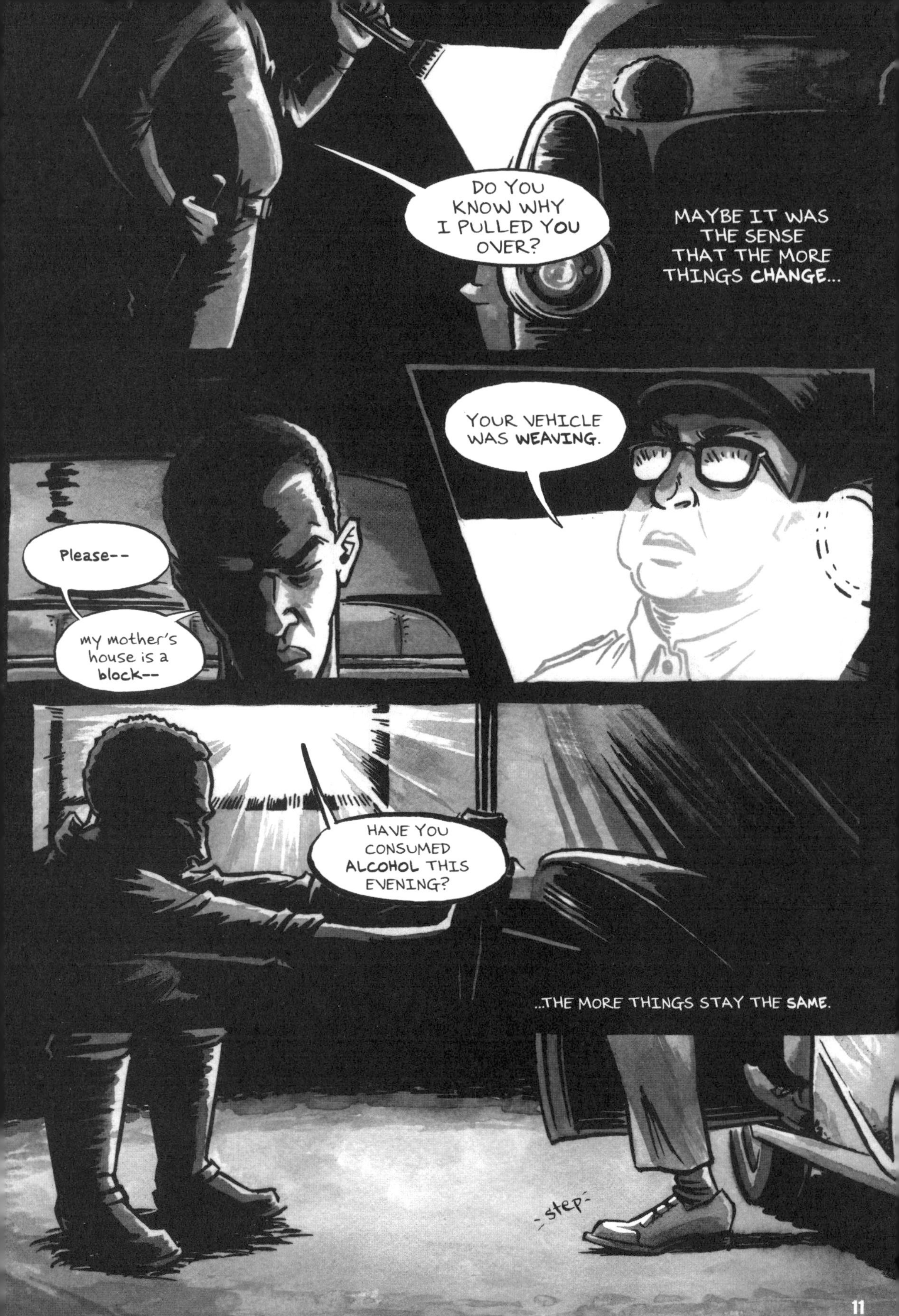
DO YOU KNOW WHY I PULLED YOU OVER?
MAYBE IT WAS THE SENSE THAT THE MORE THINGS CHANGE...
YOUR VEHICLE WAS WEAVING.
Please--
my mother's house is a block--
HAVE YOU CONSUMED ALCOHOL THIS EVENING?
...THE MORE THINGS STAY THE SAME.
-step-

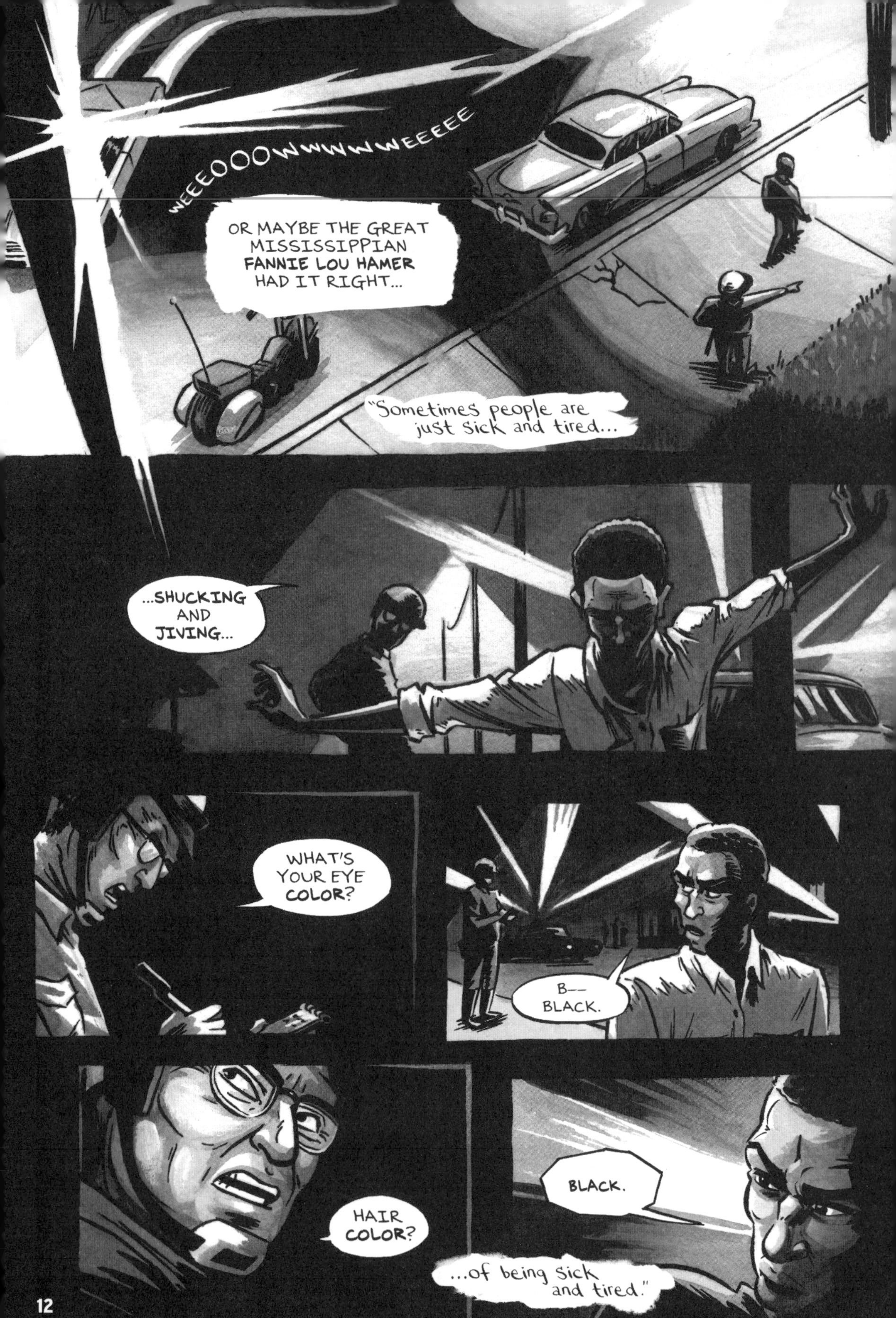
WEEEOOOWWWWWWEEEEE
OR MAYBE THE GREAT MISSISSIPPIAN **FANNIE LOU HAMER** HAD IT RIGHT...
"Sometimes people are just sick and tired...
...SHUCKING AND JIVING...
WHAT'S YOUR EYE **COLOR**?
B-- BLACK.
HAIR **COLOR**?
BLACK.
...of being sick and tired."

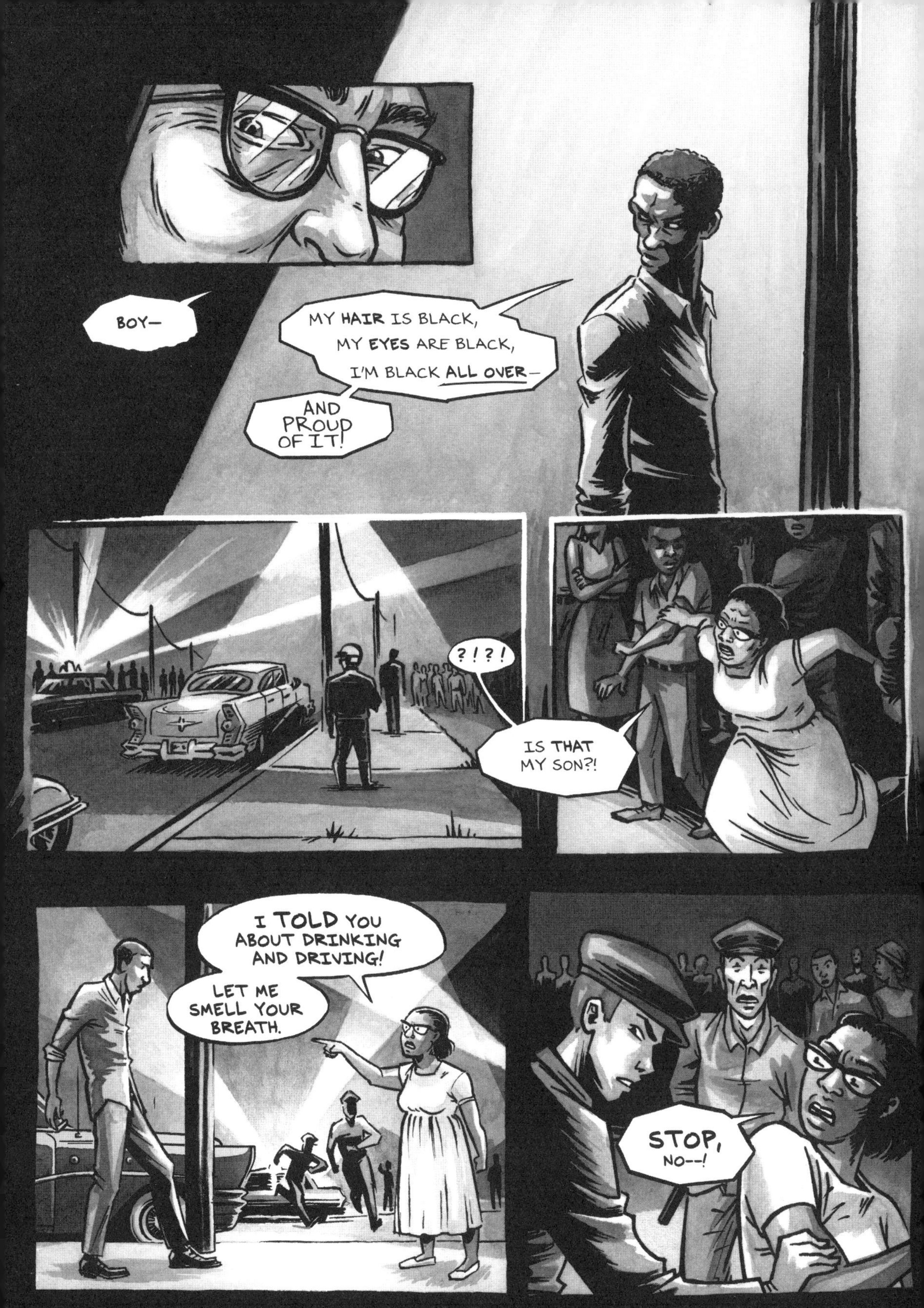
BOY—
MY HAIR IS BLACK, MY EYES ARE BLACK, I'M BLACK ALL OVER—
AND PROUD OF IT!
?!?!
IS THAT MY SON?!
I TOLD YOU ABOUT DRINKING AND DRIVING!
LET ME SMELL YOUR BREATH.
STOP, NO--!

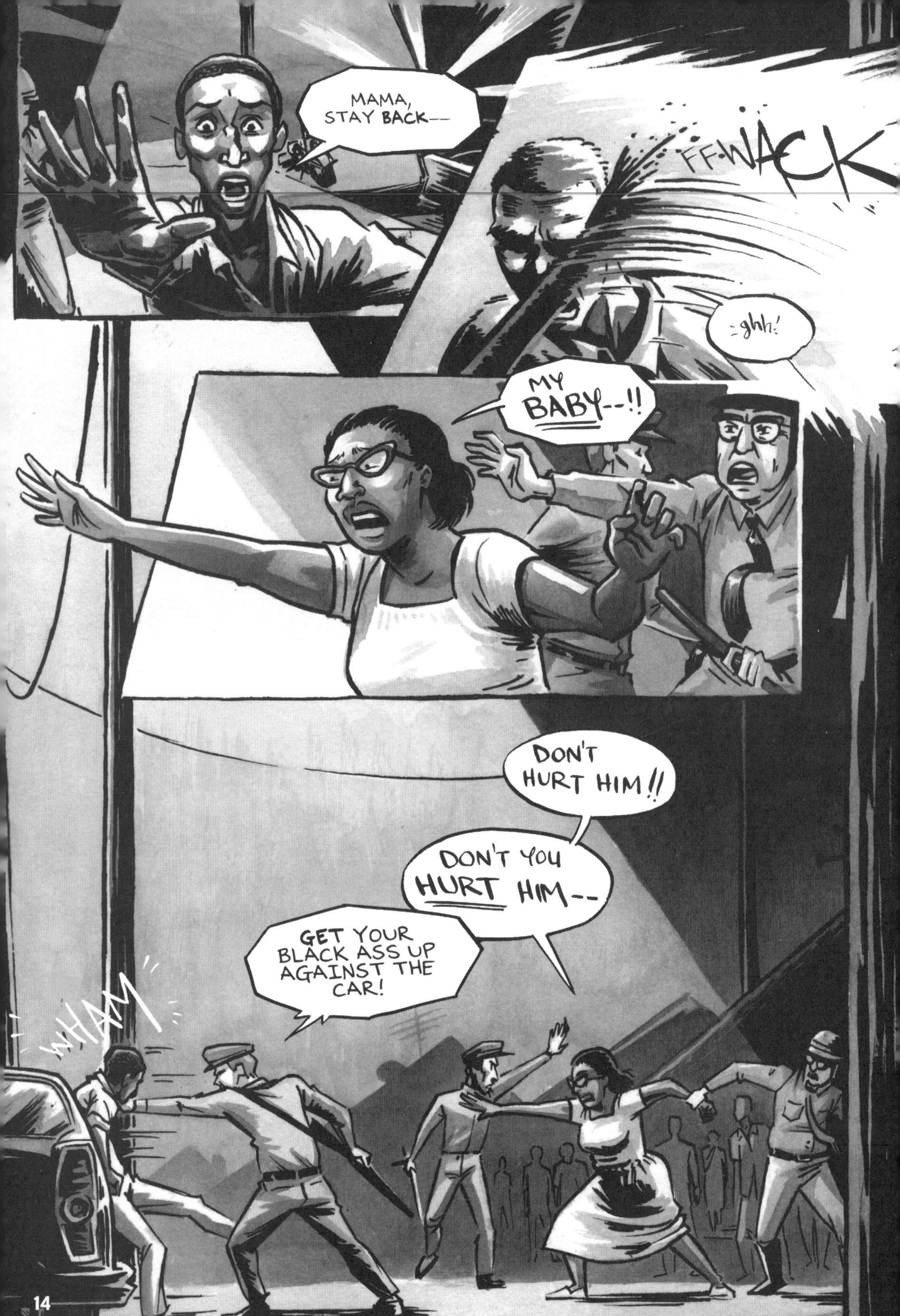
MAMA, STAY BACK--
FF-WACK
ghh!
MY BABY--!!
DON'T HURT HIM!!
DON'T YOU HURT HIM--
GET YOUR BLACK ASS UP AGAINST THE CAR!
WHAM

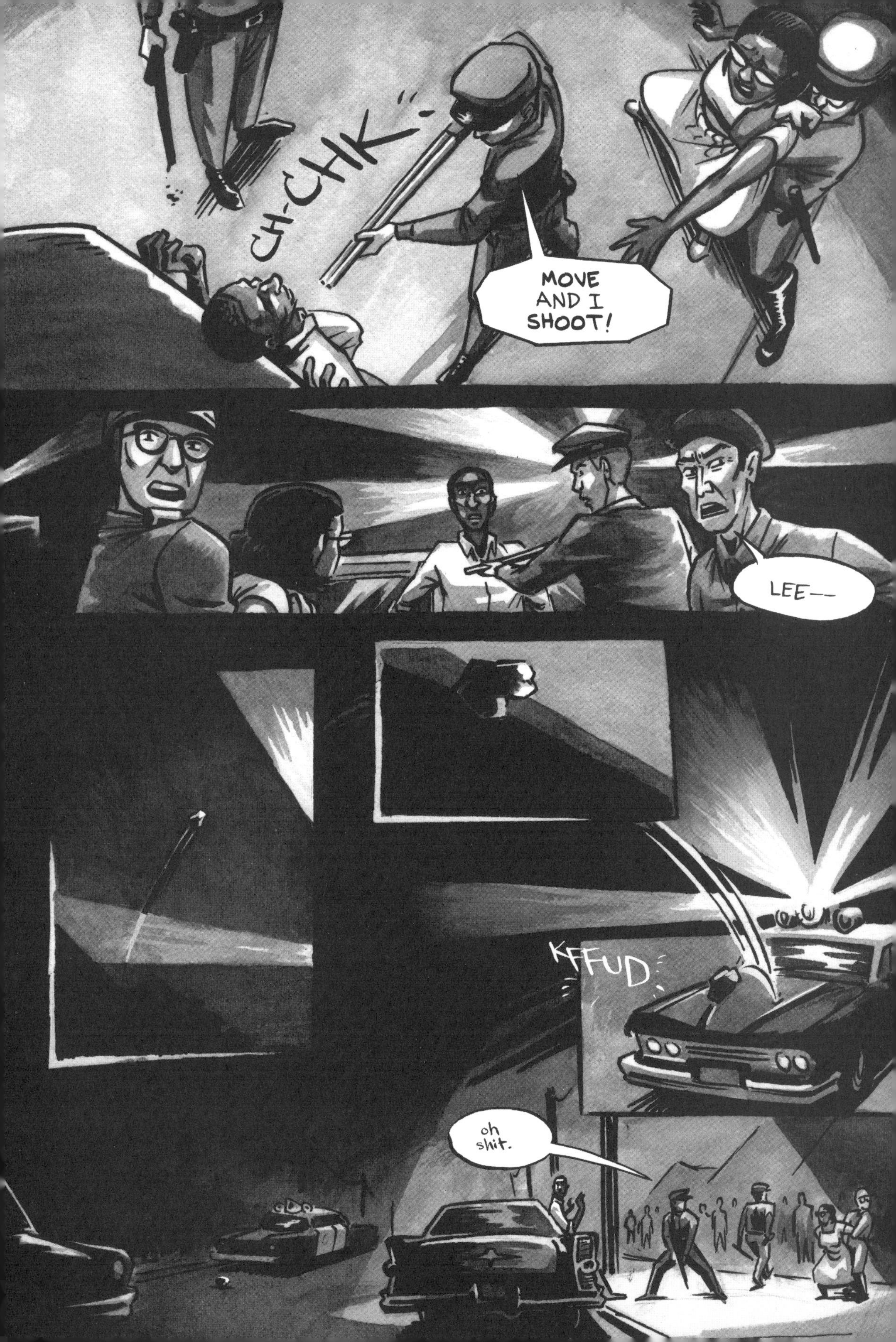
CH-CHK
MOVE AND I SHOOT!
LEE--
KFFUD
oh shit.

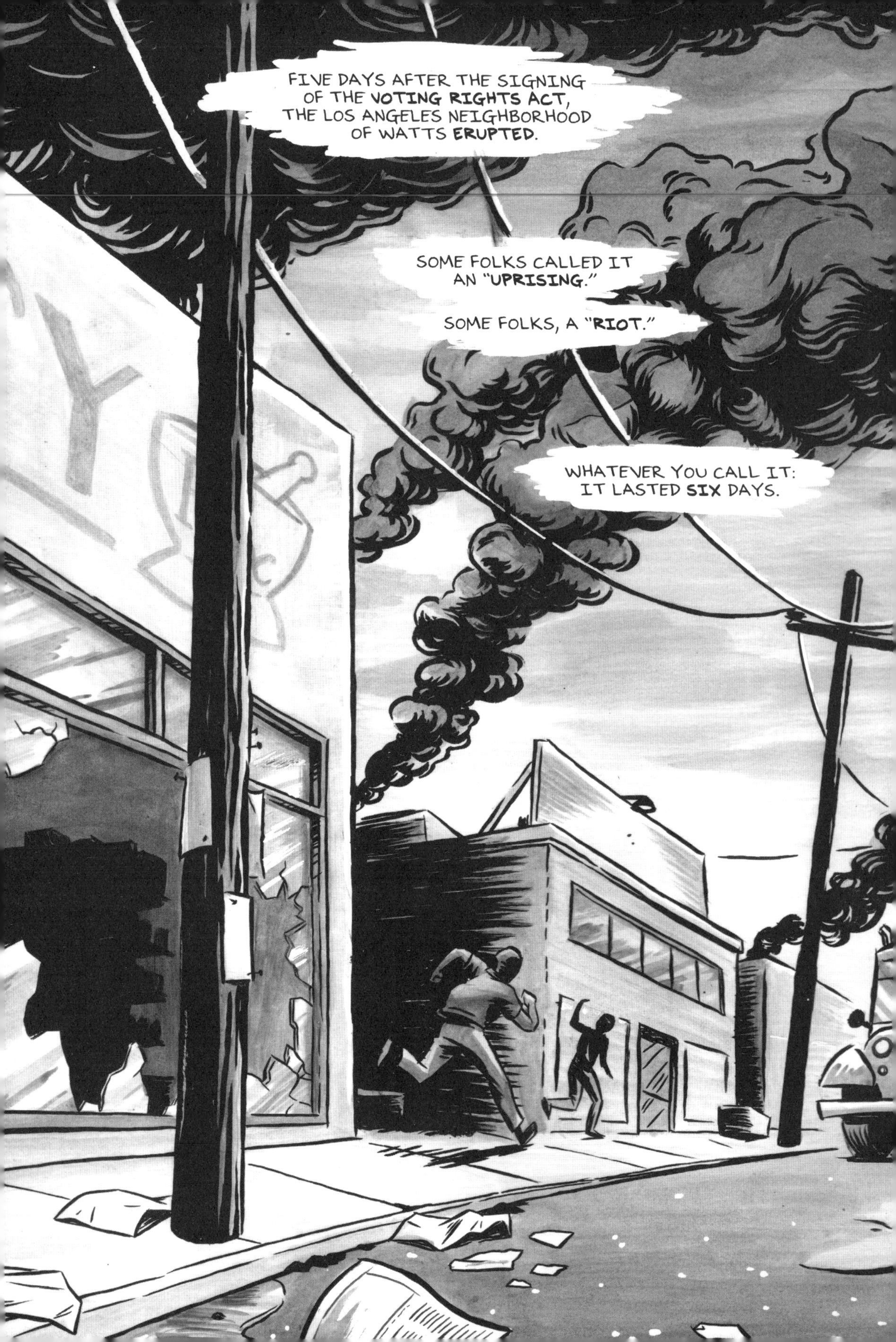
FIVE DAYS AFTER THE SIGNING OF THE **VOTING RIGHTS ACT**, THE LOS ANGELES NEIGHBORHOOD OF WATTS **ERUPTED**.
SOME FOLKS CALLED IT AN "**UPRISING**."
SOME FOLKS, A "**RIOT**."
WHATEVER YOU CALL IT: IT LASTED **SIX** DAYS.

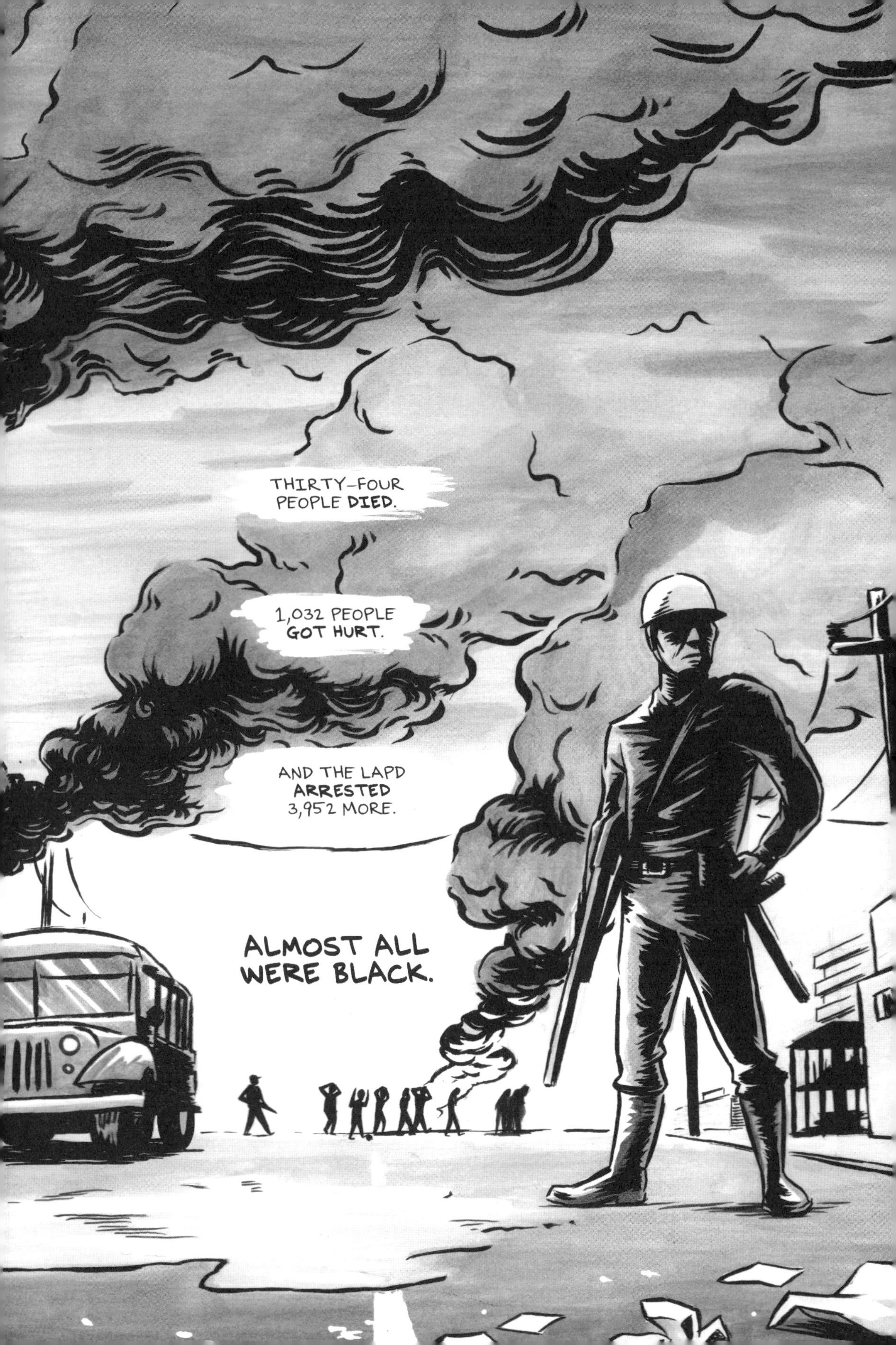
THIRTY-FOUR PEOPLE **DIED**.
1,032 PEOPLE **GOT HURT**.
AND THE LAPD **ARRESTED** 3,952 MORE.
ALMOST ALL WERE BLACK.

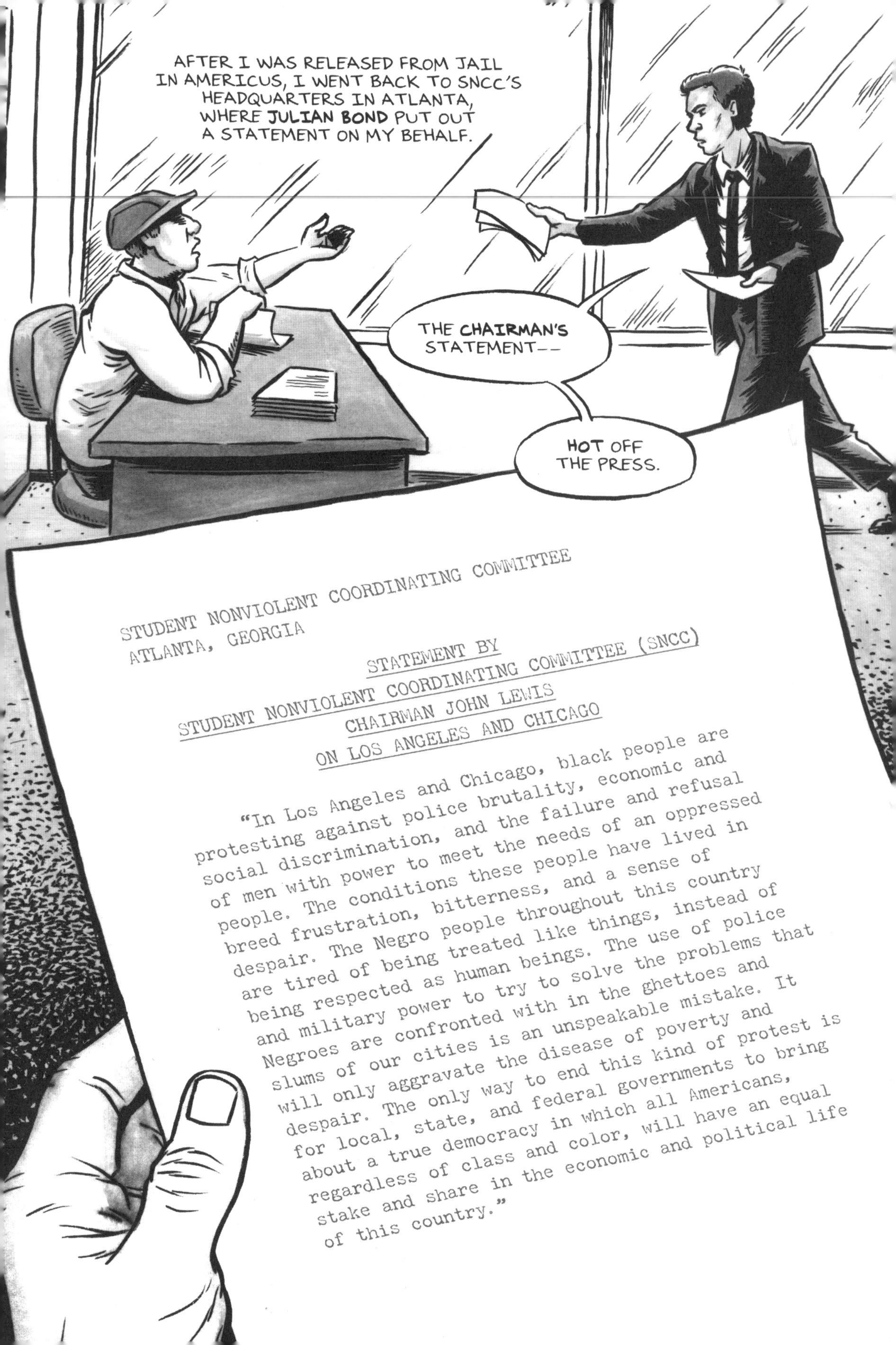
AFTER I WAS RELEASED FROM JAIL IN AMERICUS, I WENT BACK TO SNCC'S HEADQUARTERS IN ATLANTA, WHERE **JULIAN BOND** PUT OUT A STATEMENT ON MY BEHALF.
THE **CHAIRMAN'S** STATEMENT--
HOT OFF THE PRESS.
STUDENT NONVIOLENT COORDINATING COMMITTEE
ATLANTA, GEORGIA
STATEMENT BY
STUDENT NONVIOLENT COORDINATING COMMITTEE (SNCC)
CHAIRMAN JOHN LEWIS
ON LOS ANGELES AND CHICAGO
"In Los Angeles and Chicago, black people are protesting against police brutality, economic and social discrimination, and the failure and refusal of men with power to meet the needs of an oppressed people. The conditions these people have lived in breed frustration, bitterness, and a sense of despair. The Negro people throughout this country are tired of being treated like things, instead of being respected as human beings. The use of police and military power to try to solve the problems that Negroes are confronted with in the ghettoes and slums of our cities is an unspeakable mistake. It will only aggravate the disease of poverty and despair. The only way to end this kind of protest is for local, state, and federal governments to bring about a true democracy in which all Americans, regardless of class and color, will have an equal stake and share in the economic and political life of this country."

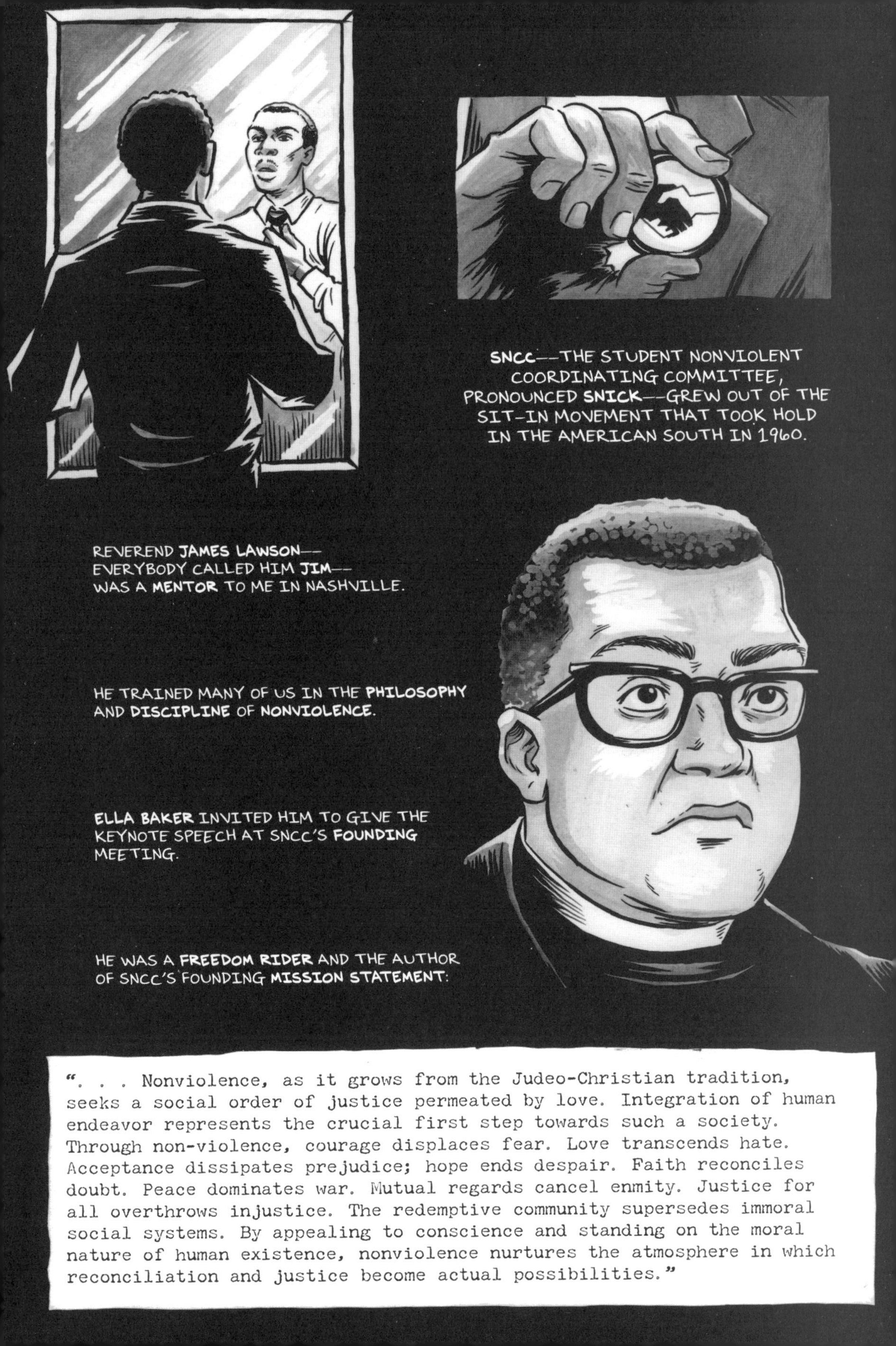
SNCC--THE STUDENT NONVIOLENT COORDINATING COMMITTEE, PRONOUNCED SNICK--GREW OUT OF THE SIT-IN MOVEMENT THAT TOOK HOLD IN THE AMERICAN SOUTH IN 1960.
REVEREND JAMES LAWSON--EVERYBODY CALLED HIM JIM--WAS A MENTOR TO ME IN NASHVILLE.
HE TRAINED MANY OF US IN THE PHILOSOPHY AND DISCIPLINE OF NONVIOLENCE.
ELLA BAKER INVITED HIM TO GIVE THE KEYNOTE SPEECH AT SNCC'S FOUNDING MEETING.
HE WAS A FREEDOM RIDER AND THE AUTHOR OF SNCC'S FOUNDING MISSION STATEMENT:
". . . Nonviolence, as it grows from the Judeo-Christian tradition, seeks a social order of justice permeated by love. Integration of human endeavor represents the crucial first step towards such a society. Through non-violence, courage displaces fear. Love transcends hate. Acceptance dissipates prejudice; hope ends despair. Faith reconciles doubt. Peace dominates war. Mutual regards cancel enmity. Justice for all overthrows injustice. The redemptive community supersedes immoral social systems. By appealing to conscience and standing on the moral nature of human existence, nonviolence nurtures the atmosphere in which reconciliation and justice become actual possibilities."

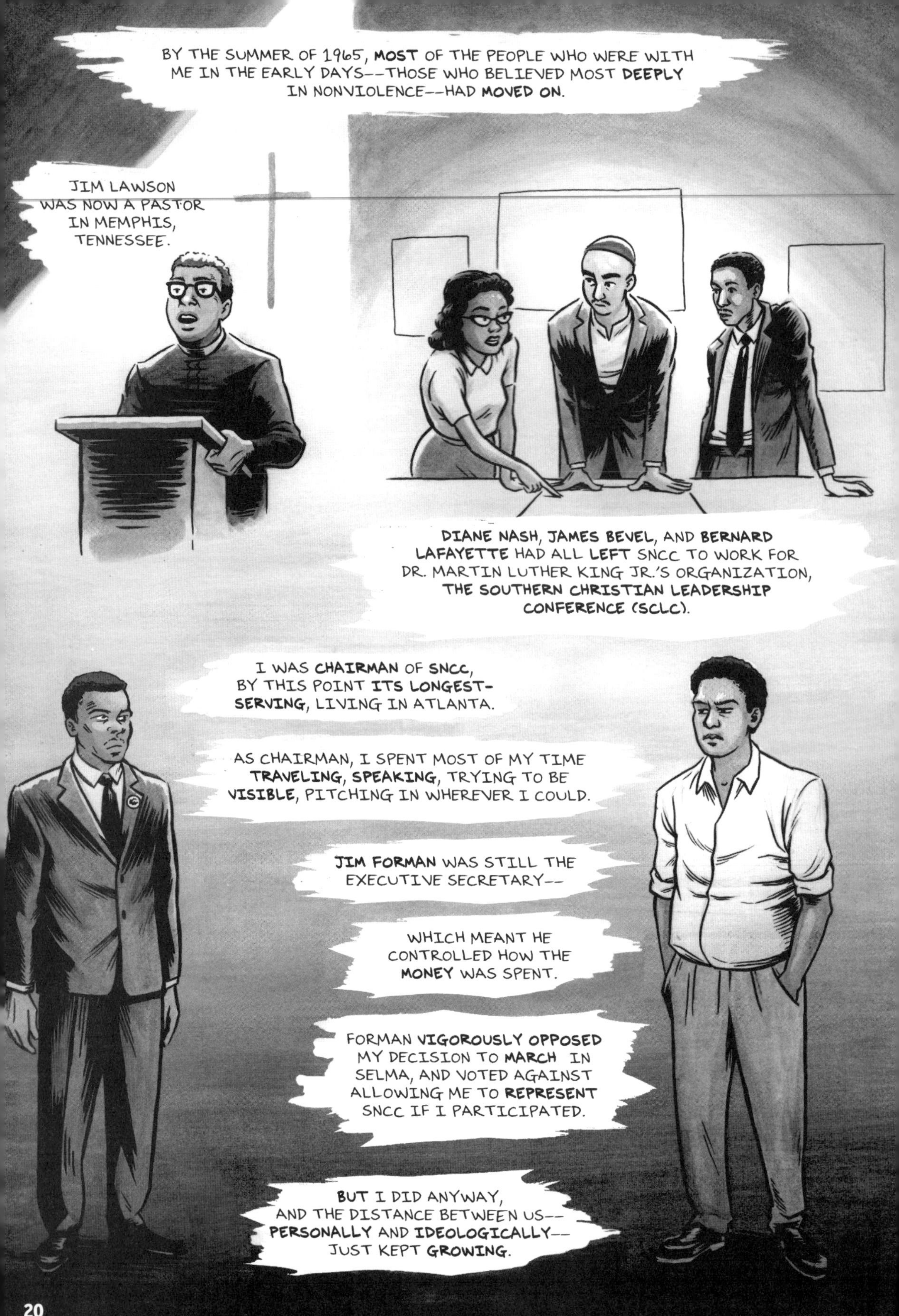
BY THE SUMMER OF 1965, MOST OF THE PEOPLE WHO WERE WITH ME IN THE EARLY DAYS--THOSE WHO BELIEVED MOST DEEPLY IN NONVIOLENCE--HAD MOVED ON.
JIM LAWSON WAS NOW A PASTOR IN MEMPHIS, TENNESSEE.
DIANE NASH, JAMES BEVEL, AND BERNARD LAFAYETTE HAD ALL LEFT SNCC TO WORK FOR DR. MARTIN LUTHER KING JR.'S ORGANIZATION, THE SOUTHERN CHRISTIAN LEADERSHIP CONFERENCE (SCLC).
I WAS CHAIRMAN OF SNCC, BY THIS POINT ITS LONGEST-SERVING, LIVING IN ATLANTA.
AS CHAIRMAN, I SPENT MOST OF MY TIME TRAVELING, SPEAKING, TRYING TO BE VISIBLE, PITCHING IN WHEREVER I COULD.
JIM FORMAN WAS STILL THE EXECUTIVE SECRETARY--
WHICH MEANT HE CONTROLLED HOW THE MONEY WAS SPENT.
FORMAN VIGOROUSLY OPPOSED MY DECISION TO MARCH IN SELMA, AND VOTED AGAINST ALLOWING ME TO REPRESENT SNCC IF I PARTICIPATED.
BUT I DID ANYWAY, AND THE DISTANCE BETWEEN US--PERSONALLY AND IDEOLOGICALLY--JUST KEPT GROWING.

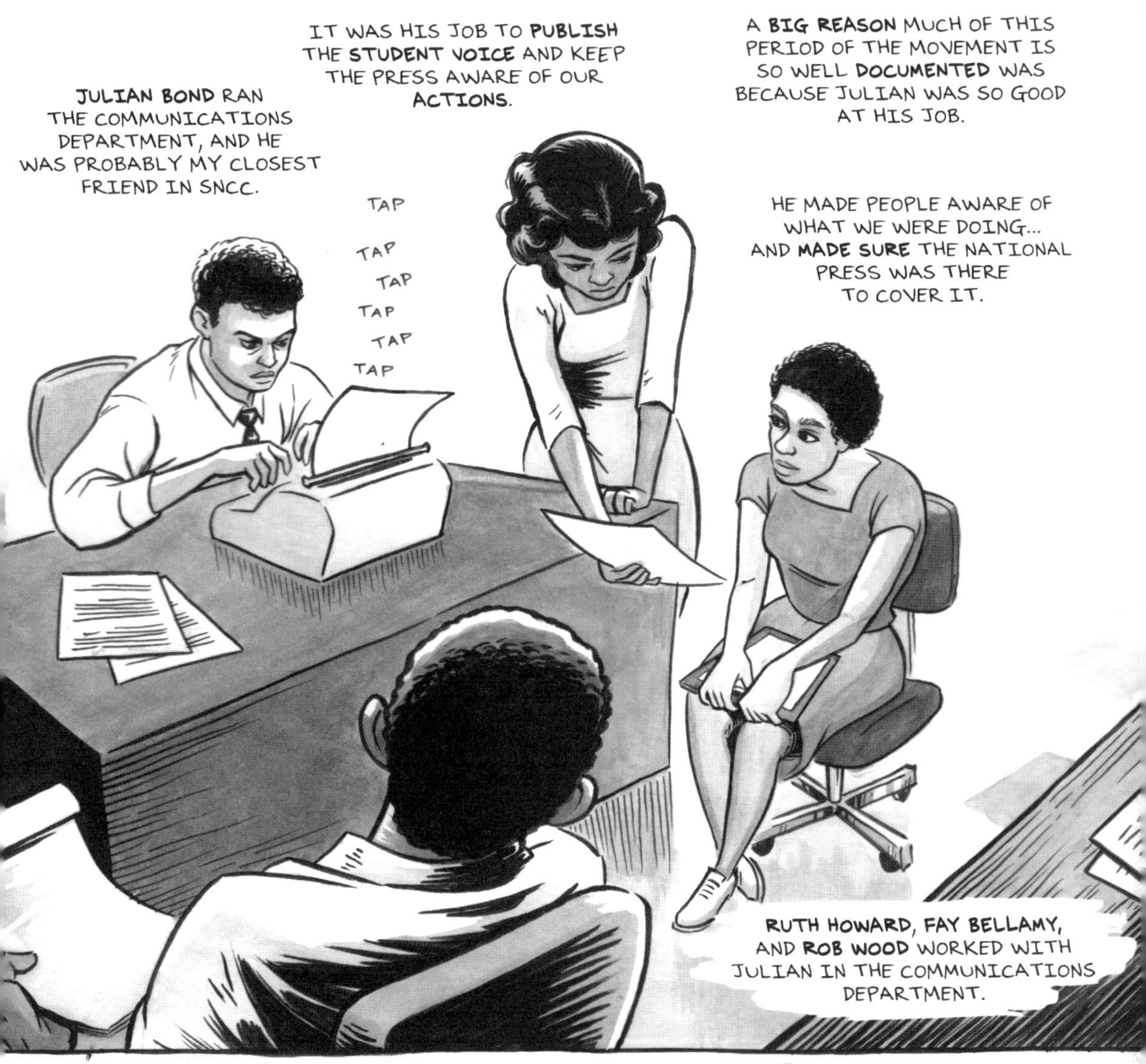
JULIAN BOND RAN THE COMMUNICATIONS DEPARTMENT, AND HE WAS PROBABLY MY CLOSEST FRIEND IN SNCC.
IT WAS HIS JOB TO PUBLISH THE STUDENT VOICE AND KEEP THE PRESS AWARE OF OUR ACTIONS.
A BIG REASON MUCH OF THIS PERIOD OF THE MOVEMENT IS SO WELL DOCUMENTED WAS BECAUSE JULIAN WAS SO GOOD AT HIS JOB.
TAP
TAP
TAP
TAP
TAP
TAP
HE MADE PEOPLE AWARE OF WHAT WE WERE DOING... AND MADE SURE THE NATIONAL PRESS WAS THERE TO COVER IT.
RUTH HOWARD, FAY BELLAMY, AND ROB WOOD WORKED WITH JULIAN IN THE COMMUNICATIONS DEPARTMENT.

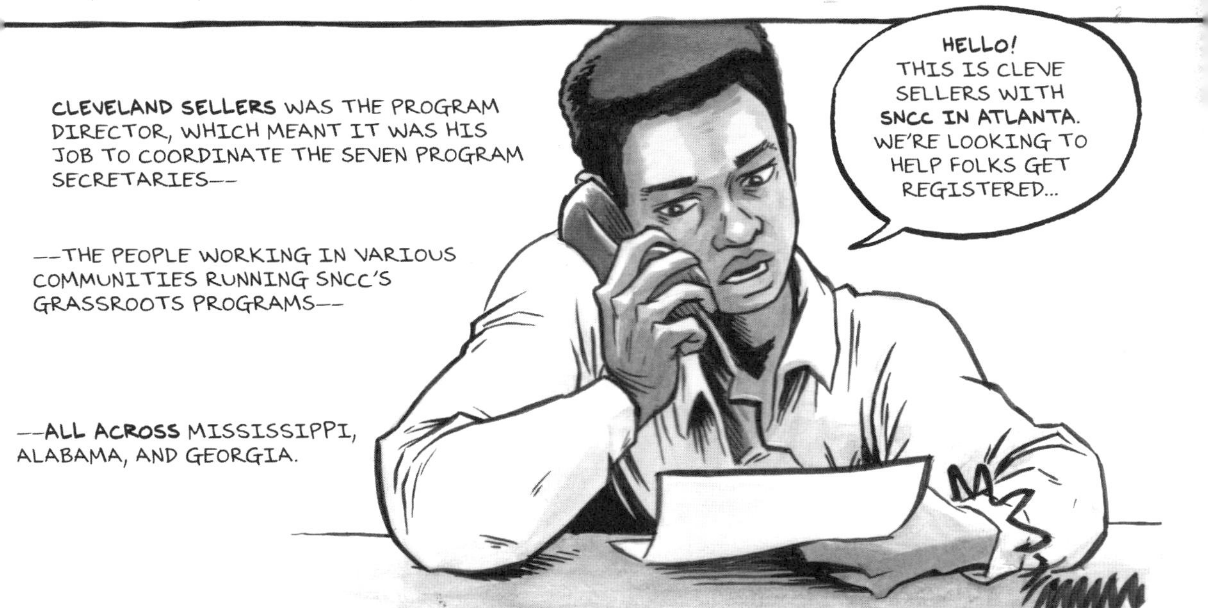
CLEVELAND SELLERS WAS THE PROGRAM DIRECTOR, WHICH MEANT IT WAS HIS JOB TO COORDINATE THE SEVEN PROGRAM SECRETARIES--
HELLO! THIS IS CLEVE SELLERS WITH SNCC IN ATLANTA. WE'RE LOOKING TO HELP FOLKS GET REGISTERED...
--THE PEOPLE WORKING IN VARIOUS COMMUNITIES RUNNING SNCC'S GRASSROOTS PROGRAMS--
--ALL ACROSS MISSISSIPPI, ALABAMA, AND GEORGIA.

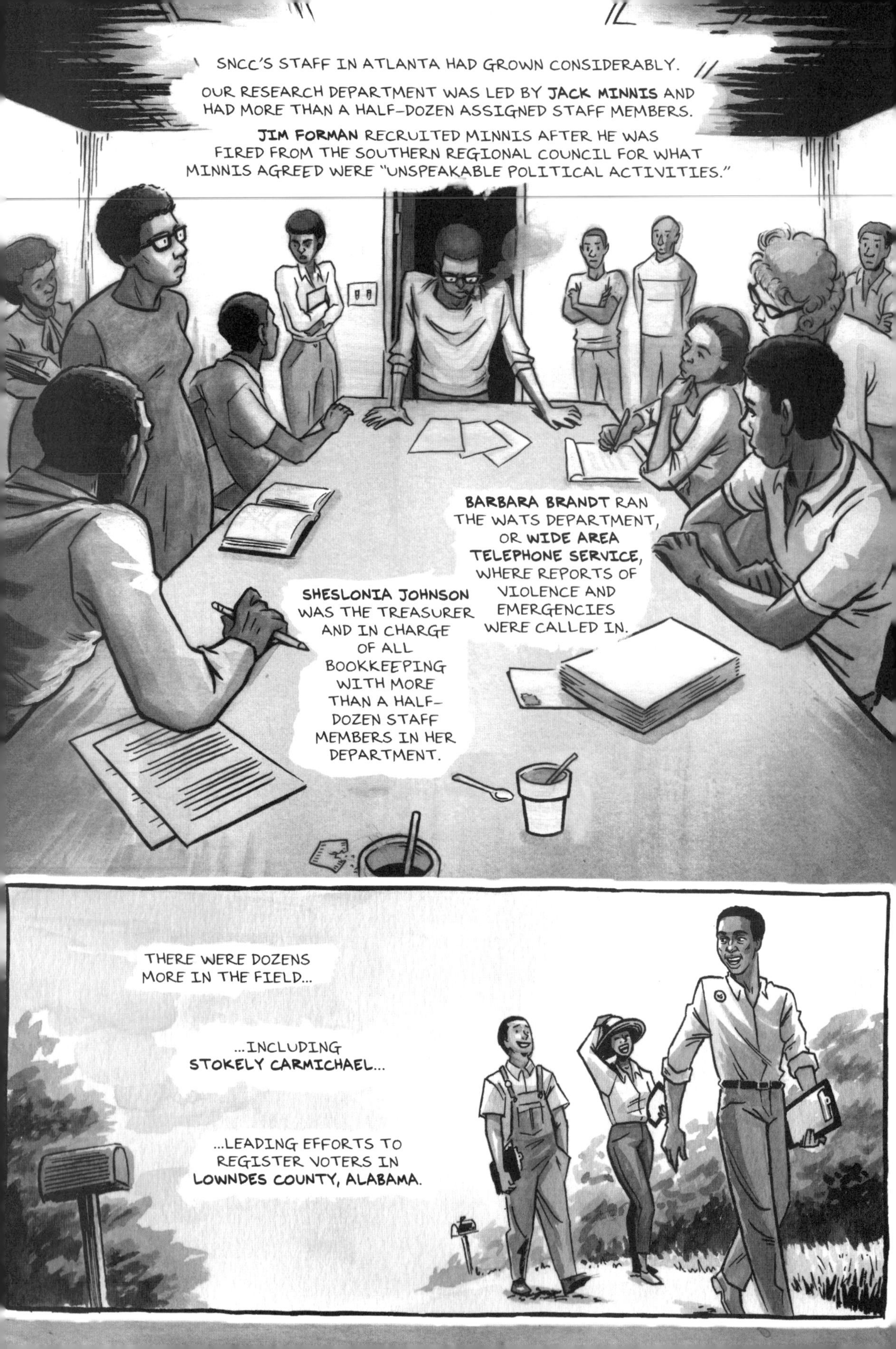
SNCC'S STAFF IN ATLANTA HAD GROWN CONSIDERABLY.
OUR RESEARCH DEPARTMENT WAS LED BY **JACK MINNIS** AND HAD MORE THAN A HALF-DOZEN ASSIGNED STAFF MEMBERS.
JIM FORMAN RECRUITED MINNIS AFTER HE WAS FIRED FROM THE SOUTHERN REGIONAL COUNCIL FOR WHAT MINNIS AGREED WERE "UNSPEAKABLE POLITICAL ACTIVITIES."
BARBARA BRANDT RAN THE WATS DEPARTMENT, OR **WIDE AREA TELEPHONE SERVICE**, WHERE REPORTS OF VIOLENCE AND EMERGENCIES WERE CALLED IN.
SHESLONIA JOHNSON WAS THE TREASURER AND IN CHARGE OF ALL BOOKKEEPING WITH MORE THAN A HALF-DOZEN STAFF MEMBERS IN HER DEPARTMENT.
THERE WERE DOZENS MORE IN THE FIELD...
...INCLUDING **STOKELY CARMICHAEL**...
...LEADING EFFORTS TO REGISTER VOTERS IN **LOWNDES COUNTY, ALABAMA**.

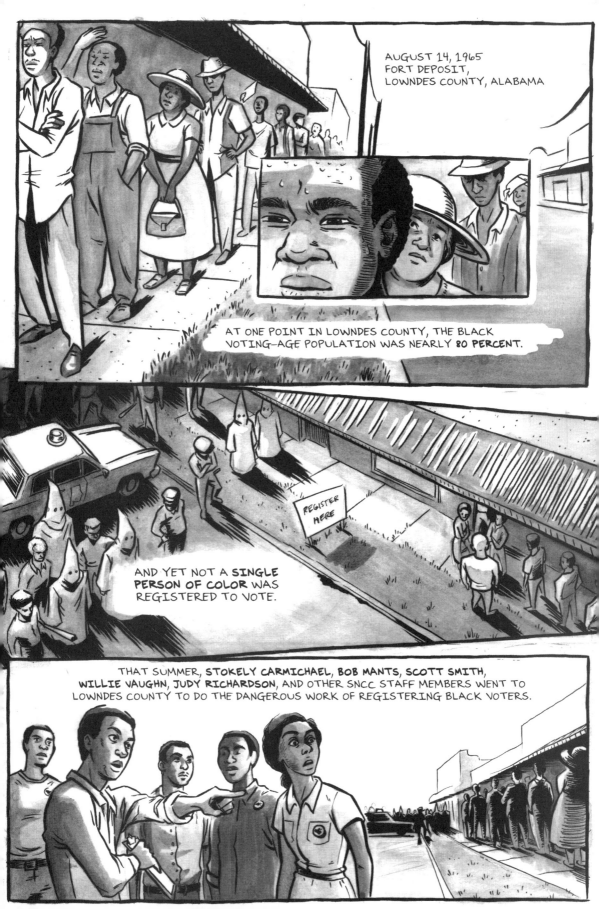

AUGUST 14, 1965
FORT DEPOSIT,
LOWNDES COUNTY, ALABAMA

AT ONE POINT IN LOWNDES COUNTY, THE BLACK VOTING-AGE POPULATION WAS NEARLY **80 PERCENT**.

REGISTER HERE

AND YET NOT A **SINGLE** PERSON OF COLOR WAS REGISTERED TO VOTE.

THAT SUMMER, **STOKELY CARMICHAEL, BOB MANTS, SCOTT SMITH, WILLIE VAUGHN, JUDY RICHARDSON,** AND OTHER SNCC STAFF MEMBERS WENT TO LOWNDES COUNTY TO DO THE DANGEROUS WORK OF REGISTERING BLACK VOTERS.

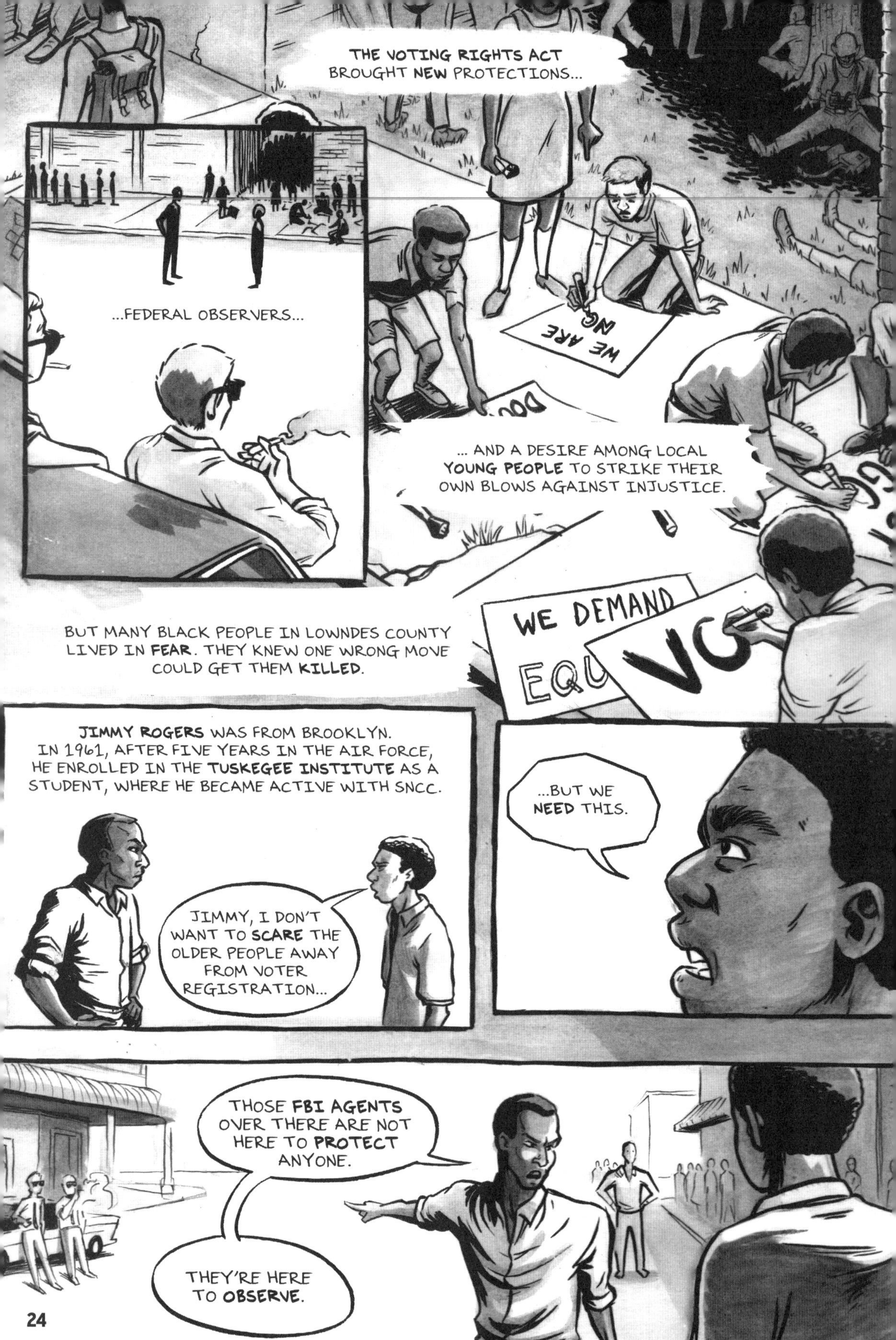
THE VOTING RIGHTS ACT BROUGHT NEW PROTECTIONS...
...FEDERAL OBSERVERS...
... AND A DESIRE AMONG LOCAL YOUNG PEOPLE TO STRIKE THEIR OWN BLOWS AGAINST INJUSTICE.
WE ARE NO
WE DEMAND
EQU
VO
BUT MANY BLACK PEOPLE IN LOWNDES COUNTY LIVED IN FEAR. THEY KNEW ONE WRONG MOVE COULD GET THEM KILLED.
JIMMY ROGERS WAS FROM BROOKLYN. IN 1961, AFTER FIVE YEARS IN THE AIR FORCE, HE ENROLLED IN THE TUSKEGEE INSTITUTE AS A STUDENT, WHERE HE BECAME ACTIVE WITH SNCC.
JIMMY, I DON'T WANT TO SCARE THE OLDER PEOPLE AWAY FROM VOTER REGISTRATION...
...BUT WE NEED THIS.
THOSE FBI AGENTS OVER THERE ARE NOT HERE TO PROTECT ANYONE.
THEY'RE HERE TO OBSERVE.

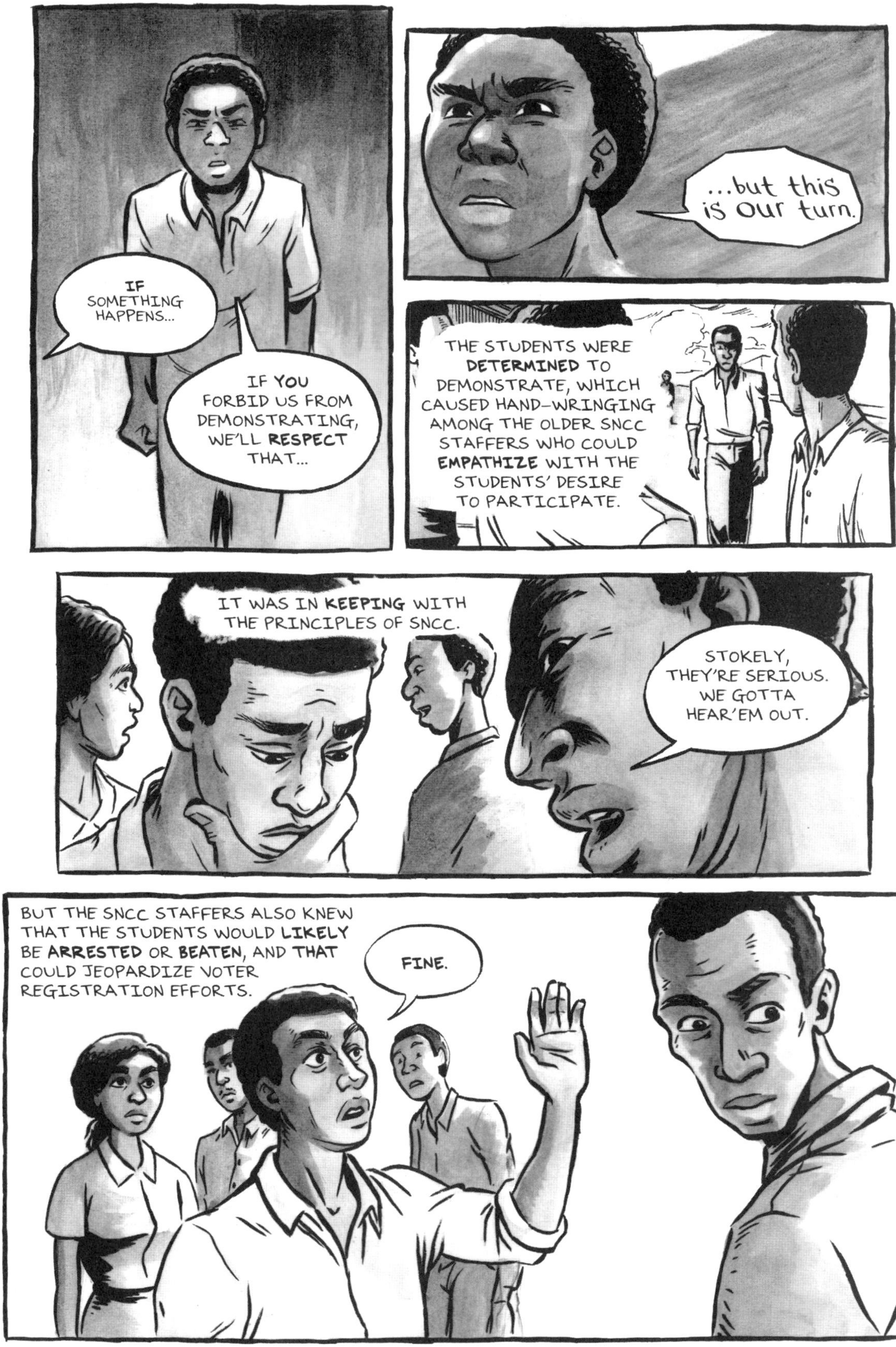
IF SOMETHING HAPPENS...
IF YOU FORBID US FROM DEMONSTRATING, WE'LL RESPECT THAT...
...but this is our turn.
THE STUDENTS WERE DETERMINED TO DEMONSTRATE, WHICH CAUSED HAND-WRINGING AMONG THE OLDER SNCC STAFFERS WHO COULD EMPATHIZE WITH THE STUDENTS' DESIRE TO PARTICIPATE.
IT WAS IN KEEPING WITH THE PRINCIPLES OF SNCC.
STOKELY, THEY'RE SERIOUS. WE GOTTA HEAR'EM OUT.
BUT THE SNCC STAFFERS ALSO KNEW THAT THE STUDENTS WOULD LIKELY BE ARRESTED OR BEATEN, AND THAT COULD JEOPARDIZE VOTER REGISTRATION EFFORTS.
FINE.

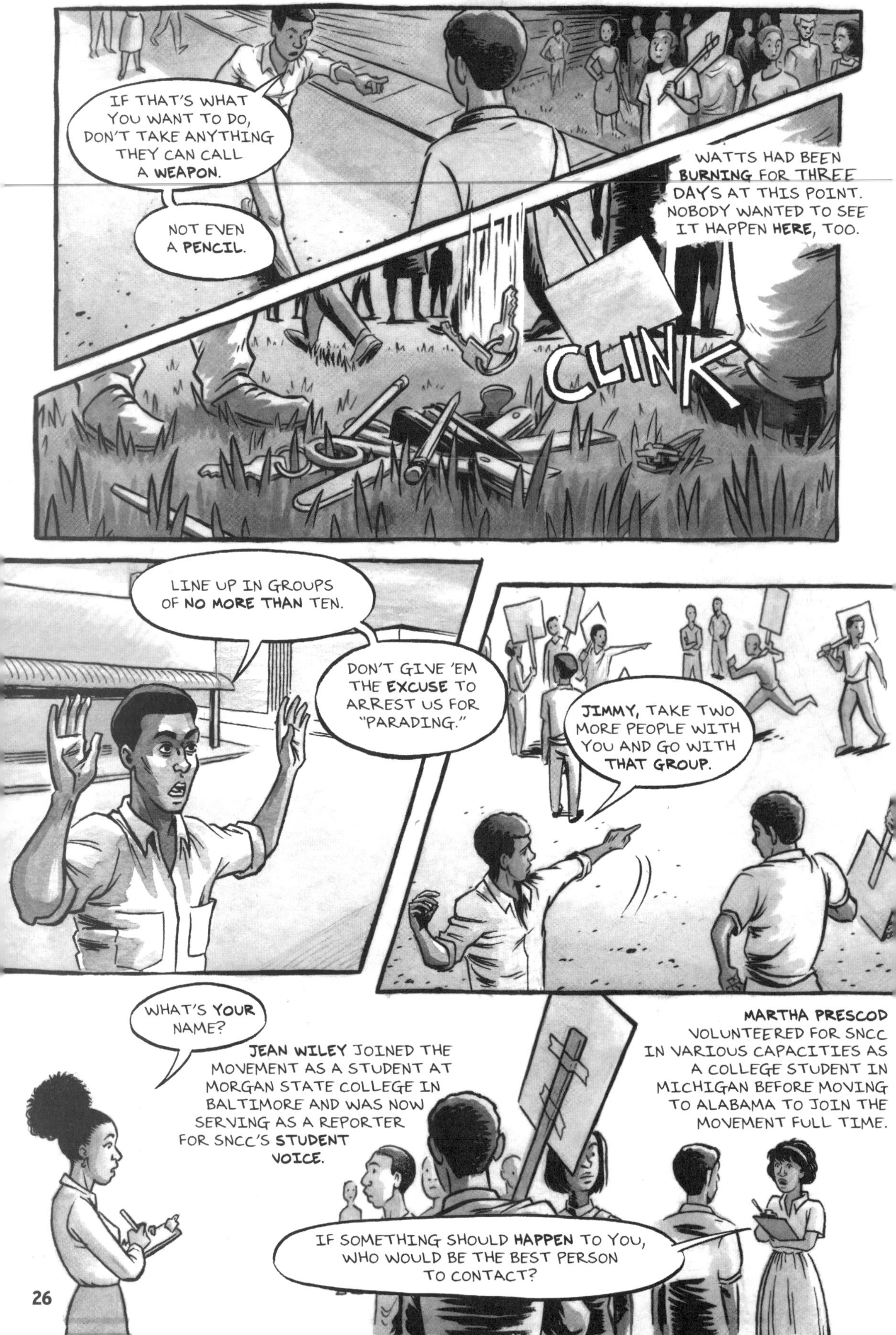

IF THAT'S WHAT YOU WANT TO DO, DON'T TAKE ANYTHING THEY CAN CALL A **WEAPON**.
NOT EVEN A **PENCIL**.
WATTS HAD BEEN **BURNING** FOR THREE DAYS AT THIS POINT. NOBODY WANTED TO SEE IT HAPPEN **HERE**, TOO.
CLINK
LINE UP IN GROUPS OF **NO MORE THAN** TEN.
DON'T GIVE 'EM THE **EXCUSE** TO ARREST US FOR "PARADING."
JIMMY, TAKE TWO MORE PEOPLE WITH YOU AND GO WITH **THAT GROUP**.
WHAT'S **YOUR** NAME?
JEAN WILEY JOINED THE MOVEMENT AS A STUDENT AT MORGAN STATE COLLEGE IN BALTIMORE AND WAS NOW SERVING AS A REPORTER FOR SNCC'S **STUDENT VOICE**.
MARTHA PRESCOD VOLUNTEERED FOR SNCC IN VARIOUS CAPACITIES AS A COLLEGE STUDENT IN MICHIGAN BEFORE MOVING TO ALABAMA TO JOIN THE MOVEMENT FULL TIME.
IF SOMETHING SHOULD **HAPPEN** TO YOU, WHO WOULD BE THE BEST PERSON TO CONTACT?

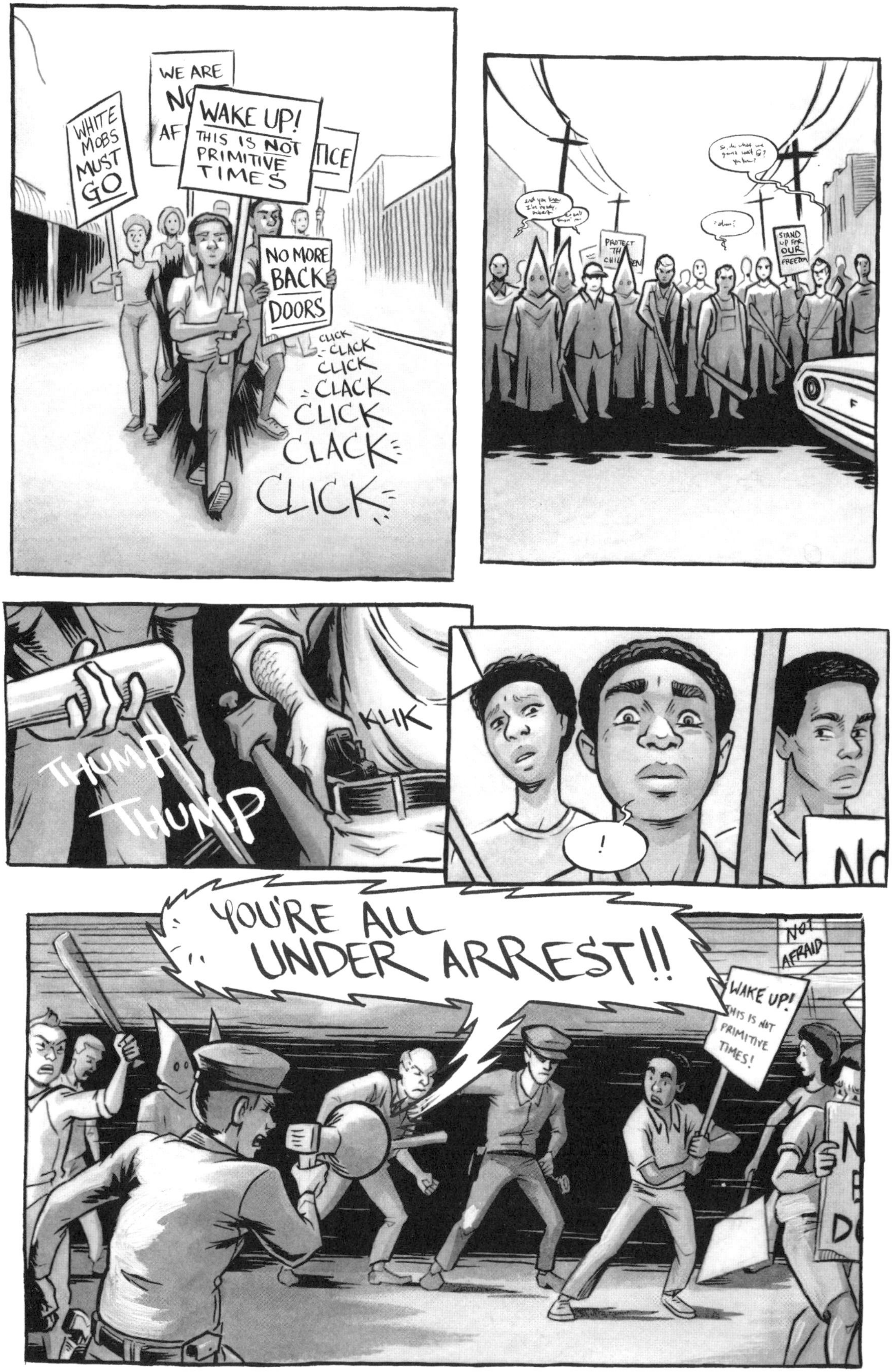
WE ARE
WHITE MOBS MUST GO
WAKE UP! THIS IS NOT PRIMITIVE TIMES
NO MORE BACK DOORS
CLICK CLACK CLICK CLACK CLICK CLACK CLICK
STAND UP FOR OUR FREEDOM
THUMP THUMP
KLIK
!
YOU'RE ALL UNDER ARREST!!
NOT AFRAID
WAKE UP! THIS IS NOT PRIMITIVE TIMES!

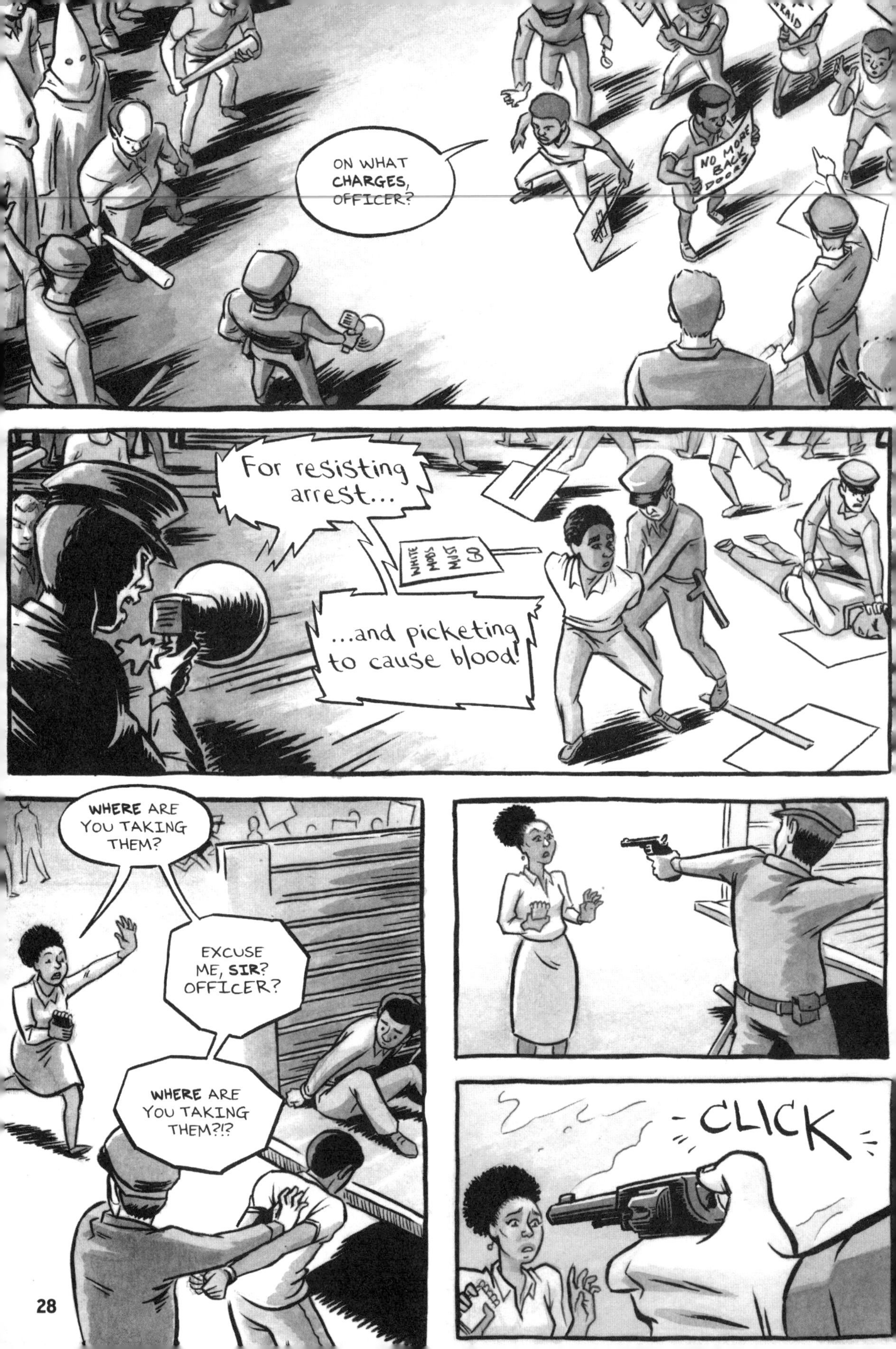
ON WHAT CHARGES, OFFICER?
NO MORE BACK DOORS
For resisting arrest...
...and picketing to cause blood!
WHITE MOBS MUST GO
WHERE ARE YOU TAKING THEM?
EXCUSE ME, SIR? OFFICER?
WHERE ARE YOU TAKING THEM?!?
CLICK

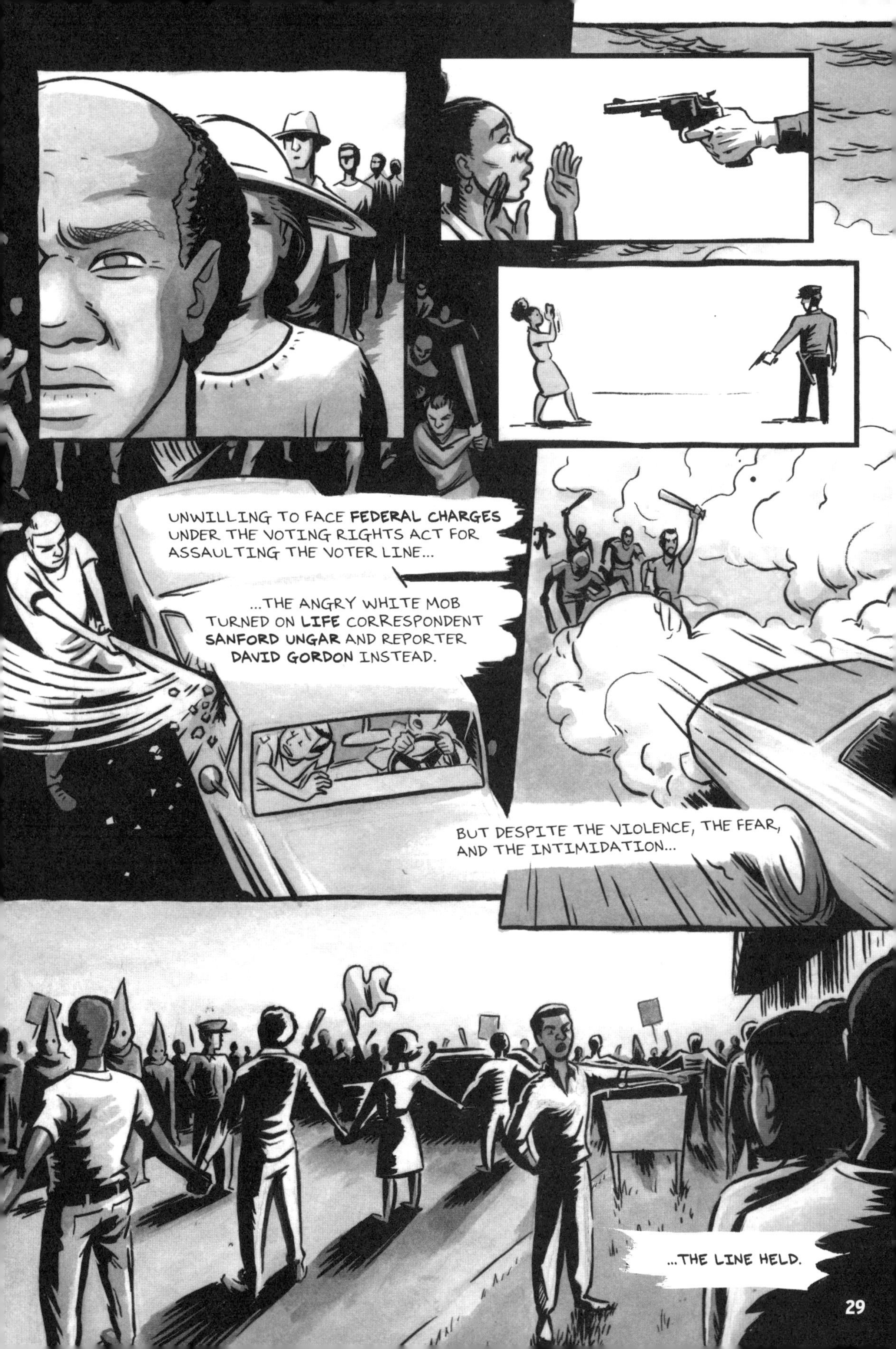
UNWILLING TO FACE FEDERAL CHARGES UNDER THE VOTING RIGHTS ACT FOR ASSAULTING THE VOTER LINE...
...THE ANGRY WHITE MOB TURNED ON LIFE CORRESPONDENT SANFORD UNGAR AND REPORTER DAVID GORDON INSTEAD.
BUT DESPITE THE VIOLENCE, THE FEAR, AND THE INTIMIDATION...
...THE LINE HELD.

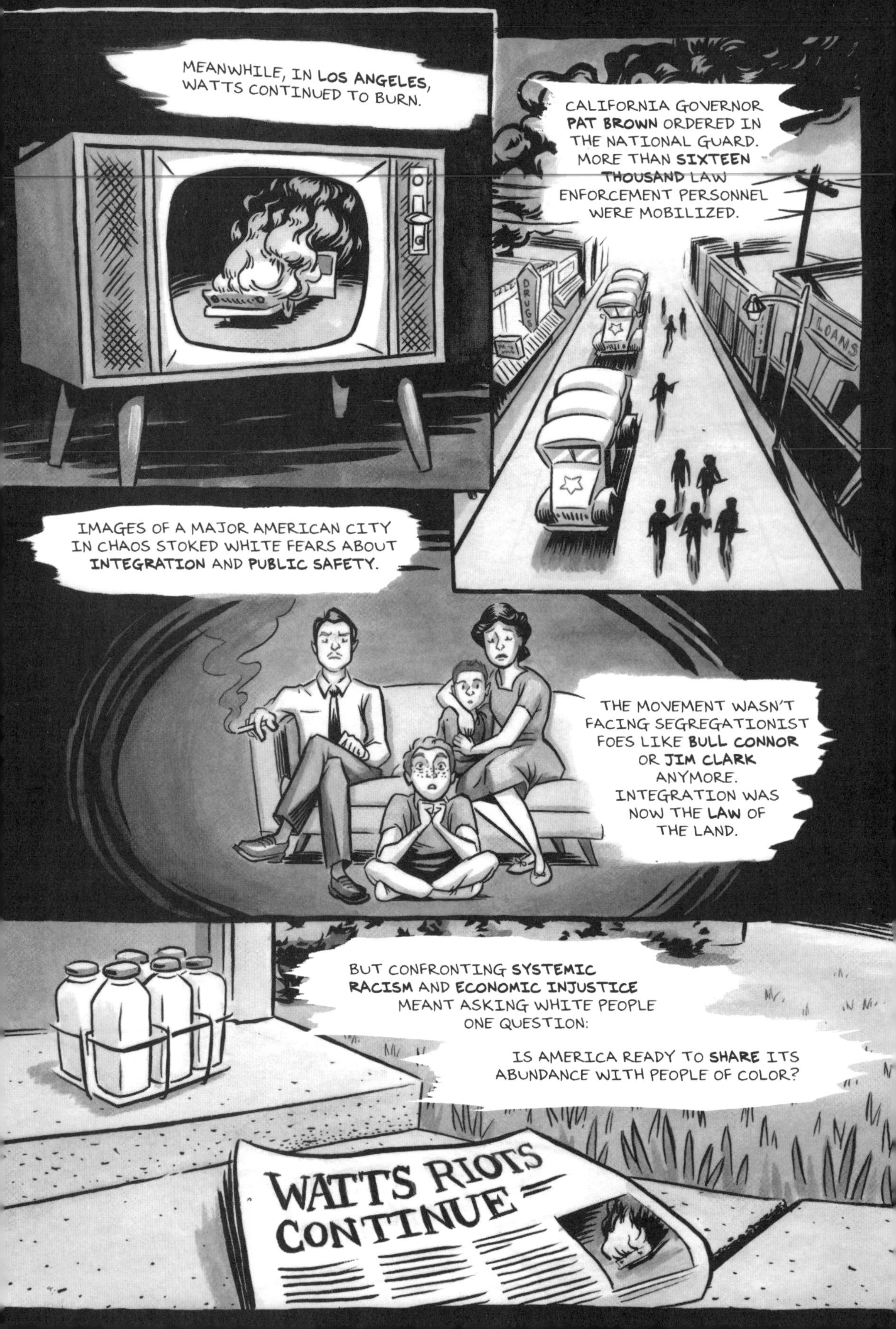
MEANWHILE, IN LOS ANGELES, WATTS CONTINUED TO BURN.
CALIFORNIA GOVERNOR PAT BROWN ORDERED IN THE NATIONAL GUARD. MORE THAN SIXTEEN THOUSAND LAW ENFORCEMENT PERSONNEL WERE MOBILIZED.
DRUGS
LOANS
IMAGES OF A MAJOR AMERICAN CITY IN CHAOS STOKED WHITE FEARS ABOUT INTEGRATION AND PUBLIC SAFETY.
THE MOVEMENT WASN'T FACING SEGREGATIONIST FOES LIKE BULL CONNOR OR JIM CLARK ANYMORE. INTEGRATION WAS NOW THE LAW OF THE LAND.
BUT CONFRONTING SYSTEMIC RACISM AND ECONOMIC INJUSTICE MEANT ASKING WHITE PEOPLE ONE QUESTION:
IS AMERICA READY TO SHARE ITS ABUNDANCE WITH PEOPLE OF COLOR?
WATTS RIOTS CONTINUE

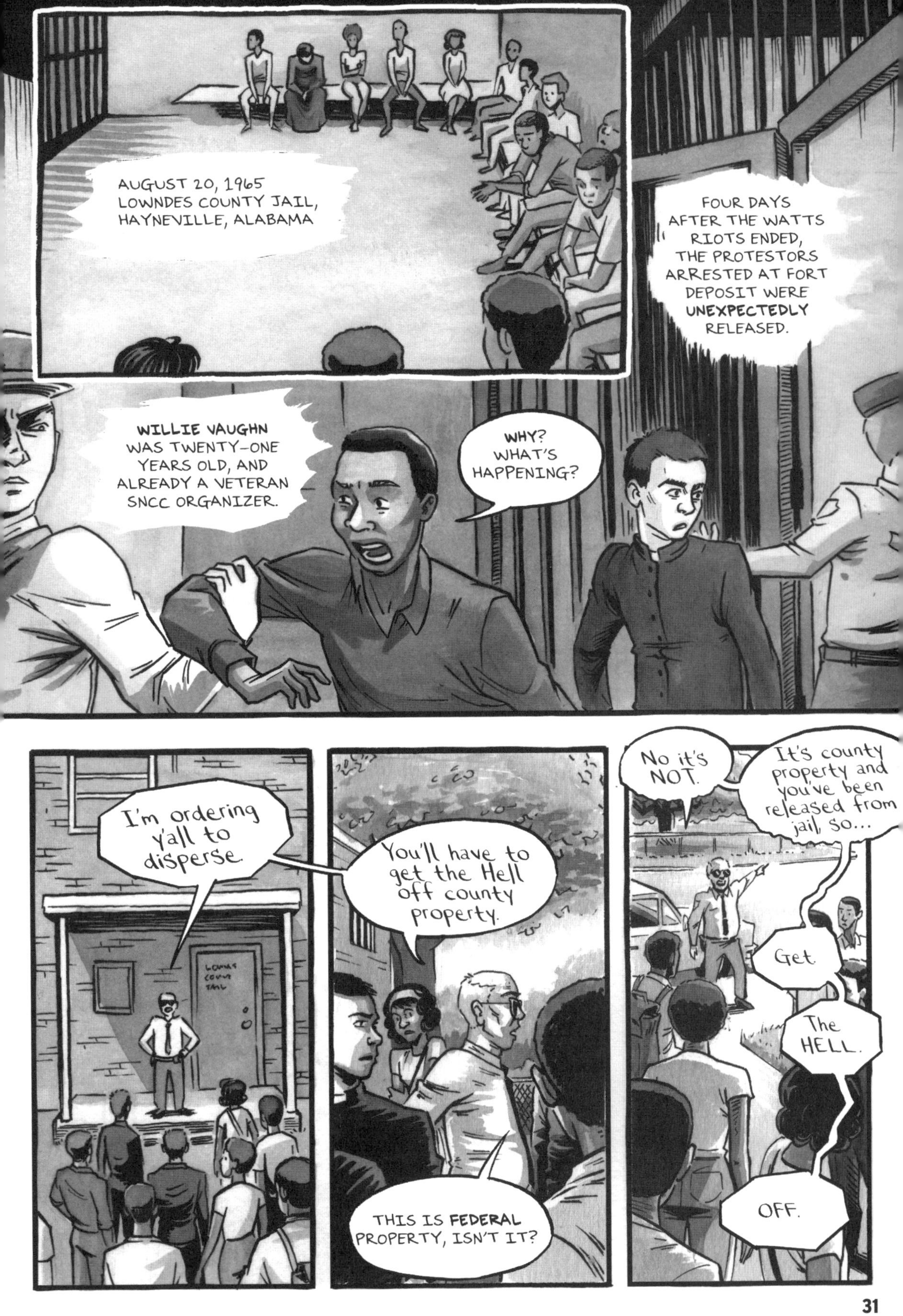
AUGUST 20, 1965
LOWNDES COUNTY JAIL, HAYNEVILLE, ALABAMA
FOUR DAYS AFTER THE WATTS RIOTS ENDED, THE PROTESTORS ARRESTED AT FORT DEPOSIT WERE UNEXPECTEDLY RELEASED.
WILLIE VAUGHN WAS TWENTY-ONE YEARS OLD, AND ALREADY A VETERAN SNCC ORGANIZER.
WHY? WHAT'S HAPPENING?
I'm ordering y'all to disperse.
You'll have to get the Hell off county property.
THIS IS FEDERAL PROPERTY, ISN'T IT?
No it's NOT.
It's county property and you've been released from jail, so...
Get.
The HELL.
OFF.

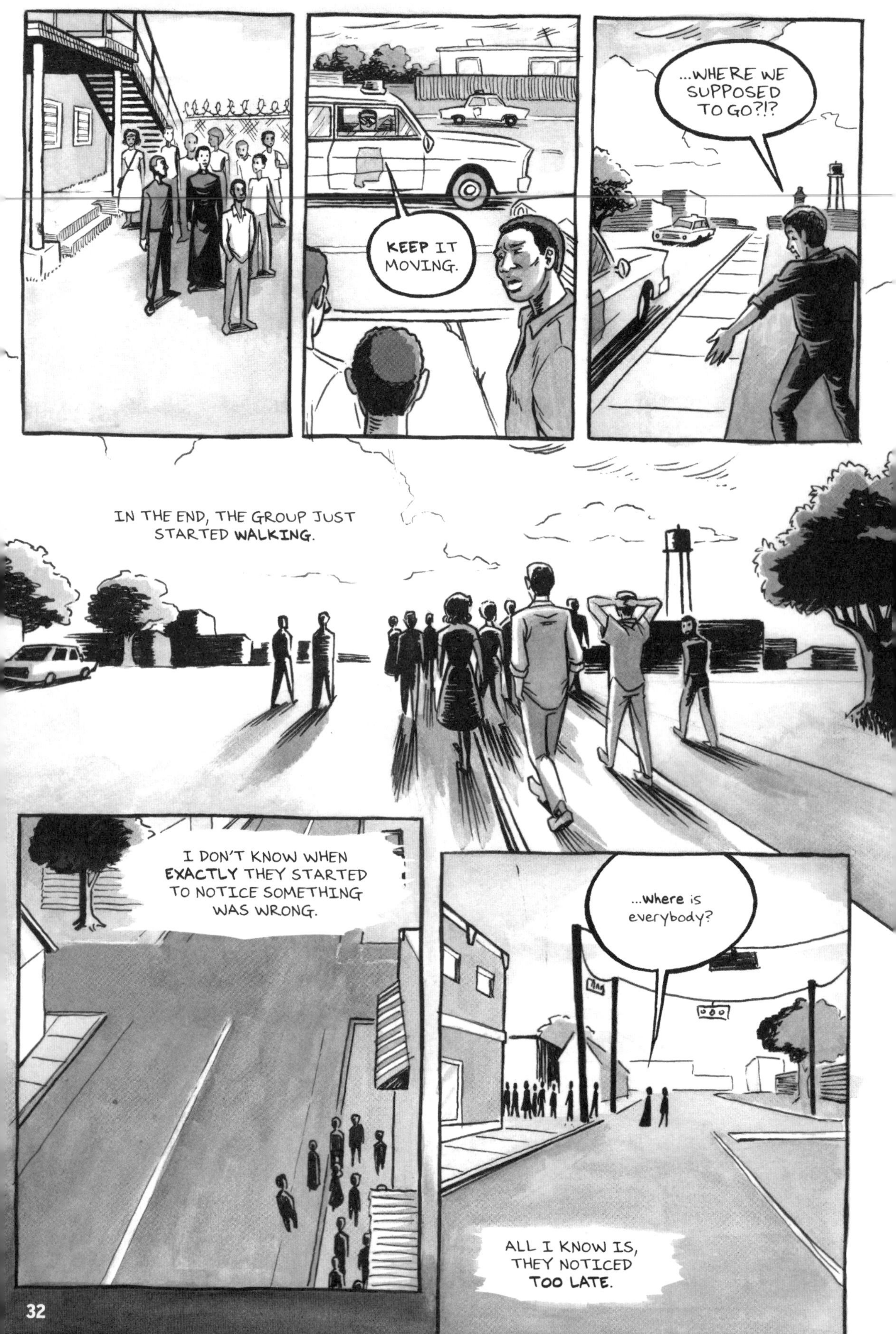
KEEP IT MOVING.
...WHERE WE SUPPOSED TO GO?!?
IN THE END, THE GROUP JUST STARTED WALKING.
I DON'T KNOW WHEN EXACTLY THEY STARTED TO NOTICE SOMETHING WAS WRONG.
...where is everybody?
ALL I KNOW IS, THEY NOTICED TOO LATE.

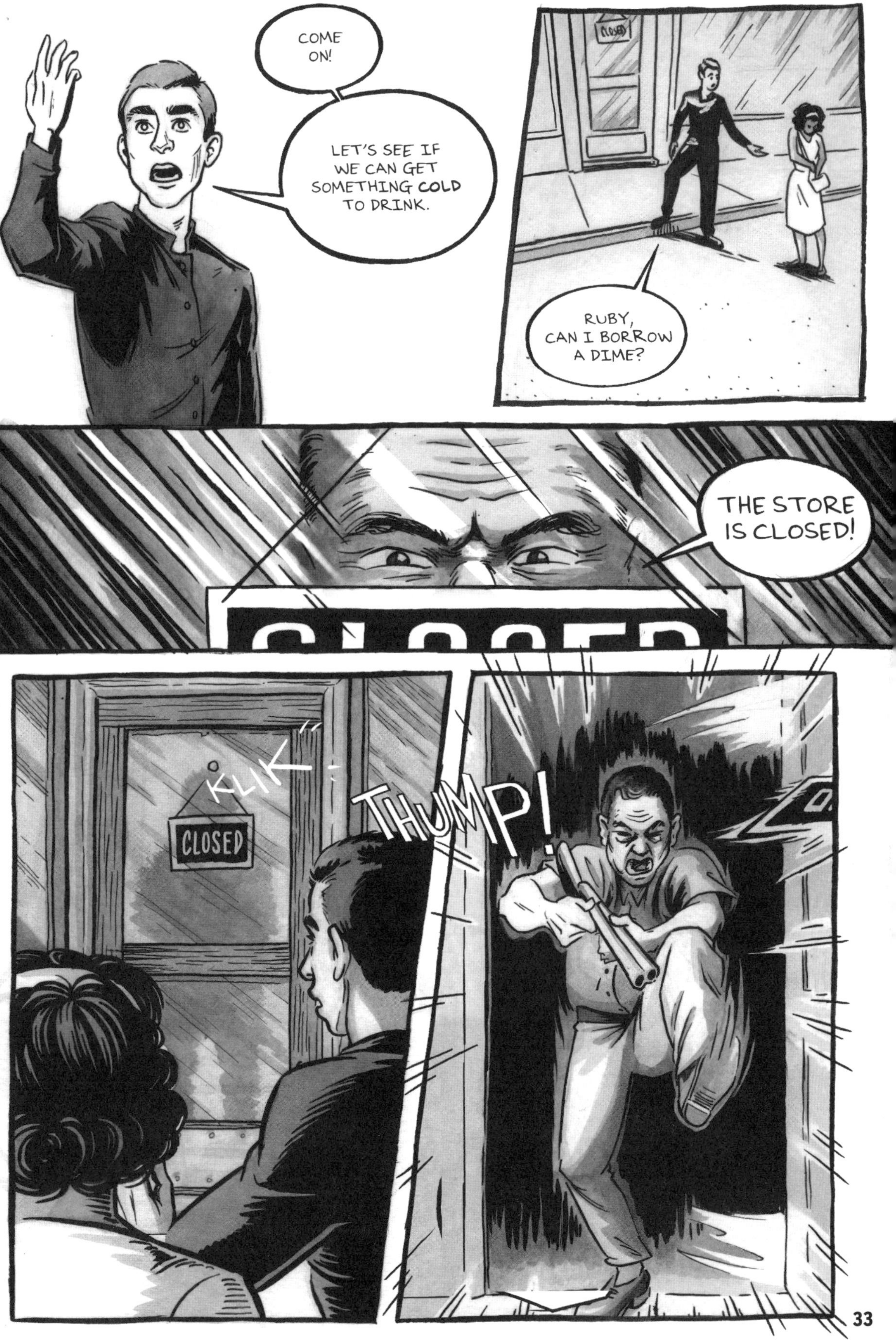
COME ON!
LET'S SEE IF WE CAN GET SOMETHING COLD TO DRINK.
CLOSED
RUBY, CAN I BORROW A DIME?
THE STORE IS CLOSED!
CLOSED
KLIK
THUMP!

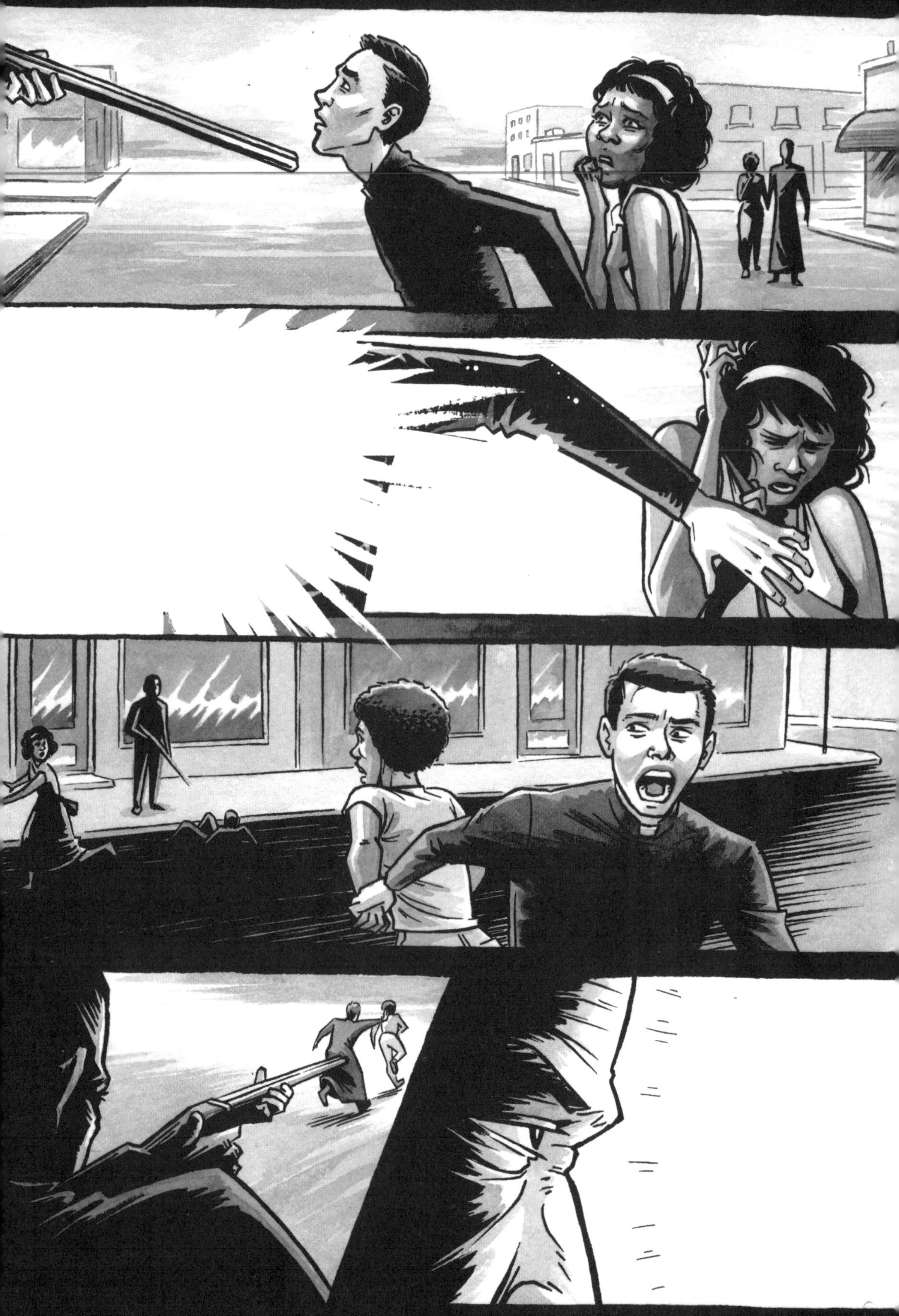

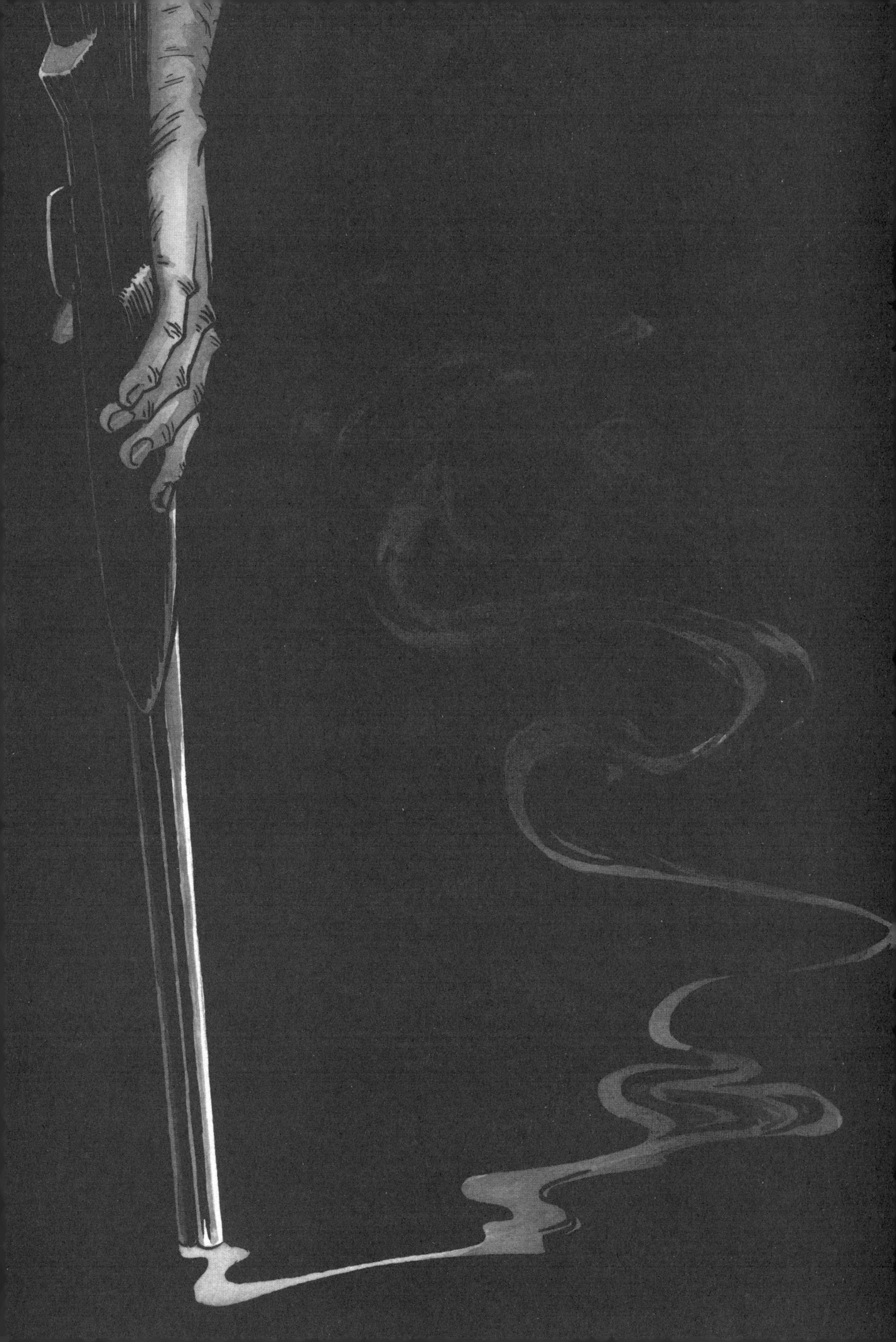

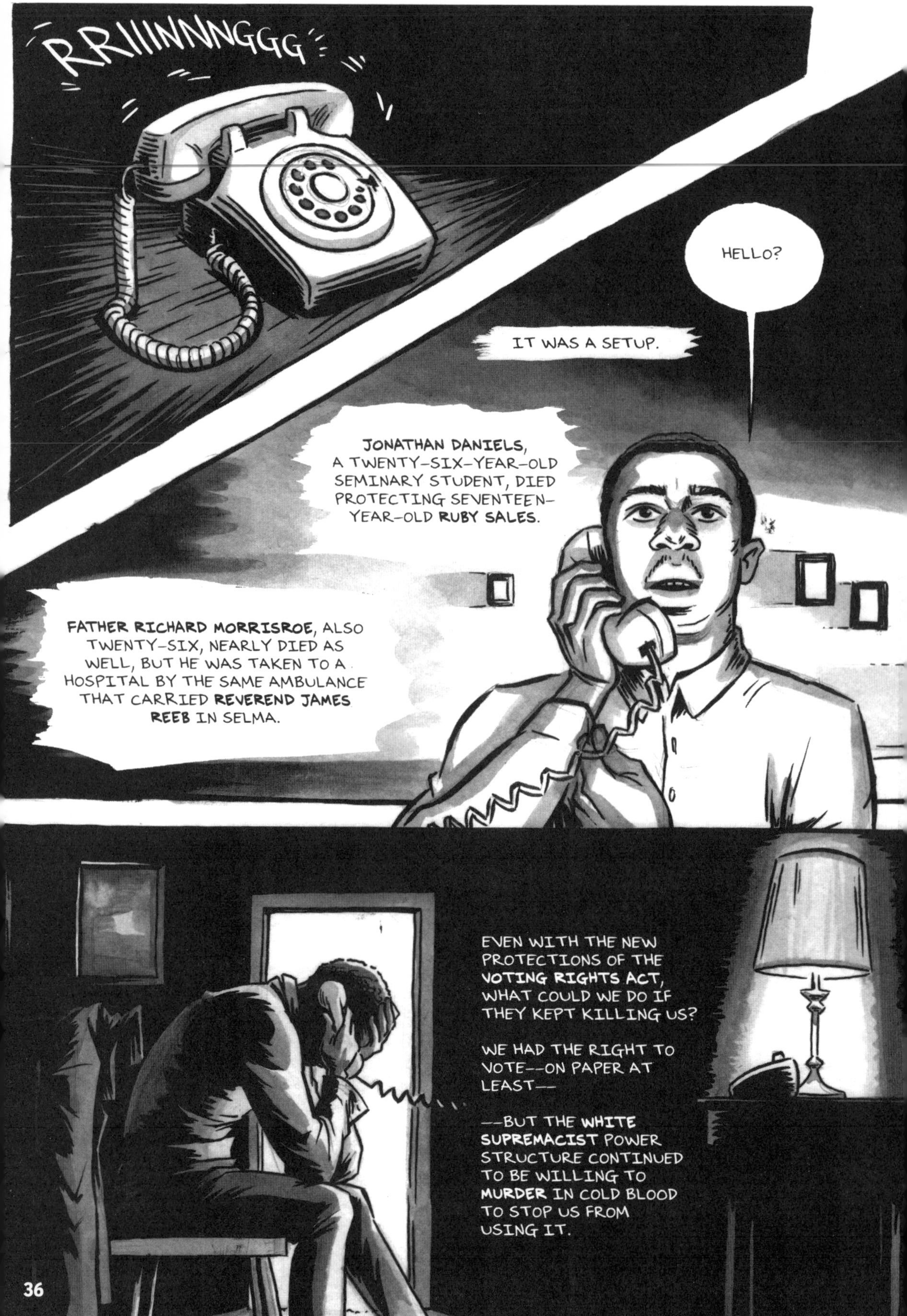
RRIIINNNGGG
HELLO?
IT WAS A SETUP.
JONATHAN DANIELS, A TWENTY-SIX-YEAR-OLD SEMINARY STUDENT, DIED PROTECTING SEVENTEEN-YEAR-OLD RUBY SALES.
FATHER RICHARD MORRISROE, ALSO TWENTY-SIX, NEARLY DIED AS WELL, BUT HE WAS TAKEN TO A HOSPITAL BY THE SAME AMBULANCE THAT CARRIED REVEREND JAMES REEB IN SELMA.
EVEN WITH THE NEW PROTECTIONS OF THE VOTING RIGHTS ACT, WHAT COULD WE DO IF THEY KEPT KILLING US?
WE HAD THE RIGHT TO VOTE--ON PAPER AT LEAST--
--BUT THE WHITE SUPREMACIST POWER STRUCTURE CONTINUED TO BE WILLING TO MURDER IN COLD BLOOD TO STOP US FROM USING IT.

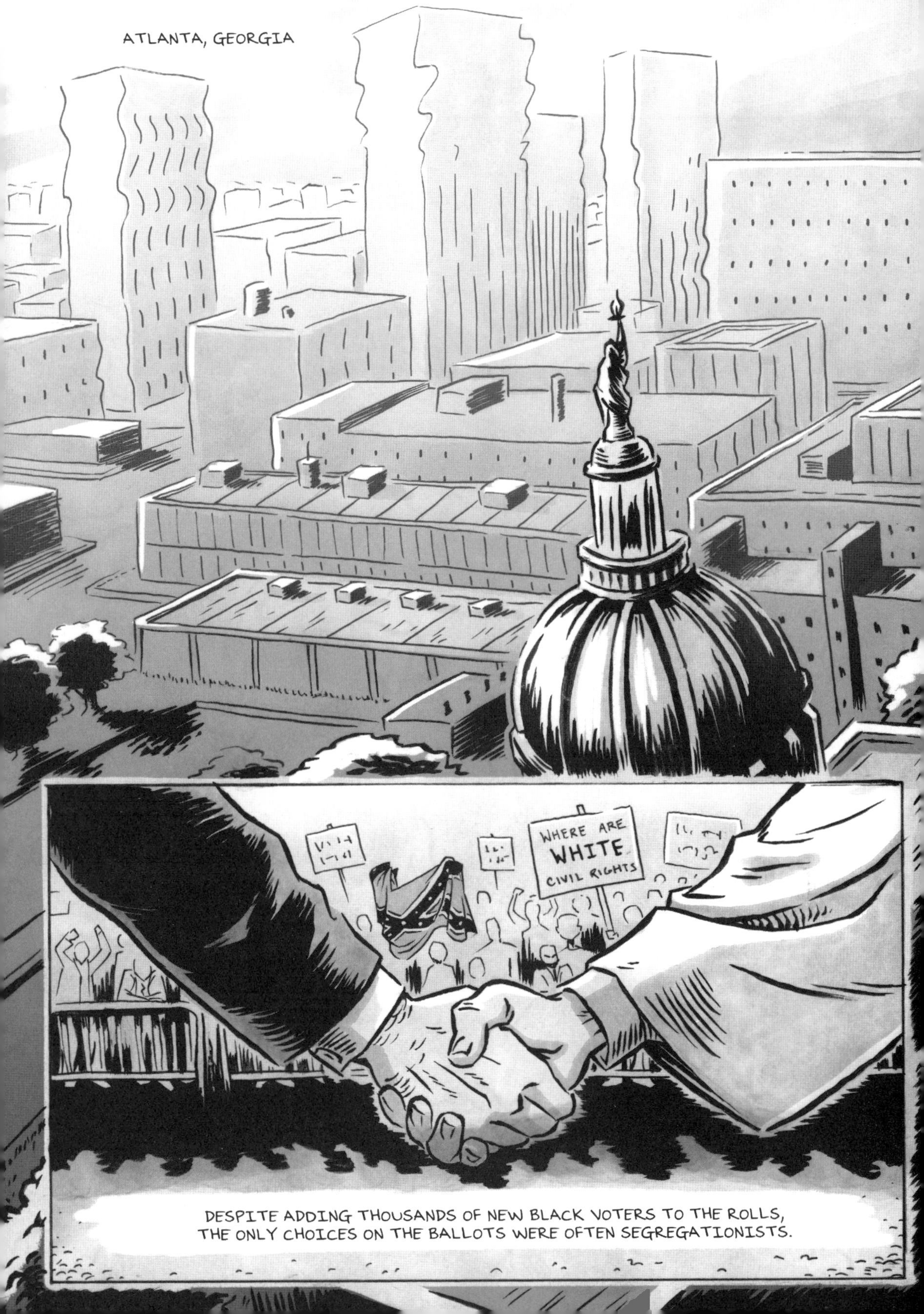
ATLANTA, GEORGIA
WHERE ARE WHITE CIVIL RIGHTS
DESPITE ADDING THOUSANDS OF NEW BLACK VOTERS TO THE ROLLS, THE ONLY CHOICES ON THE BALLOTS WERE OFTEN SEGREGATIONISTS.

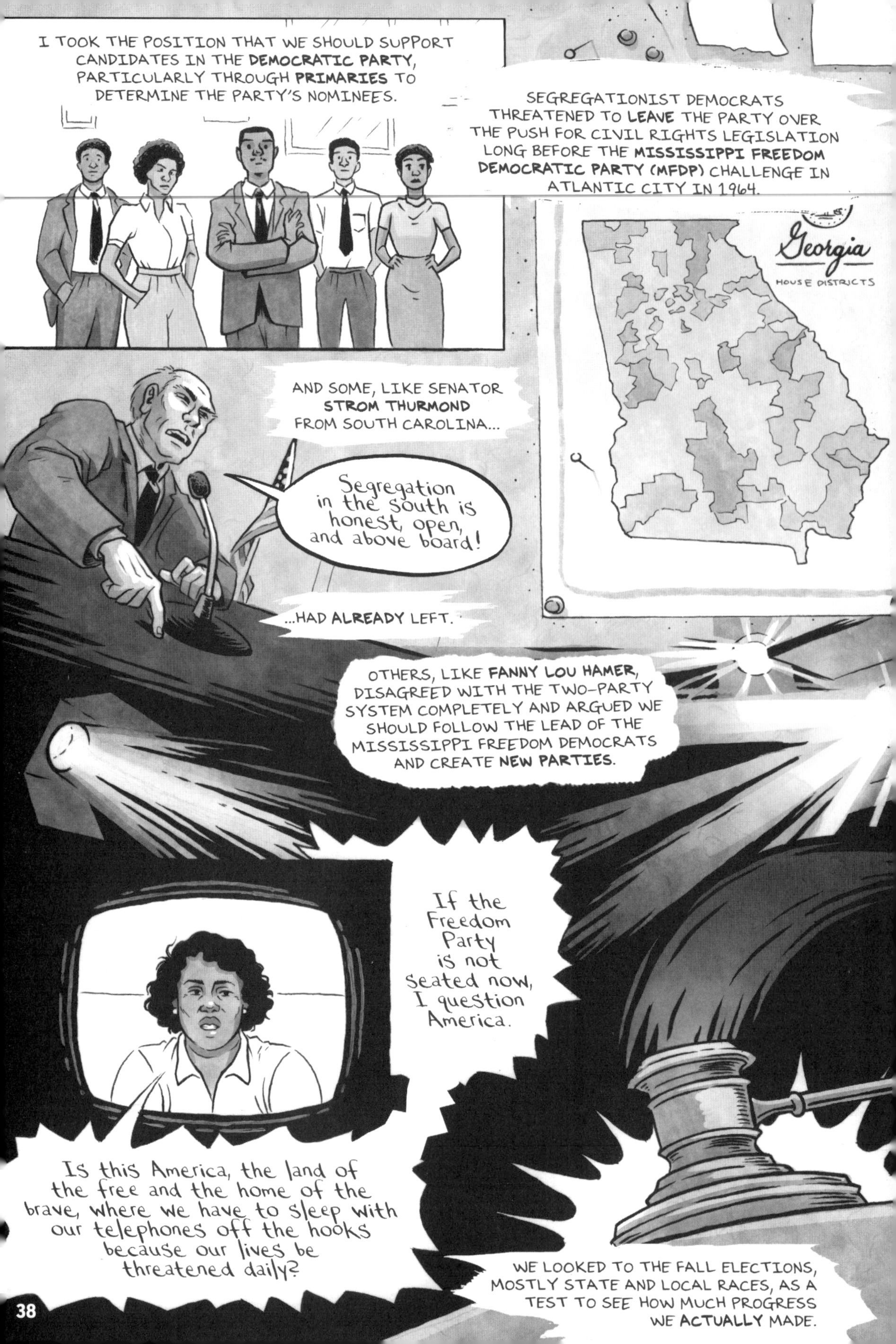

I TOOK THE POSITION THAT WE SHOULD SUPPORT CANDIDATES IN THE **DEMOCRATIC PARTY**, PARTICULARLY THROUGH **PRIMARIES** TO DETERMINE THE PARTY'S NOMINEES.
SEGREGATIONIST DEMOCRATS THREATENED TO **LEAVE** THE PARTY OVER THE PUSH FOR CIVIL RIGHTS LEGISLATION LONG BEFORE THE **MISSISSIPPI FREEDOM DEMOCRATIC PARTY (MFDP)** CHALLENGE IN ATLANTIC CITY IN 1964.
Georgia
HOUSE DISTRICTS
AND SOME, LIKE SENATOR **STROM THURMOND** FROM SOUTH CAROLINA...
Segregation in the South is honest, open, and above board!
...HAD **ALREADY** LEFT.
OTHERS, LIKE **FANNY LOU HAMER**, DISAGREED WITH THE TWO-PARTY SYSTEM COMPLETELY AND ARGUED WE SHOULD FOLLOW THE LEAD OF THE MISSISSIPPI FREEDOM DEMOCRATS AND CREATE **NEW PARTIES**.
If the Freedom Party is not seated now, I question America.
Is this America, the land of the free and the home of the brave, where we have to sleep with our telephones off the hooks because our lives be threatened daily?
WE LOOKED TO THE FALL ELECTIONS, MOSTLY STATE AND LOCAL RACES, AS A TEST TO SEE HOW MUCH PROGRESS WE **ACTUALLY** MADE.

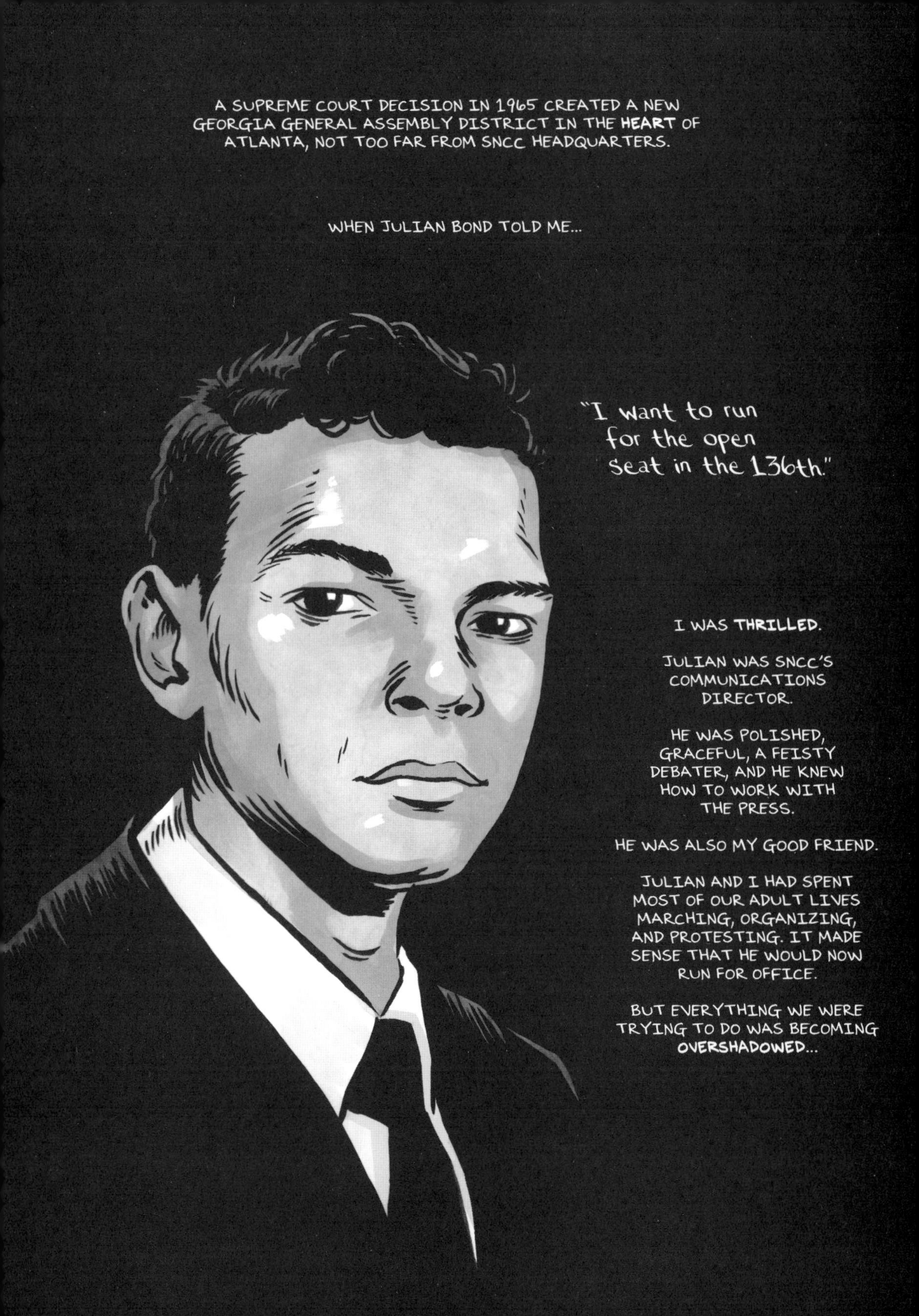
A SUPREME COURT DECISION IN 1965 CREATED A NEW GEORGIA GENERAL ASSEMBLY DISTRICT IN THE **HEART** OF ATLANTA, NOT TOO FAR FROM SNCC HEADQUARTERS.
WHEN JULIAN BOND TOLD ME...
"I want to run for the open seat in the 136th."
I WAS **THRILLED**.
JULIAN WAS SNCC'S COMMUNICATIONS DIRECTOR.
HE WAS POLISHED, GRACEFUL, A FEISTY DEBATER, AND HE KNEW HOW TO WORK WITH THE PRESS.
HE WAS ALSO MY GOOD FRIEND.
JULIAN AND I HAD SPENT MOST OF OUR ADULT LIVES MARCHING, ORGANIZING, AND PROTESTING. IT MADE SENSE THAT HE WOULD NOW RUN FOR OFFICE.
BUT EVERYTHING WE WERE TRYING TO DO WAS BECOMING **OVERSHADOWED**...

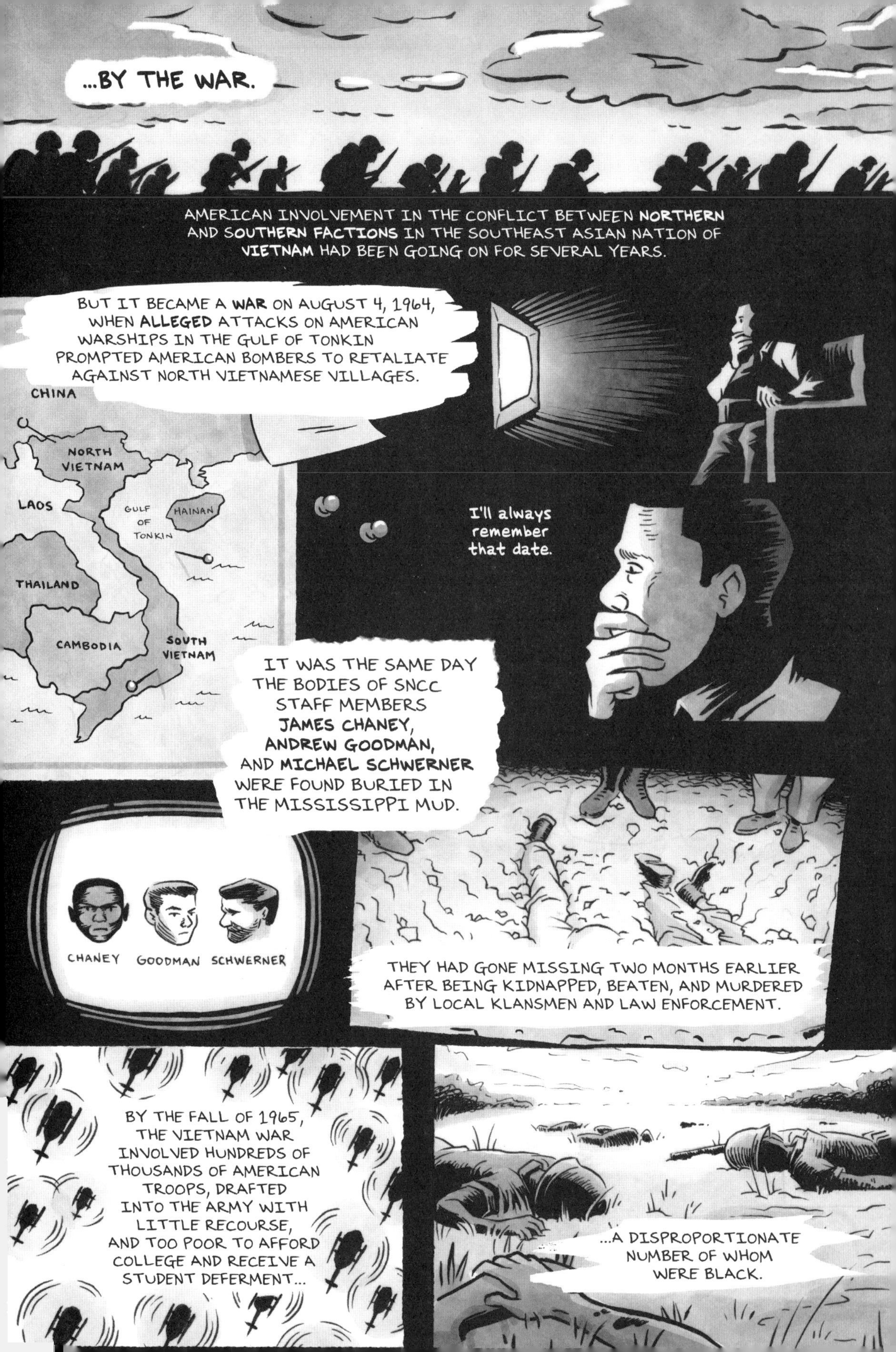
...BY THE WAR.
AMERICAN INVOLVEMENT IN THE CONFLICT BETWEEN NORTHERN AND SOUTHERN FACTIONS IN THE SOUTHEAST ASIAN NATION OF VIETNAM HAD BEEN GOING ON FOR SEVERAL YEARS.
BUT IT BECAME A WAR ON AUGUST 4, 1964, WHEN ALLEGED ATTACKS ON AMERICAN WARSHIPS IN THE GULF OF TONKIN PROMPTED AMERICAN BOMBERS TO RETALIATE AGAINST NORTH VIETNAMESE VILLAGES.
CHINA
NORTH VIETNAM
LAOS
GULF OF TONKIN
HAINAN
THAILAND
CAMBODIA
SOUTH VIETNAM
I'll always remember that date.
IT WAS THE SAME DAY THE BODIES OF SNCC STAFF MEMBERS JAMES CHANEY, ANDREW GOODMAN, AND MICHAEL SCHWERNER WERE FOUND BURIED IN THE MISSISSIPPI MUD.
CHANEY
GOODMAN
SCHWERNER
THEY HAD GONE MISSING TWO MONTHS EARLIER AFTER BEING KIDNAPPED, BEATEN, AND MURDERED BY LOCAL KLANSMEN AND LAW ENFORCEMENT.
BY THE FALL OF 1965, THE VIETNAM WAR INVOLVED HUNDREDS OF THOUSANDS OF AMERICAN TROOPS, DRAFTED INTO THE ARMY WITH LITTLE RECOURSE, AND TOO POOR TO AFFORD COLLEGE AND RECEIVE A STUDENT DEFERMENT...
...A DISPROPORTIONATE NUMBER OF WHOM WERE BLACK.

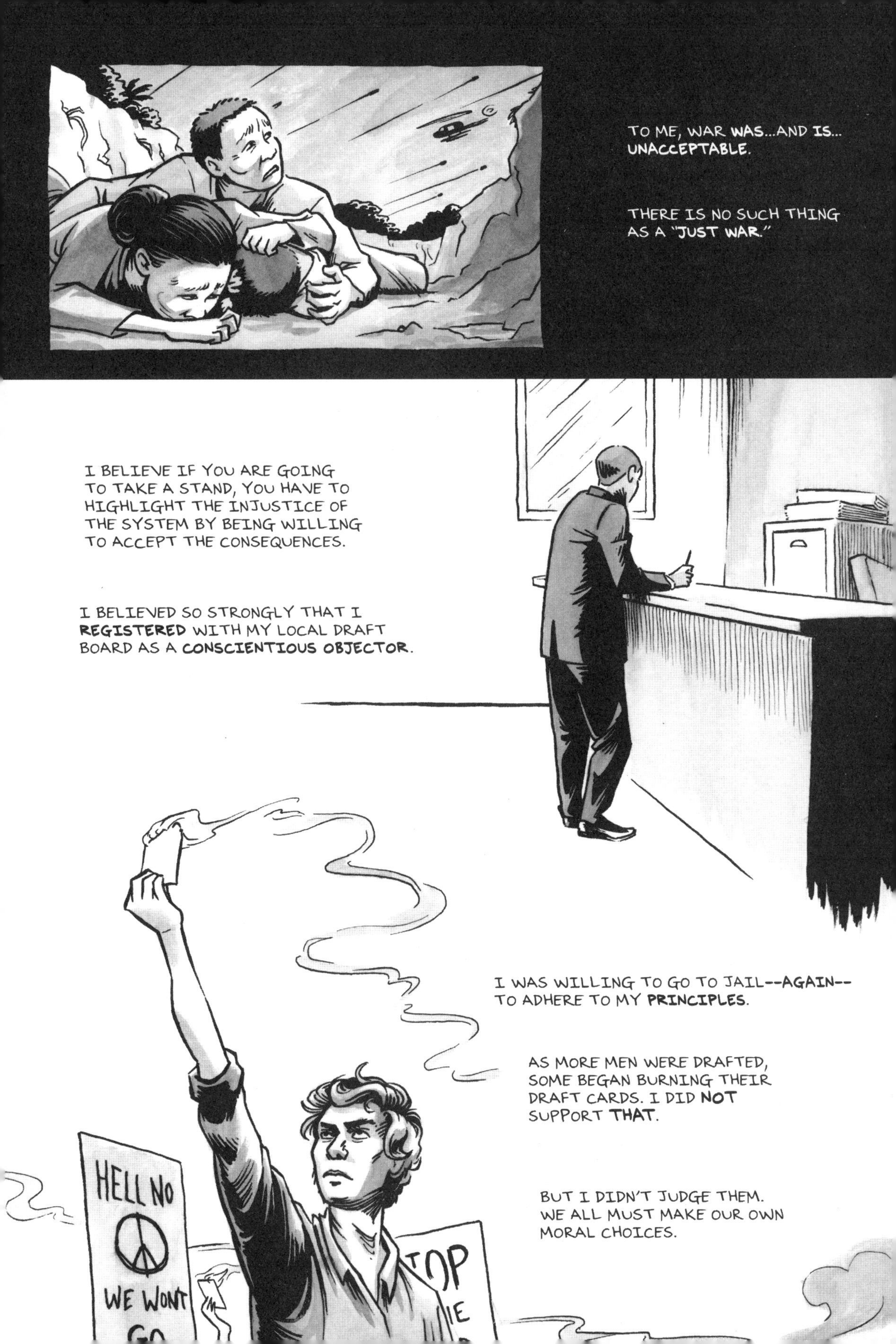

TO ME, WAR WAS...AND IS... UNACCEPTABLE.
THERE IS NO SUCH THING AS A "JUST WAR."
I BELIEVE IF YOU ARE GOING TO TAKE A STAND, YOU HAVE TO HIGHLIGHT THE INJUSTICE OF THE SYSTEM BY BEING WILLING TO ACCEPT THE CONSEQUENCES.
I BELIEVED SO STRONGLY THAT I REGISTERED WITH MY LOCAL DRAFT BOARD AS A CONSCIENTIOUS OBJECTOR.
I WAS WILLING TO GO TO JAIL--AGAIN--TO ADHERE TO MY PRINCIPLES.
AS MORE MEN WERE DRAFTED, SOME BEGAN BURNING THEIR DRAFT CARDS. I DID NOT SUPPORT THAT.
BUT I DIDN'T JUDGE THEM. WE ALL MUST MAKE OUR OWN MORAL CHOICES.
HELL NO
WE WONT

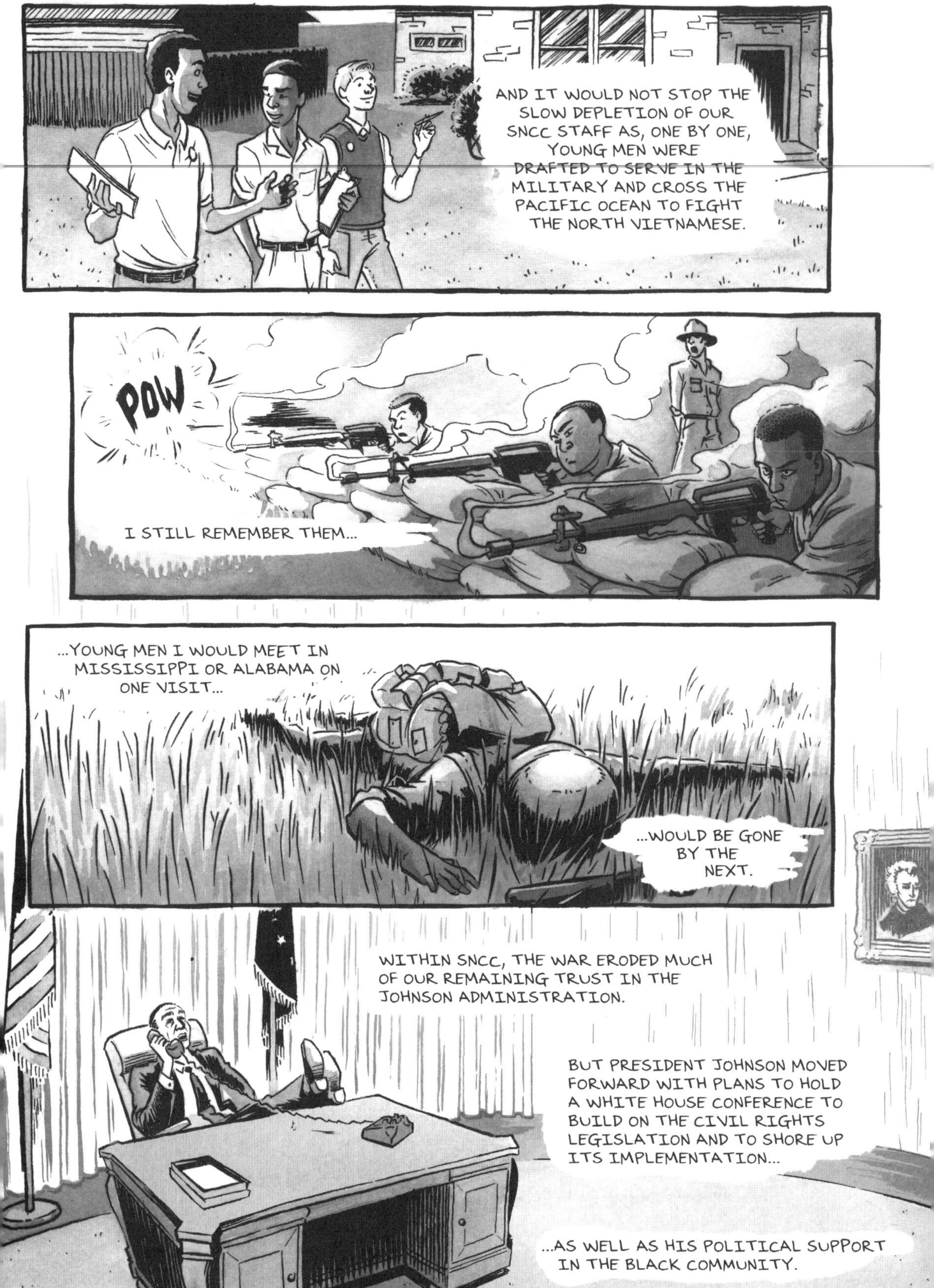
AND IT WOULD NOT STOP THE SLOW DEPLETION OF OUR SNCC STAFF AS, ONE BY ONE, YOUNG MEN WERE DRAFTED TO SERVE IN THE MILITARY AND CROSS THE PACIFIC OCEAN TO FIGHT THE NORTH VIETNAMESE.
POW
I STILL REMEMBER THEM...
...YOUNG MEN I WOULD MEET IN MISSISSIPPI OR ALABAMA ON ONE VISIT...
...WOULD BE GONE BY THE NEXT.
WITHIN SNCC, THE WAR ERODED MUCH OF OUR REMAINING TRUST IN THE JOHNSON ADMINISTRATION.
BUT PRESIDENT JOHNSON MOVED FORWARD WITH PLANS TO HOLD A WHITE HOUSE CONFERENCE TO BUILD ON THE CIVIL RIGHTS LEGISLATION AND TO SHORE UP ITS IMPLEMENTATION...
...AS WELL AS HIS POLITICAL SUPPORT IN THE BLACK COMMUNITY.

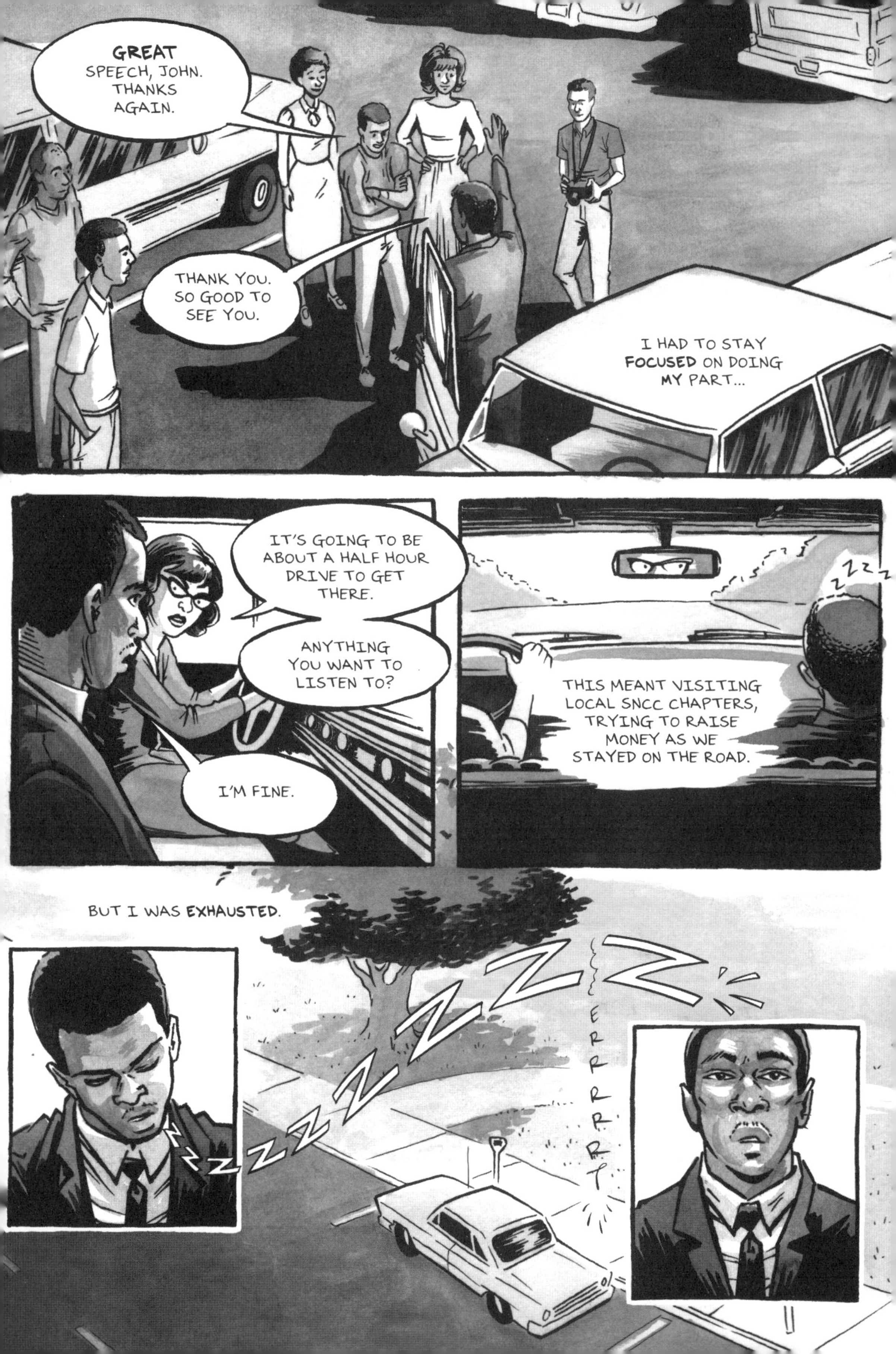
GREAT SPEECH, JOHN. THANKS AGAIN.
THANK YOU. SO GOOD TO SEE YOU.
I HAD TO STAY FOCUSED ON DOING MY PART...
IT'S GOING TO BE ABOUT A HALF HOUR DRIVE TO GET THERE.
ANYTHING YOU WANT TO LISTEN TO?
I'M FINE.
ZZZ
THIS MEANT VISITING LOCAL SNCC CHAPTERS, TRYING TO RAISE MONEY AS WE STAYED ON THE ROAD.
BUT I WAS EXHAUSTED.
ZZZZZZZZ
ERRRRRT

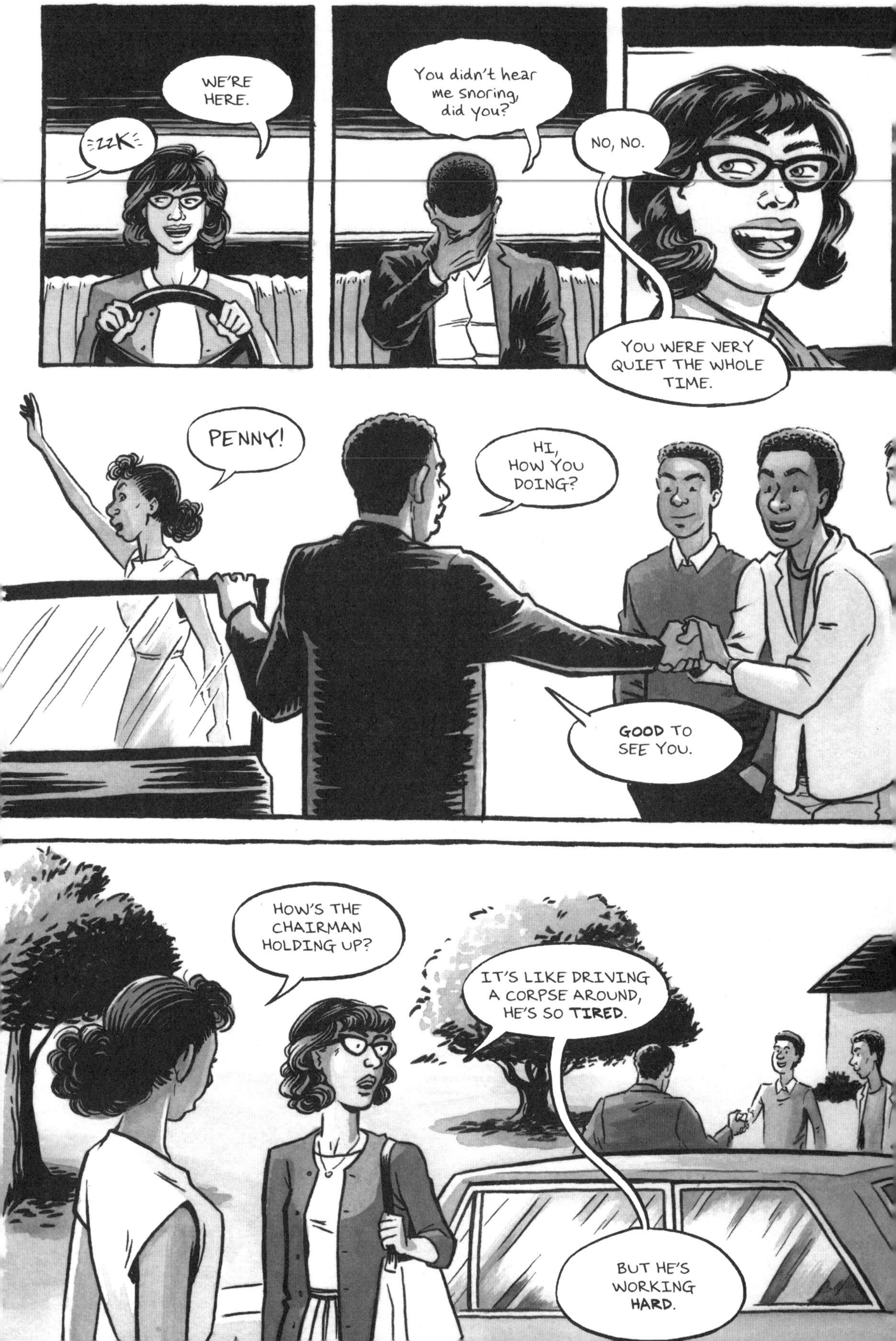
WE'RE HERE.
ZZK
You didn't hear me snoring, did you?
NO, NO.
YOU WERE VERY QUIET THE WHOLE TIME.
PENNY!
HI, HOW YOU DOING?
GOOD TO SEE YOU.
HOW'S THE CHAIRMAN HOLDING UP?
IT'S LIKE DRIVING A CORPSE AROUND, HE'S SO TIRED.
BUT HE'S WORKING HARD.

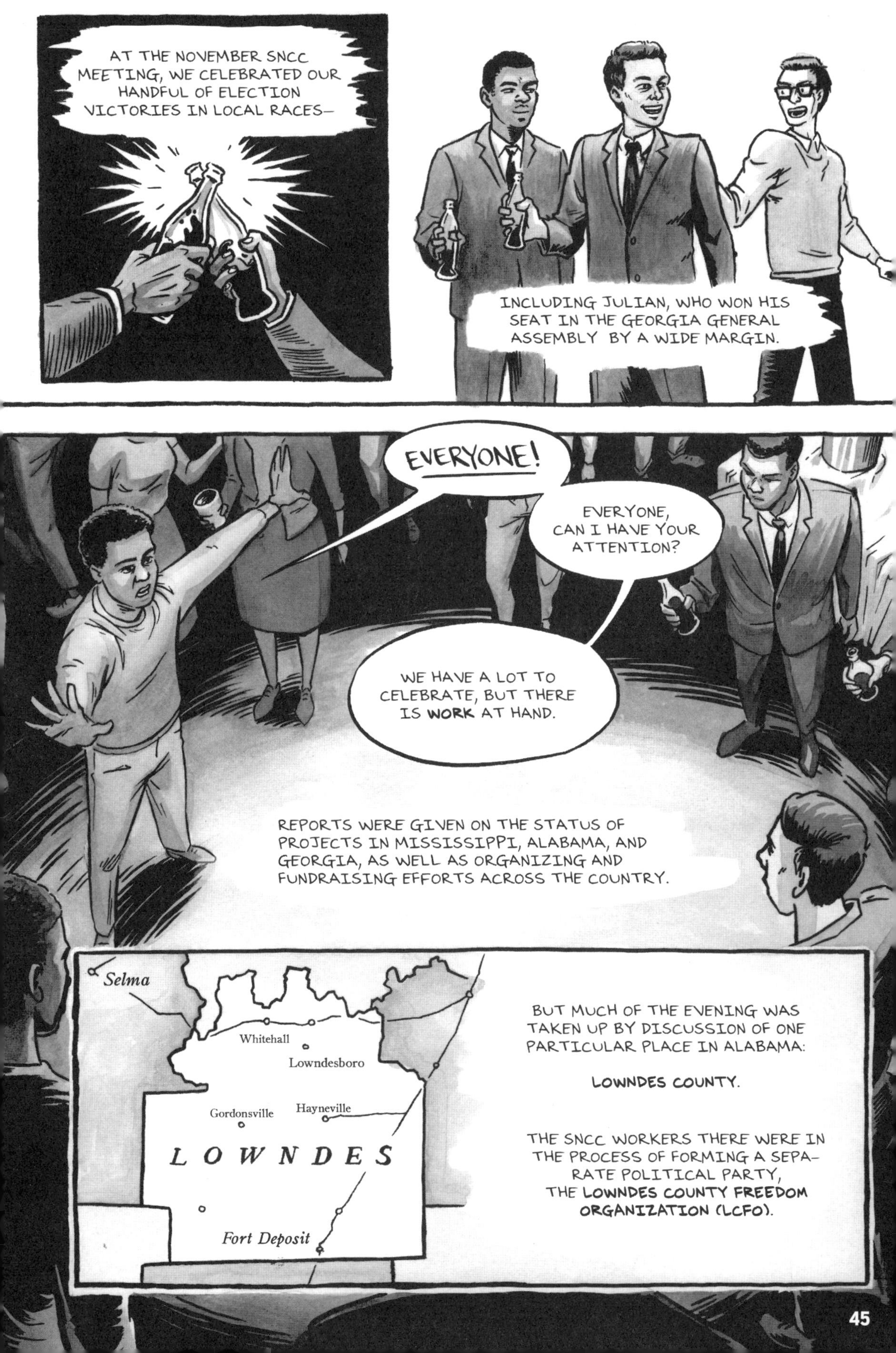
AT THE NOVEMBER SNCC MEETING, WE CELEBRATED OUR HANDFUL OF ELECTION VICTORIES IN LOCAL RACES–
INCLUDING JULIAN, WHO WON HIS SEAT IN THE GEORGIA GENERAL ASSEMBLY BY A WIDE MARGIN.
EVERYONE!
EVERYONE, CAN I HAVE YOUR ATTENTION?
WE HAVE A LOT TO CELEBRATE, BUT THERE IS **WORK** AT HAND.
REPORTS WERE GIVEN ON THE STATUS OF PROJECTS IN MISSISSIPPI, ALABAMA, AND GEORGIA, AS WELL AS ORGANIZING AND FUNDRAISING EFFORTS ACROSS THE COUNTRY.
Selma
Whitehall
Lowndesboro
Gordonsville
Hayneville
LOWNDES
Fort Deposit
BUT MUCH OF THE EVENING WAS TAKEN UP BY DISCUSSION OF ONE PARTICULAR PLACE IN ALABAMA:
LOWNDES COUNTY.
THE SNCC WORKERS THERE WERE IN THE PROCESS OF FORMING A SEPARATE POLITICAL PARTY, THE **LOWNDES COUNTY FREEDOM ORGANIZATION (LCFO).**

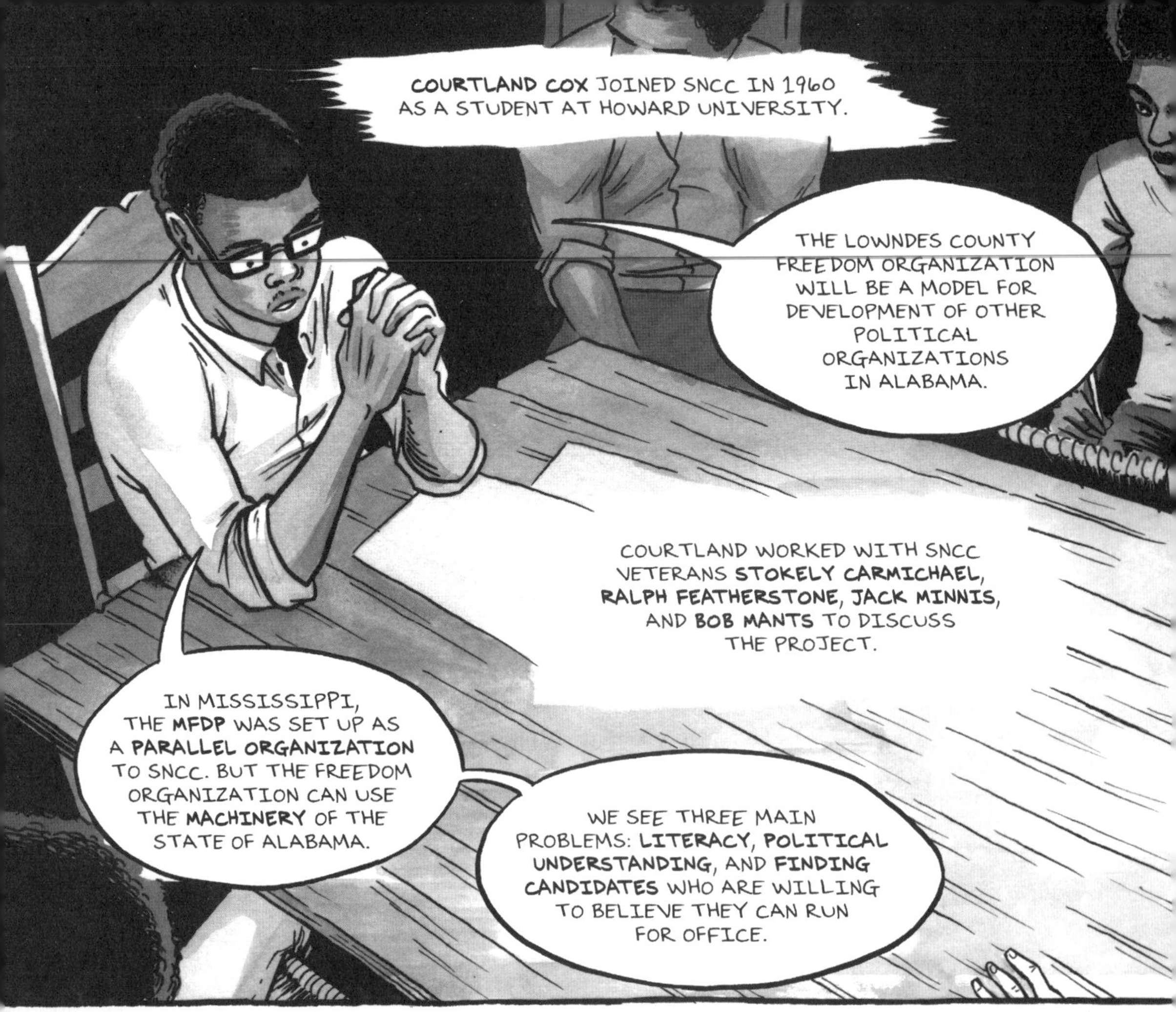
COURTLAND COX JOINED SNCC IN 1960 AS A STUDENT AT HOWARD UNIVERSITY.
THE LOWNDES COUNTY FREEDOM ORGANIZATION WILL BE A MODEL FOR DEVELOPMENT OF OTHER POLITICAL ORGANIZATIONS IN ALABAMA.
COURTLAND WORKED WITH SNCC VETERANS STOKELY CARMICHAEL, RALPH FEATHERSTONE, JACK MINNIS, AND BOB MANTS TO DISCUSS THE PROJECT.
IN MISSISSIPPI, THE MFDP WAS SET UP AS A PARALLEL ORGANIZATION TO SNCC. BUT THE FREEDOM ORGANIZATION CAN USE THE MACHINERY OF THE STATE OF ALABAMA.
WE SEE THREE MAIN PROBLEMS: LITERACY, POLITICAL UNDERSTANDING, AND FINDING CANDIDATES WHO ARE WILLING TO BELIEVE THEY CAN RUN FOR OFFICE.

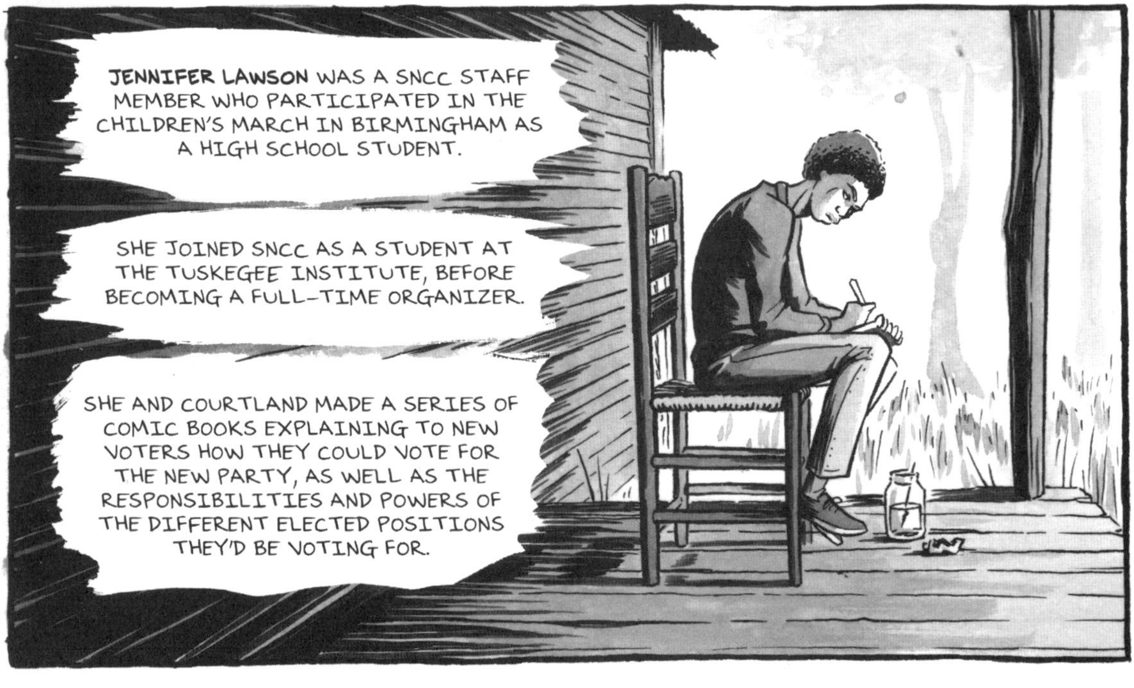
JENNIFER LAWSON WAS A SNCC STAFF MEMBER WHO PARTICIPATED IN THE CHILDREN'S MARCH IN BIRMINGHAM AS A HIGH SCHOOL STUDENT.
SHE JOINED SNCC AS A STUDENT AT THE TUSKEGEE INSTITUTE, BEFORE BECOMING A FULL-TIME ORGANIZER.
SHE AND COURTLAND MADE A SERIES OF COMIC BOOKS EXPLAINING TO NEW VOTERS HOW THEY COULD VOTE FOR THE NEW PARTY, AS WELL AS THE RESPONSIBILITIES AND POWERS OF THE DIFFERENT ELECTED POSITIONS THEY'D BE VOTING FOR.

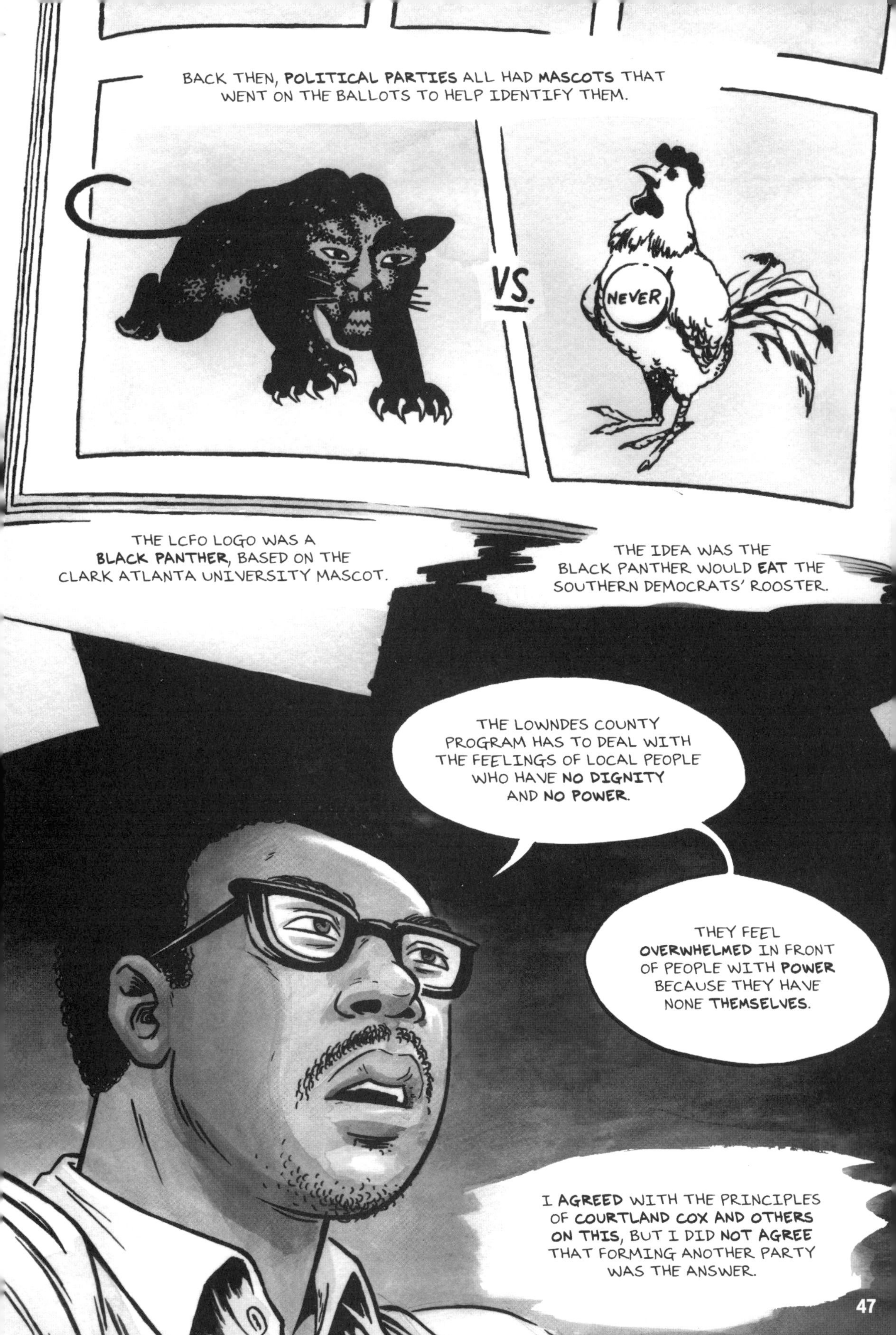
BACK THEN, POLITICAL PARTIES ALL HAD MASCOTS THAT WENT ON THE BALLOTS TO HELP IDENTIFY THEM.
VS.
NEVER
THE LCFO LOGO WAS A BLACK PANTHER, BASED ON THE CLARK ATLANTA UNIVERSITY MASCOT.
THE IDEA WAS THE BLACK PANTHER WOULD EAT THE SOUTHERN DEMOCRATS' ROOSTER.
THE LOWNDES COUNTY PROGRAM HAS TO DEAL WITH THE FEELINGS OF LOCAL PEOPLE WHO HAVE NO DIGNITY AND NO POWER.
THEY FEEL OVERWHELMED IN FRONT OF PEOPLE WITH POWER BECAUSE THEY HAVE NONE THEMSELVES.
I AGREED WITH THE PRINCIPLES OF COURTLAND COX AND OTHERS ON THIS, BUT I DID NOT AGREE THAT FORMING ANOTHER PARTY WAS THE ANSWER.

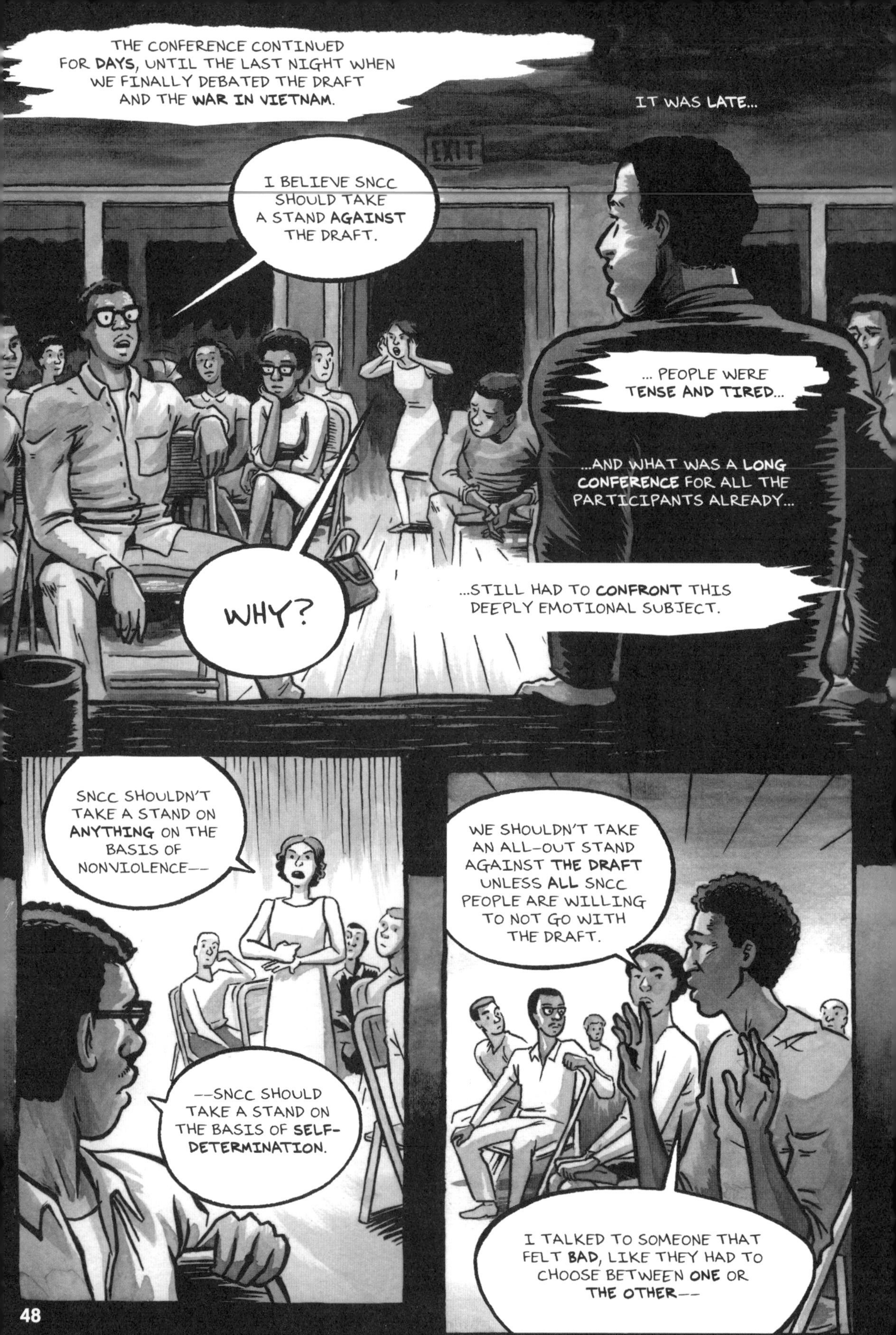
THE CONFERENCE CONTINUED FOR DAYS, UNTIL THE LAST NIGHT WHEN WE FINALLY DEBATED THE DRAFT AND THE WAR IN VIETNAM.
IT WAS LATE...
EXIT
I BELIEVE SNCC SHOULD TAKE A STAND AGAINST THE DRAFT.
... PEOPLE WERE TENSE AND TIRED...
...AND WHAT WAS A LONG CONFERENCE FOR ALL THE PARTICIPANTS ALREADY...
WHY?
...STILL HAD TO CONFRONT THIS DEEPLY EMOTIONAL SUBJECT.
SNCC SHOULDN'T TAKE A STAND ON ANYTHING ON THE BASIS OF NONVIOLENCE--
--SNCC SHOULD TAKE A STAND ON THE BASIS OF SELF-DETERMINATION.
WE SHOULDN'T TAKE AN ALL-OUT STAND AGAINST THE DRAFT UNLESS ALL SNCC PEOPLE ARE WILLING TO NOT GO WITH THE DRAFT.
I TALKED TO SOMEONE THAT FELT BAD, LIKE THEY HAD TO CHOOSE BETWEEN ONE OR THE OTHER--

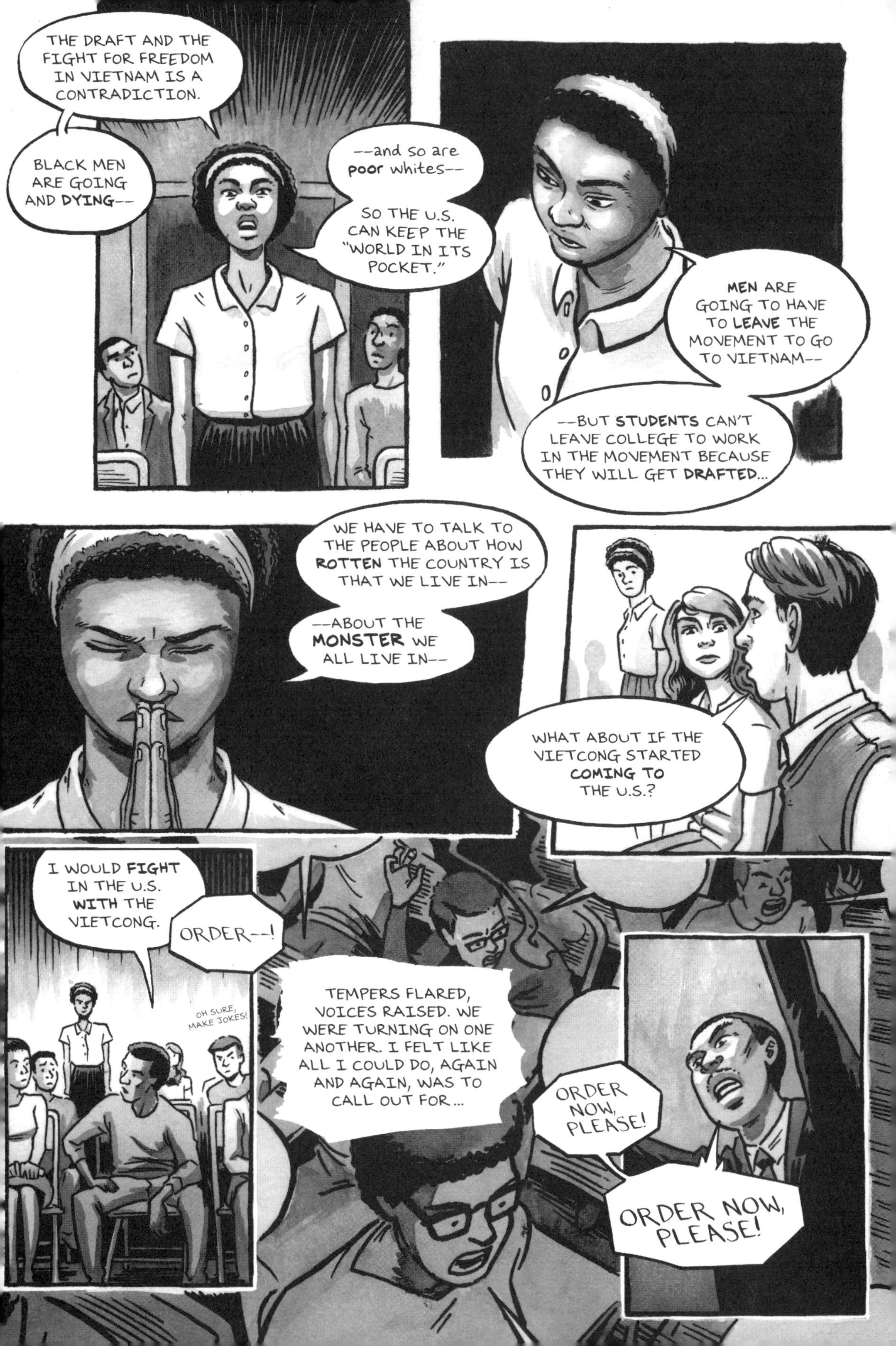
THE DRAFT AND THE FIGHT FOR FREEDOM IN VIETNAM IS A CONTRADICTION.
BLACK MEN ARE GOING AND **DYING**--
--and so are **poor** whites--
SO THE U.S. CAN KEEP THE "WORLD IN ITS POCKET."
MEN ARE GOING TO HAVE TO **LEAVE** THE MOVEMENT TO GO TO VIETNAM--
--BUT **STUDENTS** CAN'T LEAVE COLLEGE TO WORK IN THE MOVEMENT BECAUSE THEY WILL GET **DRAFTED**...
WE HAVE TO TALK TO THE PEOPLE ABOUT HOW **ROTTEN** THE COUNTRY IS THAT WE LIVE IN--
--ABOUT THE **MONSTER** WE ALL LIVE IN--
WHAT ABOUT IF THE VIETCONG STARTED **COMING TO** THE U.S.?
I WOULD **FIGHT** IN THE U.S. **WITH** THE VIETCONG.
ORDER--!
OH SURE, MAKE JOKES!
TEMPERS FLARED, VOICES RAISED. WE WERE TURNING ON ONE ANOTHER. I FELT LIKE ALL I COULD DO, AGAIN AND AGAIN, WAS TO CALL OUT FOR...
ORDER NOW, PLEASE!
ORDER NOW, PLEASE!

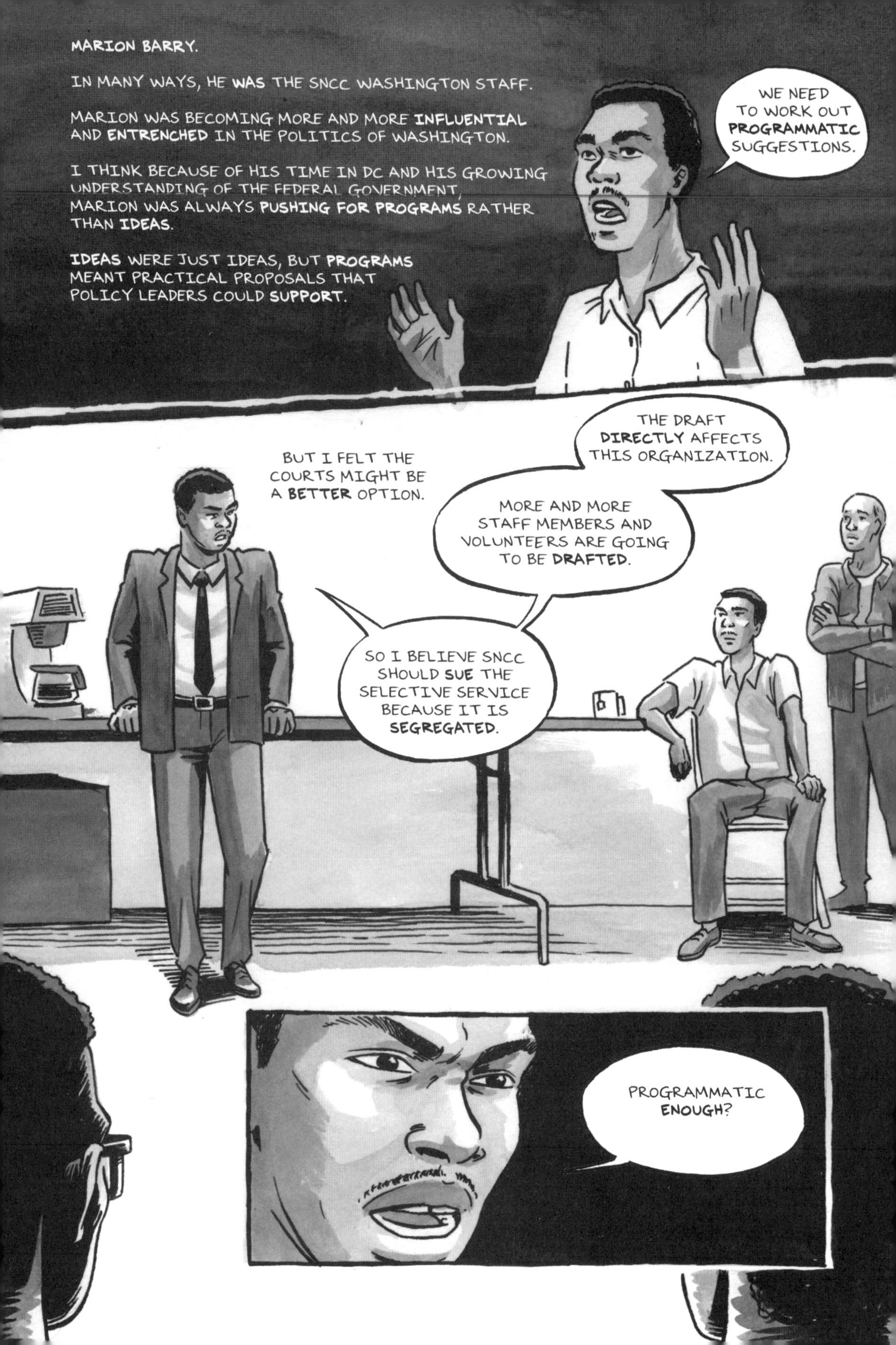
MARION BARRY.
IN MANY WAYS, HE WAS THE SNCC WASHINGTON STAFF.
MARION WAS BECOMING MORE AND MORE INFLUENTIAL AND ENTRENCHED IN THE POLITICS OF WASHINGTON.
I THINK BECAUSE OF HIS TIME IN DC AND HIS GROWING UNDERSTANDING OF THE FEDERAL GOVERNMENT, MARION WAS ALWAYS PUSHING FOR PROGRAMS RATHER THAN IDEAS.
IDEAS WERE JUST IDEAS, BUT PROGRAMS MEANT PRACTICAL PROPOSALS THAT POLICY LEADERS COULD SUPPORT.
WE NEED TO WORK OUT PROGRAMMATIC SUGGESTIONS.
THE DRAFT DIRECTLY AFFECTS THIS ORGANIZATION.
MORE AND MORE STAFF MEMBERS AND VOLUNTEERS ARE GOING TO BE DRAFTED.
BUT I FELT THE COURTS MIGHT BE A BETTER OPTION.
SO I BELIEVE SNCC SHOULD SUE THE SELECTIVE SERVICE BECAUSE IT IS SEGREGATED.
PROGRAMMATIC ENOUGH?

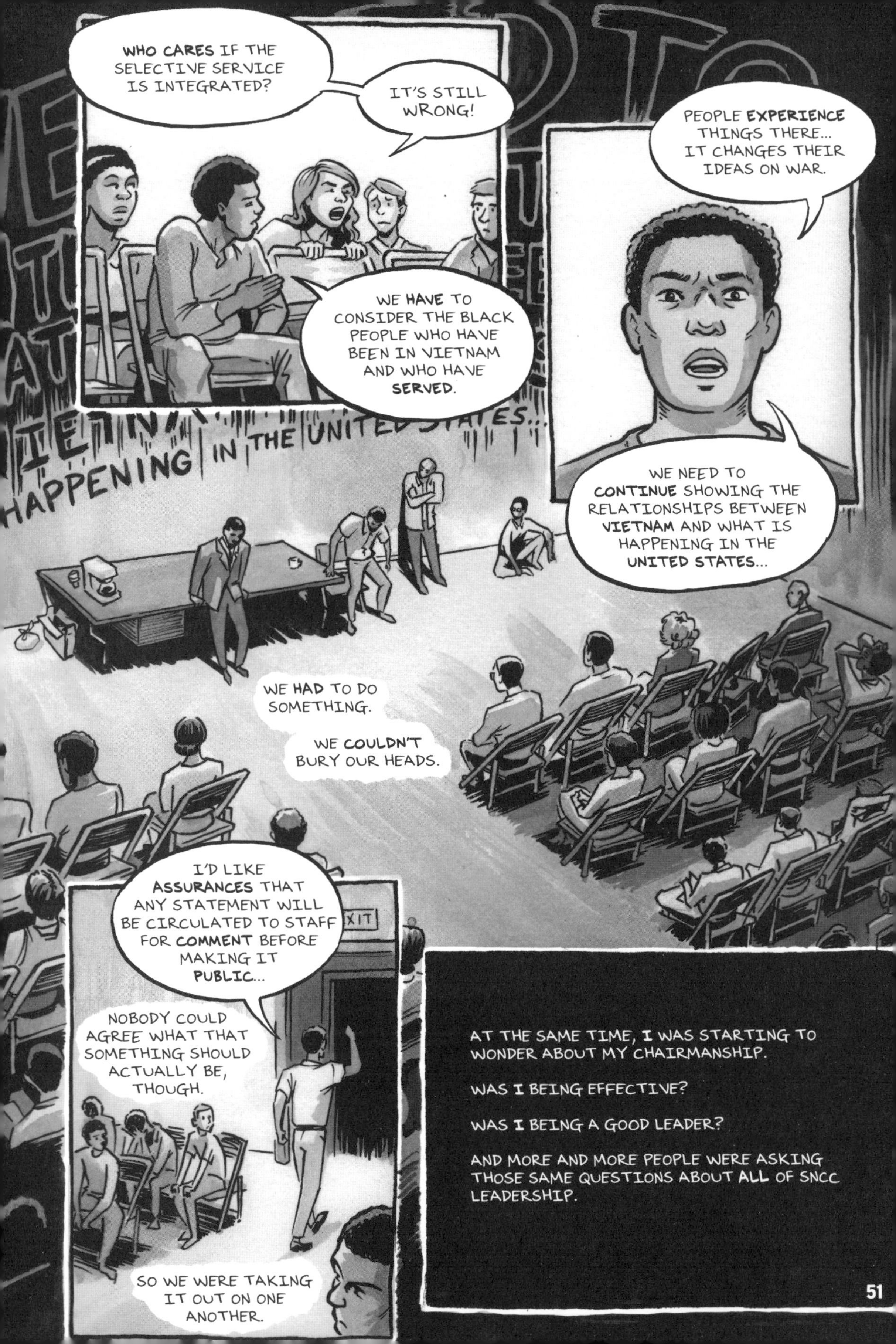
WHO CARES IF THE SELECTIVE SERVICE IS INTEGRATED?
IT'S STILL WRONG!
WE HAVE TO CONSIDER THE BLACK PEOPLE WHO HAVE BEEN IN VIETNAM AND WHO HAVE SERVED.
PEOPLE EXPERIENCE THINGS THERE... IT CHANGES THEIR IDEAS ON WAR.
WE NEED TO CONTINUE SHOWING THE RELATIONSHIPS BETWEEN VIETNAM AND WHAT IS HAPPENING IN THE UNITED STATES...
HAPPENING IN THE UNITED STATES...
WE HAD TO DO SOMETHING.
WE COULDN'T BURY OUR HEADS.
I'D LIKE ASSURANCES THAT ANY STATEMENT WILL BE CIRCULATED TO STAFF FOR COMMENT BEFORE MAKING IT PUBLIC...
EXIT
NOBODY COULD AGREE WHAT THAT SOMETHING SHOULD ACTUALLY BE, THOUGH.
SO WE WERE TAKING IT OUT ON ONE ANOTHER.
AT THE SAME TIME, I WAS STARTING TO WONDER ABOUT MY CHAIRMANSHIP.
WAS I BEING EFFECTIVE?
WAS I BEING A GOOD LEADER?
AND MORE AND MORE PEOPLE WERE ASKING THOSE SAME QUESTIONS ABOUT ALL OF SNCC LEADERSHIP.

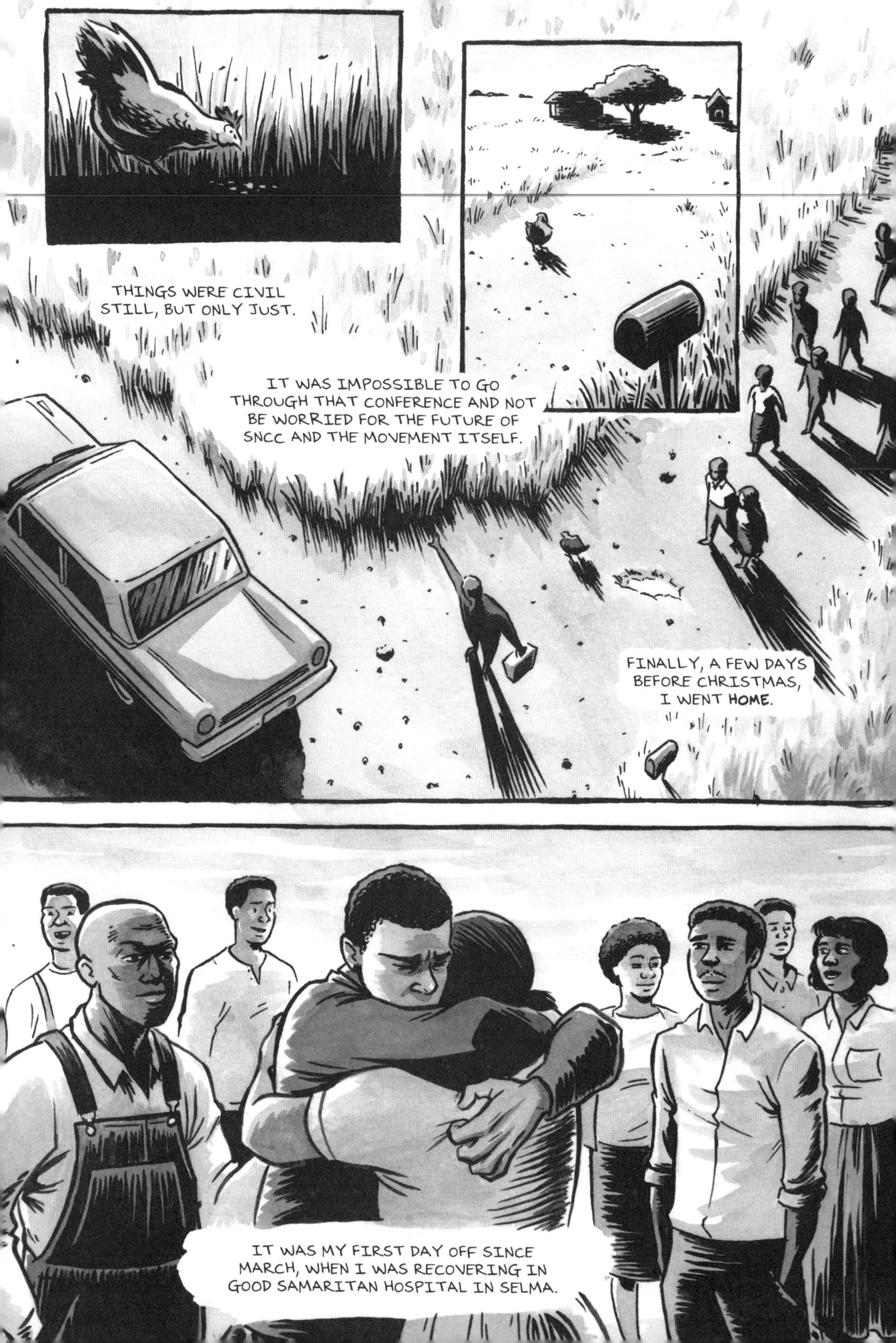
THINGS WERE CIVIL STILL, BUT ONLY JUST.
IT WAS IMPOSSIBLE TO GO THROUGH THAT CONFERENCE AND NOT BE WORRIED FOR THE FUTURE OF SNCC AND THE MOVEMENT ITSELF.
FINALLY, A FEW DAYS BEFORE CHRISTMAS, I WENT HOME.
IT WAS MY FIRST DAY OFF SINCE MARCH, WHEN I WAS RECOVERING IN GOOD SAMARITAN HOSPITAL IN SELMA.

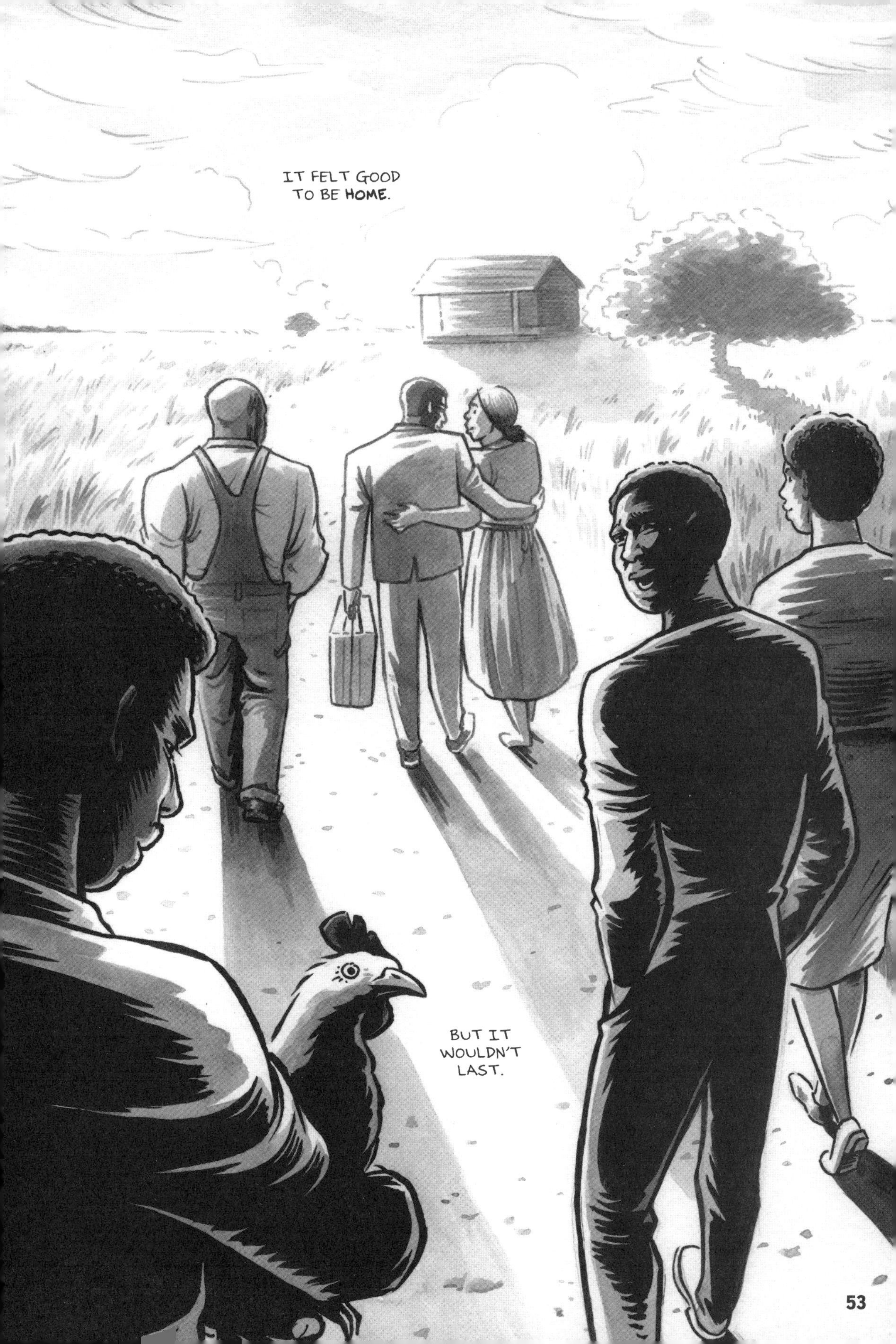
IT FELT GOOD
TO BE HOME.
BUT IT
WOULDN'T
LAST.

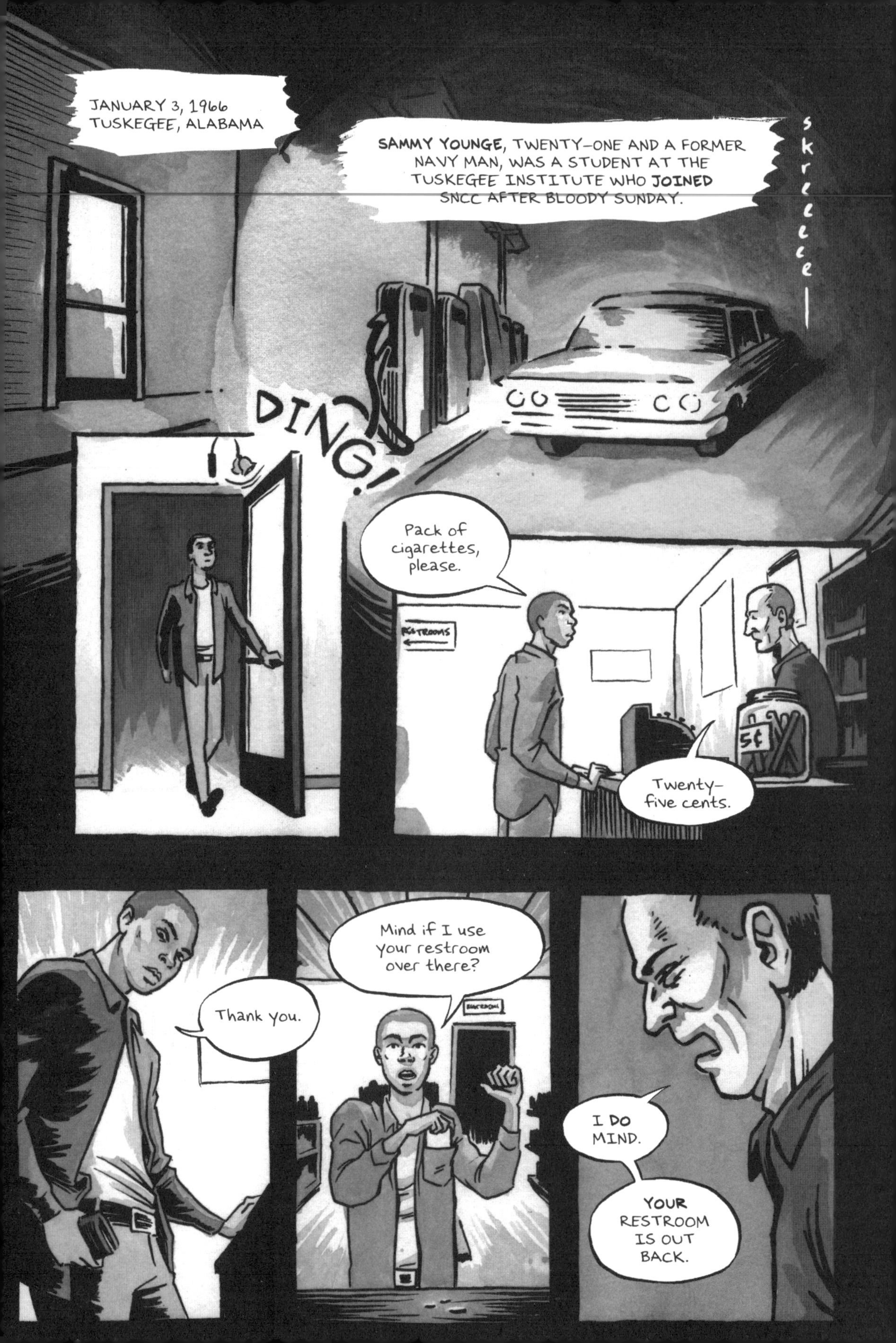
JANUARY 3, 1966
TUSKEGEE, ALABAMA
SAMMY YOUNGE, TWENTY-ONE AND A FORMER NAVY MAN, WAS A STUDENT AT THE TUSKEGEE INSTITUTE WHO JOINED SNCC AFTER BLOODY SUNDAY.
skreeeee
DING!
Pack of cigarettes, please.
RESTROOMS
Twenty-five cents.
5¢
Thank you.
Mind if I use your restroom over there?
I DO MIND.
YOUR RESTROOM IS OUT BACK.

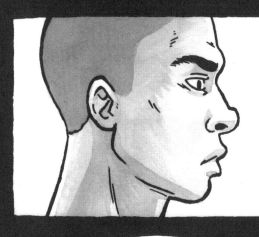

SAMMY YOUNGE HAD SPENT HIS DAY HELPING VOTERS REGISTER AT THE COURTHOUSE IN DOWNTOWN TUSKEGEE.

I KNEW SAMMY PERSONALLY.

HAVEN'T YOU HEARD OF THE **CIVIL RIGHTS** ACT?

HAVEN'T YOU HEARD OF GIT THE **HELL** OFF MY PROPERTY?

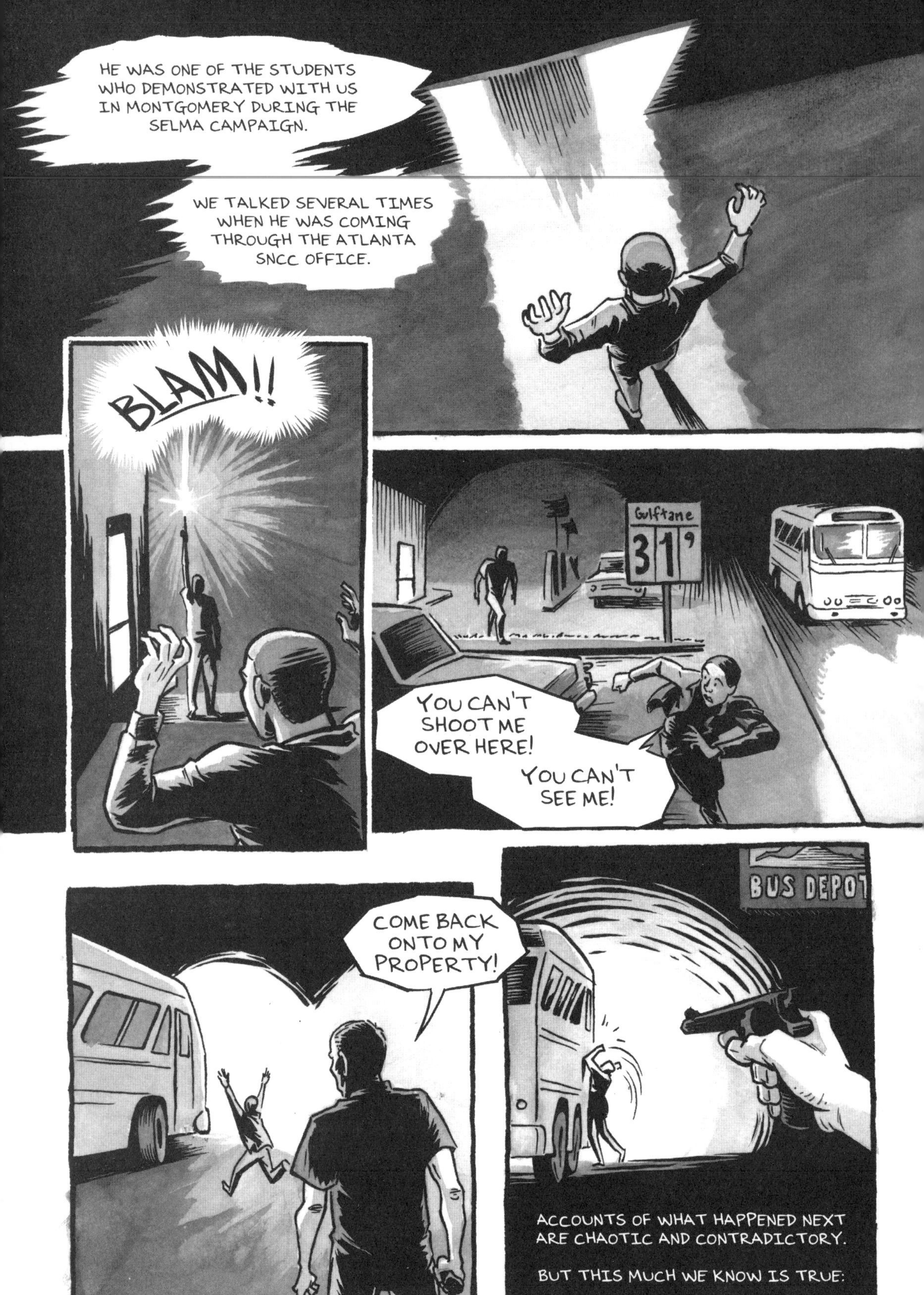
HE WAS ONE OF THE STUDENTS WHO DEMONSTRATED WITH US IN MONTGOMERY DURING THE SELMA CAMPAIGN.
WE TALKED SEVERAL TIMES WHEN HE WAS COMING THROUGH THE ATLANTA SNCC OFFICE.
BLAM!!
Gulftane
31 9
YOU CAN'T SHOOT ME OVER HERE!
YOU CAN'T SEE ME!
BUS DEPOT
COME BACK ONTO MY PROPERTY!
ACCOUNTS OF WHAT HAPPENED NEXT ARE CHAOTIC AND CONTRADICTORY.
BUT THIS MUCH WE KNOW IS TRUE:

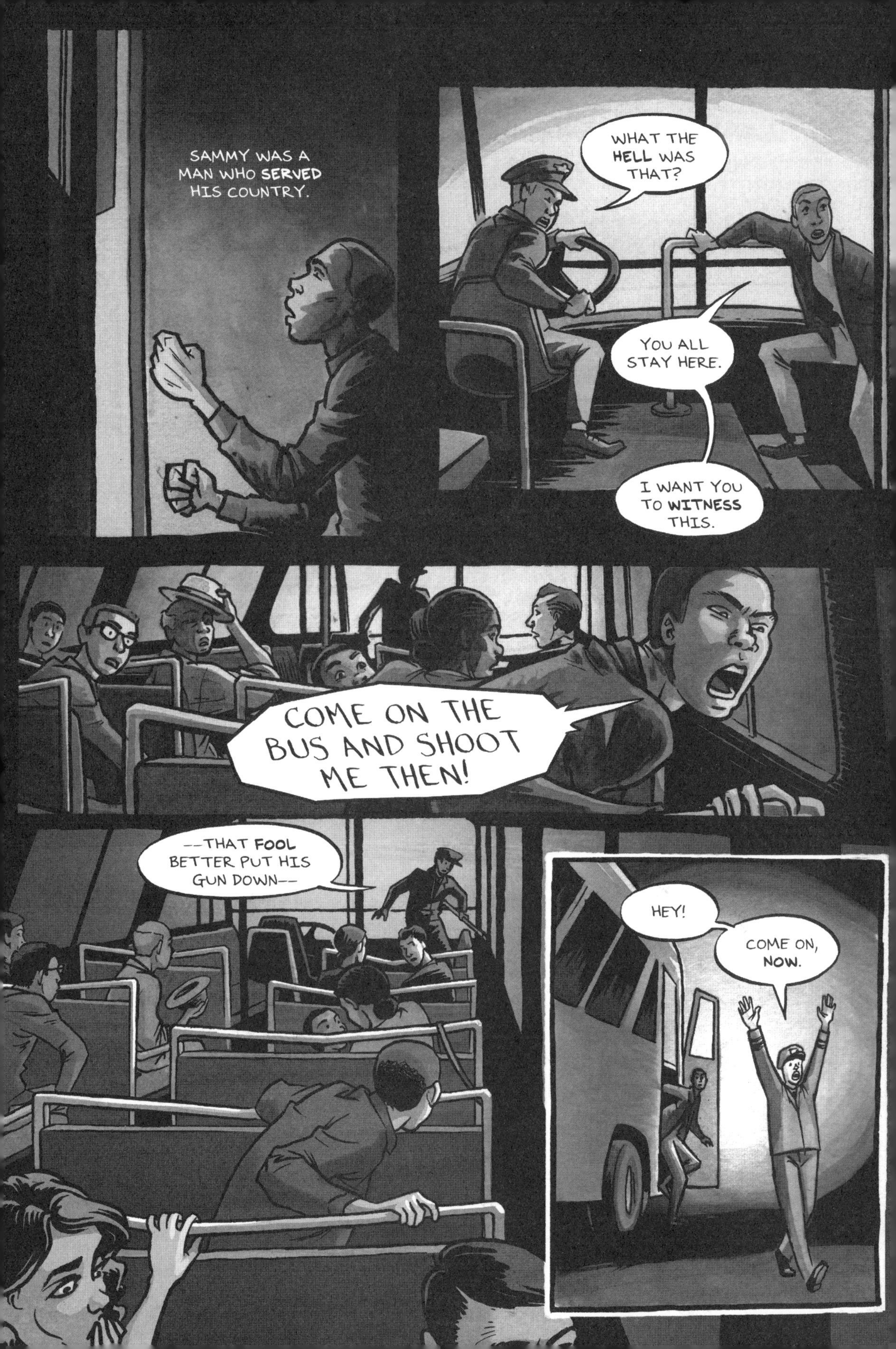
SAMMY WAS A MAN WHO SERVED HIS COUNTRY.
WHAT THE HELL WAS THAT?
YOU ALL STAY HERE.
I WANT YOU TO WITNESS THIS.
COME ON THE BUS AND SHOOT ME THEN!
--THAT FOOL BETTER PUT HIS GUN DOWN--
HEY!
COME ON, NOW.

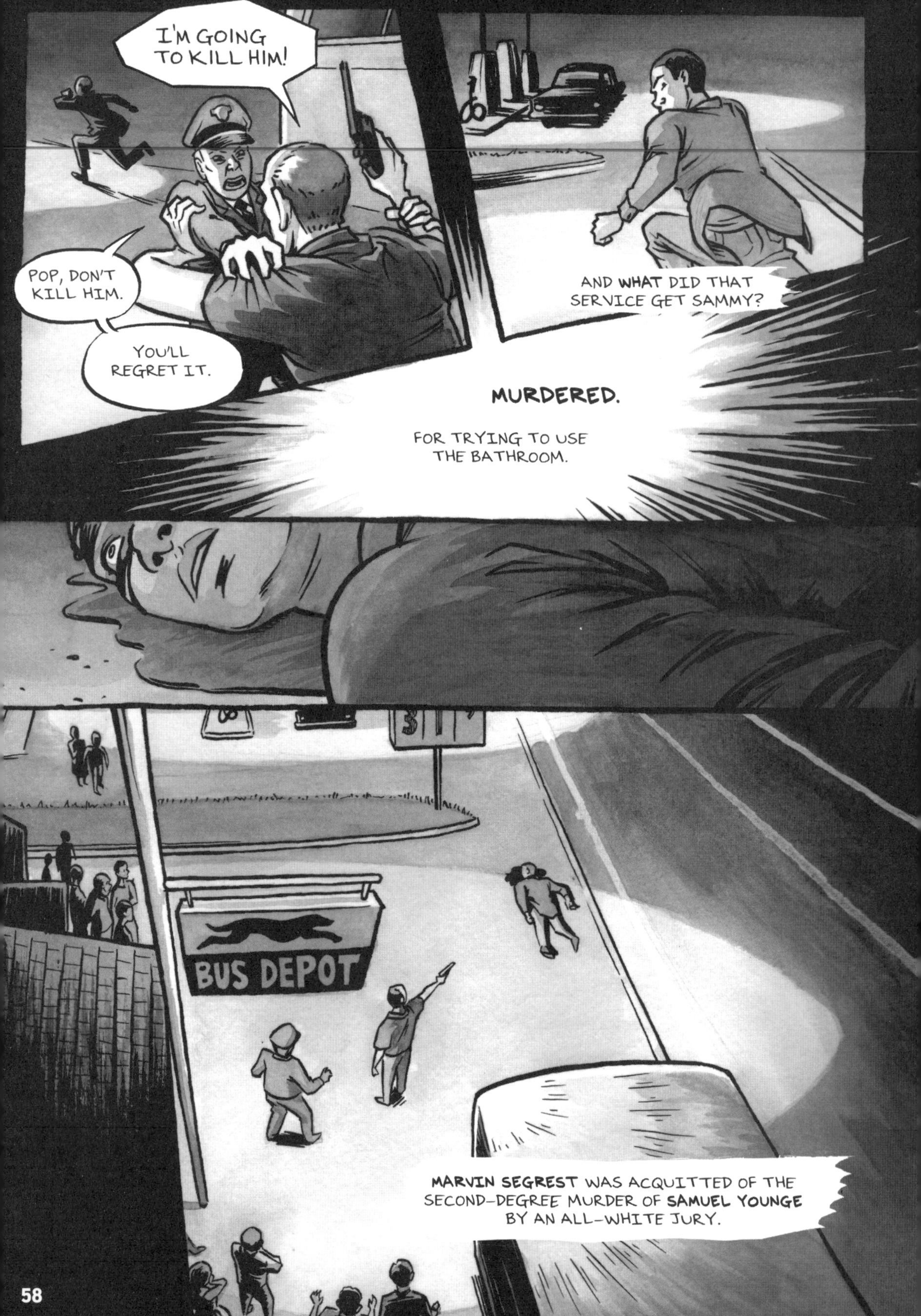
I'M GOING TO KILL HIM!
POP, DON'T KILL HIM.
YOU'LL REGRET IT.
AND WHAT DID THAT SERVICE GET SAMMY?
MURDERED.
FOR TRYING TO USE THE BATHROOM.
BUS DEPOT
MARVIN SEGREST WAS ACQUITTED OF THE SECOND-DEGREE MURDER OF SAMUEL YOUNGE BY AN ALL-WHITE JURY.

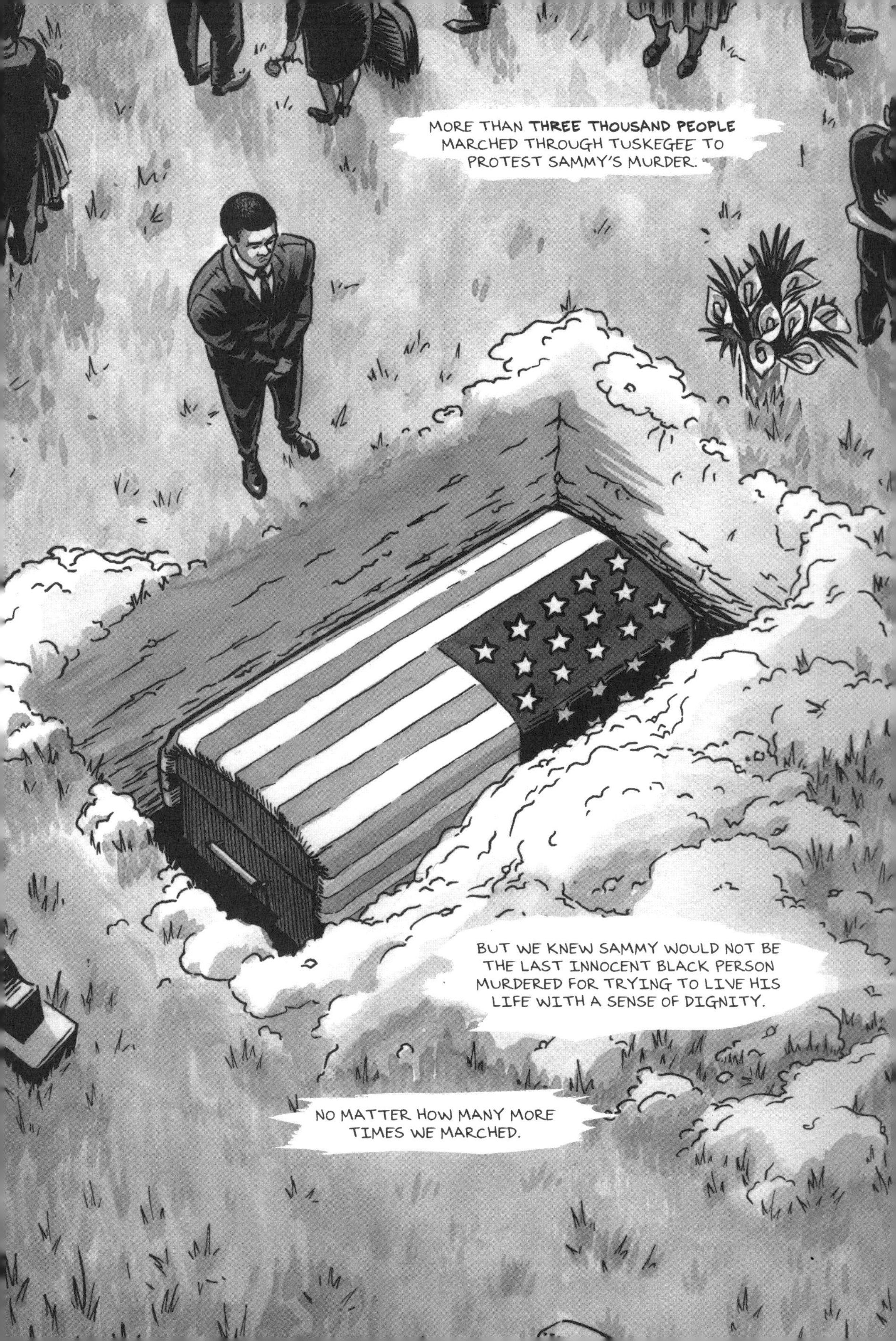
MORE THAN **THREE THOUSAND PEOPLE** MARCHED THROUGH TUSKEGEE TO PROTEST SAMMY'S MURDER.
BUT WE KNEW SAMMY WOULD NOT BE THE LAST INNOCENT BLACK PERSON MURDERED FOR TRYING TO LIVE HIS LIFE WITH A SENSE OF DIGNITY.
NO MATTER HOW MANY MORE TIMES WE MARCHED.

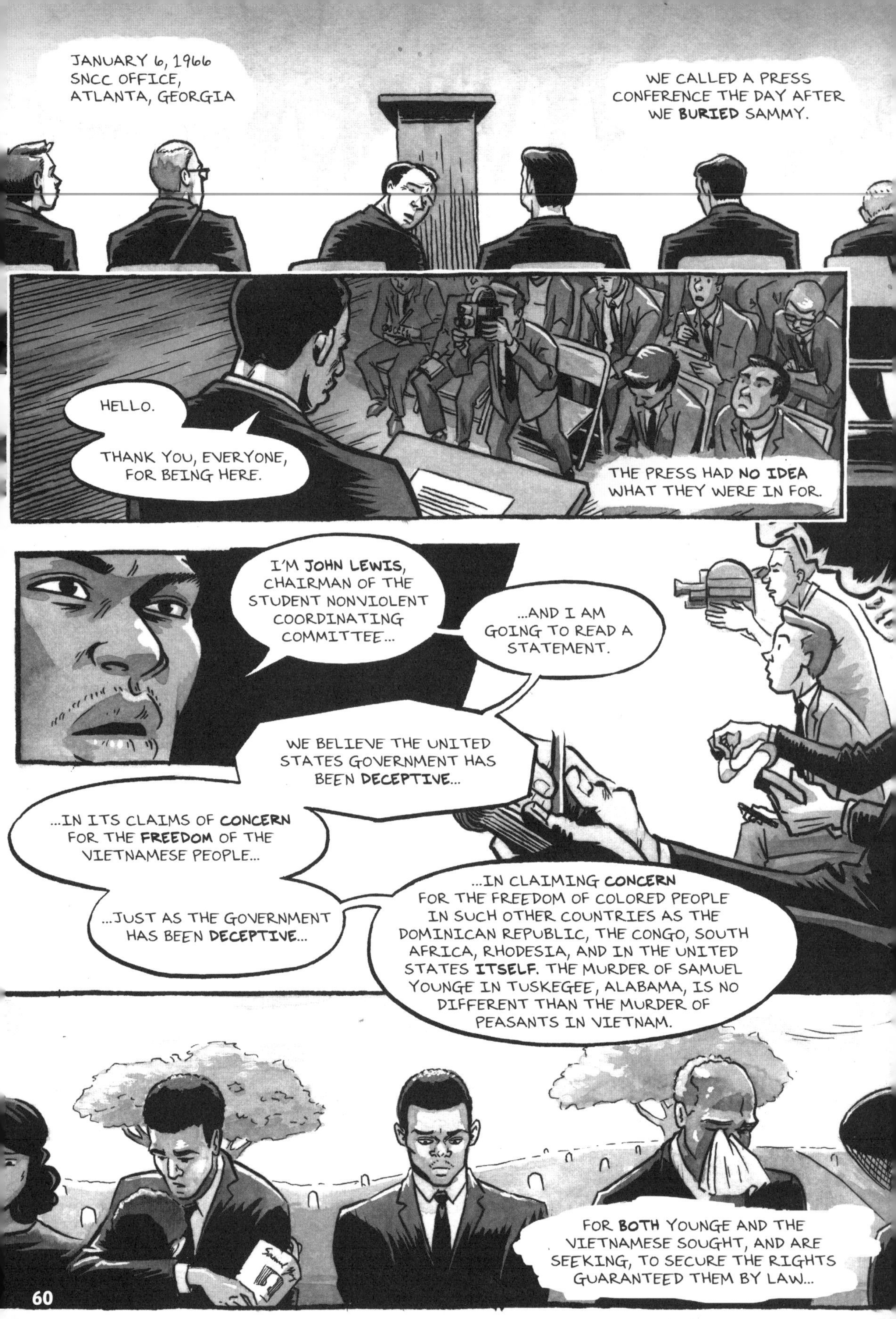

JANUARY 6, 1966 SNCC OFFICE, ATLANTA, GEORGIA
WE CALLED A PRESS CONFERENCE THE DAY AFTER WE BURIED SAMMY.
HELLO.
THANK YOU, EVERYONE, FOR BEING HERE.
THE PRESS HAD NO IDEA WHAT THEY WERE IN FOR.
I'M JOHN LEWIS, CHAIRMAN OF THE STUDENT NONVIOLENT COORDINATING COMMITTEE...
...AND I AM GOING TO READ A STATEMENT.
WE BELIEVE THE UNITED STATES GOVERNMENT HAS BEEN DECEPTIVE...
...IN ITS CLAIMS OF CONCERN FOR THE FREEDOM OF THE VIETNAMESE PEOPLE...
...JUST AS THE GOVERNMENT HAS BEEN DECEPTIVE...
...IN CLAIMING CONCERN FOR THE FREEDOM OF COLORED PEOPLE IN SUCH OTHER COUNTRIES AS THE DOMINICAN REPUBLIC, THE CONGO, SOUTH AFRICA, RHODESIA, AND IN THE UNITED STATES ITSELF. THE MURDER OF SAMUEL YOUNGE IN TUSKEGEE, ALABAMA, IS NO DIFFERENT THAN THE MURDER OF PEASANTS IN VIETNAM.
FOR BOTH YOUNGE AND THE VIETNAMESE SOUGHT, AND ARE SEEKING, TO SECURE THE RIGHTS GUARANTEED THEM BY LAW...

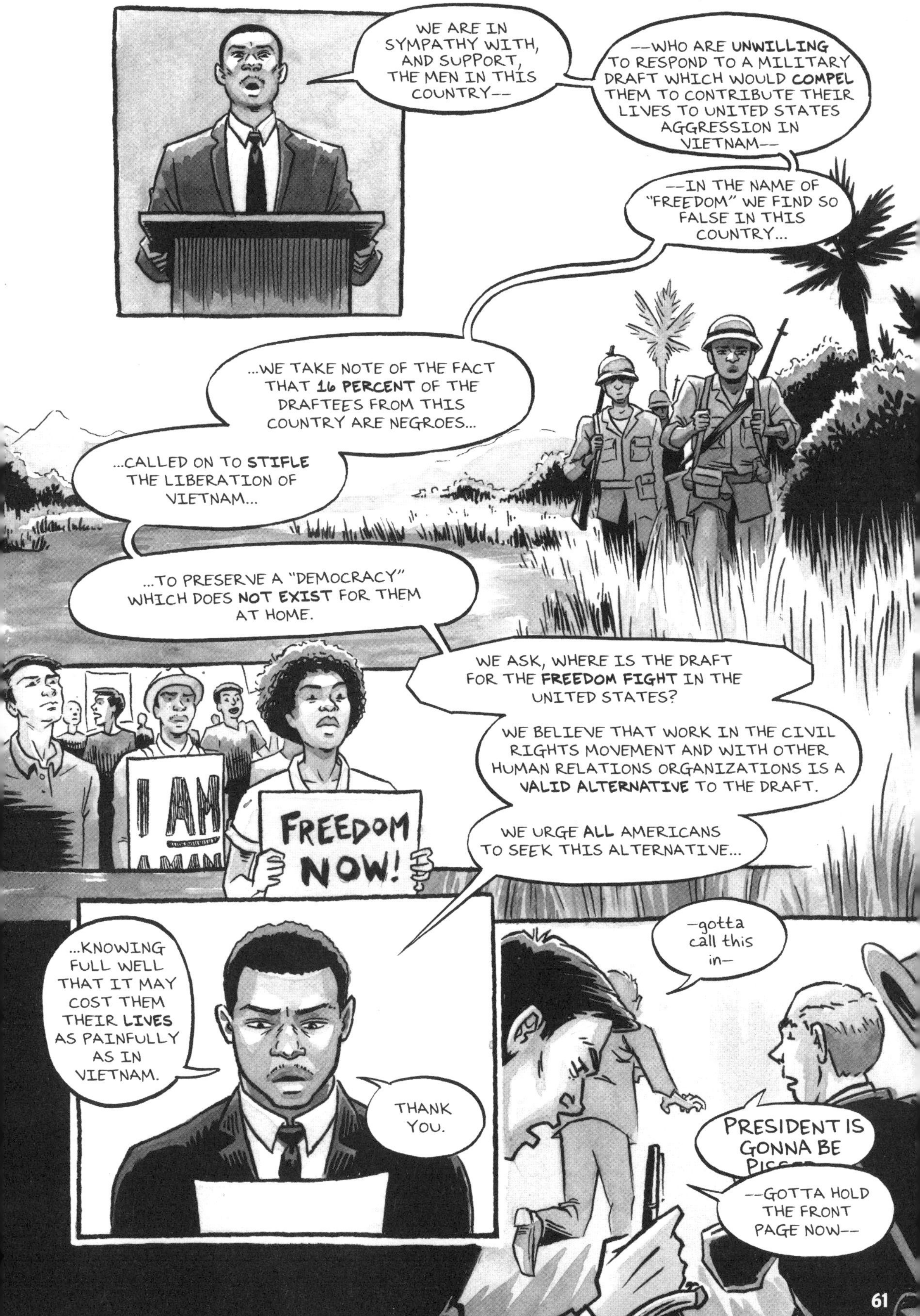

WE ARE IN SYMPATHY WITH, AND SUPPORT, THE MEN IN THIS COUNTRY--
--WHO ARE UNWILLING TO RESPOND TO A MILITARY DRAFT WHICH WOULD COMPEL THEM TO CONTRIBUTE THEIR LIVES TO UNITED STATES AGGRESSION IN VIETNAM--
--IN THE NAME OF "FREEDOM" WE FIND SO FALSE IN THIS COUNTRY...
...WE TAKE NOTE OF THE FACT THAT 16 PERCENT OF THE DRAFTEES FROM THIS COUNTRY ARE NEGROES...
...CALLED ON TO STIFLE THE LIBERATION OF VIETNAM...
...TO PRESERVE A "DEMOCRACY" WHICH DOES NOT EXIST FOR THEM AT HOME.
WE ASK, WHERE IS THE DRAFT FOR THE FREEDOM FIGHT IN THE UNITED STATES?
WE BELIEVE THAT WORK IN THE CIVIL RIGHTS MOVEMENT AND WITH OTHER HUMAN RELATIONS ORGANIZATIONS IS A VALID ALTERNATIVE TO THE DRAFT.
WE URGE ALL AMERICANS TO SEEK THIS ALTERNATIVE...
I AM
FREEDOM NOW!
...KNOWING FULL WELL THAT IT MAY COST THEM THEIR LIVES AS PAINFULLY AS IN VIETNAM.
THANK YOU.
-gotta call this in-
PRESIDENT IS GONNA BE
--GOTTA HOLD THE FRONT PAGE NOW--

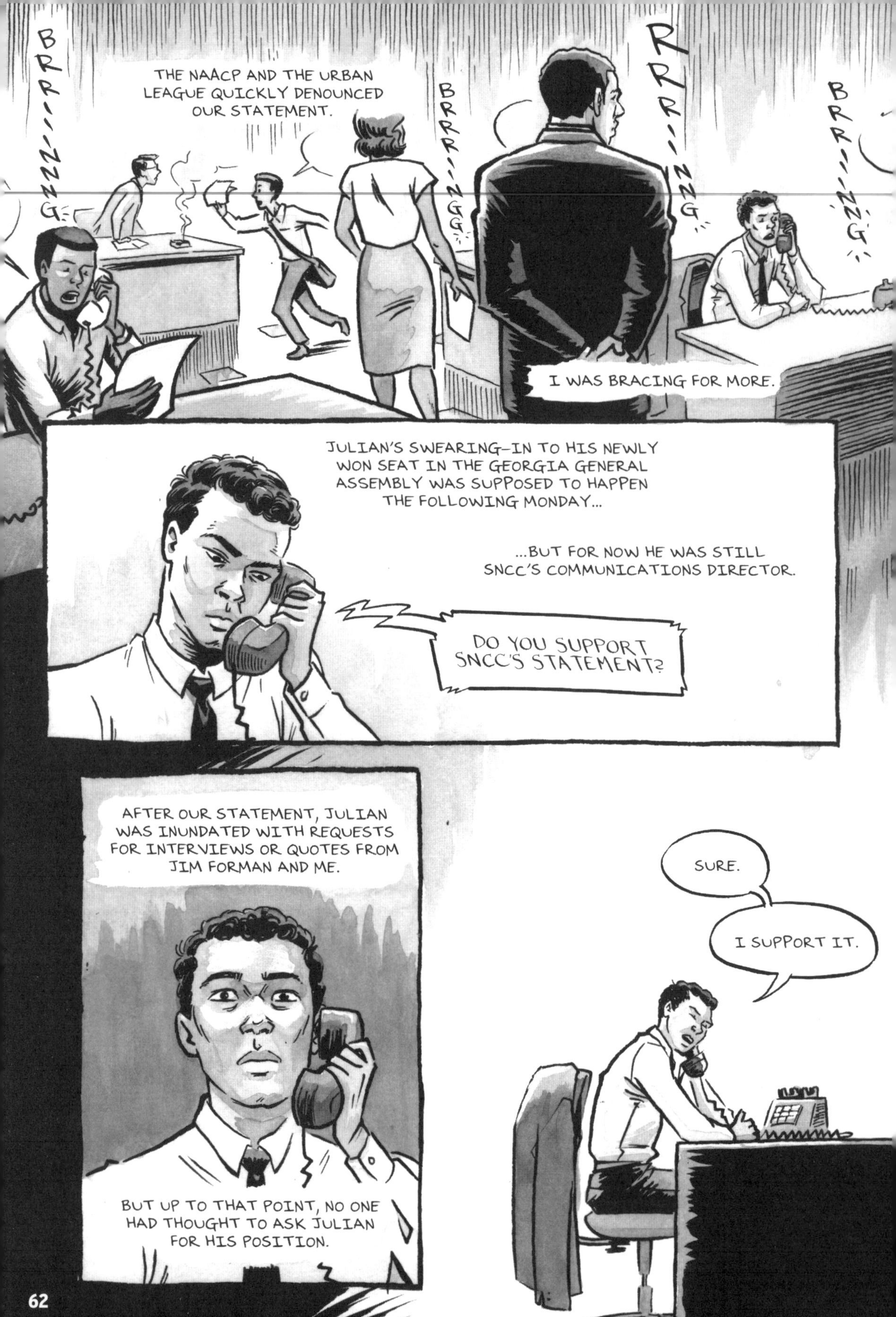
BRRIINNNG
THE NAACP AND THE URBAN LEAGUE QUICKLY DENOUNCED OUR STATEMENT.
BRRRIINGG
RRRIINNG
BRRIINNG
I WAS BRACING FOR MORE.
JULIAN'S SWEARING-IN TO HIS NEWLY WON SEAT IN THE GEORGIA GENERAL ASSEMBLY WAS SUPPOSED TO HAPPEN THE FOLLOWING MONDAY...
...BUT FOR NOW HE WAS STILL SNCC'S COMMUNICATIONS DIRECTOR.
DO YOU SUPPORT SNCC'S STATEMENT?
AFTER OUR STATEMENT, JULIAN WAS INUNDATED WITH REQUESTS FOR INTERVIEWS OR QUOTES FROM JIM FORMAN AND ME.
BUT UP TO THAT POINT, NO ONE HAD THOUGHT TO ASK JULIAN FOR HIS POSITION.
SURE.
I SUPPORT IT.

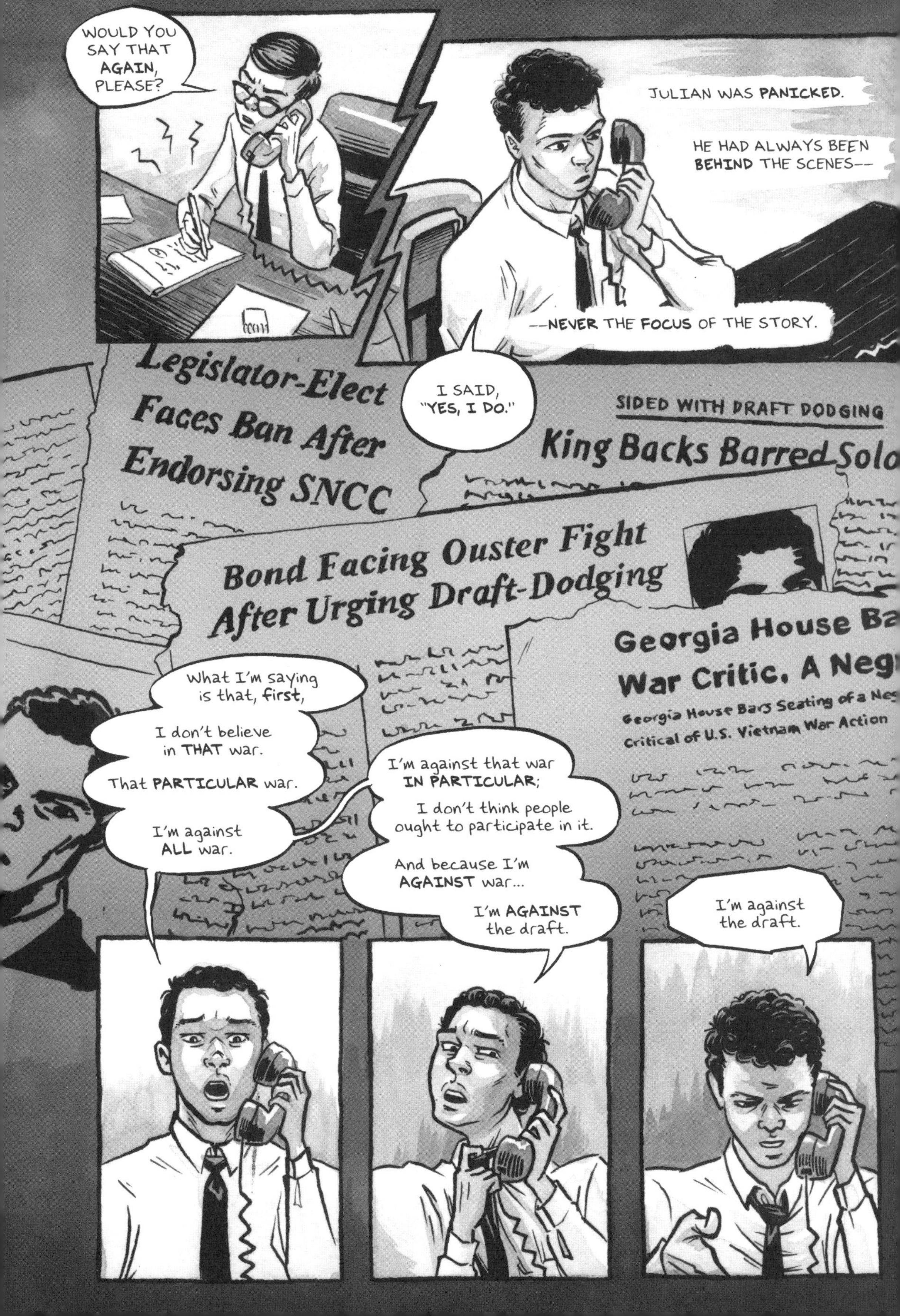
WOULD YOU SAY THAT AGAIN, PLEASE?
JULIAN WAS PANICKED.
HE HAD ALWAYS BEEN BEHIND THE SCENES--
--NEVER THE FOCUS OF THE STORY.
Legislator-Elect Faces Ban After Endorsing SNCC
I SAID, "YES, I DO."
SIDED WITH DRAFT DODGING
King Backs Barred Solo
Bond Facing Ouster Fight After Urging Draft-Dodging
Georgia House Ba
War Critic, A Neg
Georgia House Bars Seating of a Ne
Critical of U.S. Vietnam War Action
What I'm saying is that, first,
I don't believe in THAT war.
That PARTICULAR war.
I'm against ALL war.
I'm against that war IN PARTICULAR;
I don't think people ought to participate in it.
And because I'm AGAINST war...
I'm AGAINST the draft.
I'm against the draft.

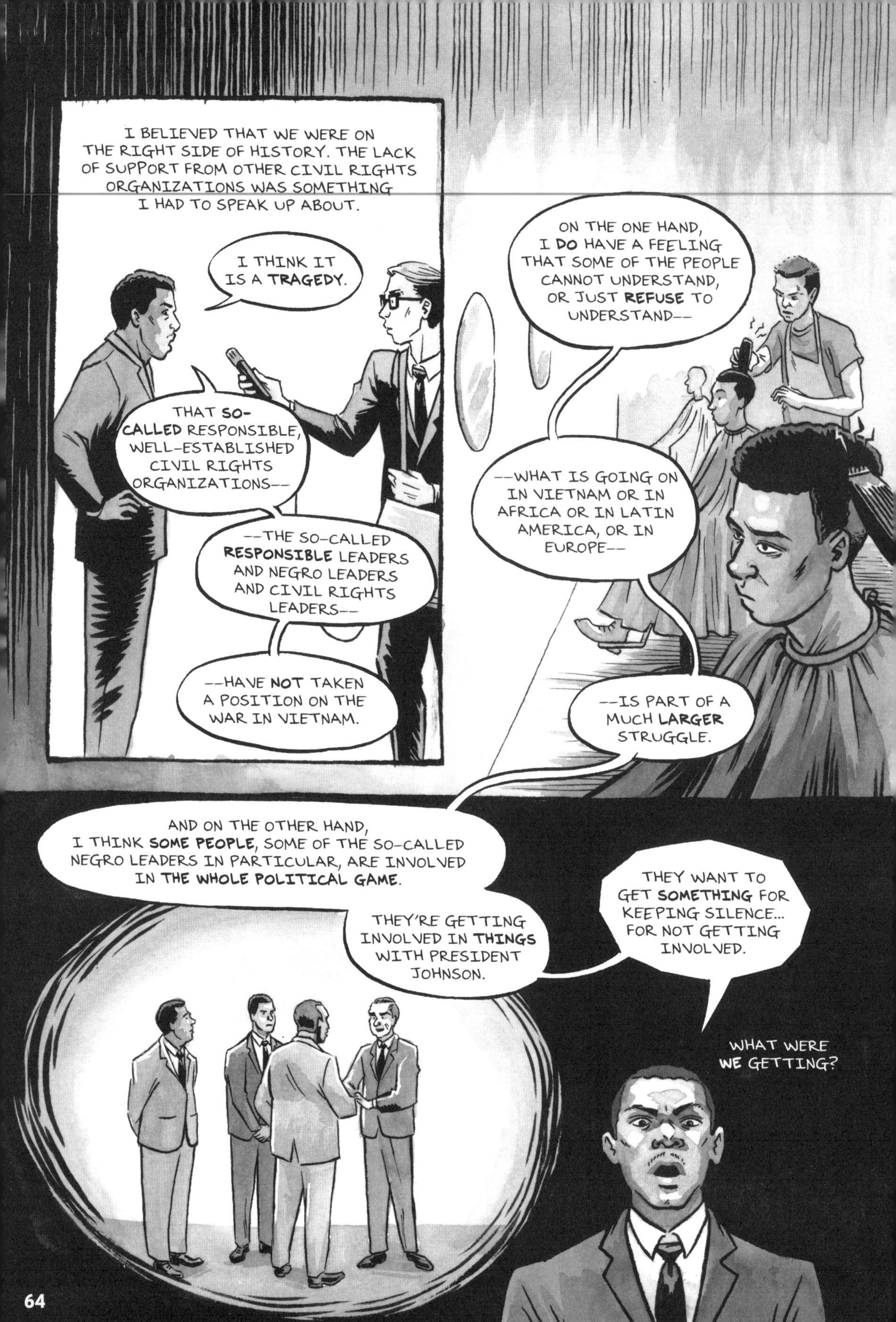

I BELIEVED THAT WE WERE ON THE RIGHT SIDE OF HISTORY. THE LACK OF SUPPORT FROM OTHER CIVIL RIGHTS ORGANIZATIONS WAS SOMETHING I HAD TO SPEAK UP ABOUT.
I THINK IT IS A **TRAGEDY**.
THAT **SO-CALLED** RESPONSIBLE, WELL-ESTABLISHED CIVIL RIGHTS ORGANIZATIONS--
--THE SO-CALLED **RESPONSIBLE** LEADERS AND NEGRO LEADERS AND CIVIL RIGHTS LEADERS--
--HAVE **NOT** TAKEN A POSITION ON THE WAR IN VIETNAM.
ON THE ONE HAND, I **DO** HAVE A FEELING THAT SOME OF THE PEOPLE CANNOT UNDERSTAND, OR JUST **REFUSE** TO UNDERSTAND--
--WHAT IS GOING ON IN VIETNAM OR IN AFRICA OR IN LATIN AMERICA, OR IN EUROPE--
--IS PART OF A MUCH **LARGER** STRUGGLE.
AND ON THE OTHER HAND, I THINK **SOME PEOPLE**, SOME OF THE SO-CALLED NEGRO LEADERS IN PARTICULAR, ARE INVOLVED IN **THE WHOLE POLITICAL GAME**.
THEY'RE GETTING INVOLVED IN **THINGS** WITH PRESIDENT JOHNSON.
THEY WANT TO GET **SOMETHING** FOR KEEPING SILENCE... FOR NOT GETTING INVOLVED.
WHAT WERE **WE** GETTING?

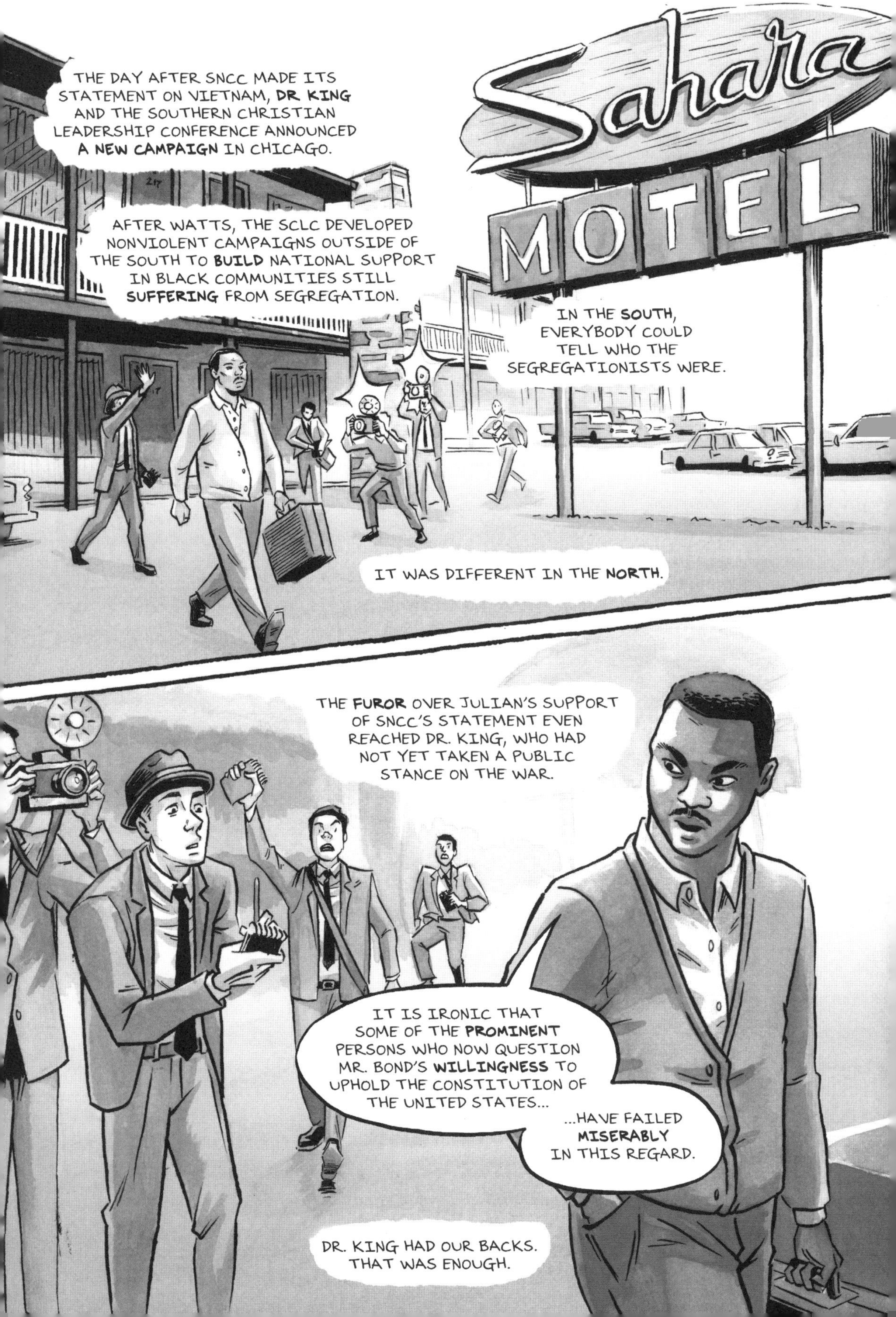
THE DAY AFTER SNCC MADE ITS STATEMENT ON VIETNAM, DR KING AND THE SOUTHERN CHRISTIAN LEADERSHIP CONFERENCE ANNOUNCED A NEW CAMPAIGN IN CHICAGO.
Sahara
MOTEL
AFTER WATTS, THE SCLC DEVELOPED NONVIOLENT CAMPAIGNS OUTSIDE OF THE SOUTH TO BUILD NATIONAL SUPPORT IN BLACK COMMUNITIES STILL SUFFERING FROM SEGREGATION.
IN THE SOUTH, EVERYBODY COULD TELL WHO THE SEGREGATIONISTS WERE.
IT WAS DIFFERENT IN THE NORTH.
THE FUROR OVER JULIAN'S SUPPORT OF SNCC'S STATEMENT EVEN REACHED DR. KING, WHO HAD NOT YET TAKEN A PUBLIC STANCE ON THE WAR.
IT IS IRONIC THAT SOME OF THE PROMINENT PERSONS WHO NOW QUESTION MR. BOND'S WILLINGNESS TO UPHOLD THE CONSTITUTION OF THE UNITED STATES...
...HAVE FAILED MISERABLY IN THIS REGARD.
DR. KING HAD OUR BACKS. THAT WAS ENOUGH.

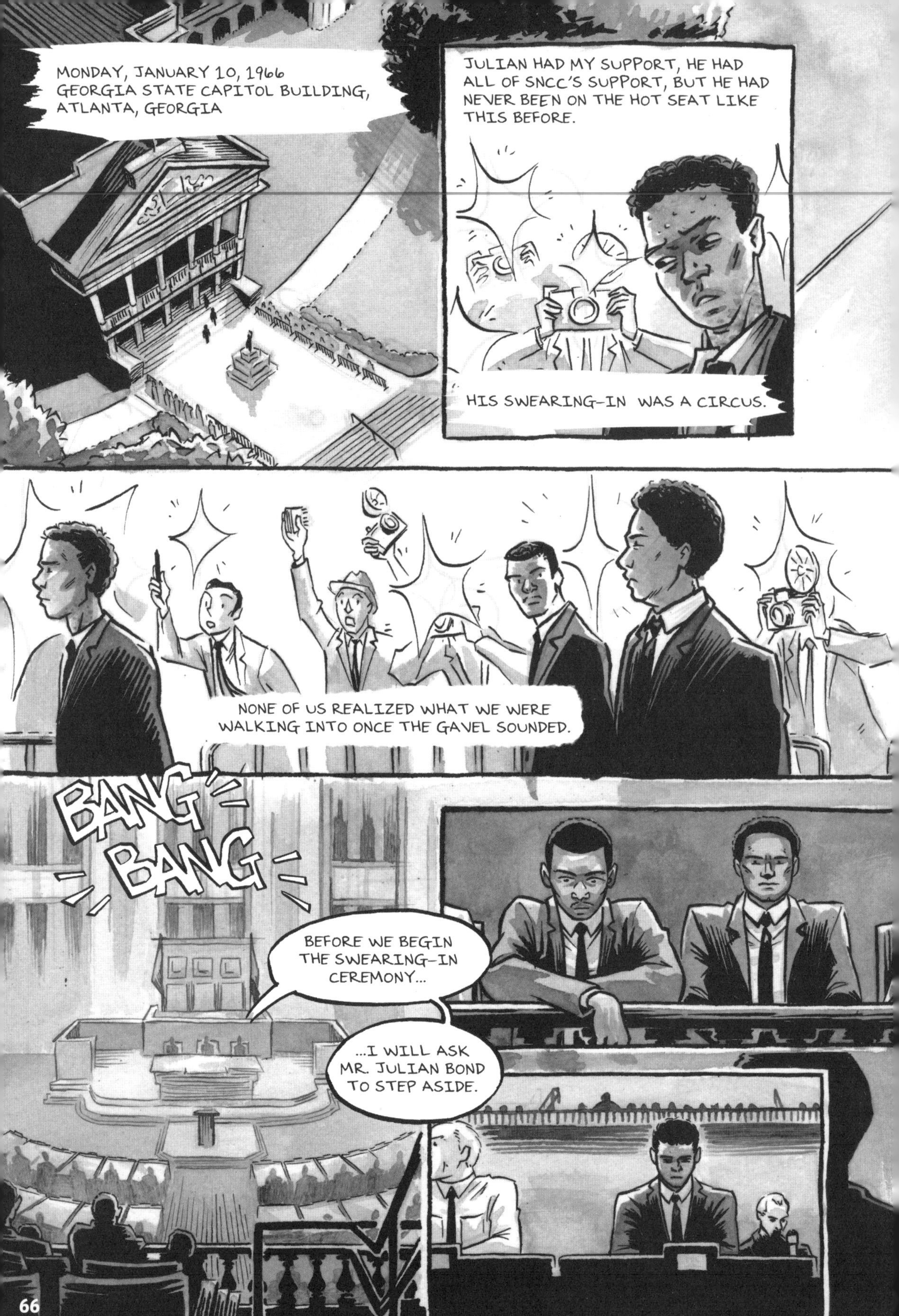
MONDAY, JANUARY 10, 1966
GEORGIA STATE CAPITOL BUILDING, ATLANTA, GEORGIA
JULIAN HAD MY SUPPORT, HE HAD ALL OF SNCC'S SUPPORT, BUT HE HAD NEVER BEEN ON THE HOT SEAT LIKE THIS BEFORE.
HIS SWEARING-IN WAS A CIRCUS.
NONE OF US REALIZED WHAT WE WERE WALKING INTO ONCE THE GAVEL SOUNDED.
BANG
BANG
BEFORE WE BEGIN THE SWEARING-IN CEREMONY...
...I WILL ASK MR. JULIAN BOND TO STEP ASIDE.

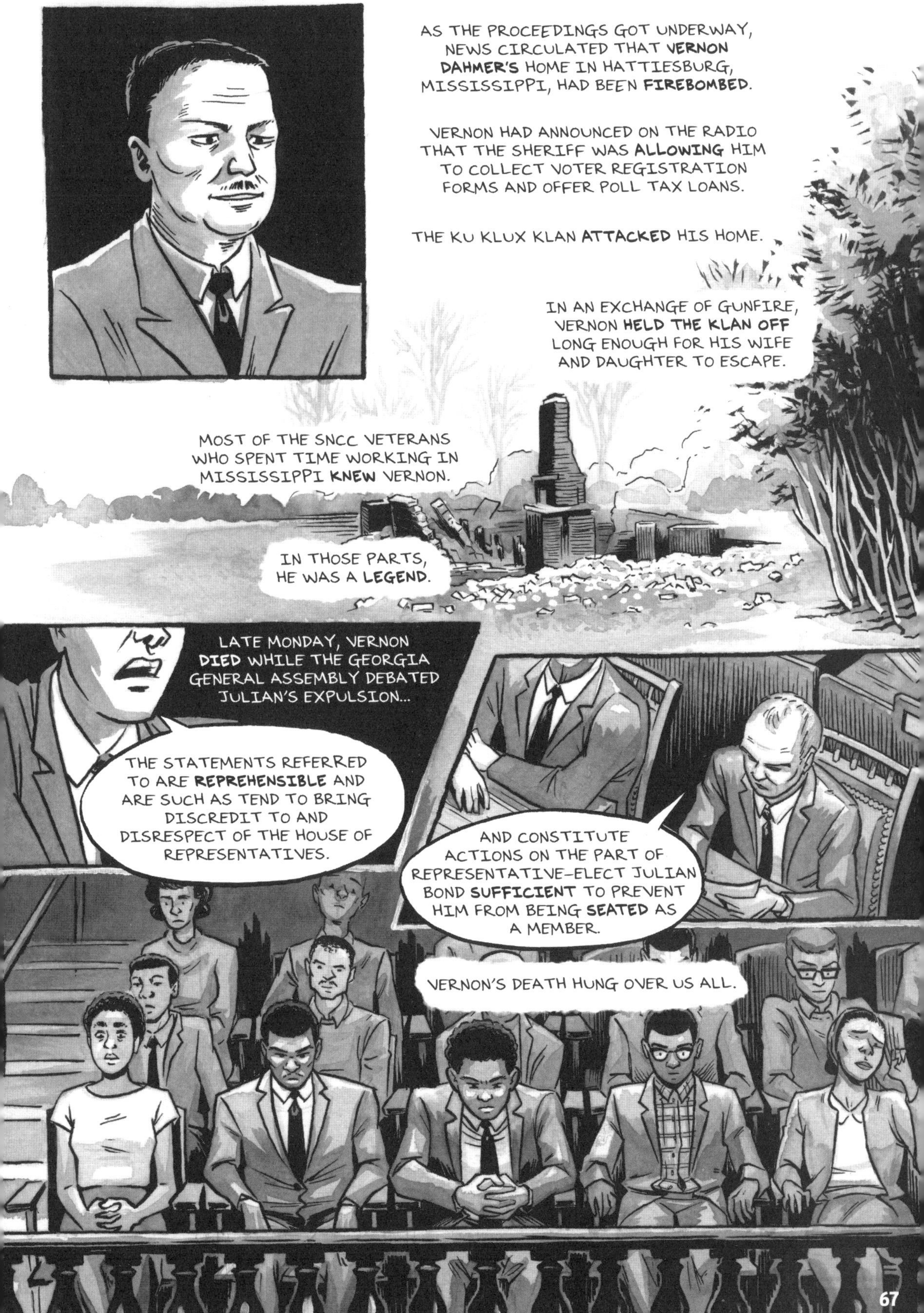
AS THE PROCEEDINGS GOT UNDERWAY, NEWS CIRCULATED THAT VERNON DAHMER'S HOME IN HATTIESBURG, MISSISSIPPI, HAD BEEN FIREBOMBED.
VERNON HAD ANNOUNCED ON THE RADIO THAT THE SHERIFF WAS ALLOWING HIM TO COLLECT VOTER REGISTRATION FORMS AND OFFER POLL TAX LOANS.
THE KU KLUX KLAN ATTACKED HIS HOME.
IN AN EXCHANGE OF GUNFIRE, VERNON HELD THE KLAN OFF LONG ENOUGH FOR HIS WIFE AND DAUGHTER TO ESCAPE.
MOST OF THE SNCC VETERANS WHO SPENT TIME WORKING IN MISSISSIPPI KNEW VERNON.
IN THOSE PARTS, HE WAS A LEGEND.
LATE MONDAY, VERNON DIED WHILE THE GEORGIA GENERAL ASSEMBLY DEBATED JULIAN'S EXPULSION...
THE STATEMENTS REFERRED TO ARE REPREHENSIBLE AND ARE SUCH AS TEND TO BRING DISCREDIT TO AND DISRESPECT OF THE HOUSE OF REPRESENTATIVES.
AND CONSTITUTE ACTIONS ON THE PART OF REPRESENTATIVE-ELECT JULIAN BOND SUFFICIENT TO PREVENT HIM FROM BEING SEATED AS A MEMBER.
VERNON'S DEATH HUNG OVER US ALL.

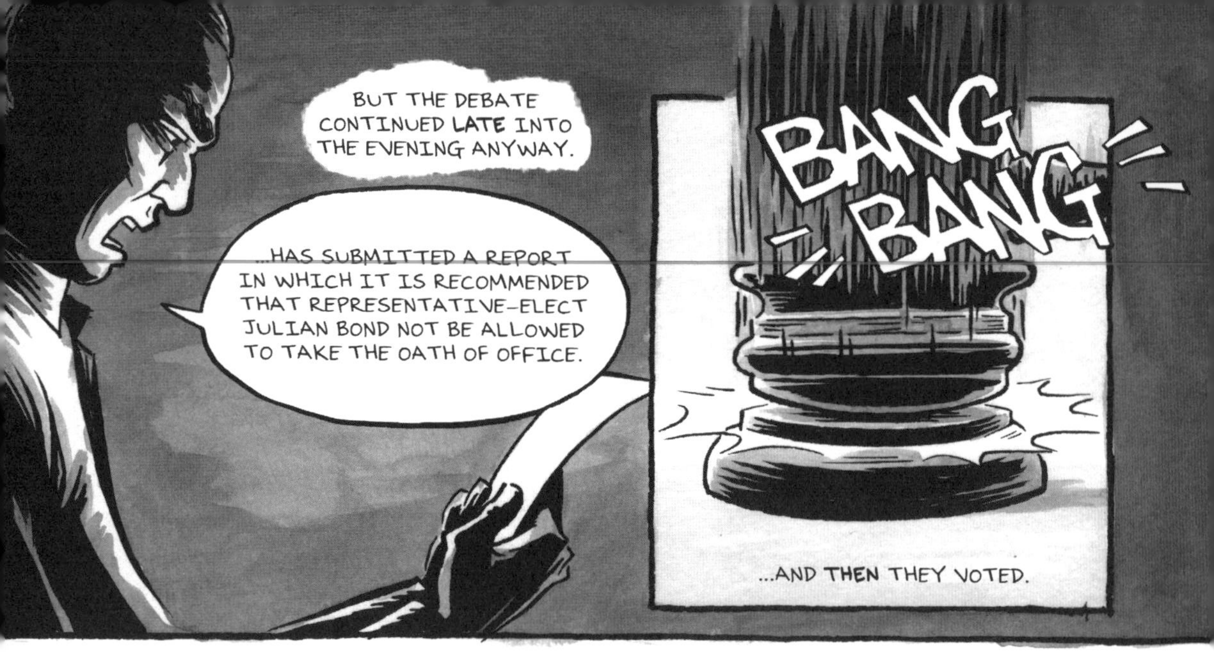
BUT THE DEBATE CONTINUED LATE INTO THE EVENING ANYWAY.
...HAS SUBMITTED A REPORT IN WHICH IT IS RECOMMENDED THAT REPRESENTATIVE-ELECT JULIAN BOND NOT BE ALLOWED TO TAKE THE OATH OF OFFICE.
BANG BANG
...AND THEN THEY VOTED.

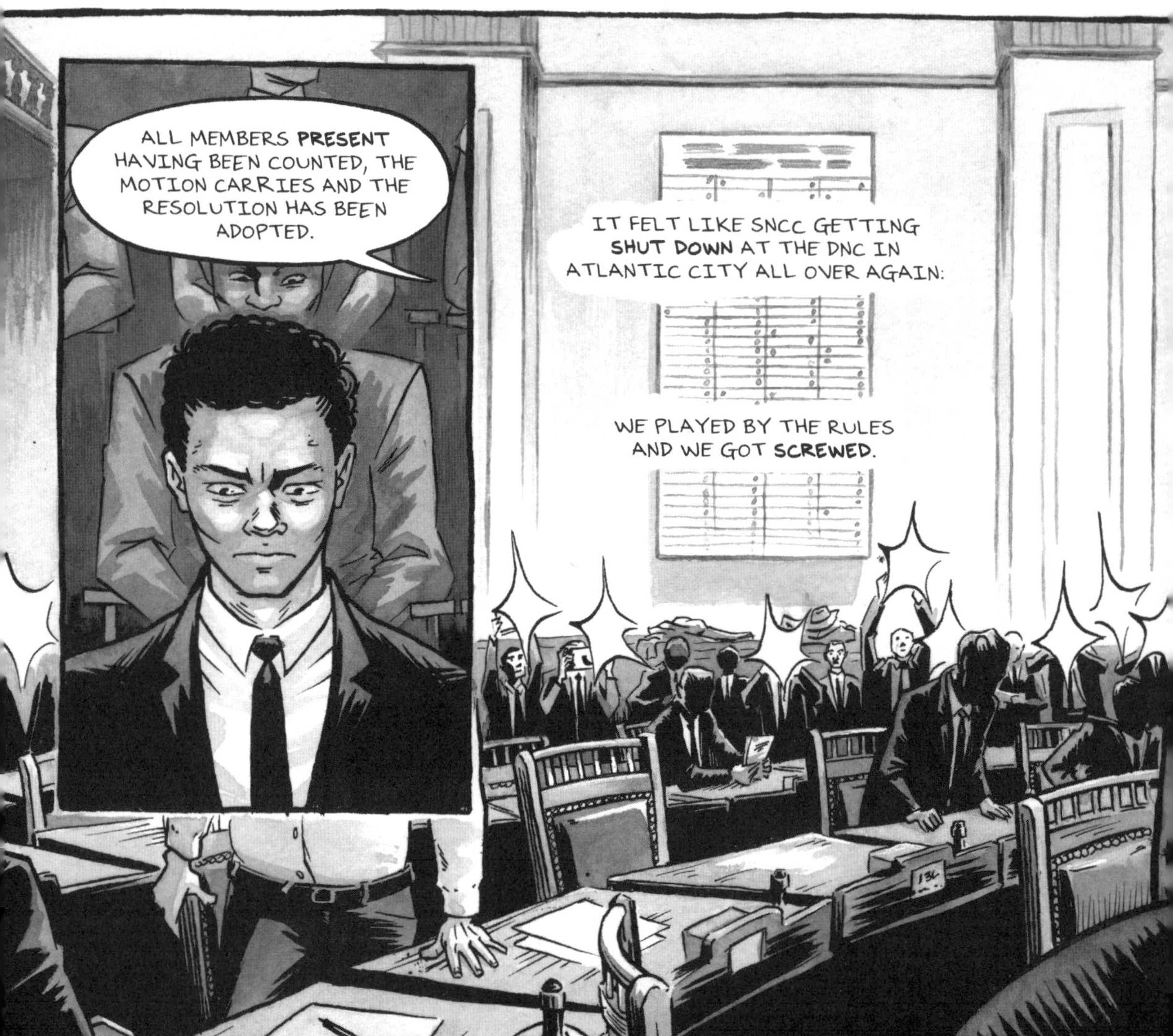
ALL MEMBERS PRESENT HAVING BEEN COUNTED, THE MOTION CARRIES AND THE RESOLUTION HAS BEEN ADOPTED.
IT FELT LIKE SNCC GETTING SHUT DOWN AT THE DNC IN ATLANTIC CITY ALL OVER AGAIN:
WE PLAYED BY THE RULES AND WE GOT SCREWED.

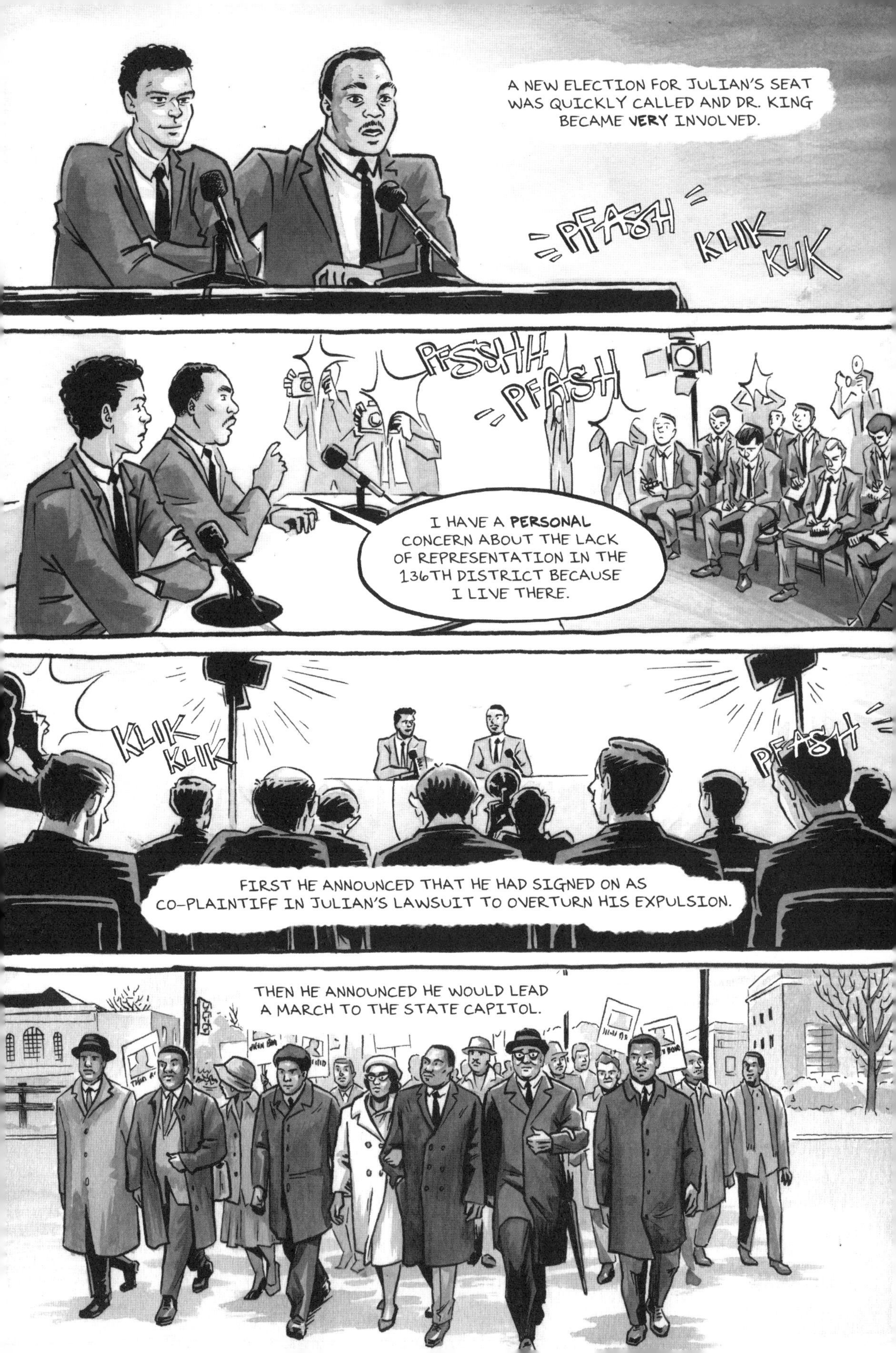
A NEW ELECTION FOR JULIAN'S SEAT WAS QUICKLY CALLED AND DR. KING BECAME **VERY** INVOLVED.
PFASH
KLIK KLIK
PFSSHH
PFASH
I HAVE A **PERSONAL** CONCERN ABOUT THE LACK OF REPRESENTATION IN THE 136TH DISTRICT BECAUSE I LIVE THERE.
KLIK KLIK
PFASH
FIRST HE ANNOUNCED THAT HE HAD SIGNED ON AS CO-PLAINTIFF IN JULIAN'S LAWSUIT TO OVERTURN HIS EXPULSION.
THEN HE ANNOUNCED HE WOULD LEAD A MARCH TO THE STATE CAPITOL.

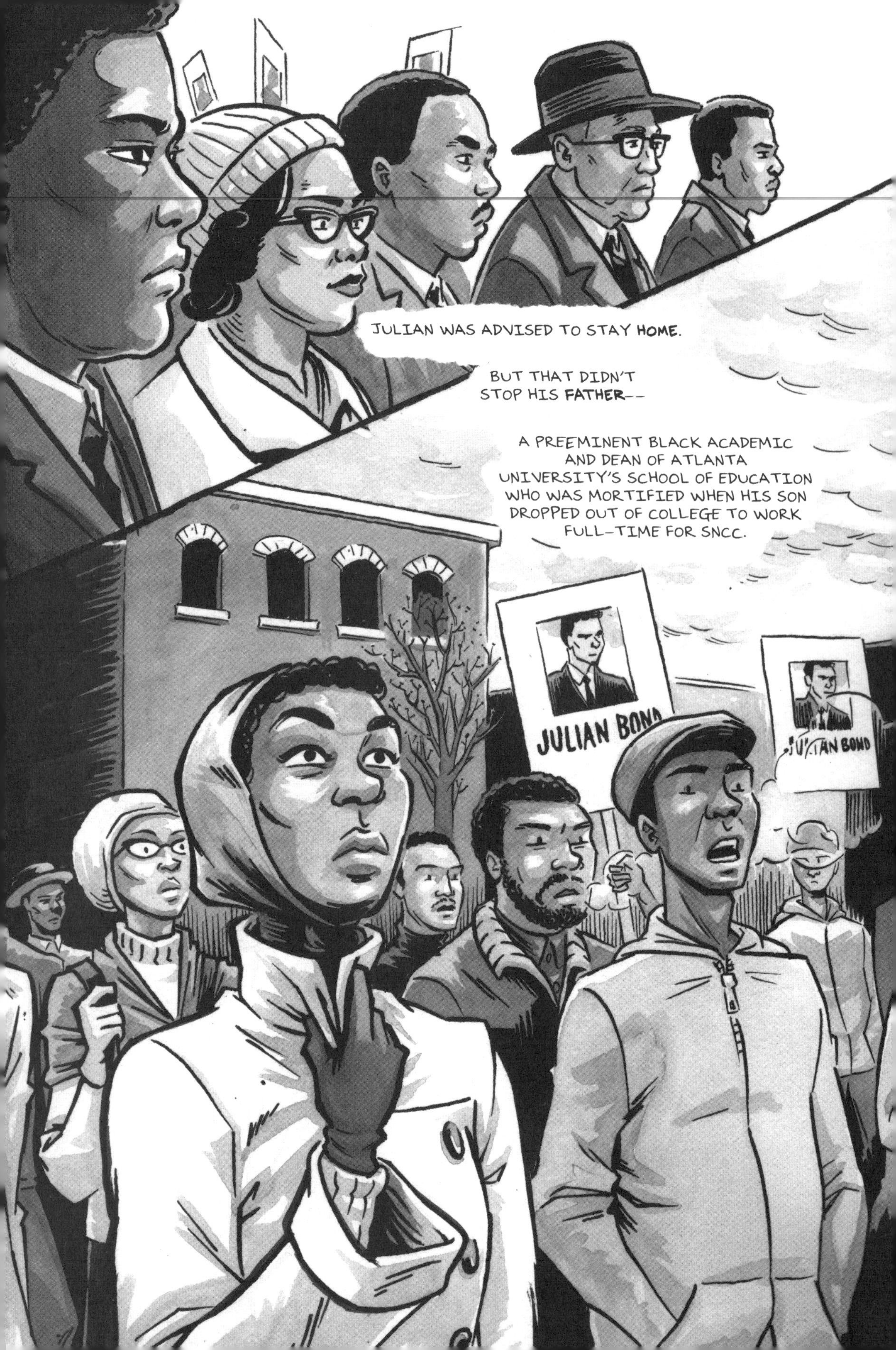
JULIAN WAS ADVISED TO STAY HOME.
BUT THAT DIDN'T STOP HIS FATHER--
A PREEMINENT BLACK ACADEMIC AND DEAN OF ATLANTA UNIVERSITY'S SCHOOL OF EDUCATION WHO WAS MORTIFIED WHEN HIS SON DROPPED OUT OF COLLEGE TO WORK FULL-TIME FOR SNCC.
JULIAN BOND
JULIAN BOND

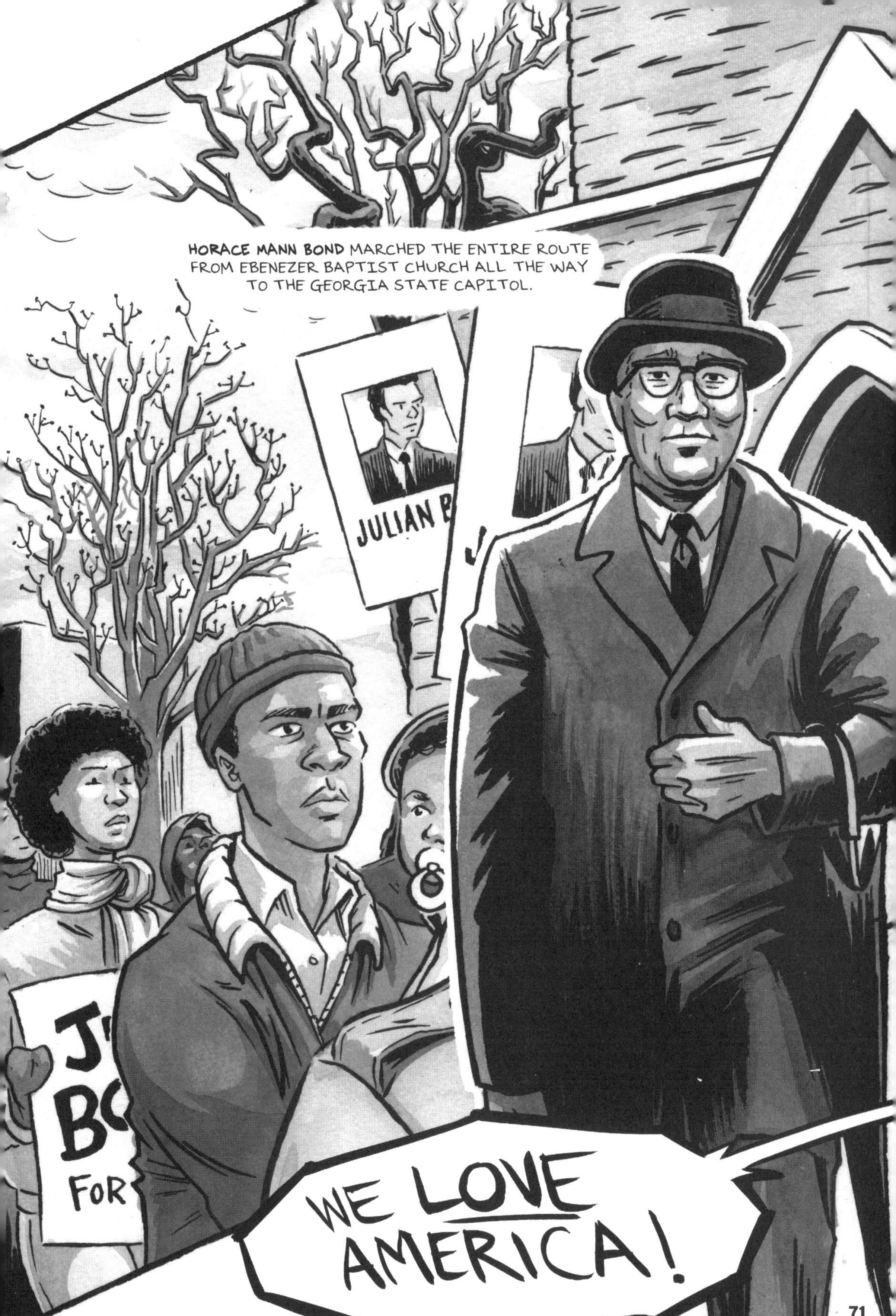
HORACE MANN BOND MARCHED THE ENTIRE ROUTE FROM EBENEZER BAPTIST CHURCH ALL THE WAY TO THE GEORGIA STATE CAPITOL.
JULIAN B
FOR
WE LOVE AMERICA!

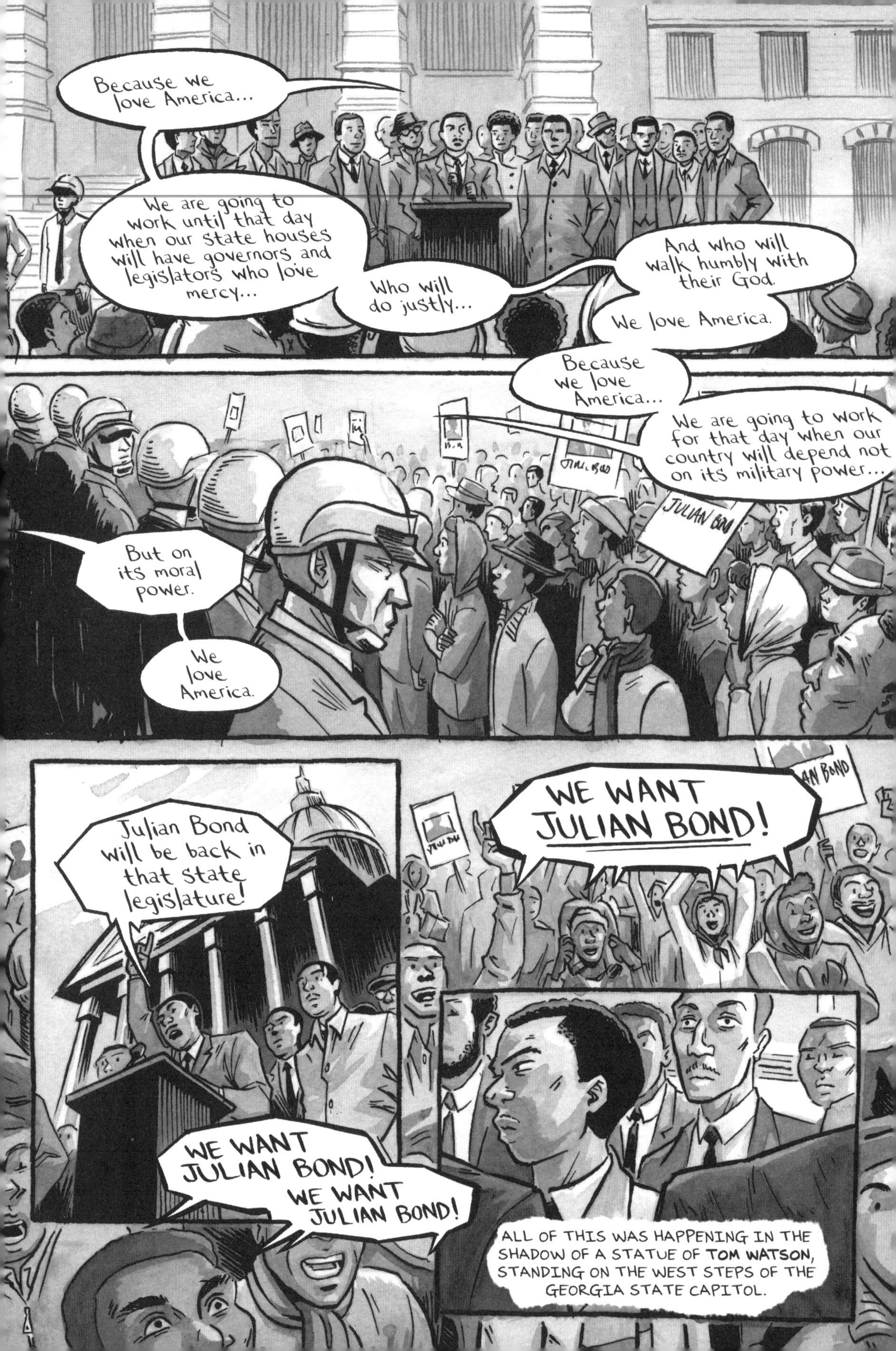
Because we love America...
We are going to work until that day when our state houses will have governors and legislators who love mercy...
Who will do justly...
And who will walk humbly with their God.
We love America.
Because we love America...
We are going to work for that day when our country will depend not on its military power...
But on its moral power.
We love America.
JULIAN BOND
Julian Bond will be back in that state legislature!
WE WANT JULIAN BOND!
WE WANT JULIAN BOND!
WE WANT JULIAN BOND!
ALL OF THIS WAS HAPPENING IN THE SHADOW OF A STATUE OF TOM WATSON, STANDING ON THE WEST STEPS OF THE GEORGIA STATE CAPITOL.

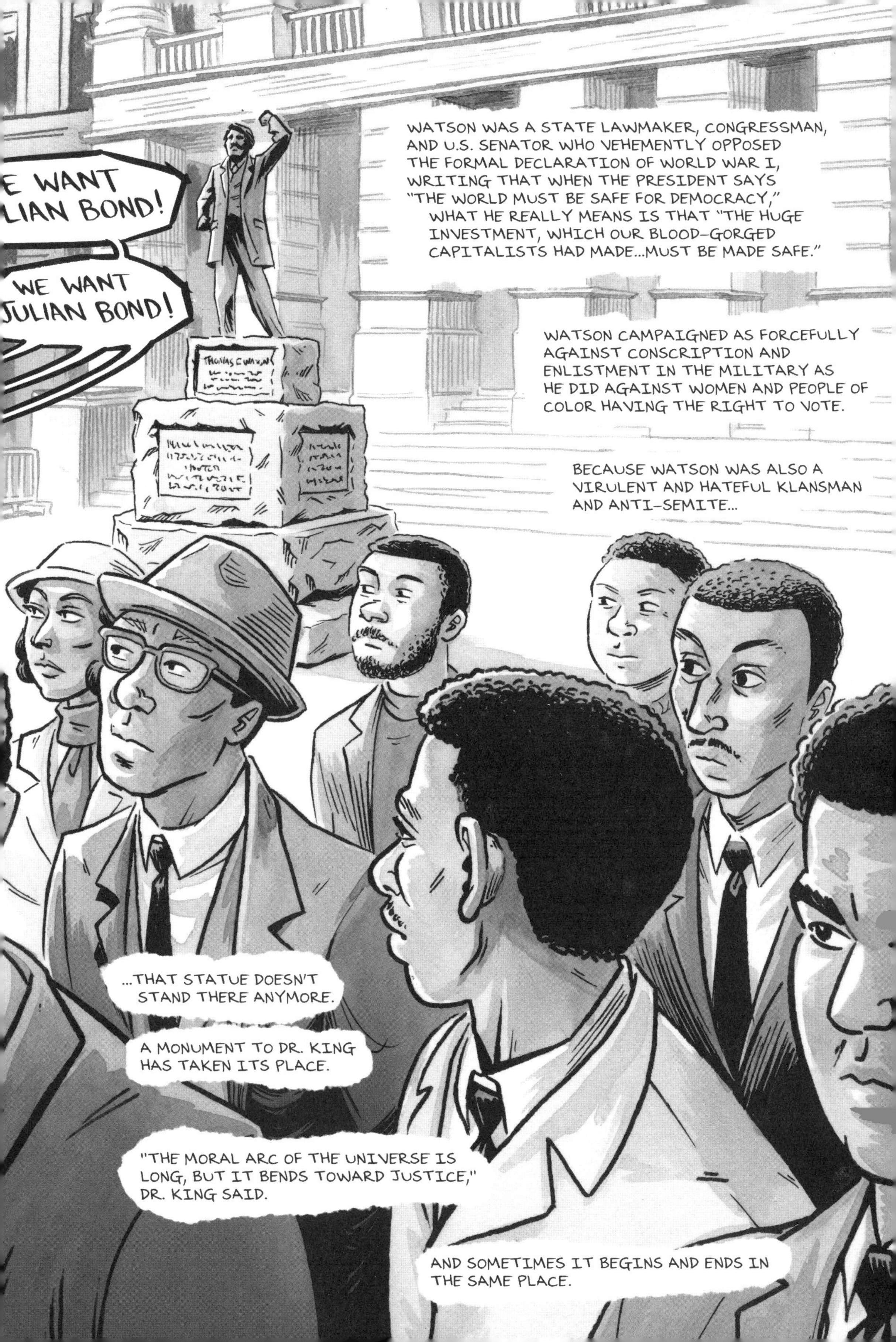
E WANT
LIAN BOND!
WE WANT
JULIAN BOND!
WATSON WAS A STATE LAWMAKER, CONGRESSMAN, AND U.S. SENATOR WHO VEHEMENTLY OPPOSED THE FORMAL DECLARATION OF WORLD WAR I, WRITING THAT WHEN THE PRESIDENT SAYS "THE WORLD MUST BE SAFE FOR DEMOCRACY," WHAT HE REALLY MEANS IS THAT "THE HUGE INVESTMENT, WHICH OUR BLOOD-GORGED CAPITALISTS HAD MADE...MUST BE MADE SAFE."
WATSON CAMPAIGNED AS FORCEFULLY AGAINST CONSCRIPTION AND ENLISTMENT IN THE MILITARY AS HE DID AGAINST WOMEN AND PEOPLE OF COLOR HAVING THE RIGHT TO VOTE.
BECAUSE WATSON WAS ALSO A VIRULENT AND HATEFUL KLANSMAN AND ANTI-SEMITE...
...THAT STATUE DOESN'T STAND THERE ANYMORE.
A MONUMENT TO DR. KING HAS TAKEN ITS PLACE.
"THE MORAL ARC OF THE UNIVERSE IS LONG, BUT IT BENDS TOWARD JUSTICE," DR. KING SAID.
AND SOMETIMES IT BEGINS AND ENDS IN THE SAME PLACE.

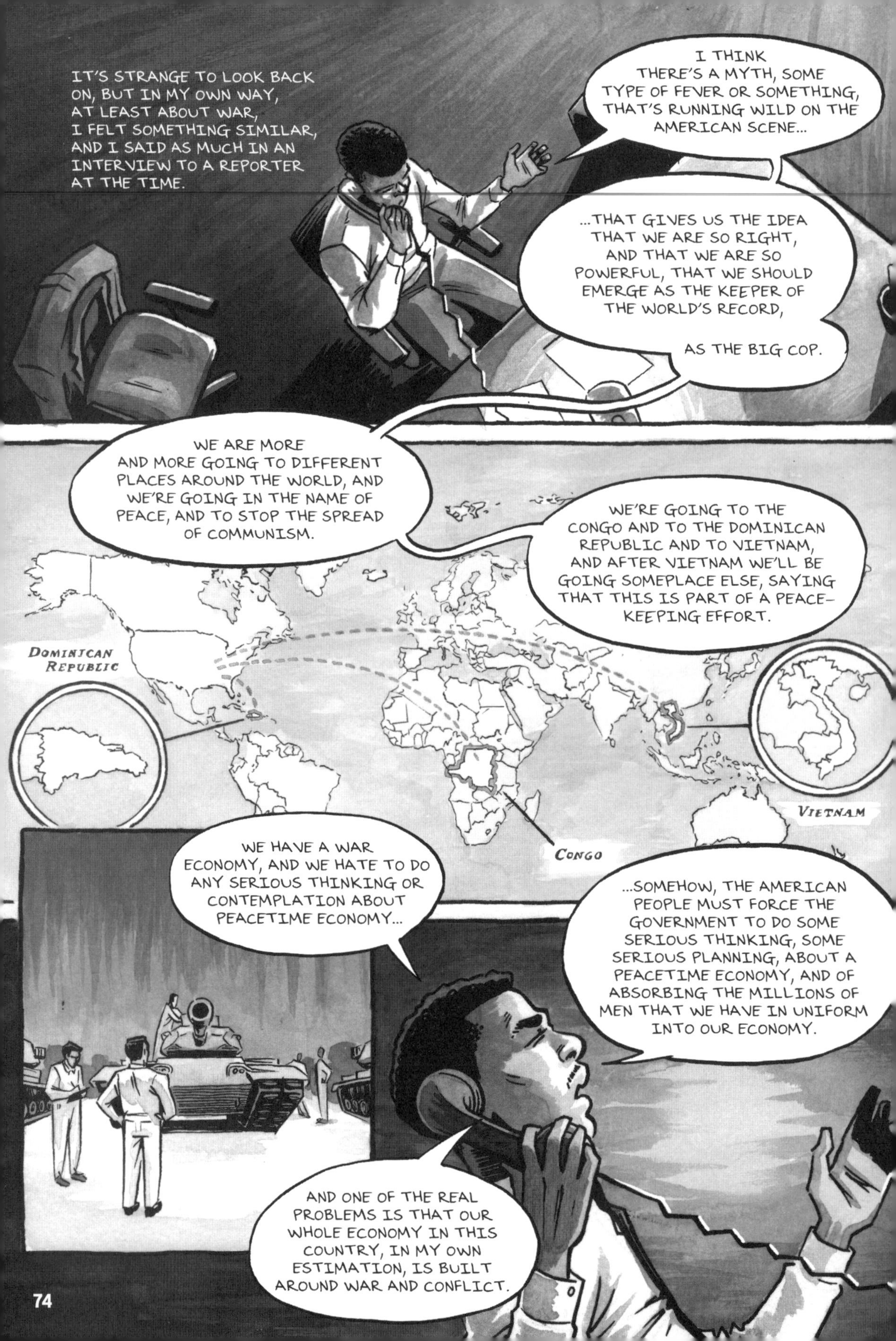
IT'S STRANGE TO LOOK BACK ON, BUT IN MY OWN WAY, AT LEAST ABOUT WAR, I FELT SOMETHING SIMILAR, AND I SAID AS MUCH IN AN INTERVIEW TO A REPORTER AT THE TIME.
I THINK THERE'S A MYTH, SOME TYPE OF FEVER OR SOMETHING, THAT'S RUNNING WILD ON THE AMERICAN SCENE...
...THAT GIVES US THE IDEA THAT WE ARE SO RIGHT, AND THAT WE ARE SO POWERFUL, THAT WE SHOULD EMERGE AS THE KEEPER OF THE WORLD'S RECORD,
AS THE BIG COP.
WE ARE MORE AND MORE GOING TO DIFFERENT PLACES AROUND THE WORLD, AND WE'RE GOING IN THE NAME OF PEACE, AND TO STOP THE SPREAD OF COMMUNISM.
WE'RE GOING TO THE CONGO AND TO THE DOMINICAN REPUBLIC AND TO VIETNAM, AND AFTER VIETNAM WE'LL BE GOING SOMEPLACE ELSE, SAYING THAT THIS IS PART OF A PEACE-KEEPING EFFORT.
DOMINICAN REPUBLIC
VIETNAM
CONGO
WE HAVE A WAR ECONOMY, AND WE HATE TO DO ANY SERIOUS THINKING OR CONTEMPLATION ABOUT PEACETIME ECONOMY...
...SOMEHOW, THE AMERICAN PEOPLE MUST FORCE THE GOVERNMENT TO DO SOME SERIOUS THINKING, SOME SERIOUS PLANNING, ABOUT A PEACETIME ECONOMY, AND OF ABSORBING THE MILLIONS OF MEN THAT WE HAVE IN UNIFORM INTO OUR ECONOMY.
AND ONE OF THE REAL PROBLEMS IS THAT OUR WHOLE ECONOMY IN THIS COUNTRY, IN MY OWN ESTIMATION, IS BUILT AROUND WAR AND CONFLICT.

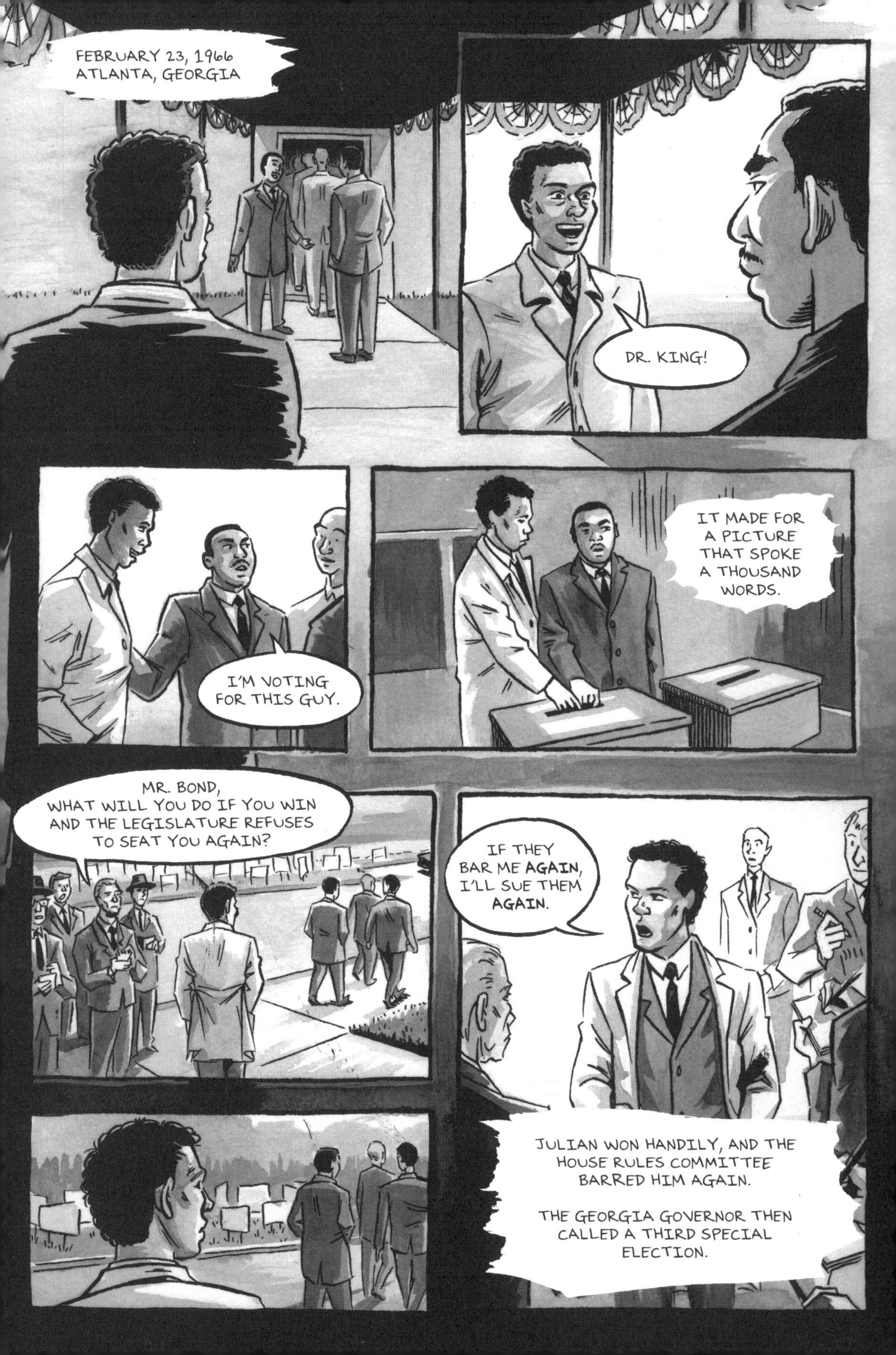
FEBRUARY 23, 1966
ATLANTA, GEORGIA
DR. KING!
I'M VOTING FOR THIS GUY.
IT MADE FOR A PICTURE THAT SPOKE A THOUSAND WORDS.
MR. BOND, WHAT WILL YOU DO IF YOU WIN AND THE LEGISLATURE REFUSES TO SEAT YOU AGAIN?
IF THEY BAR ME **AGAIN**, I'LL SUE THEM **AGAIN**.
JULIAN WON HANDILY, AND THE HOUSE RULES COMMITTEE BARRED HIM AGAIN.
THE GEORGIA GOVERNOR THEN CALLED A THIRD SPECIAL ELECTION.

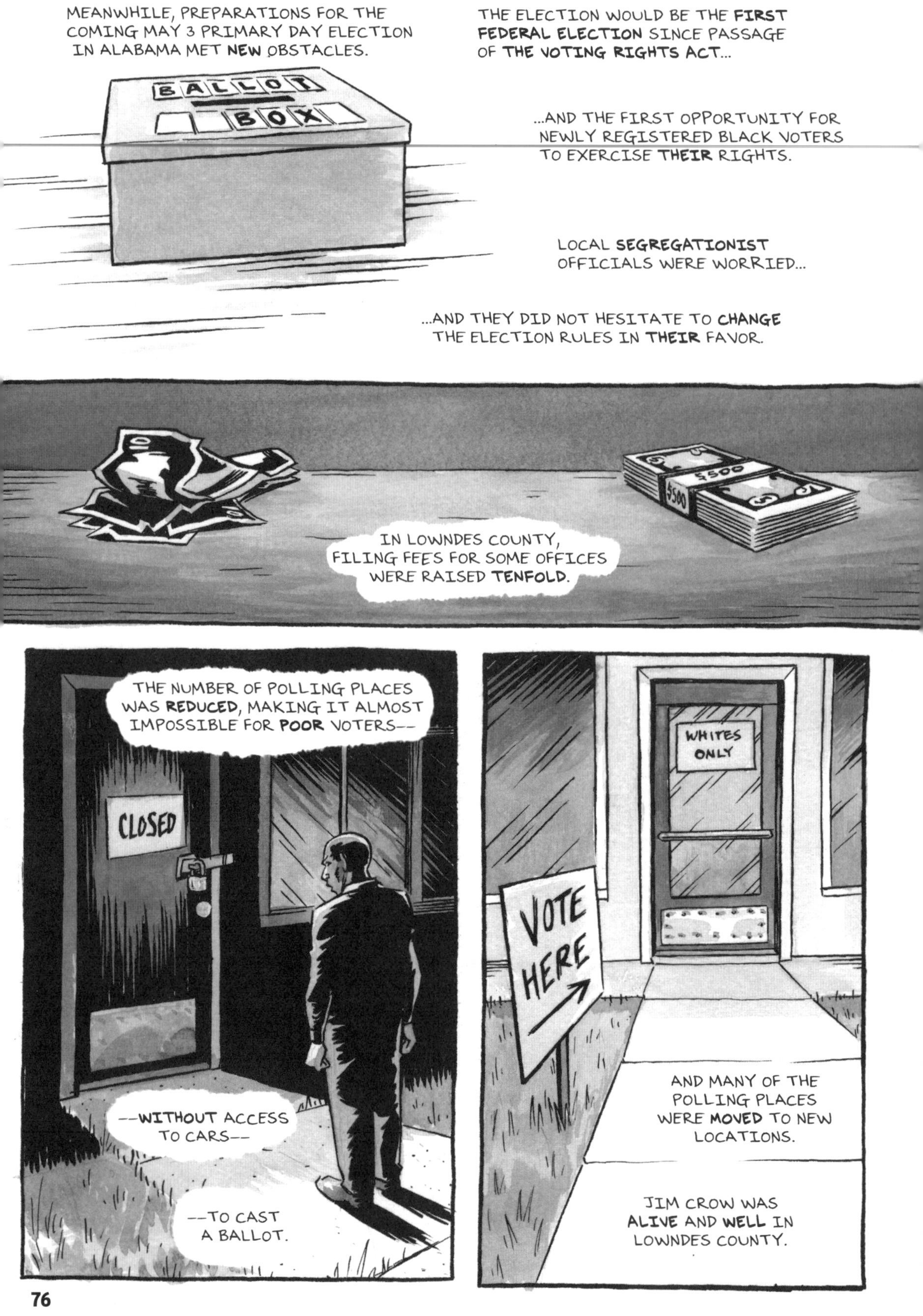
MEANWHILE, PREPARATIONS FOR THE COMING MAY 3 PRIMARY DAY ELECTION IN ALABAMA MET **NEW** OBSTACLES.
BALLOT BOX
THE ELECTION WOULD BE THE **FIRST FEDERAL ELECTION** SINCE PASSAGE OF **THE VOTING RIGHTS ACT**...
...AND THE FIRST OPPORTUNITY FOR NEWLY REGISTERED BLACK VOTERS TO EXERCISE **THEIR** RIGHTS.
LOCAL **SEGREGATIONIST** OFFICIALS WERE WORRIED...
...AND THEY DID NOT HESITATE TO **CHANGE** THE ELECTION RULES IN **THEIR** FAVOR.
$500
$500
IN LOWNDES COUNTY, FILING FEES FOR SOME OFFICES WERE RAISED **TENFOLD**.
THE NUMBER OF POLLING PLACES WAS **REDUCED**, MAKING IT ALMOST IMPOSSIBLE FOR **POOR** VOTERS--
CLOSED
--**WITHOUT** ACCESS TO CARS--
--TO CAST A BALLOT.
WHITES ONLY
VOTE HERE
AND MANY OF THE POLLING PLACES WERE **MOVED** TO NEW LOCATIONS.
JIM CROW WAS **ALIVE** AND **WELL** IN LOWNDES COUNTY.

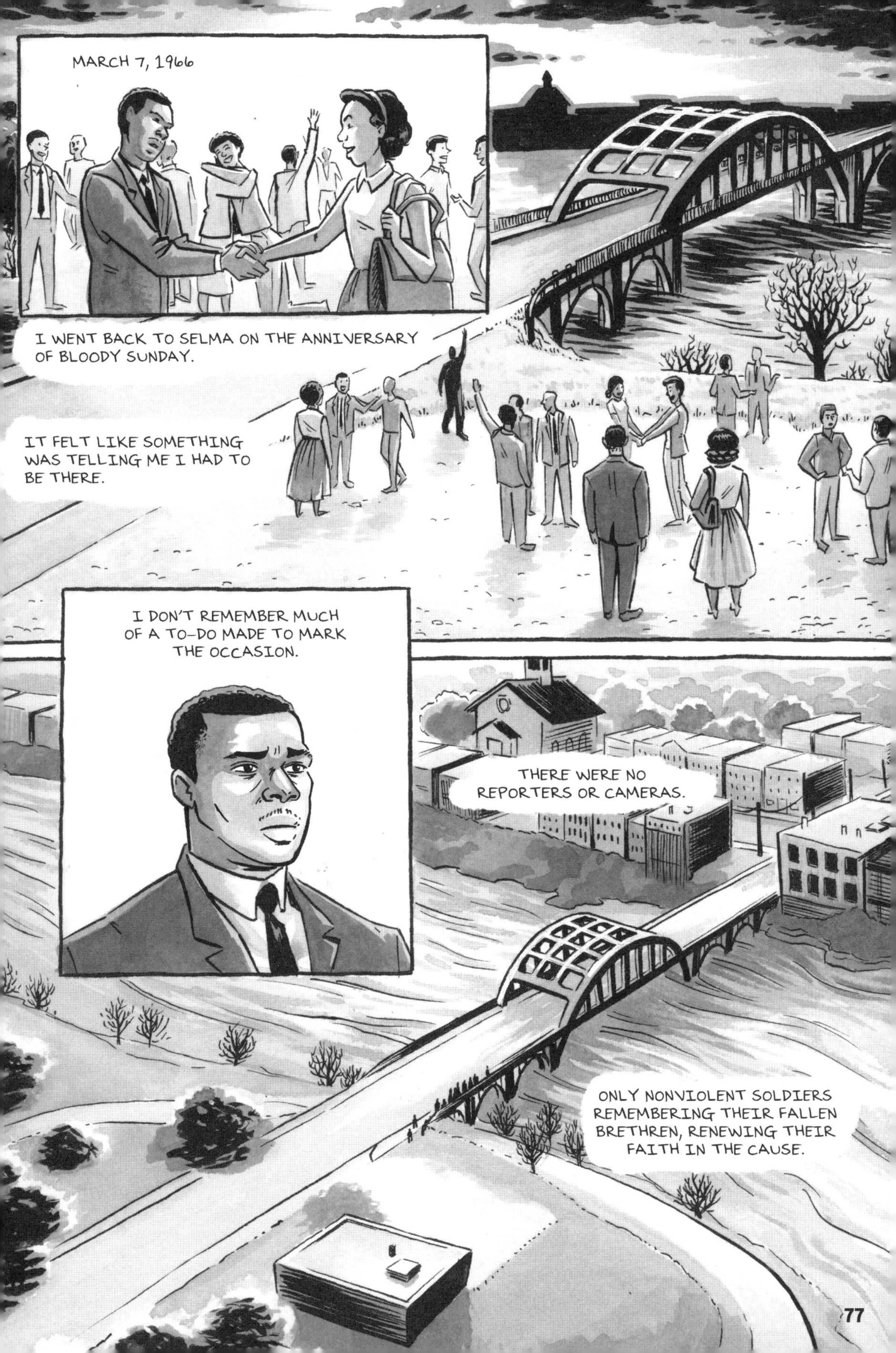

MARCH 7, 1966
I WENT BACK TO SELMA ON THE ANNIVERSARY OF BLOODY SUNDAY.
IT FELT LIKE SOMETHING WAS TELLING ME I HAD TO BE THERE.
I DON'T REMEMBER MUCH OF A TO-DO MADE TO MARK THE OCCASION.
THERE WERE NO REPORTERS OR CAMERAS.
ONLY NONVIOLENT SOLDIERS REMEMBERING THEIR FALLEN BRETHREN, RENEWING THEIR FAITH IN THE CAUSE.

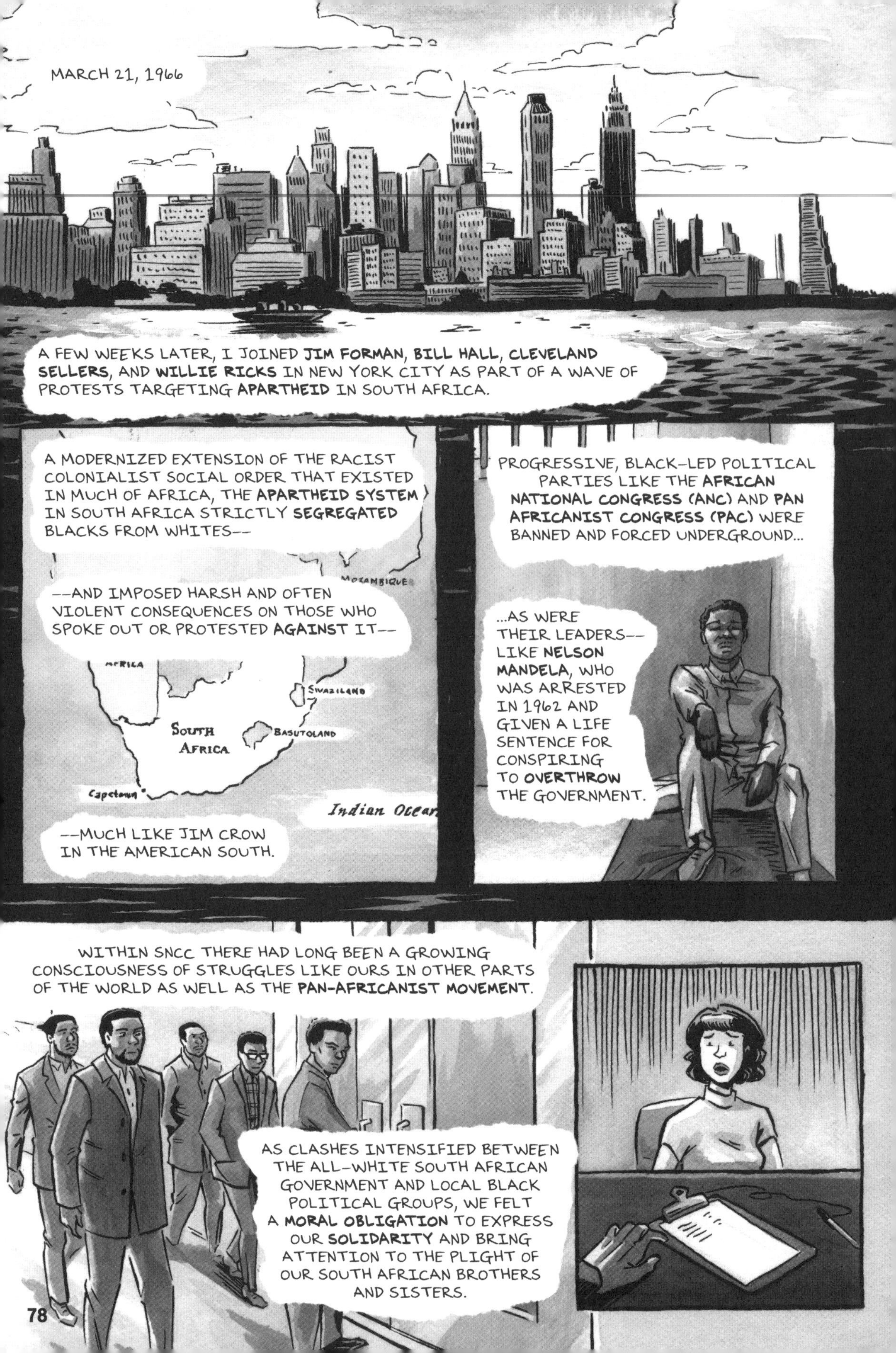
MARCH 21, 1966
A FEW WEEKS LATER, I JOINED **JIM FORMAN**, **BILL HALL**, **CLEVELAND SELLERS**, AND **WILLIE RICKS** IN NEW YORK CITY AS PART OF A WAVE OF PROTESTS TARGETING **APARTHEID** IN SOUTH AFRICA.
A MODERNIZED EXTENSION OF THE RACIST COLONIALIST SOCIAL ORDER THAT EXISTED IN MUCH OF AFRICA, THE **APARTHEID SYSTEM** IN SOUTH AFRICA STRICTLY **SEGREGATED** BLACKS FROM WHITES--
MOZAMBIQUE
--AND IMPOSED HARSH AND OFTEN VIOLENT CONSEQUENCES ON THOSE WHO SPOKE OUT OR PROTESTED **AGAINST** IT--
AFRICA
SWAZILAND
SOUTH AFRICA
BASUTOLAND
Capetown
Indian Ocea
--MUCH LIKE JIM CROW IN THE AMERICAN SOUTH.
PROGRESSIVE, BLACK-LED POLITICAL PARTIES LIKE THE **AFRICAN NATIONAL CONGRESS (ANC)** AND **PAN AFRICANIST CONGRESS (PAC)** WERE BANNED AND FORCED UNDERGROUND...
...AS WERE THEIR LEADERS-- LIKE **NELSON MANDELA**, WHO WAS ARRESTED IN 1962 AND GIVEN A LIFE SENTENCE FOR CONSPIRING TO **OVERTHROW** THE GOVERNMENT.
WITHIN SNCC THERE HAD LONG BEEN A GROWING CONSCIOUSNESS OF STRUGGLES LIKE OURS IN OTHER PARTS OF THE WORLD AS WELL AS THE **PAN-AFRICANIST MOVEMENT**.
AS CLASHES INTENSIFIED BETWEEN THE ALL-WHITE SOUTH AFRICAN GOVERNMENT AND LOCAL BLACK POLITICAL GROUPS, WE FELT A **MORAL OBLIGATION** TO EXPRESS OUR **SOLIDARITY** AND BRING ATTENTION TO THE PLIGHT OF OUR SOUTH AFRICAN BROTHERS AND SISTERS.

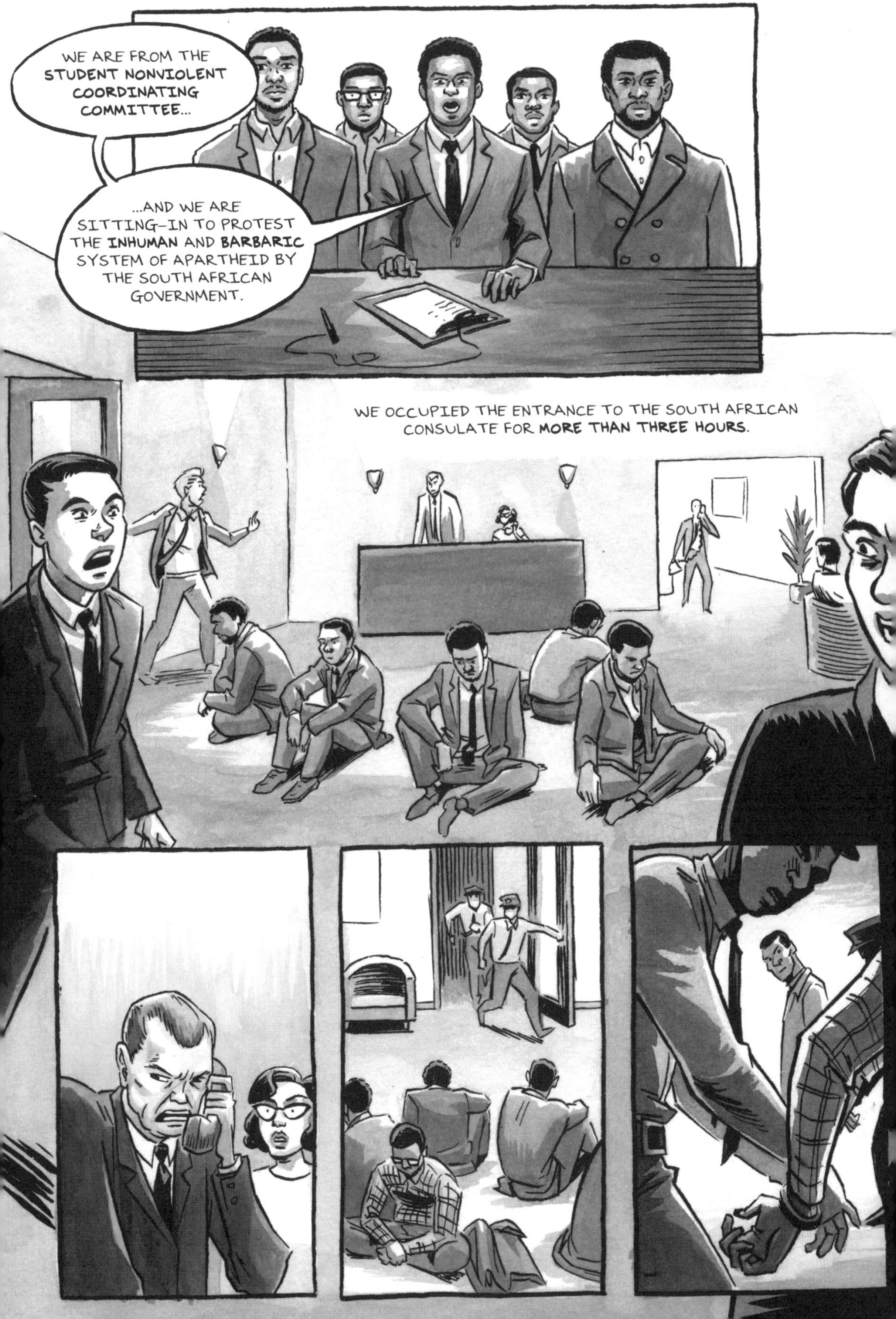
WE ARE FROM THE **STUDENT NONVIOLENT COORDINATING COMMITTEE...**
...AND WE ARE SITTING-IN TO PROTEST THE **INHUMAN** AND **BARBARIC** SYSTEM OF APARTHEID BY THE SOUTH AFRICAN GOVERNMENT.
WE OCCUPIED THE ENTRANCE TO THE SOUTH AFRICAN CONSULATE FOR **MORE THAN THREE HOURS.**

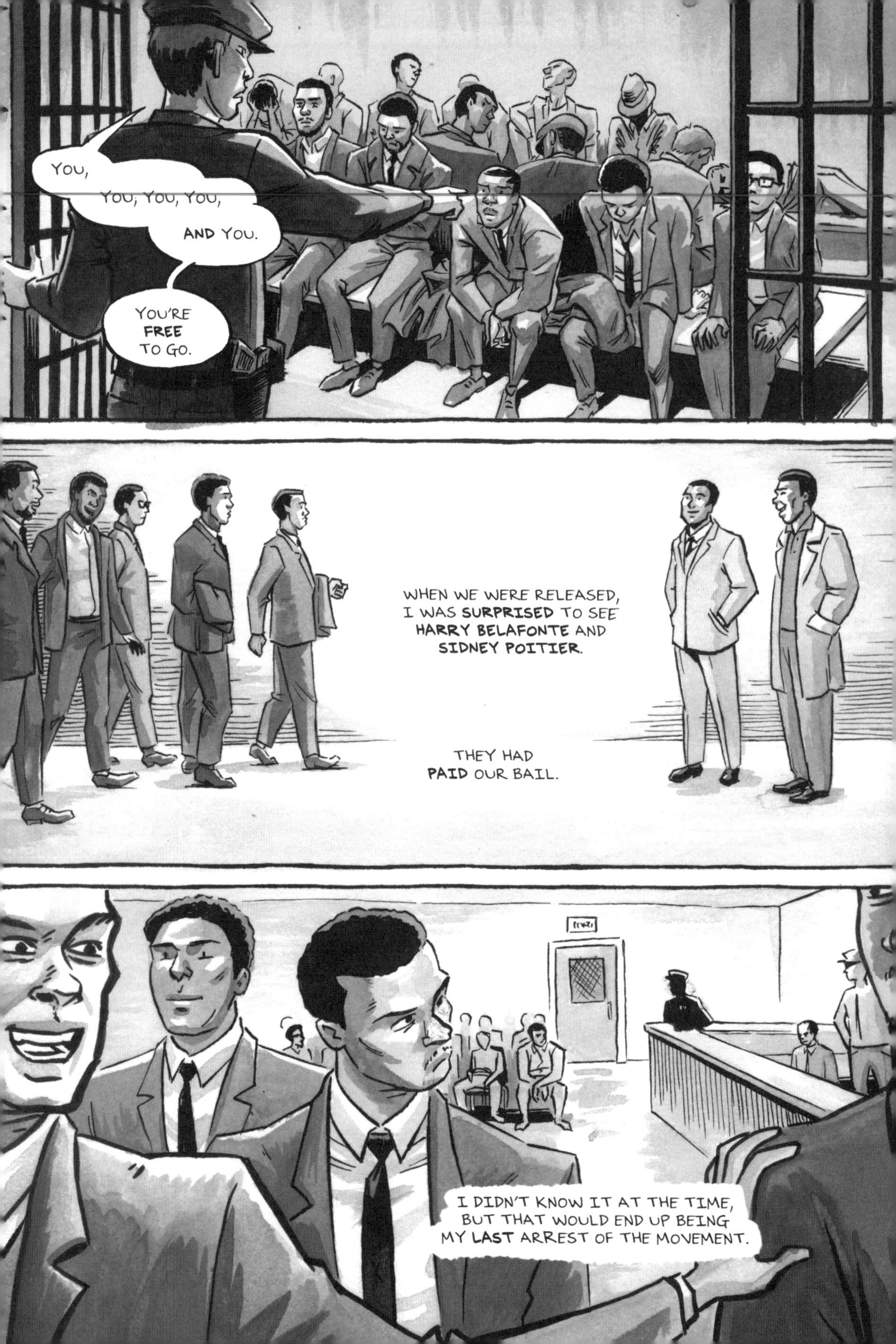
YOU,
YOU, YOU, YOU,
AND YOU.
YOU'RE FREE TO GO.
WHEN WE WERE RELEASED, I WAS SURPRISED TO SEE HARRY BELAFONTE AND SIDNEY POITIER.
THEY HAD PAID OUR BAIL.
I DIDN'T KNOW IT AT THE TIME, BUT THAT WOULD END UP BEING MY LAST ARREST OF THE MOVEMENT.

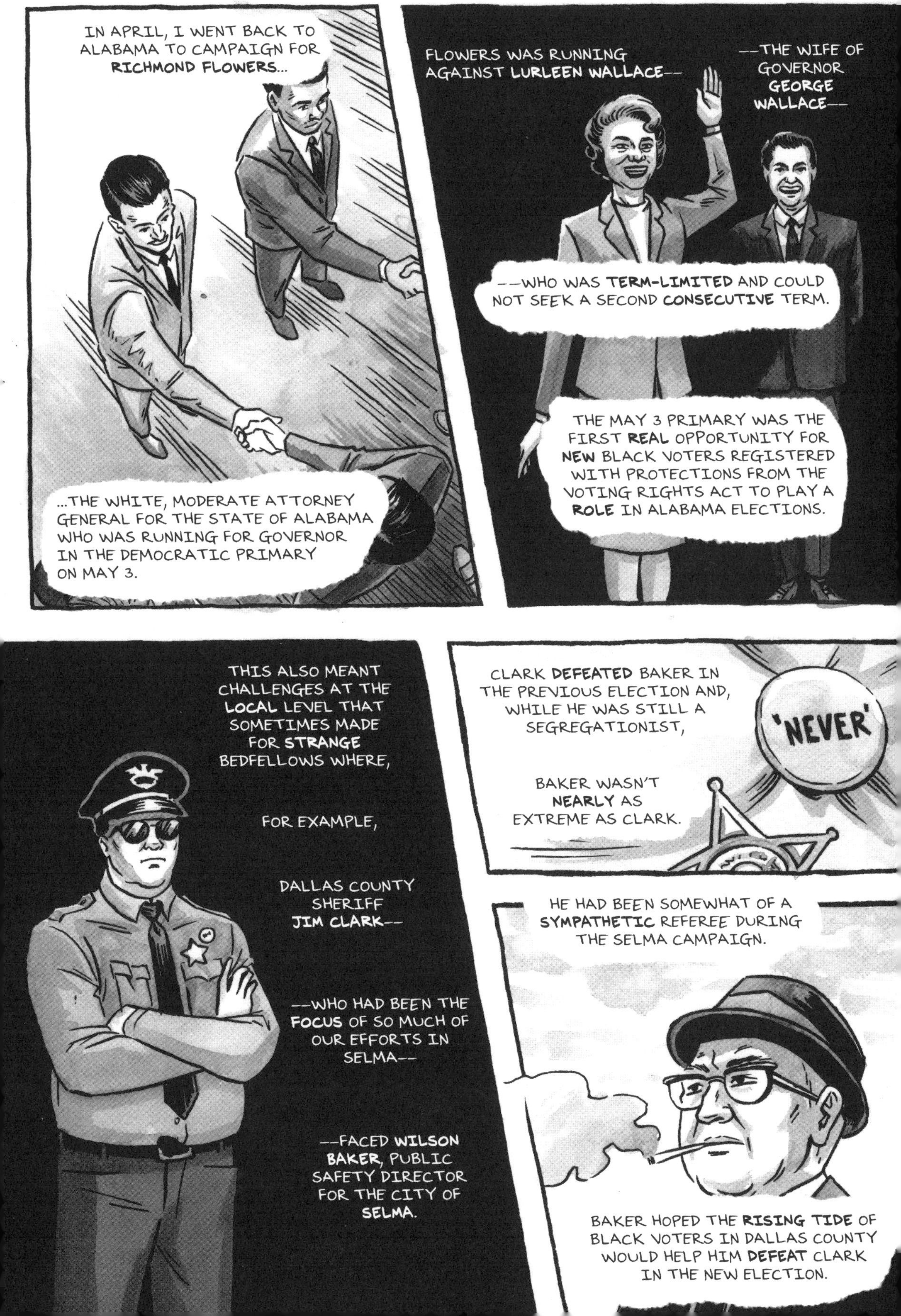
IN APRIL, I WENT BACK TO ALABAMA TO CAMPAIGN FOR **RICHMOND FLOWERS**...
...THE WHITE, MODERATE ATTORNEY GENERAL FOR THE STATE OF ALABAMA WHO WAS RUNNING FOR GOVERNOR IN THE DEMOCRATIC PRIMARY ON MAY 3.
FLOWERS WAS RUNNING AGAINST **LURLEEN WALLACE**--
--THE WIFE OF GOVERNOR **GEORGE WALLACE**--
--WHO WAS **TERM-LIMITED** AND COULD NOT SEEK A SECOND **CONSECUTIVE** TERM.
THE MAY 3 PRIMARY WAS THE FIRST **REAL** OPPORTUNITY FOR **NEW** BLACK VOTERS REGISTERED WITH PROTECTIONS FROM THE VOTING RIGHTS ACT TO PLAY A **ROLE** IN ALABAMA ELECTIONS.
THIS ALSO MEANT CHALLENGES AT THE **LOCAL** LEVEL THAT SOMETIMES MADE FOR **STRANGE** BEDFELLOWS WHERE,
FOR EXAMPLE,
DALLAS COUNTY SHERIFF **JIM CLARK**--
--WHO HAD BEEN THE **FOCUS** OF SO MUCH OF OUR EFFORTS IN SELMA--
--FACED **WILSON BAKER**, PUBLIC SAFETY DIRECTOR FOR THE CITY OF **SELMA**.
CLARK **DEFEATED** BAKER IN THE PREVIOUS ELECTION AND, WHILE HE WAS STILL A SEGREGATIONIST,
'NEVER'
BAKER WASN'T **NEARLY** AS EXTREME AS CLARK.
HE HAD BEEN SOMEWHAT OF A **SYMPATHETIC** REFEREE DURING THE SELMA CAMPAIGN.
BAKER HOPED THE **RISING TIDE** OF BLACK VOTERS IN DALLAS COUNTY WOULD HELP HIM **DEFEAT** CLARK IN THE NEW ELECTION.

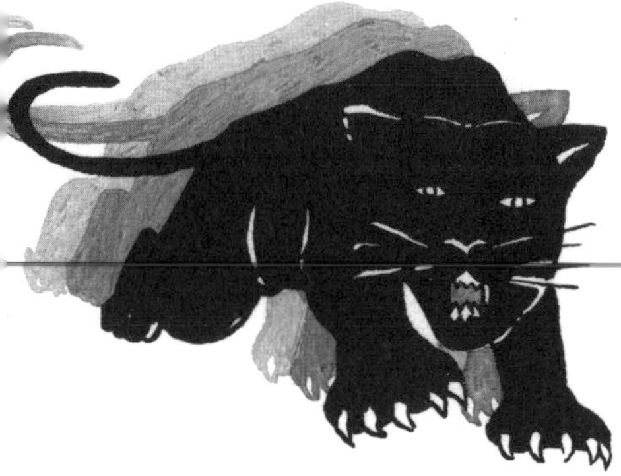

MEANWHILE, IN LOWNDES COUNTY, THE LCFO--

--WHICH WAS BECOMING KNOWN AS THE "BLACK PANTHER PARTY" BECAUSE OF ITS **MASCOT**--

--PREPARED FOR ITS **OWN** PRIMARY ELECTIONS ON MAY 3, IN ACCORDANCE WITH ALABAMA STATE ELECTIONS LAW, TO **OFFICIALLY** NOMINATE ITS SLATE OF CANDIDATES TO APPEAR ON THE FALL GENERAL ELECTION BALLOT.

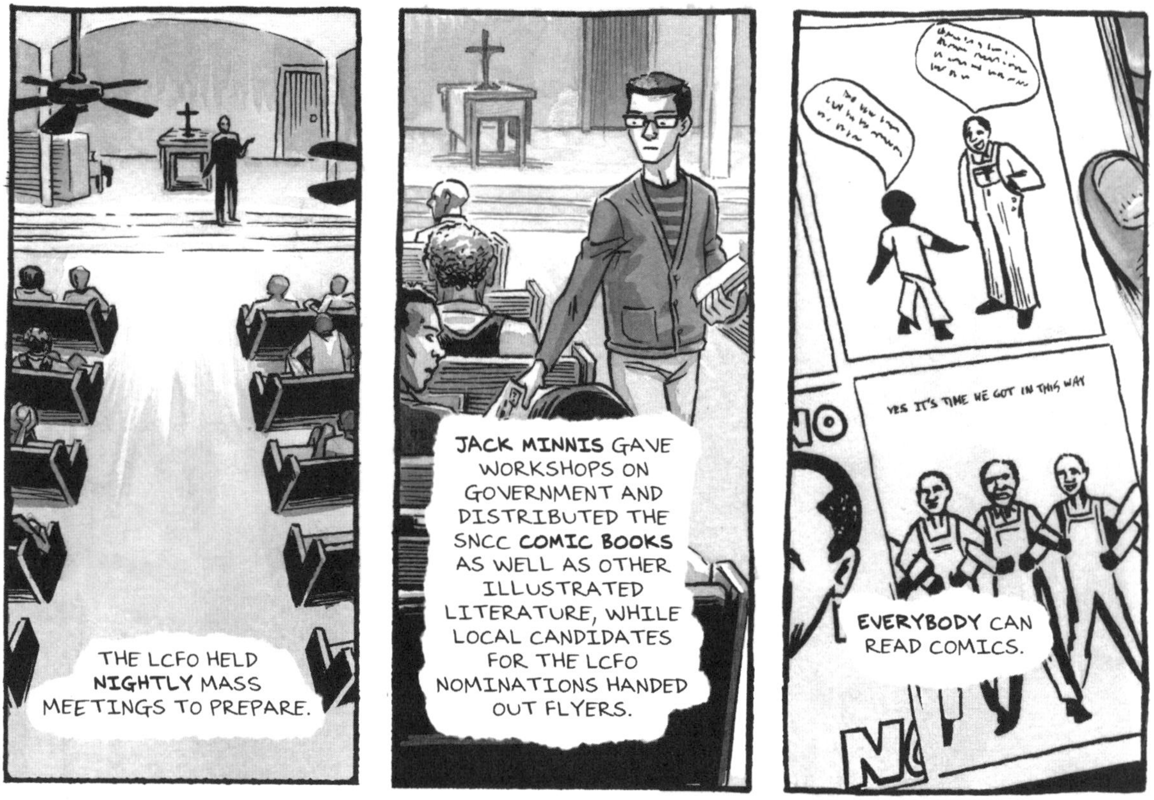
THE LCFO HELD **NIGHTLY** MASS MEETINGS TO PREPARE.
JACK MINNIS GAVE WORKSHOPS ON GOVERNMENT AND DISTRIBUTED THE SNCC **COMIC BOOKS** AS WELL AS OTHER ILLUSTRATED LITERATURE, WHILE LOCAL CANDIDATES FOR THE LCFO NOMINATIONS HANDED OUT FLYERS.
YES IT'S TIME WE GOT IN THIS WAY
EVERYBODY CAN READ COMICS.

DR. KING **AVOIDED** LOWNDES COUNTY-- **AS DID I**--STAYING **SILENT** ON THE LCFO EFFORTS TO WORK OUTSIDE OF THE DEMOCRATIC PARTY.

THESE EFFORTS WERE **DENOUNCED** BY SOME AS "EXTREMISM FOR THE SAKE FOR EXTREMISM" AND "DESTRUCTIVE MISCHIEF-MAKING."

BUT LOCAL ORGANIZERS REMAINED **STEADFAST**...

...EVEN WHEN WORD CAME THAT LOCAL WHITES WERE PREPARING FOR **VIOLENCE**.

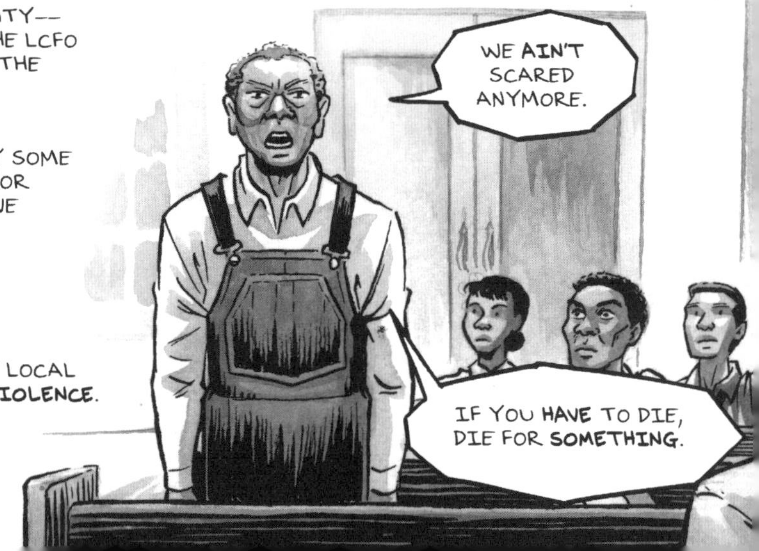
WE **AIN'T** SCARED ANYMORE.
IF YOU **HAVE** TO DIE, DIE FOR **SOMETHING**.

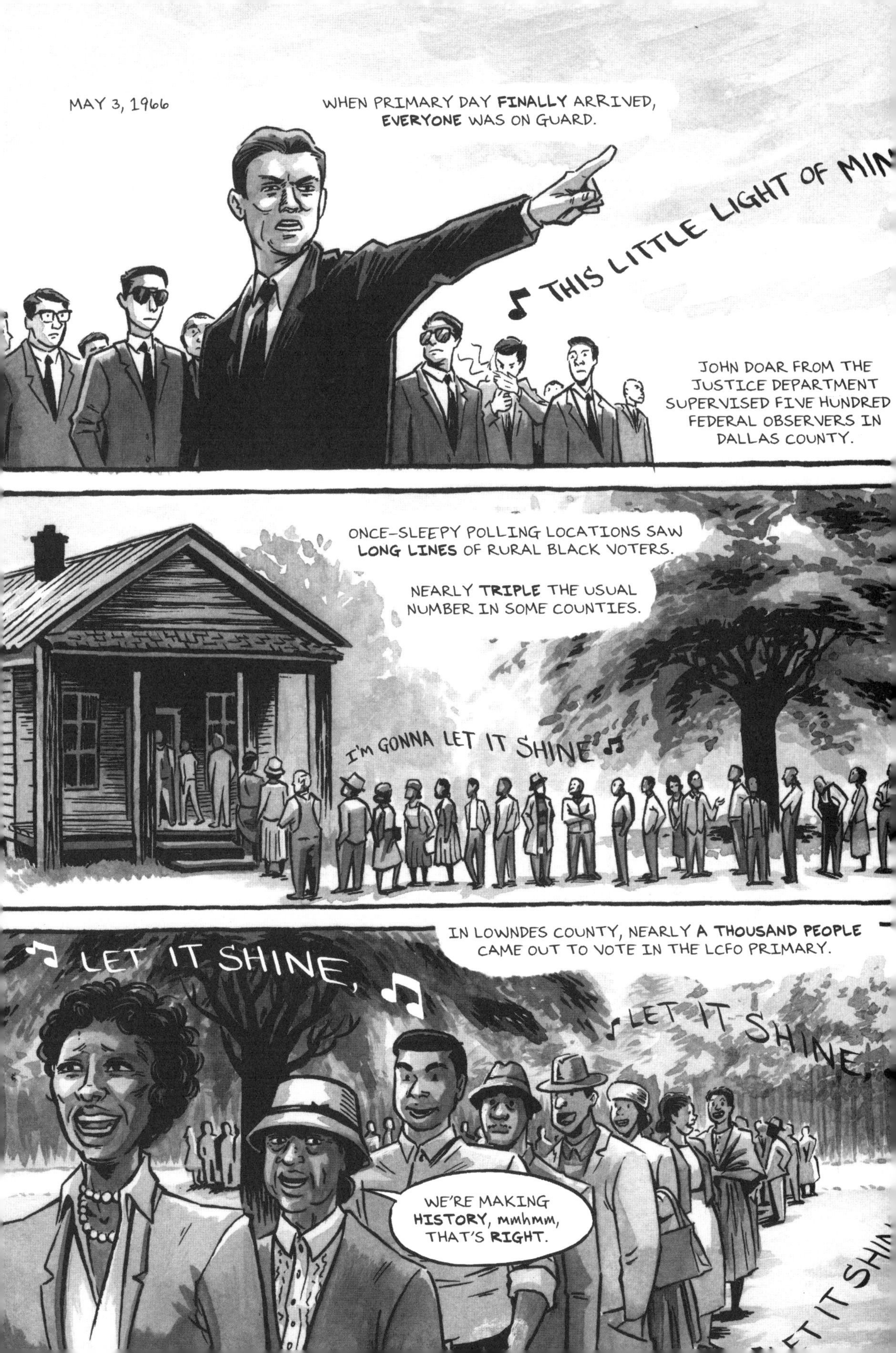
MAY 3, 1966
WHEN PRIMARY DAY **FINALLY** ARRIVED, **EVERYONE** WAS ON GUARD.
♪ THIS LITTLE LIGHT OF MIN
JOHN DOAR FROM THE JUSTICE DEPARTMENT SUPERVISED FIVE HUNDRED FEDERAL OBSERVERS IN DALLAS COUNTY.
ONCE-SLEEPY POLLING LOCATIONS SAW **LONG LINES** OF RURAL BLACK VOTERS.
NEARLY **TRIPLE** THE USUAL NUMBER IN SOME COUNTIES.
I'M GONNA LET IT SHINE ♪
IN LOWNDES COUNTY, NEARLY **A THOUSAND PEOPLE** CAME OUT TO VOTE IN THE LCFO PRIMARY.
♪ LET IT SHINE, ♪
♪ LET IT SHINE,
WE'RE MAKING **HISTORY**, mmhmm, THAT'S **RIGHT**.
ET IT SHIN

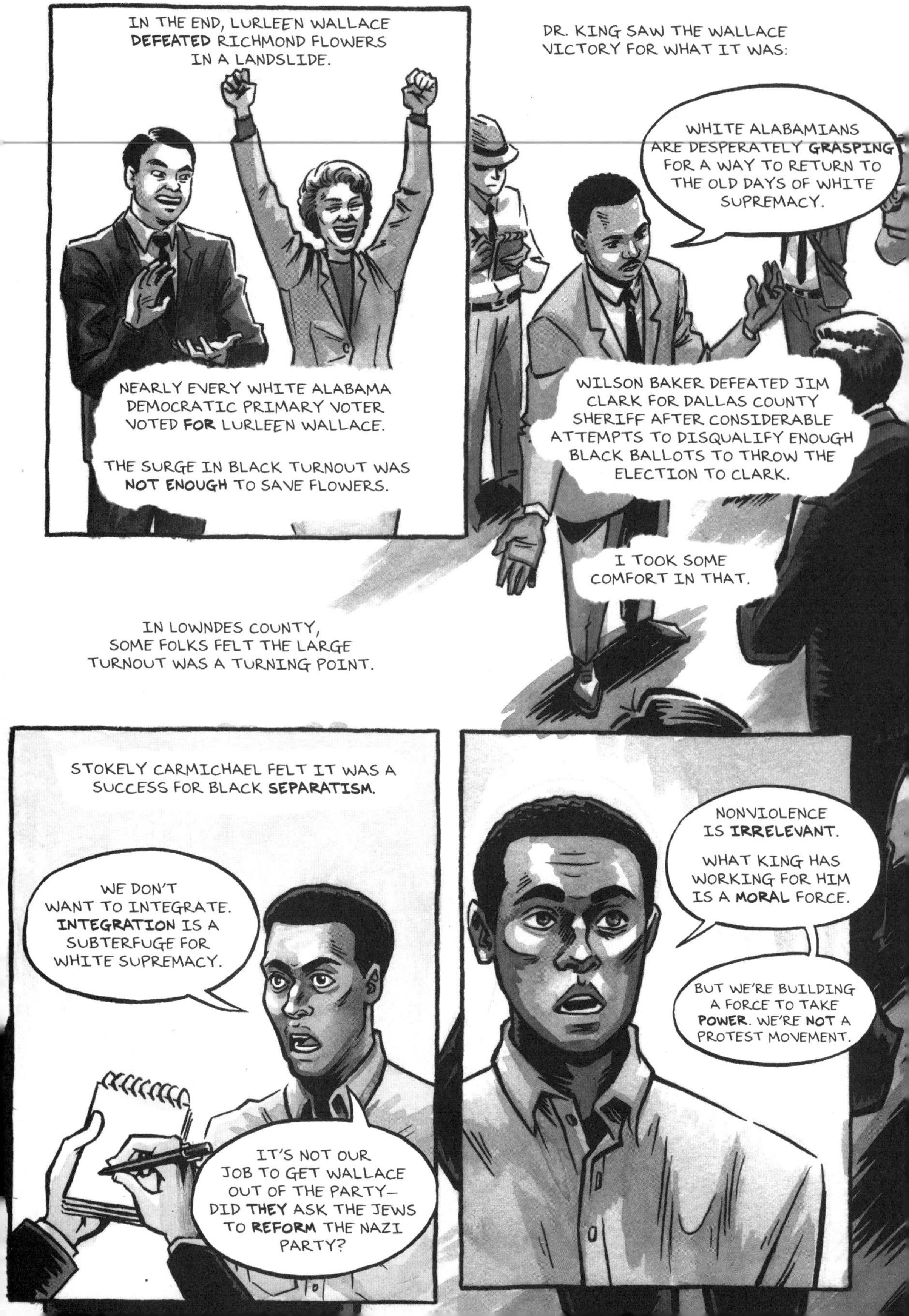
IN THE END, LURLEEN WALLACE **DEFEATED** RICHMOND FLOWERS IN A LANDSLIDE.
NEARLY EVERY WHITE ALABAMA DEMOCRATIC PRIMARY VOTER VOTED **FOR** LURLEEN WALLACE.
THE SURGE IN BLACK TURNOUT WAS **NOT ENOUGH** TO SAVE FLOWERS.
DR. KING SAW THE WALLACE VICTORY FOR WHAT IT WAS:
WHITE ALABAMIANS ARE DESPERATELY **GRASPING** FOR A WAY TO RETURN TO THE OLD DAYS OF WHITE SUPREMACY.
WILSON BAKER DEFEATED JIM CLARK FOR DALLAS COUNTY SHERIFF AFTER CONSIDERABLE ATTEMPTS TO DISQUALIFY ENOUGH BLACK BALLOTS TO THROW THE ELECTION TO CLARK.
I TOOK SOME COMFORT IN THAT.
IN LOWNDES COUNTY, SOME FOLKS FELT THE LARGE TURNOUT WAS A TURNING POINT.
STOKELY CARMICHAEL FELT IT WAS A SUCCESS FOR BLACK **SEPARATISM**.
WE DON'T WANT TO INTEGRATE. **INTEGRATION** IS A SUBTERFUGE FOR WHITE SUPREMACY.
IT'S NOT OUR JOB TO GET WALLACE OUT OF THE PARTY— DID **THEY** ASK THE JEWS TO **REFORM** THE NAZI PARTY?
NONVIOLENCE IS **IRRELEVANT**.
WHAT KING HAS WORKING FOR HIM IS A **MORAL** FORCE.
BUT WE'RE BUILDING A FORCE TO TAKE **POWER**. WE'RE **NOT** A PROTEST MOVEMENT.

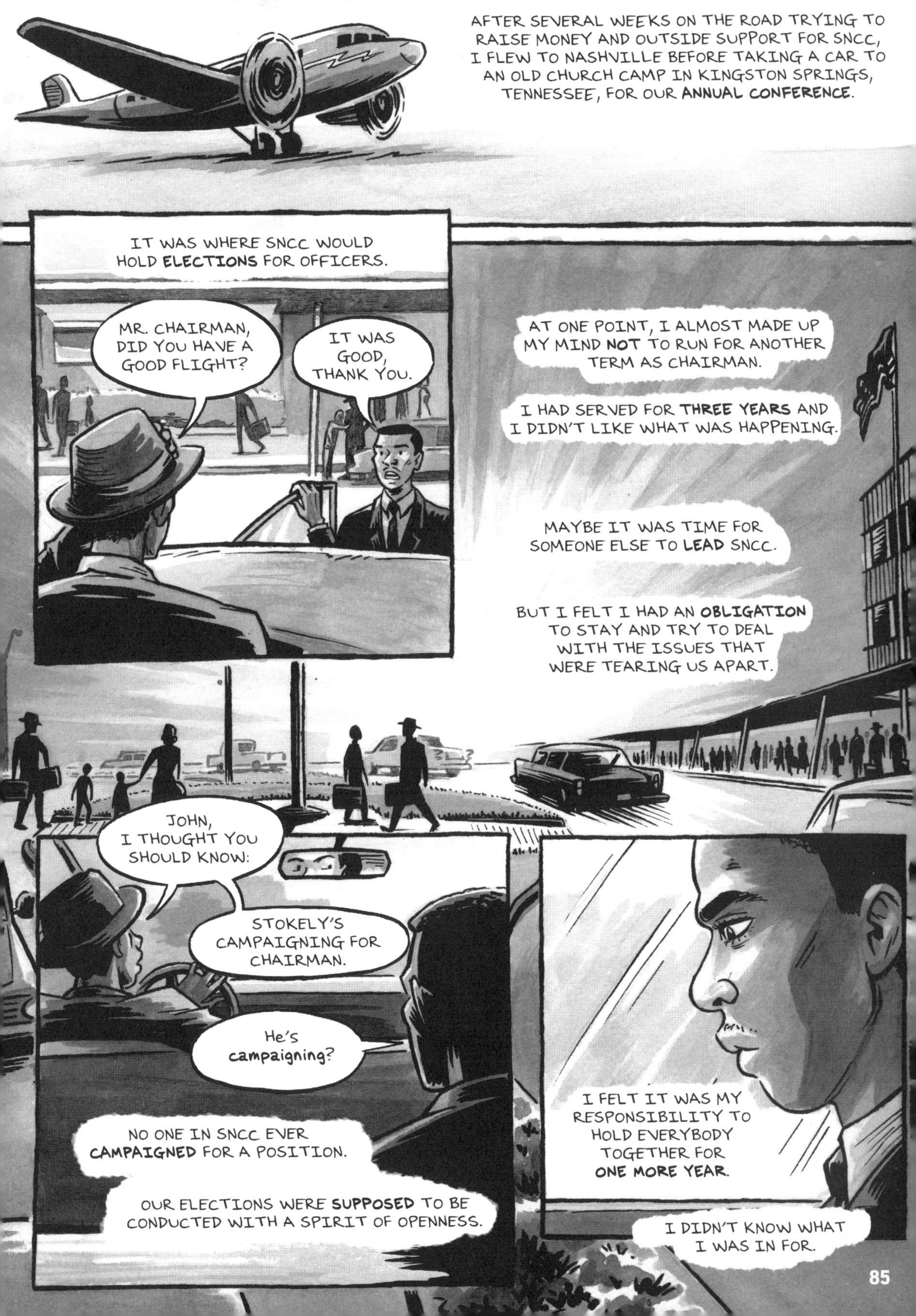

AFTER SEVERAL WEEKS ON THE ROAD TRYING TO RAISE MONEY AND OUTSIDE SUPPORT FOR SNCC, I FLEW TO NASHVILLE BEFORE TAKING A CAR TO AN OLD CHURCH CAMP IN KINGSTON SPRINGS, TENNESSEE, FOR OUR **ANNUAL CONFERENCE**.
IT WAS WHERE SNCC WOULD HOLD **ELECTIONS** FOR OFFICERS.
MR. CHAIRMAN, DID YOU HAVE A GOOD FLIGHT?
IT WAS GOOD, THANK YOU.
AT ONE POINT, I ALMOST MADE UP MY MIND **NOT** TO RUN FOR ANOTHER TERM AS CHAIRMAN.
I HAD SERVED FOR **THREE YEARS** AND I DIDN'T LIKE WHAT WAS HAPPENING.
MAYBE IT WAS TIME FOR SOMEONE ELSE TO **LEAD** SNCC.
BUT I FELT I HAD AN **OBLIGATION** TO STAY AND TRY TO DEAL WITH THE ISSUES THAT WERE TEARING US APART.
JOHN, I THOUGHT YOU SHOULD KNOW:
STOKELY'S CAMPAIGNING FOR CHAIRMAN.
He's **campaigning**?
NO ONE IN SNCC EVER **CAMPAIGNED** FOR A POSITION.
OUR ELECTIONS WERE **SUPPOSED** TO BE CONDUCTED WITH A SPIRIT OF OPENNESS.
I FELT IT WAS MY RESPONSIBILITY TO HOLD EVERYBODY TOGETHER FOR **ONE MORE YEAR**.
I DIDN'T KNOW WHAT I WAS IN FOR.

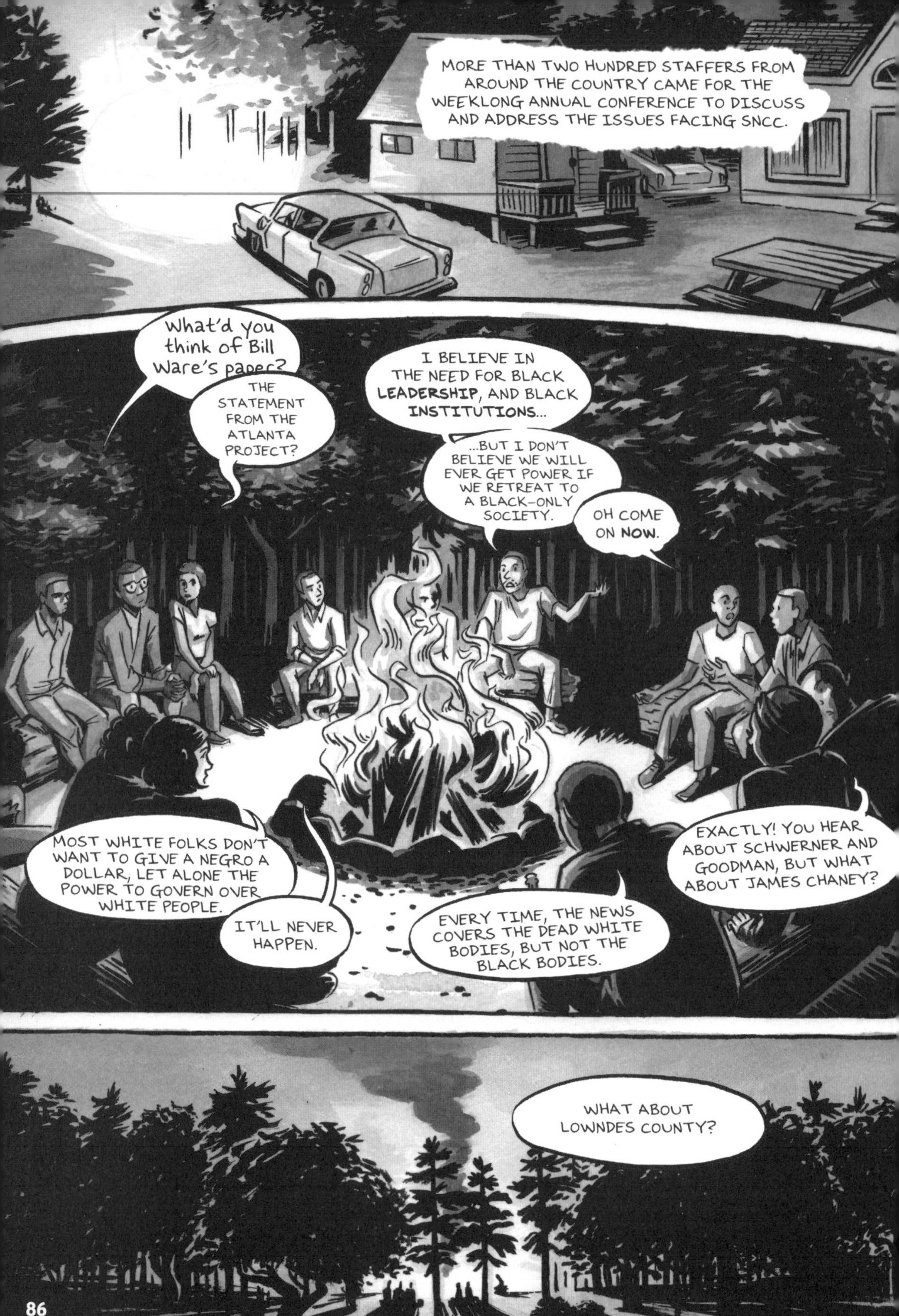
MORE THAN TWO HUNDRED STAFFERS FROM AROUND THE COUNTRY CAME FOR THE WEEKLONG ANNUAL CONFERENCE TO DISCUSS AND ADDRESS THE ISSUES FACING SNCC.
What'd you think of Bill Ware's paper?
THE STATEMENT FROM THE ATLANTA PROJECT?
I BELIEVE IN THE NEED FOR BLACK **LEADERSHIP**, AND BLACK **INSTITUTIONS**...
...BUT I DON'T BELIEVE WE WILL EVER GET POWER IF WE RETREAT TO A BLACK-ONLY SOCIETY.
OH COME ON **NOW**.
MOST WHITE FOLKS DON'T WANT TO GIVE A NEGRO A DOLLAR, LET ALONE THE POWER TO GOVERN OVER WHITE PEOPLE.
IT'LL NEVER HAPPEN.
EVERY TIME, THE NEWS COVERS THE DEAD WHITE BODIES, BUT NOT THE BLACK BODIES.
EXACTLY! YOU HEAR ABOUT SCHWERNER AND GOODMAN, BUT WHAT ABOUT JAMES CHANEY?
WHAT ABOUT LOWNDES COUNTY?

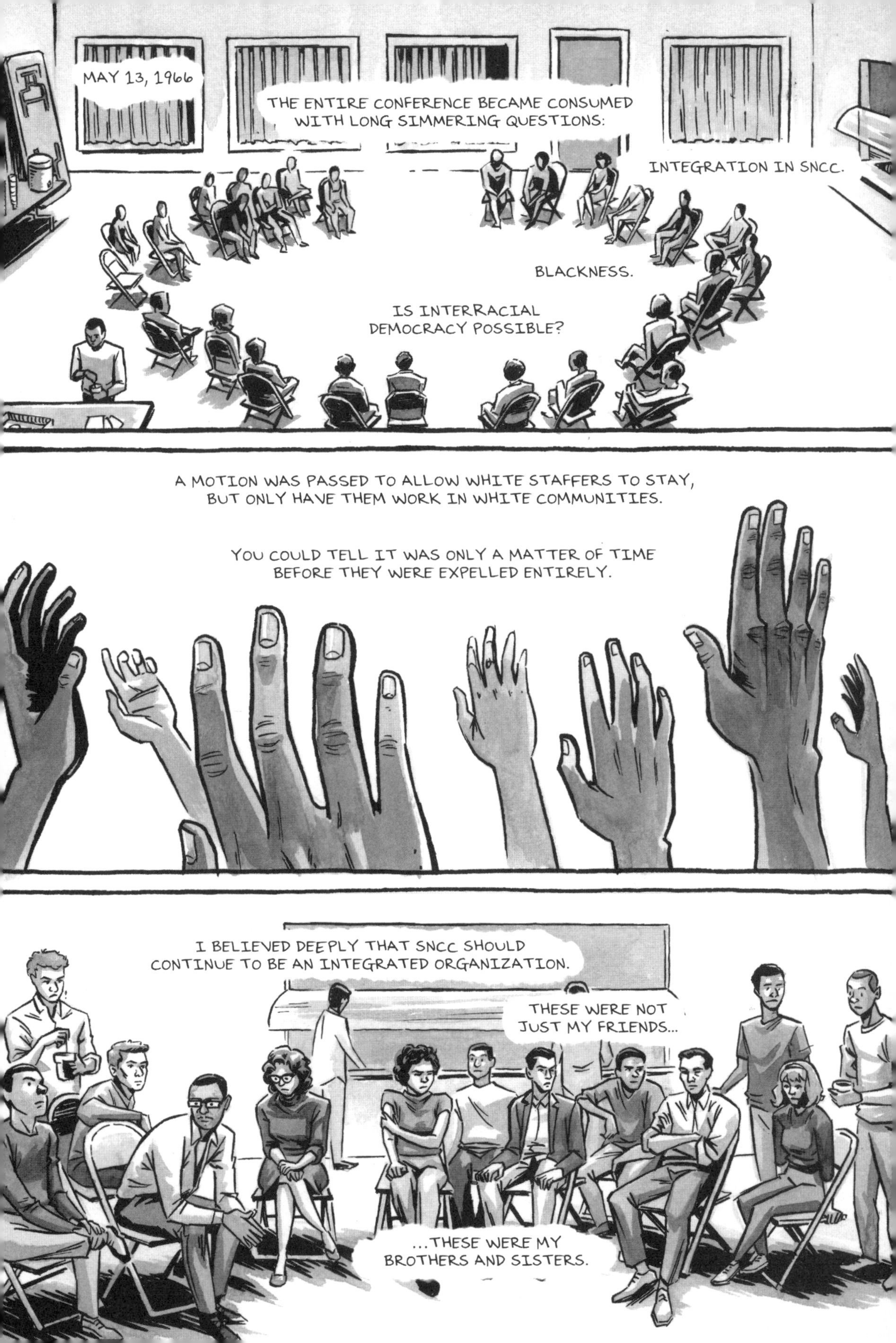
MAY 13, 1966
THE ENTIRE CONFERENCE BECAME CONSUMED WITH LONG SIMMERING QUESTIONS:
INTEGRATION IN SNCC.
BLACKNESS.
IS INTERRACIAL DEMOCRACY POSSIBLE?
A MOTION WAS PASSED TO ALLOW WHITE STAFFERS TO STAY, BUT ONLY HAVE THEM WORK IN WHITE COMMUNITIES.
YOU COULD TELL IT WAS ONLY A MATTER OF TIME BEFORE THEY WERE EXPELLED ENTIRELY.
I BELIEVED DEEPLY THAT SNCC SHOULD CONTINUE TO BE AN INTEGRATED ORGANIZATION.
THESE WERE NOT JUST MY FRIENDS...
...THESE WERE MY BROTHERS AND SISTERS.

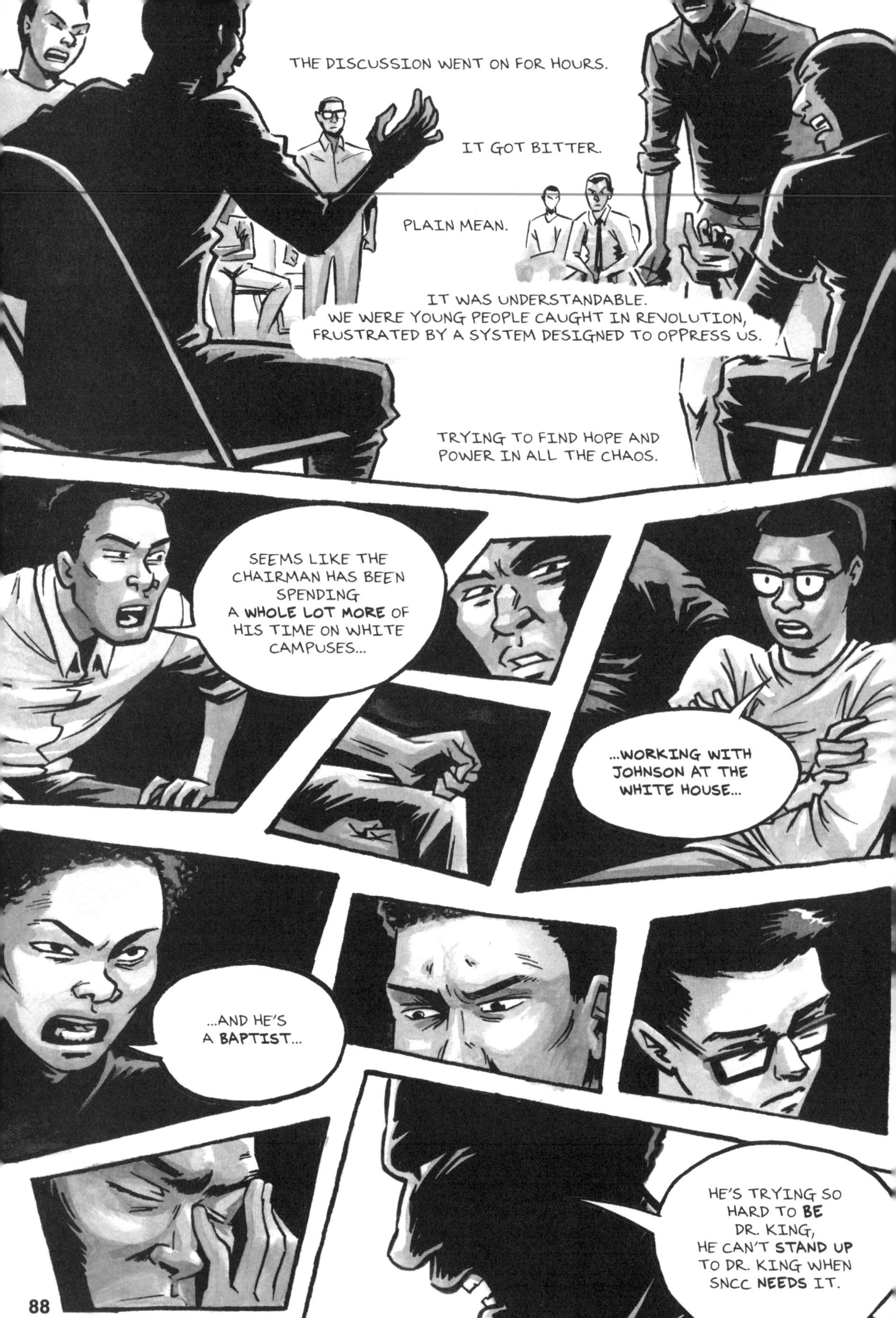

THE DISCUSSION WENT ON FOR HOURS.
IT GOT BITTER.
PLAIN MEAN.
IT WAS UNDERSTANDABLE. WE WERE YOUNG PEOPLE CAUGHT IN REVOLUTION, FRUSTRATED BY A SYSTEM DESIGNED TO OPPRESS US.
TRYING TO FIND HOPE AND POWER IN ALL THE CHAOS.
SEEMS LIKE THE CHAIRMAN HAS BEEN SPENDING A WHOLE LOT MORE OF HIS TIME ON WHITE CAMPUSES...
...WORKING WITH JOHNSON AT THE WHITE HOUSE...
...AND HE'S A BAPTIST...
HE'S TRYING SO HARD TO BE DR. KING, HE CAN'T STAND UP TO DR. KING WHEN SNCC NEEDS IT.

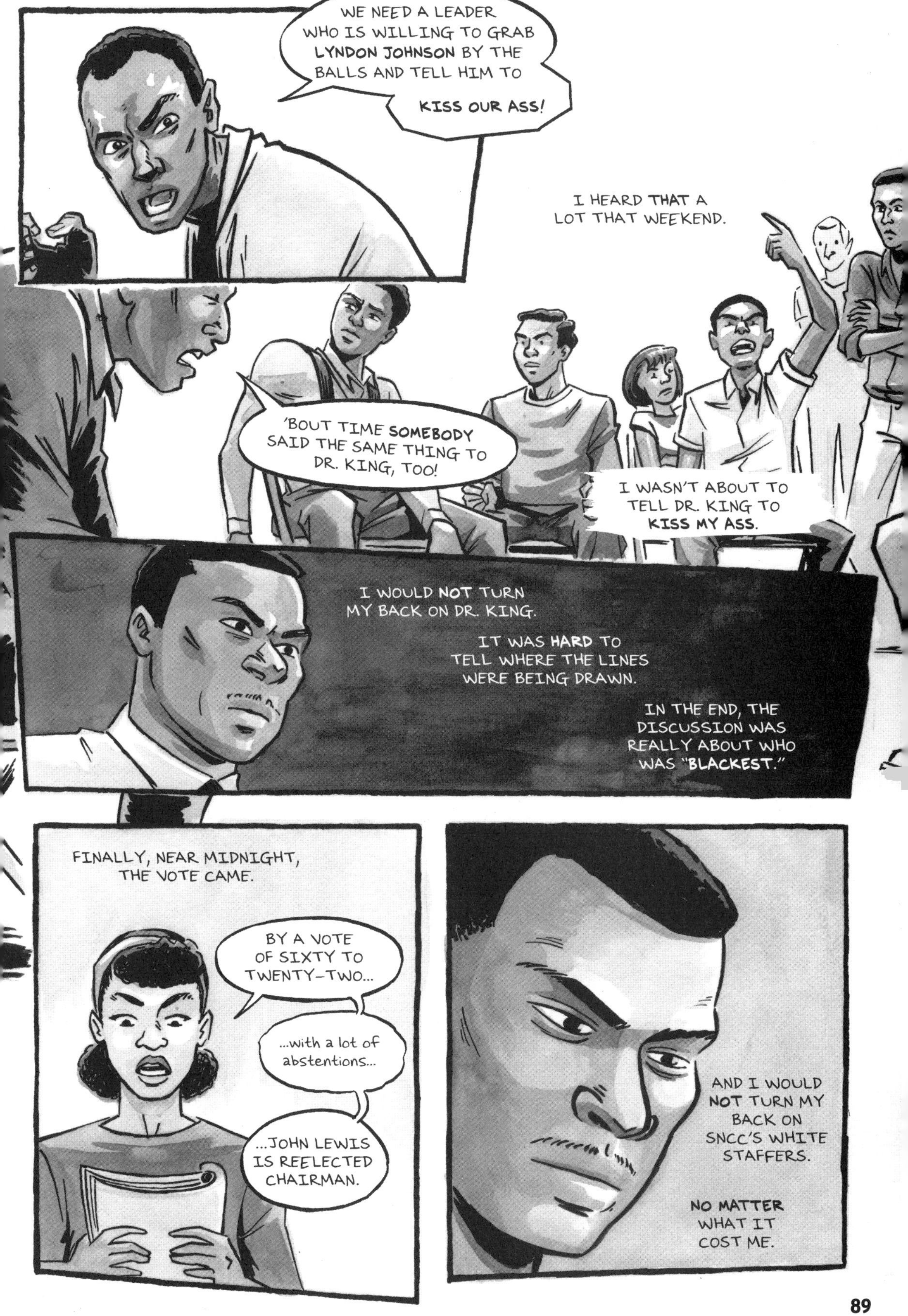
WE NEED A LEADER WHO IS WILLING TO GRAB LYNDON JOHNSON BY THE BALLS AND TELL HIM TO
KISS OUR ASS!
I HEARD THAT A LOT THAT WEEKEND.
'BOUT TIME SOMEBODY SAID THE SAME THING TO DR. KING, TOO!
I WASN'T ABOUT TO TELL DR. KING TO KISS MY ASS.
I WOULD NOT TURN MY BACK ON DR. KING.
IT WAS HARD TO TELL WHERE THE LINES WERE BEING DRAWN.
IN THE END, THE DISCUSSION WAS REALLY ABOUT WHO WAS "BLACKEST."
FINALLY, NEAR MIDNIGHT, THE VOTE CAME.
BY A VOTE OF SIXTY TO TWENTY-TWO...
...with a lot of abstentions...
...JOHN LEWIS IS REELECTED CHAIRMAN.
AND I WOULD NOT TURN MY BACK ON SNCC'S WHITE STAFFERS.
NO MATTER WHAT IT COST ME.

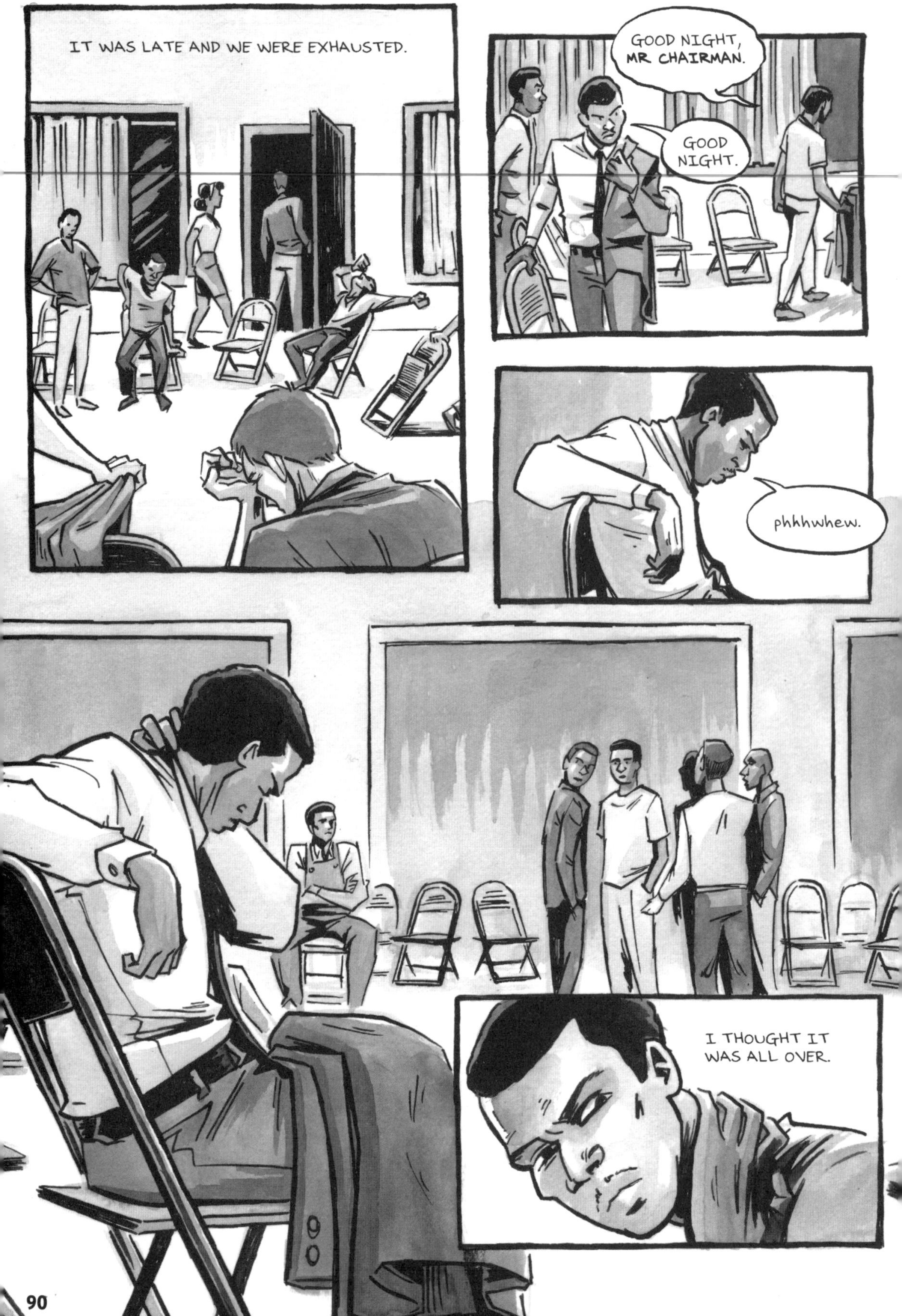
IT WAS LATE AND WE WERE EXHAUSTED.
GOOD NIGHT, MR CHAIRMAN.
GOOD NIGHT.
phhhwhew.
I THOUGHT IT WAS ALL OVER.

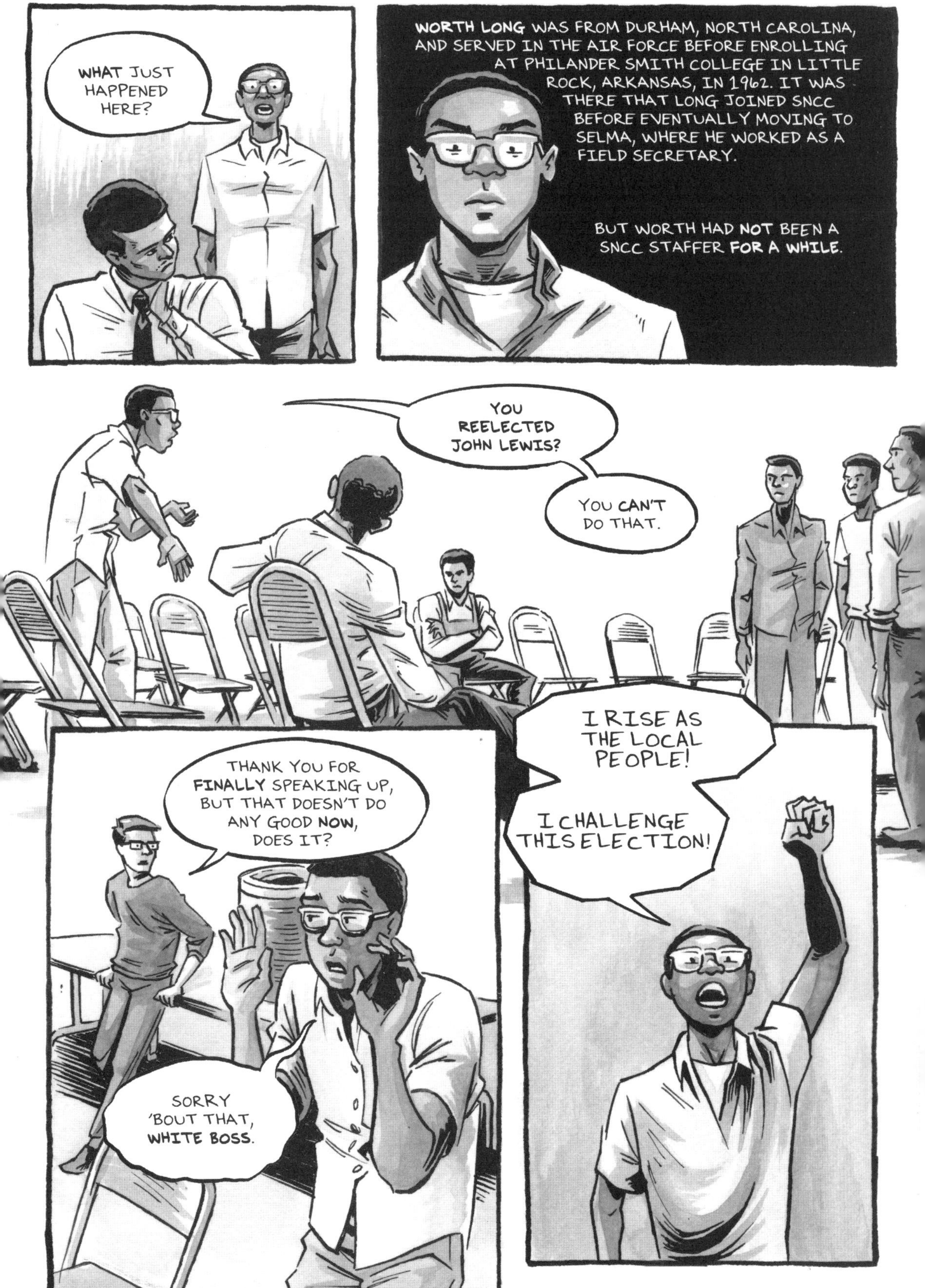
WHAT JUST HAPPENED HERE?
WORTH LONG WAS FROM DURHAM, NORTH CAROLINA, AND SERVED IN THE AIR FORCE BEFORE ENROLLING AT PHILANDER SMITH COLLEGE IN LITTLE ROCK, ARKANSAS, IN 1962. IT WAS THERE THAT LONG JOINED SNCC BEFORE EVENTUALLY MOVING TO SELMA, WHERE HE WORKED AS A FIELD SECRETARY.
BUT WORTH HAD NOT BEEN A SNCC STAFFER FOR A WHILE.
YOU REELECTED JOHN LEWIS?
YOU CAN'T DO THAT.
THANK YOU FOR FINALLY SPEAKING UP, BUT THAT DOESN'T DO ANY GOOD NOW, DOES IT?
SORRY 'BOUT THAT, WHITE BOSS.
I RISE AS THE LOCAL PEOPLE!
I CHALLENGE THIS ELECTION!

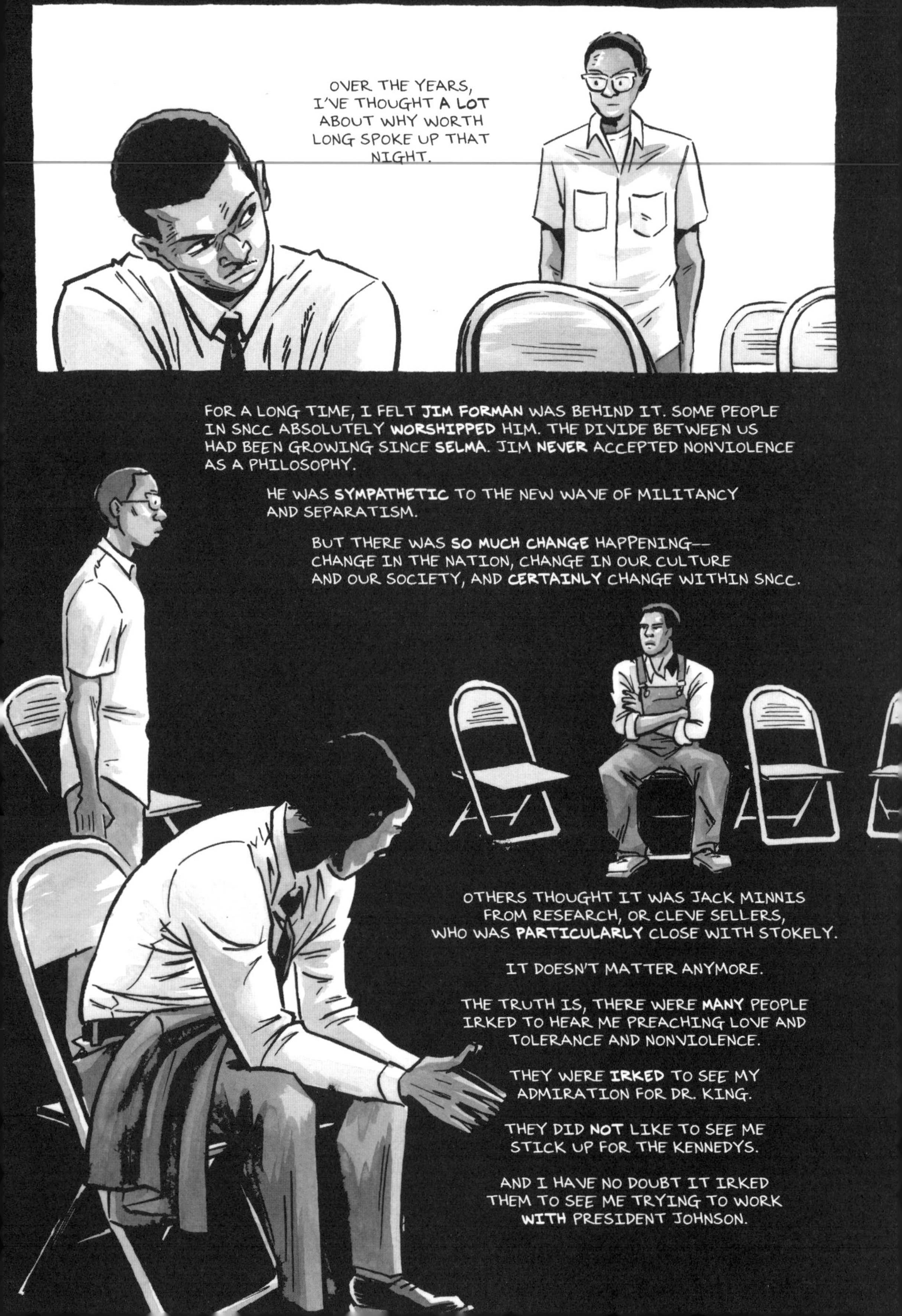
OVER THE YEARS, I'VE THOUGHT A LOT ABOUT WHY WORTH LONG SPOKE UP THAT NIGHT.
FOR A LONG TIME, I FELT JIM FORMAN WAS BEHIND IT. SOME PEOPLE IN SNCC ABSOLUTELY WORSHIPPED HIM. THE DIVIDE BETWEEN US HAD BEEN GROWING SINCE SELMA. JIM NEVER ACCEPTED NONVIOLENCE AS A PHILOSOPHY.
HE WAS SYMPATHETIC TO THE NEW WAVE OF MILITANCY AND SEPARATISM.
BUT THERE WAS SO MUCH CHANGE HAPPENING-- CHANGE IN THE NATION, CHANGE IN OUR CULTURE AND OUR SOCIETY, AND CERTAINLY CHANGE WITHIN SNCC.
OTHERS THOUGHT IT WAS JACK MINNIS FROM RESEARCH, OR CLEVE SELLERS, WHO WAS PARTICULARLY CLOSE WITH STOKELY.
IT DOESN'T MATTER ANYMORE.
THE TRUTH IS, THERE WERE MANY PEOPLE IRKED TO HEAR ME PREACHING LOVE AND TOLERANCE AND NONVIOLENCE.
THEY WERE IRKED TO SEE MY ADMIRATION FOR DR. KING.
THEY DID NOT LIKE TO SEE ME STICK UP FOR THE KENNEDYS.
AND I HAVE NO DOUBT IT IRKED THEM TO SEE ME TRYING TO WORK WITH PRESIDENT JOHNSON.

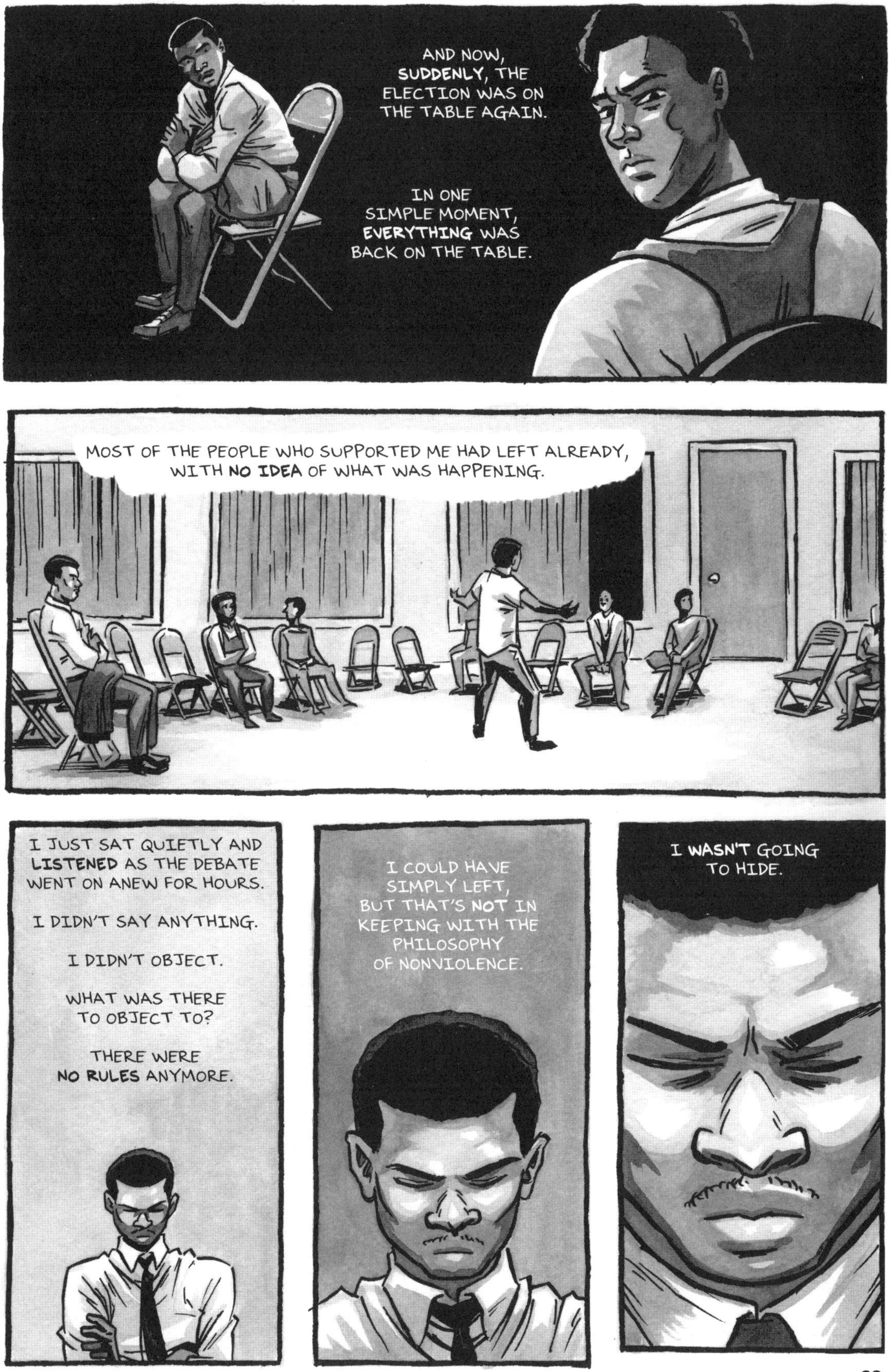
AND NOW, **SUDDENLY**, THE ELECTION WAS ON THE TABLE AGAIN.
IN ONE SIMPLE MOMENT, **EVERYTHING** WAS BACK ON THE TABLE.
MOST OF THE PEOPLE WHO SUPPORTED ME HAD LEFT ALREADY, WITH **NO IDEA** OF WHAT WAS HAPPENING.
I JUST SAT QUIETLY AND **LISTENED** AS THE DEBATE WENT ON ANEW FOR HOURS.
I DIDN'T SAY ANYTHING.
I DIDN'T OBJECT.
WHAT WAS THERE TO OBJECT TO?
THERE WERE **NO RULES** ANYMORE.
I COULD HAVE SIMPLY LEFT, BUT THAT'S **NOT** IN KEEPING WITH THE PHILOSOPHY OF NONVIOLENCE.
I **WASN'T** GOING TO HIDE.

RUBY AND CLEVE "RESIGNED" THEIR POSITIONS AROUND 5:30 THAT NEXT MORNING TO PAVE THE WAY FOR **A NEW VOTE** TO BE TAKEN, EVEN THOUGH MOST EVERYONE HAD LEFT AND GONE TO BED.

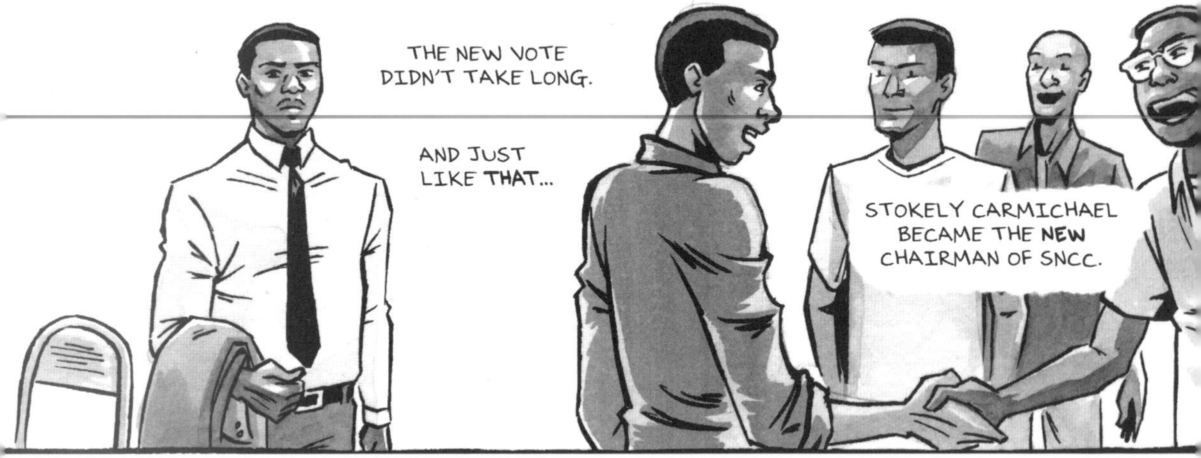
THE NEW VOTE DIDN'T TAKE LONG.
AND JUST LIKE THAT...
STOKELY CARMICHAEL BECAME THE NEW CHAIRMAN OF SNCC.

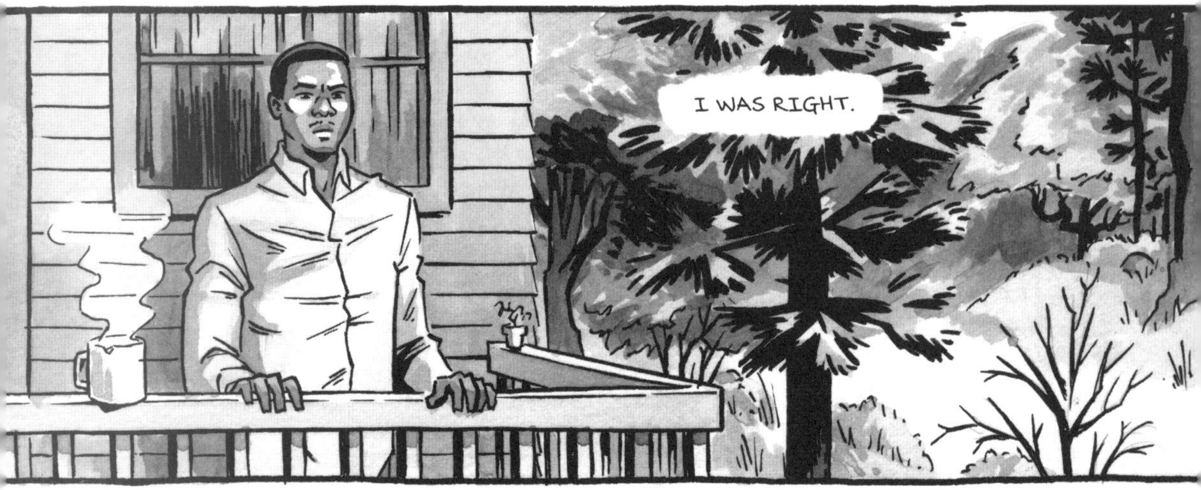
I WAS RIGHT.

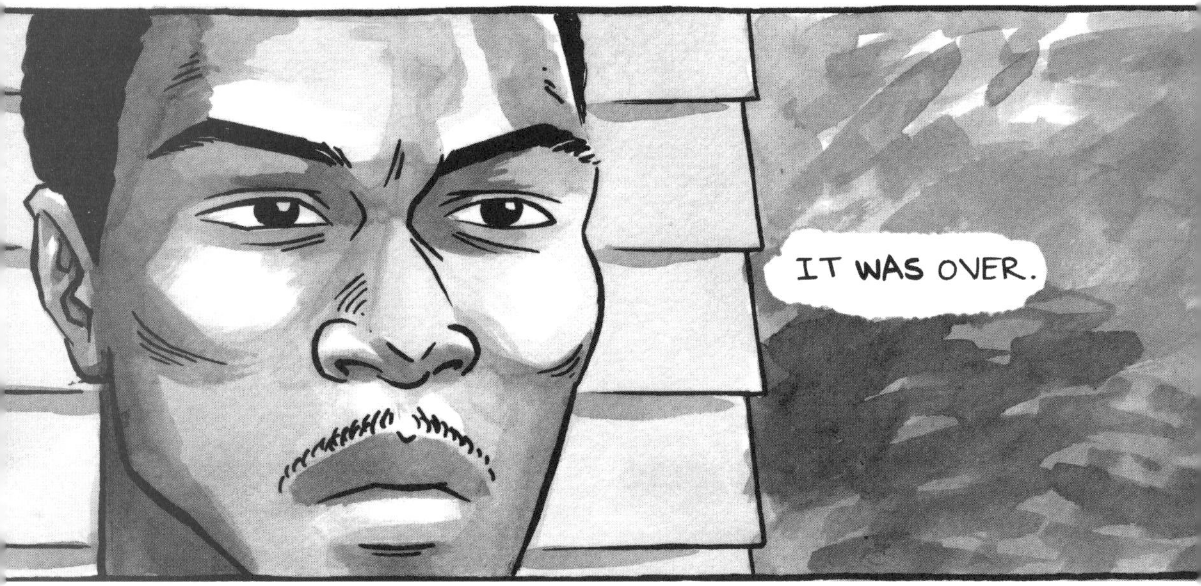
IT WAS OVER.

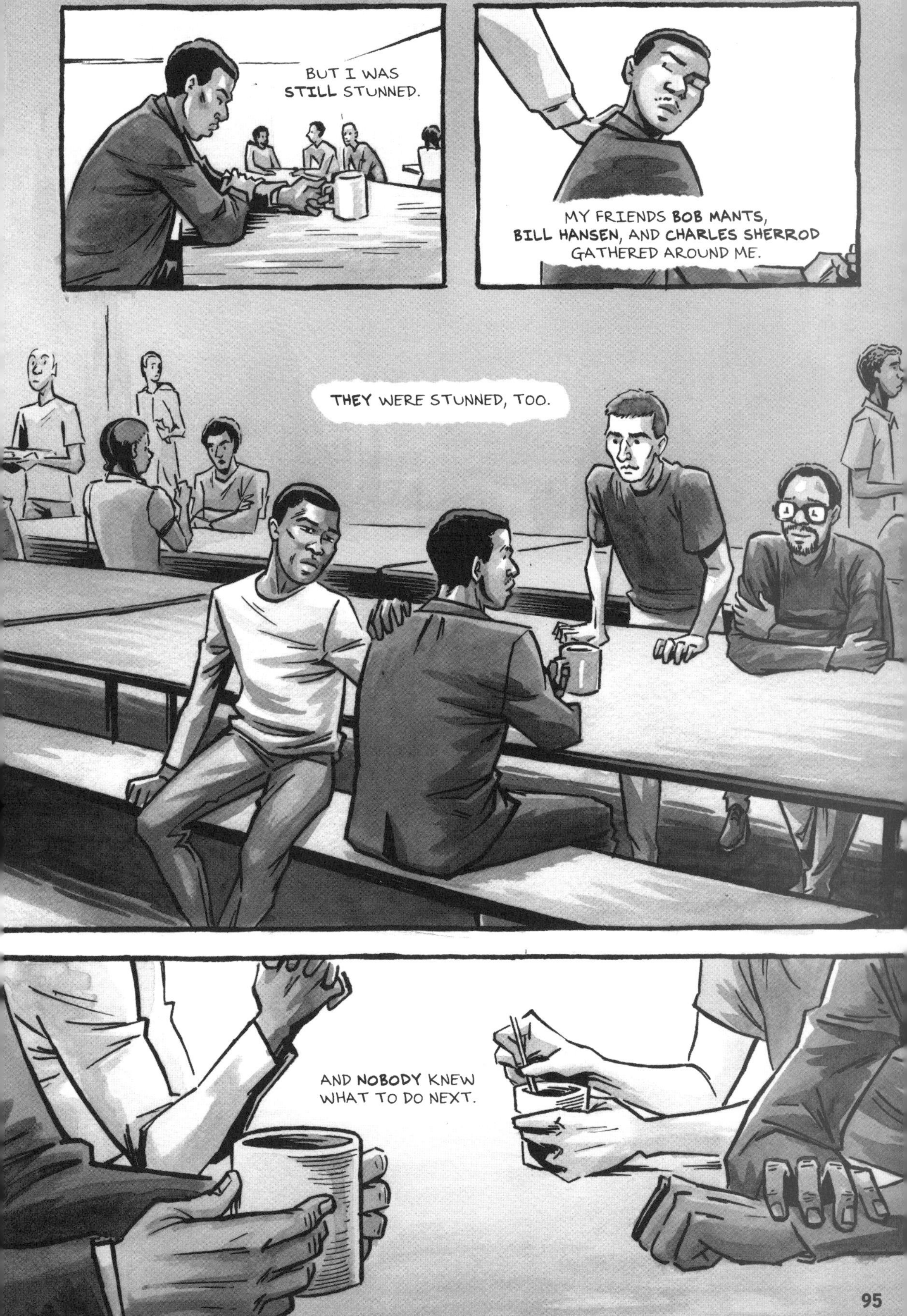
BUT I WAS STILL STUNNED.
MY FRIENDS BOB MANTS, BILL HANSEN, AND CHARLES SHERROD GATHERED AROUND ME.
THEY WERE STUNNED, TOO.
AND NOBODY KNEW WHAT TO DO NEXT.

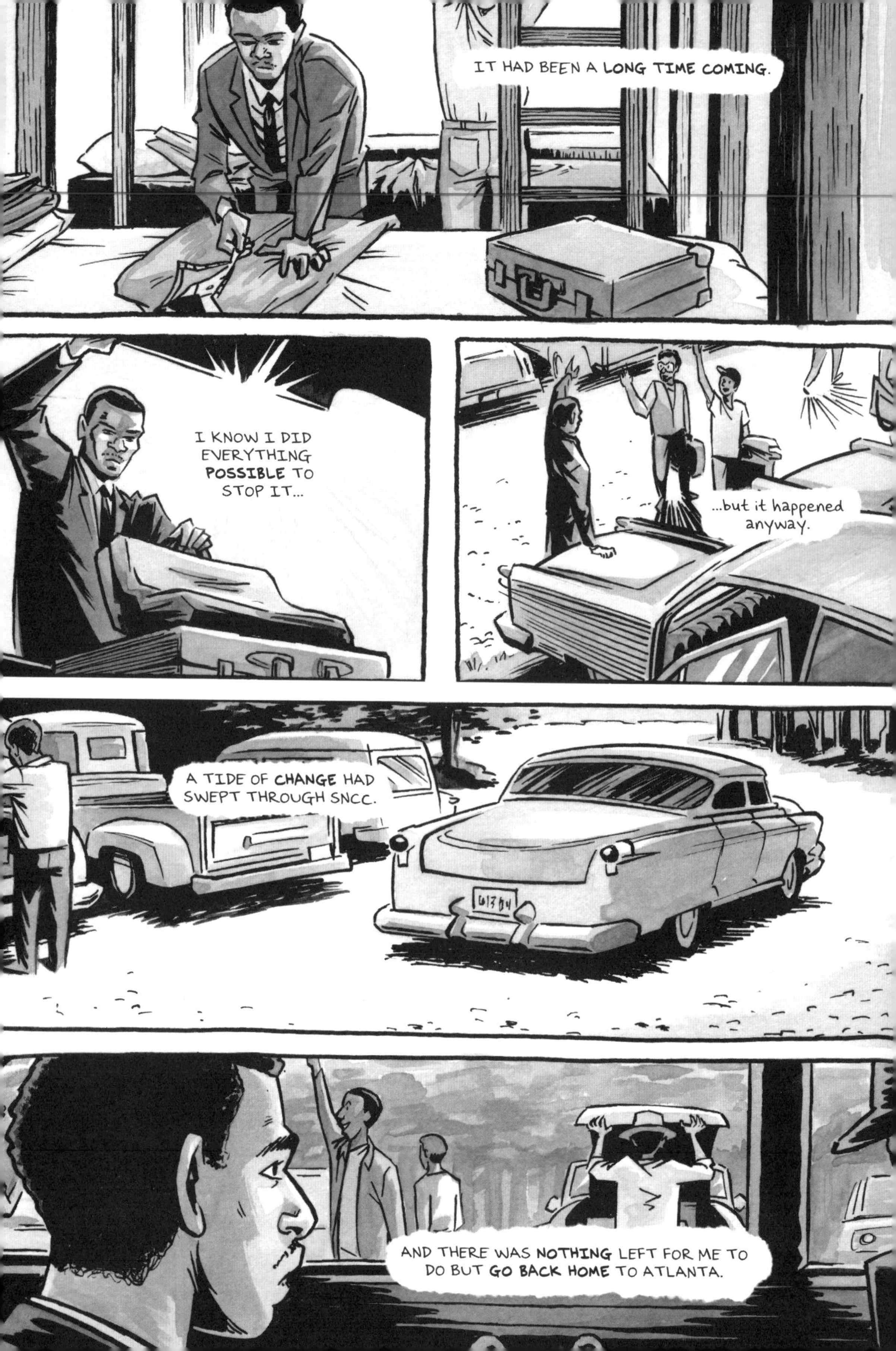
IT HAD BEEN A LONG TIME COMING.
I KNOW I DID EVERYTHING POSSIBLE TO STOP IT...
...but it happened anyway.
A TIDE OF CHANGE HAD SWEPT THROUGH SNCC.
AND THERE WAS NOTHING LEFT FOR ME TO DO BUT GO BACK HOME TO ATLANTA.

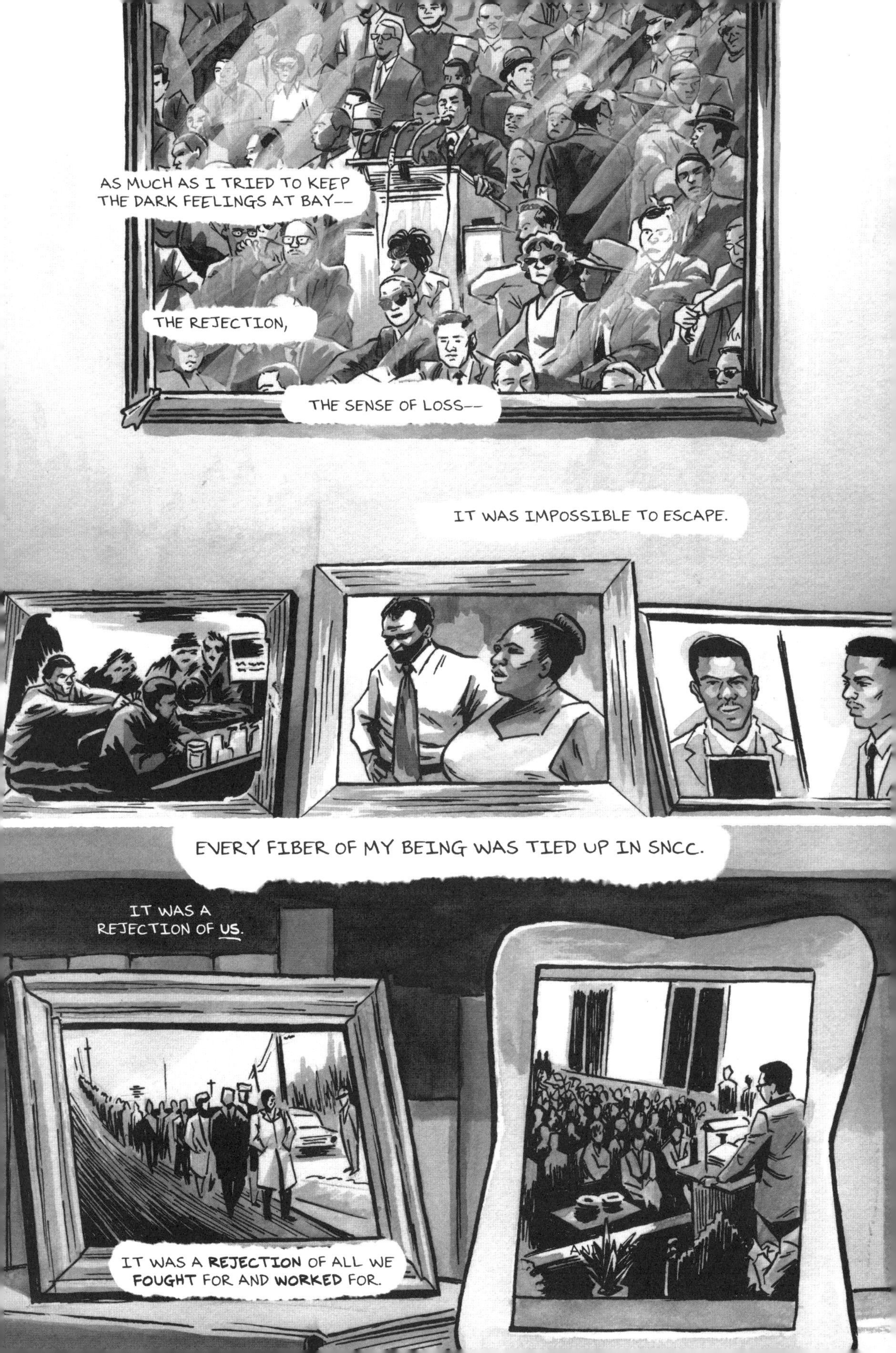

AS MUCH AS I TRIED TO KEEP THE DARK FEELINGS AT BAY--
THE REJECTION,
THE SENSE OF LOSS--
IT WAS IMPOSSIBLE TO ESCAPE.
EVERY FIBER OF MY BEING WAS TIED UP IN SNCC.
IT WAS A REJECTION OF US.
IT WAS A REJECTION OF ALL WE FOUGHT FOR AND WORKED FOR.

BY THE TIME I GOT BACK TO THE ATLANTA OFFICE, I HAD A **NEW ASSIGNMENT** TO LEAD SNCC'S RECENTLY FORMED **INTERNATIONAL AFFAIRS COMMISSION.**

I was being put out to **pasture.**

BUT I WAS HOLDING ON BECAUSE I BELIEVED IN THE **POSSIBILITY** THAT SOME GOOD COULD STILL COME FROM THIS.

I THOUGHT I COULD HELP **HEAL** SOME OF THE WOUNDS **WITHIN** SNCC.

BUT THE TRUTH IS, **NO ONE** COULD.

ewis, Forman Replaced
**SNCC Dumps 2 Top Leaders,
Names 'Black Panther' Chairman**

**'BLACK PANTHER' NEW
SNCC HEAD; LEWIS OUT**

Julian Bond Leaving, Too?
**SNCC Ousts Lewis;
'Black Panther' Elected**

Rights Uni

**Rights Unit
Also Ousts
Forman**

'Let's Put Po

SNCC...From Page A1
SNCC Chooses Younger Leadership

I WAS BESIEGED WITH PRESS REQUESTS, BUT I SAID **NOTHING.** I DIDN'T WANT TO DO **ANYTHING** TO HURT SNCC.

NEWS FROM ....

STUDENT NONVIOLENT COORDINATING COMMITTEE
360 Nelson St., SW Atlanta, Georgia
(404) 688-0331

MAY 16, 1966

FOR IMMEDIATE RELEASE

ATLANTA, GEORGIA.   The staff of the Student Nonviolent Coordinating Committee at its sixth annual Spring Conference, held near Nashville, Tennessee, elected Stokely Carmichael as SNCC's fourth chairman. The three man SNCC Secretariate was completed with the election of Mrs. Ruby Doris Robinson as SNCC's third Executive Secretary and Cleveland Sellers who was re-elected to the position of Program Secretary.

ional changes reduced the Central Committee from 21 to 10 members and created by the Chairman, will

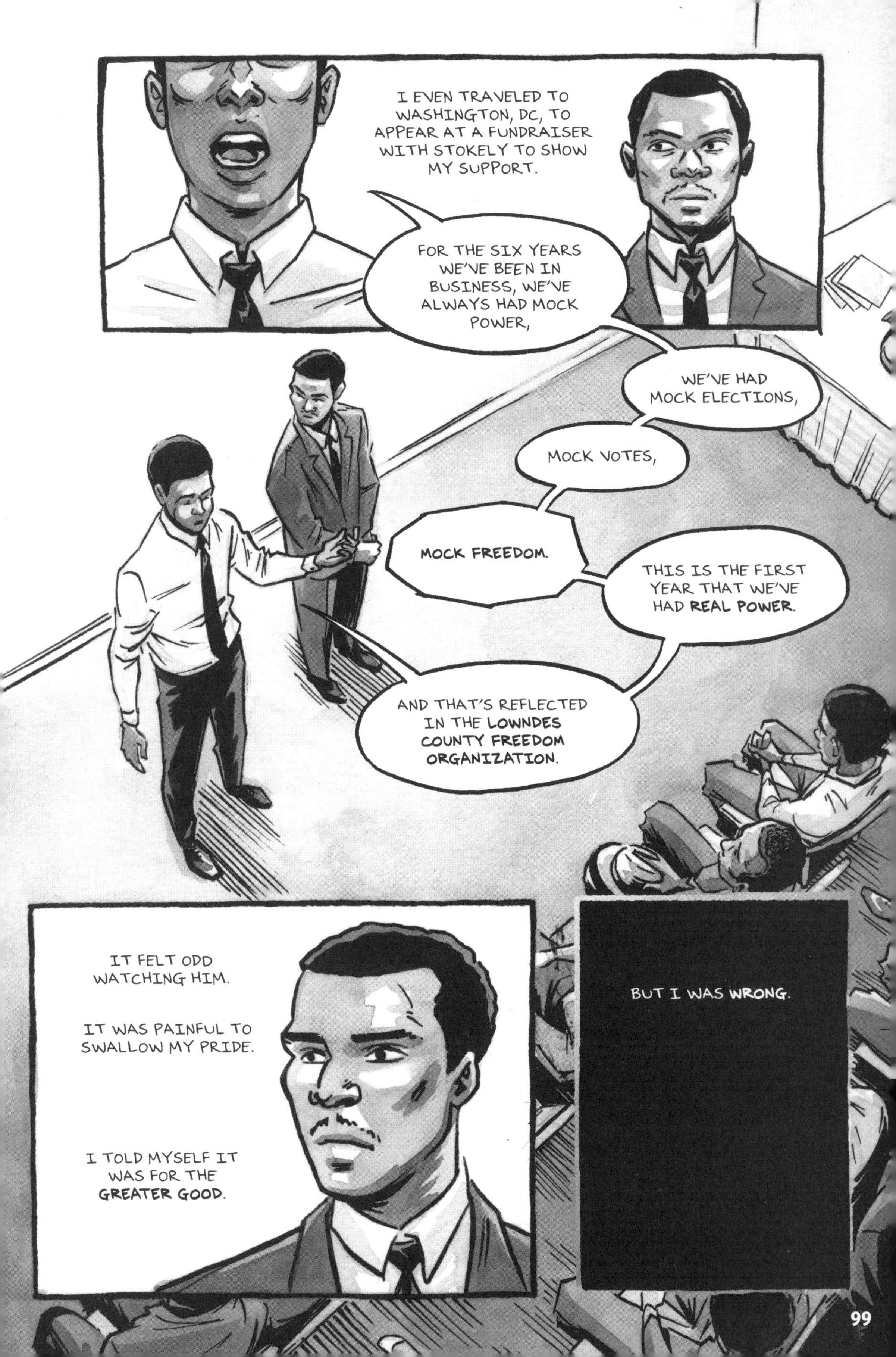
I EVEN TRAVELED TO WASHINGTON, DC, TO APPEAR AT A FUNDRAISER WITH STOKELY TO SHOW MY SUPPORT.
FOR THE SIX YEARS WE'VE BEEN IN BUSINESS, WE'VE ALWAYS HAD MOCK POWER,
WE'VE HAD MOCK ELECTIONS,
MOCK VOTES,
MOCK FREEDOM.
THIS IS THE FIRST YEAR THAT WE'VE HAD **REAL POWER.**
AND THAT'S REFLECTED IN THE **LOWNDES COUNTY FREEDOM ORGANIZATION.**
IT FELT ODD WATCHING HIM.
IT WAS PAINFUL TO SWALLOW MY PRIDE.
I TOLD MYSELF IT WAS FOR THE **GREATER GOOD.**
BUT I WAS **WRONG.**

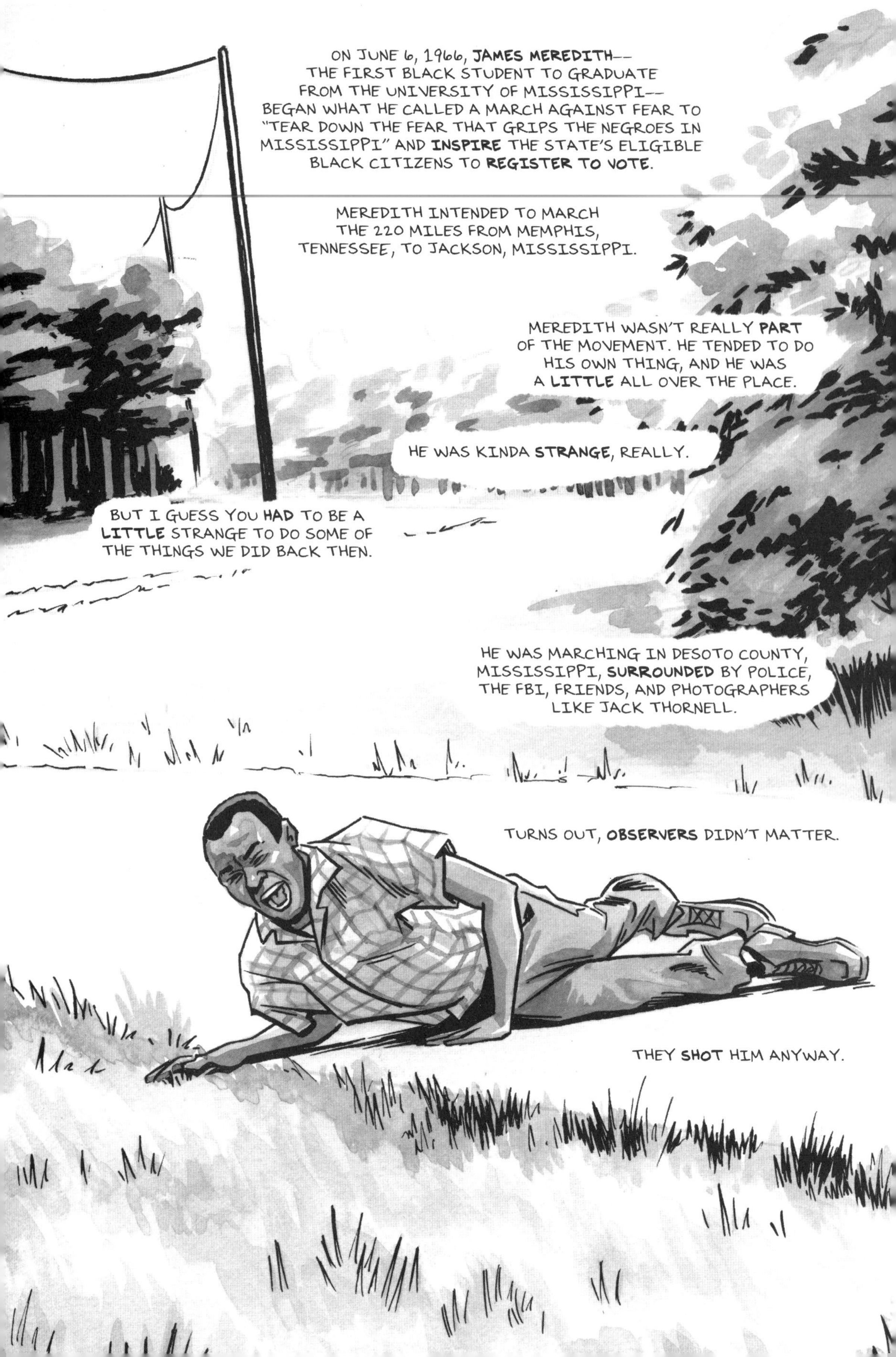
ON JUNE 6, 1966, **JAMES MEREDITH**-- THE FIRST BLACK STUDENT TO GRADUATE FROM THE UNIVERSITY OF MISSISSIPPI-- BEGAN WHAT HE CALLED A MARCH AGAINST FEAR TO "TEAR DOWN THE FEAR THAT GRIPS THE NEGROES IN MISSISSIPPI" AND **INSPIRE** THE STATE'S ELIGIBLE BLACK CITIZENS TO **REGISTER TO VOTE**.
MEREDITH INTENDED TO MARCH THE 220 MILES FROM MEMPHIS, TENNESSEE, TO JACKSON, MISSISSIPPI.
MEREDITH WASN'T REALLY **PART** OF THE MOVEMENT. HE TENDED TO DO HIS OWN THING, AND HE WAS A **LITTLE** ALL OVER THE PLACE.
HE WAS KINDA **STRANGE**, REALLY.
BUT I GUESS YOU **HAD** TO BE A **LITTLE** STRANGE TO DO SOME OF THE THINGS WE DID BACK THEN.
HE WAS MARCHING IN DESOTO COUNTY, MISSISSIPPI, **SURROUNDED** BY POLICE, THE FBI, FRIENDS, AND PHOTOGRAPHERS LIKE JACK THORNELL.
TURNS OUT, **OBSERVERS** DIDN'T MATTER.
THEY **SHOT** HIM ANYWAY.

JAMES **SURVIVED**.

AND ALL CORNERS OF THE MOVEMENT CAME TO CONTINUE **HIS** MARCH.

DR. KING CAME.

SO DID THE NEW DIRECTOR OF THE CONGRESS OF RACIAL EQUALITY (CORE)--**FLOYD MCKISSICK**, WHO REPLACED JAMES FARMER IN MUCH THE SAME WAY STOKELY REPLACED ME.

MCKISSICK CALLED NONVIOLENCE "A DYING PHILOSOPHY" THAT HAD "OUTLIVED ITS USEFULNESS."

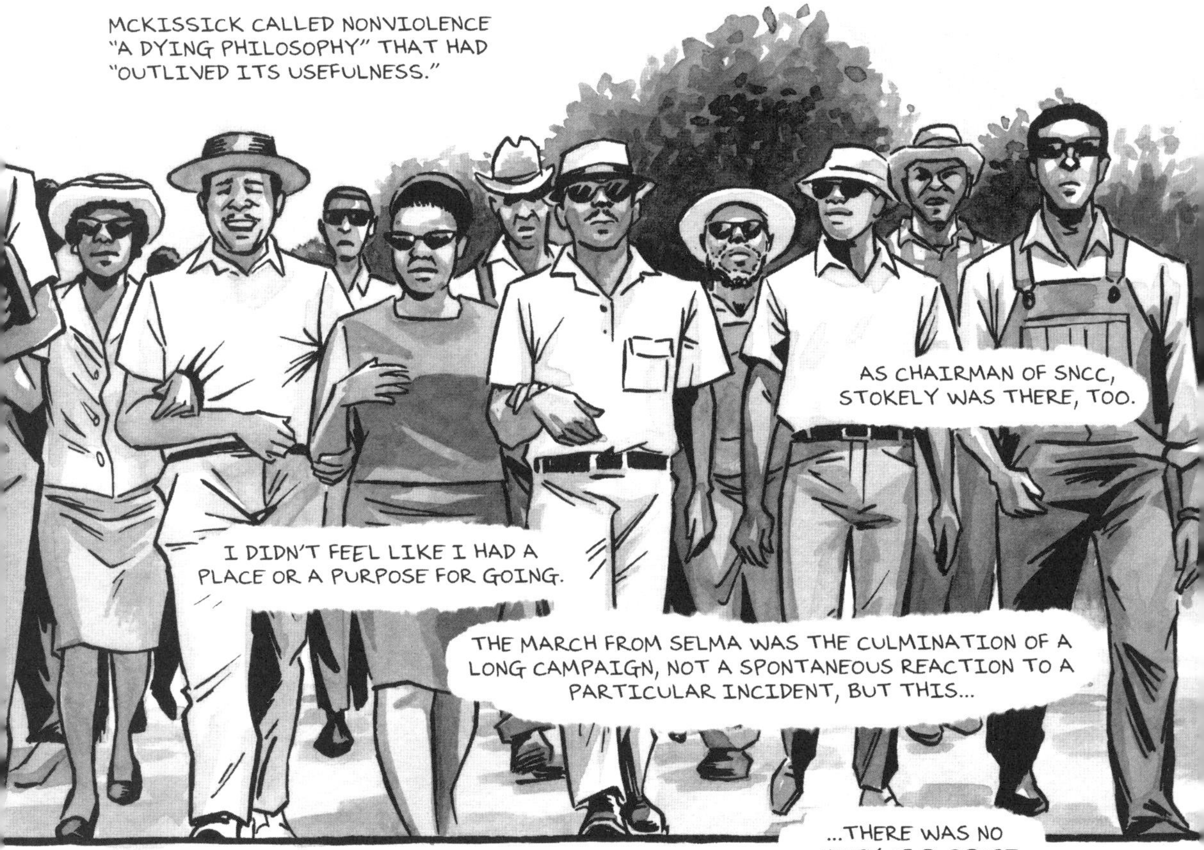

AS CHAIRMAN OF SNCC, STOKELY WAS THERE, TOO.
I DIDN'T FEEL LIKE I HAD A PLACE OR A PURPOSE FOR GOING.
THE MARCH FROM SELMA WAS THE CULMINATION OF A LONG CAMPAIGN, NOT A SPONTANEOUS REACTION TO A PARTICULAR INCIDENT, BUT THIS...
...THERE WAS NO UNITY OF PURPOSE.

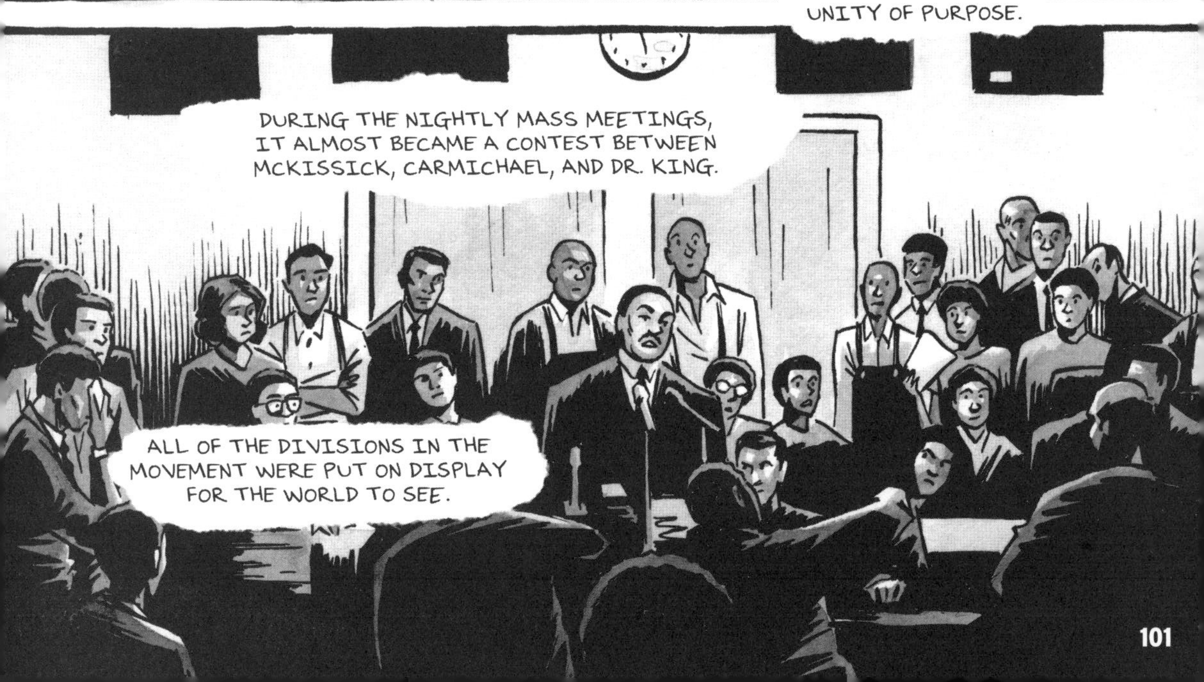

DURING THE NIGHTLY MASS MEETINGS, IT ALMOST BECAME A CONTEST BETWEEN MCKISSICK, CARMICHAEL, AND DR. KING.
ALL OF THE DIVISIONS IN THE MOVEMENT WERE PUT ON DISPLAY FOR THE WORLD TO SEE.

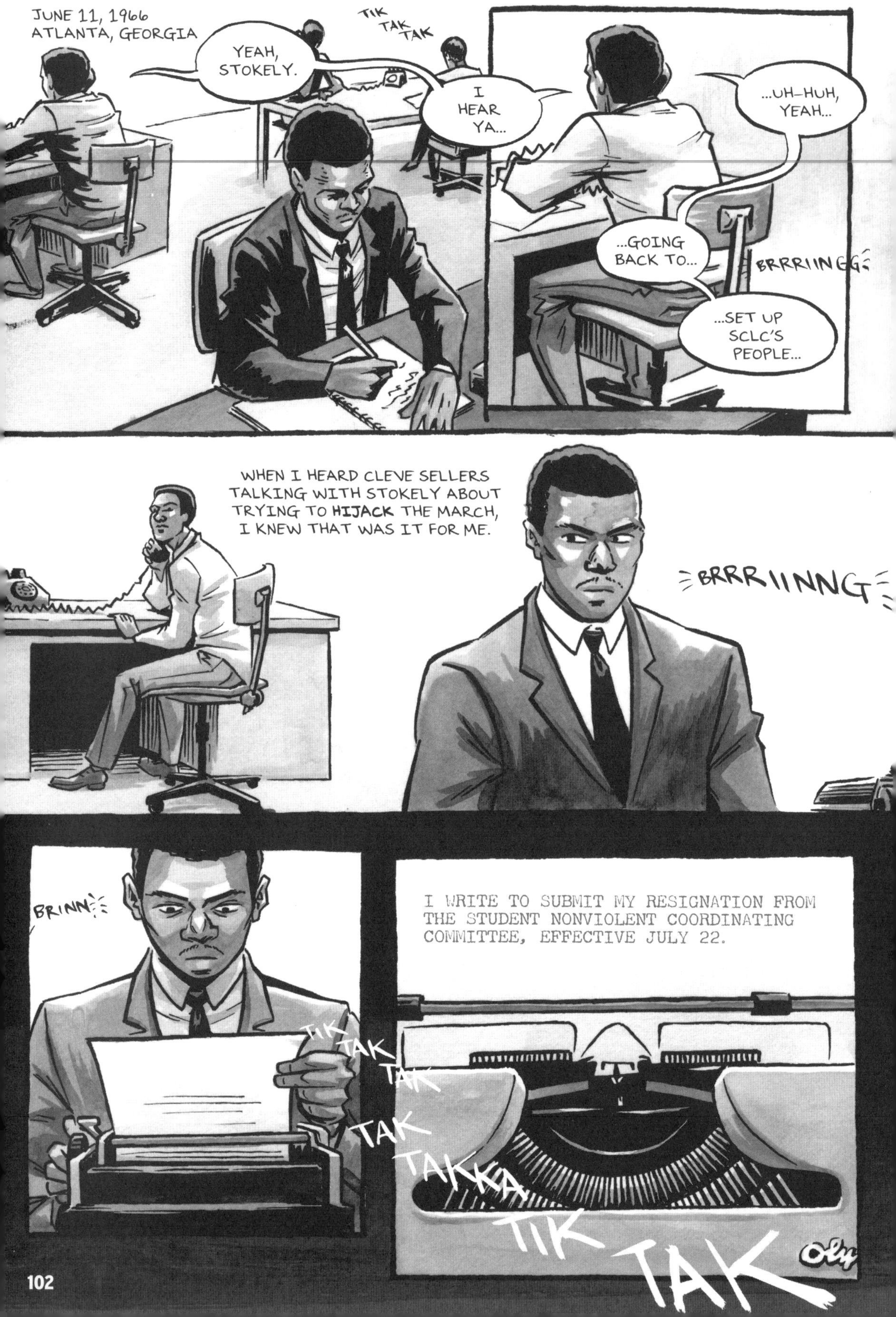

JUNE 11, 1966
ATLANTA, GEORGIA
YEAH, STOKELY.
TIK TAK TAK
I HEAR YA...
...UH-HUH, YEAH...
...GOING BACK TO...
BRRRIINGG
...SET UP SCLC'S PEOPLE...
WHEN I HEARD CLEVE SELLERS TALKING WITH STOKELY ABOUT TRYING TO **HIJACK** THE MARCH, I KNEW THAT WAS IT FOR ME.
BRRRIINNG
BRINN
I WRITE TO SUBMIT MY RESIGNATION FROM THE STUDENT NONVIOLENT COORDINATING COMMITTEE, EFFECTIVE JULY 22.
TIK TAK TAK
TAK
TAKKA
TIK
TAK

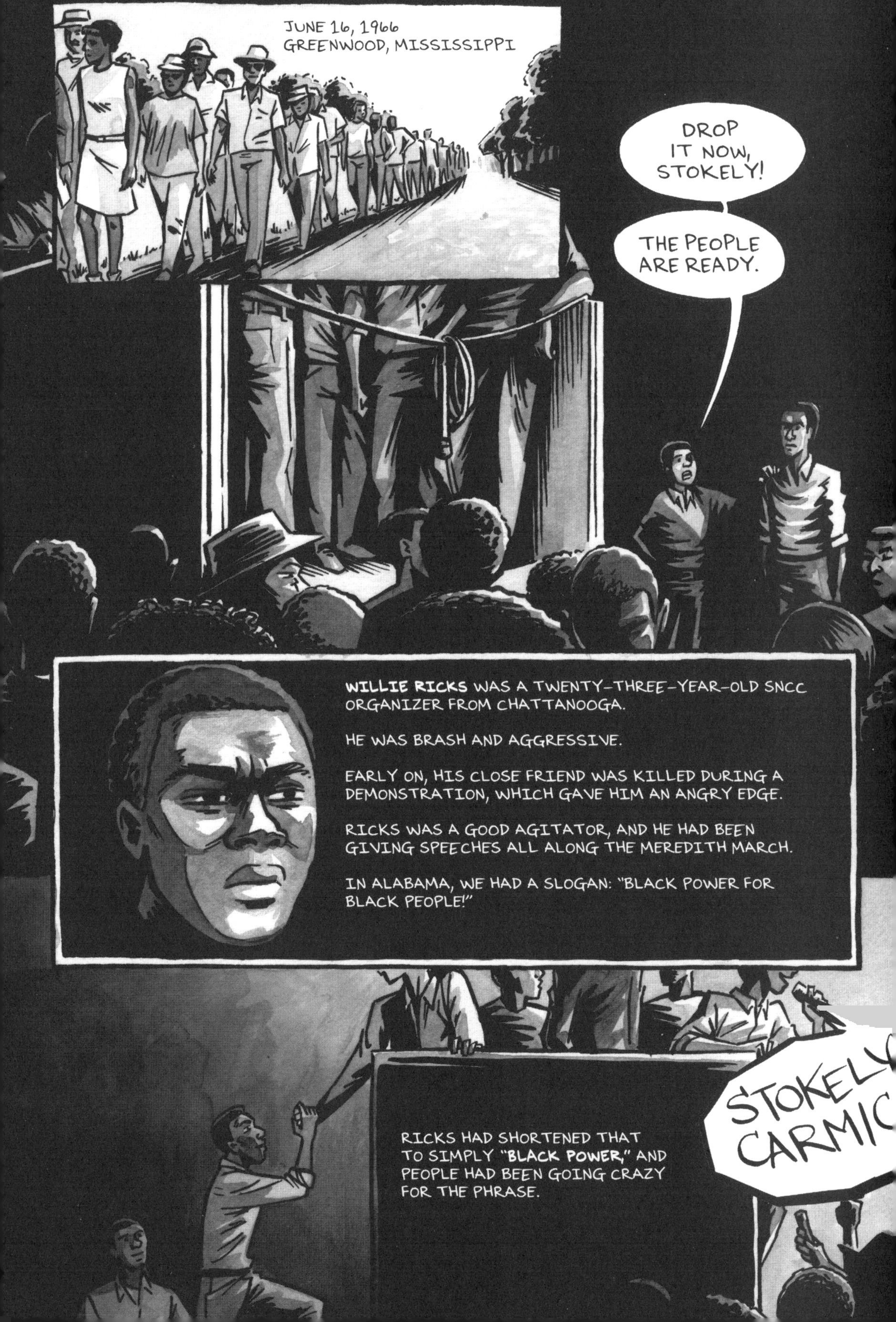
JUNE 16, 1966
GREENWOOD, MISSISSIPPI
DROP IT NOW, STOKELY!
THE PEOPLE ARE READY.
WILLIE RICKS WAS A TWENTY-THREE-YEAR-OLD SNCC ORGANIZER FROM CHATTANOOGA.
HE WAS BRASH AND AGGRESSIVE.
EARLY ON, HIS CLOSE FRIEND WAS KILLED DURING A DEMONSTRATION, WHICH GAVE HIM AN ANGRY EDGE.
RICKS WAS A GOOD AGITATOR, AND HE HAD BEEN GIVING SPEECHES ALL ALONG THE MEREDITH MARCH.
IN ALABAMA, WE HAD A SLOGAN: "BLACK POWER FOR BLACK PEOPLE!"
RICKS HAD SHORTENED THAT TO SIMPLY "BLACK POWER," AND PEOPLE HAD BEEN GOING CRAZY FOR THE PHRASE.

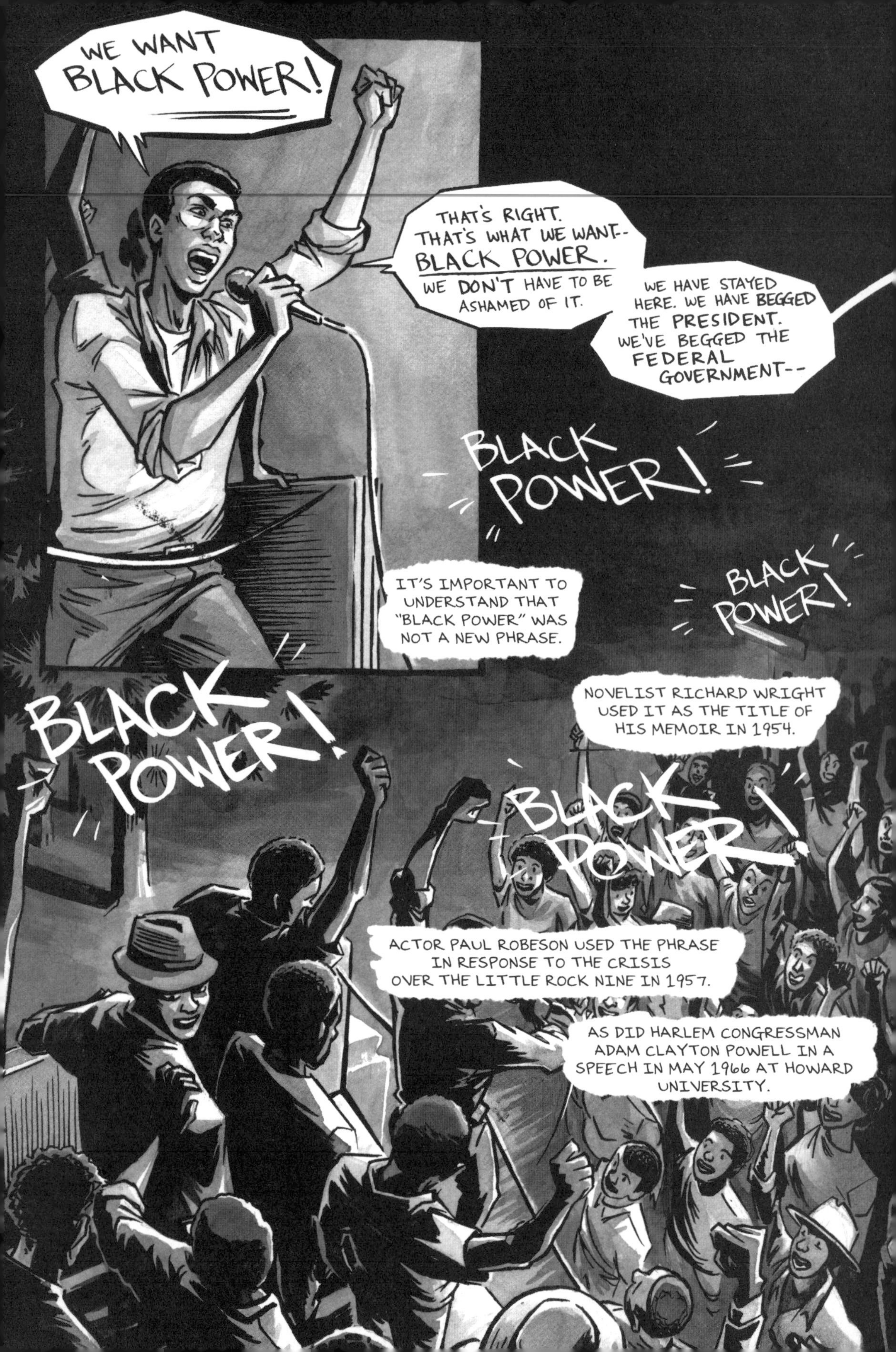
WE WANT BLACK POWER!
THAT'S RIGHT. THAT'S WHAT WE WANT-- BLACK POWER.
WE DON'T HAVE TO BE ASHAMED OF IT.
WE HAVE STAYED HERE. WE HAVE BEGGED THE PRESIDENT. WE'VE BEGGED THE FEDERAL GOVERNMENT--
BLACK POWER!
IT'S IMPORTANT TO UNDERSTAND THAT "BLACK POWER" WAS NOT A NEW PHRASE.
BLACK POWER!
BLACK POWER!
NOVELIST RICHARD WRIGHT USED IT AS THE TITLE OF HIS MEMOIR IN 1954.
BLACK POWER!
ACTOR PAUL ROBESON USED THE PHRASE IN RESPONSE TO THE CRISIS OVER THE LITTLE ROCK NINE IN 1957.
AS DID HARLEM CONGRESSMAN ADAM CLAYTON POWELL IN A SPEECH IN MAY 1966 AT HOWARD UNIVERSITY.

--THAT'S ALL WE'VE BEEN DOING, BEGGING AND BEGGING. IT'S TIME WE STAND UP AND TAKE OVER!

~BLACK POWER!~

BLACK POWER!

~BLACK POWER

~BLACK POWER

EVERY COURTHOUSE IN MISSISSIPPI OUGHT TO BE BURNED DOWN TOMORROW TO GET RID OF THE DIRT AND THE MESS.

~BLACK POWER

BLACK POWER!

FROM NOW ON, WHEN THEY ASK YOU WHAT YOU WANT, YOU KNOW WHAT TO TELL 'EM!

WHAT DO YOU WANT?!

But that night, it struck a nerve and captured a moment.

BLACK POWER!

BLACK POWER!

BLACK POWER!

BLACK POWER!

BLACK POWER!

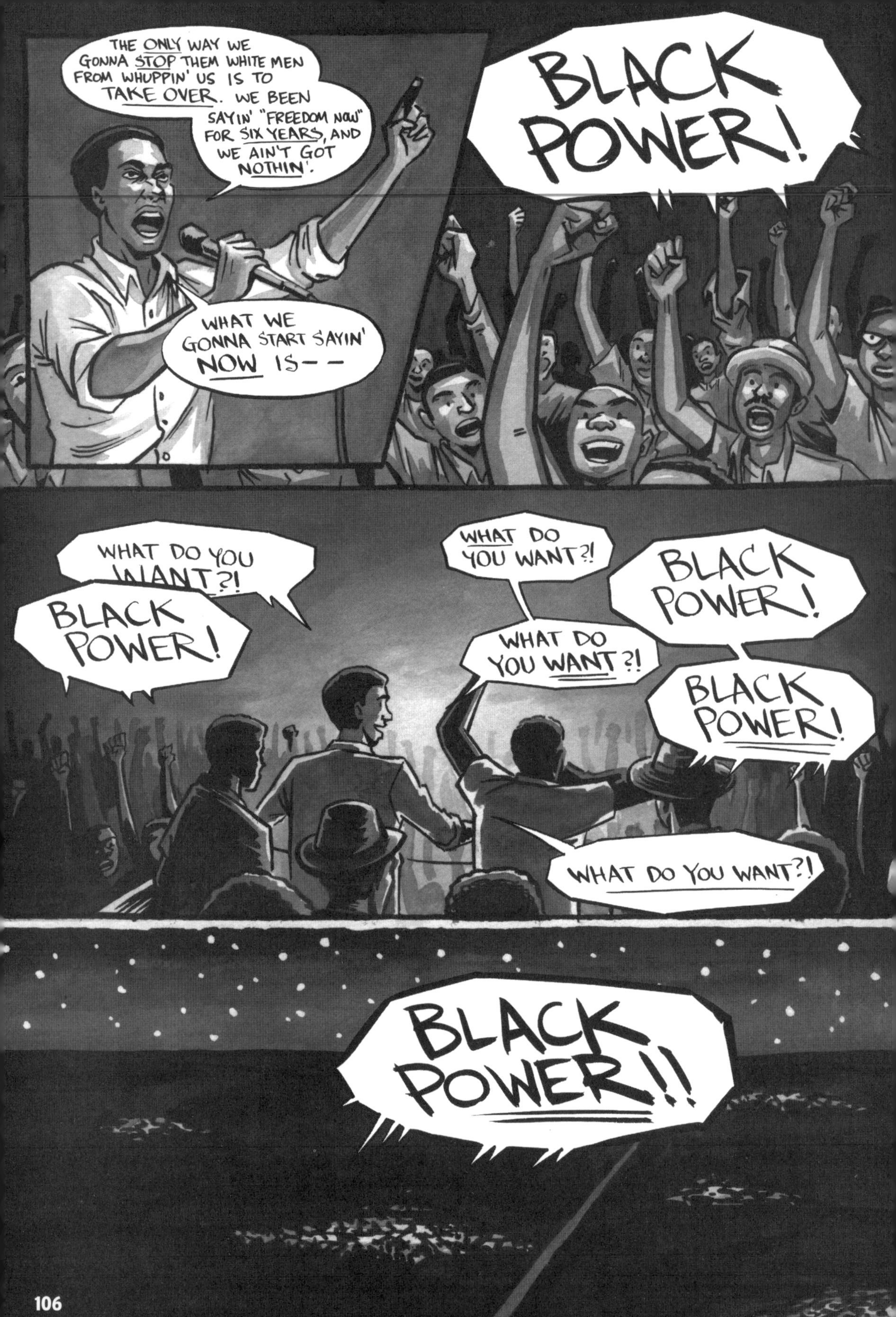
THE ONLY WAY WE GONNA STOP THEM WHITE MEN FROM WHUPPIN' US IS TO TAKE OVER. WE BEEN SAYIN' "FREEDOM NOW" FOR SIX YEARS, AND WE AIN'T GOT NOTHIN'.
WHAT WE GONNA START SAYIN' NOW IS--
BLACK POWER!
WHAT DO YOU WANT?!
BLACK POWER!
WHAT DO YOU WANT?!
BLACK POWER!
WHAT DO YOU WANT?!
BLACK POWER!
WHAT DO YOU WANT?!
BLACK POWER!!

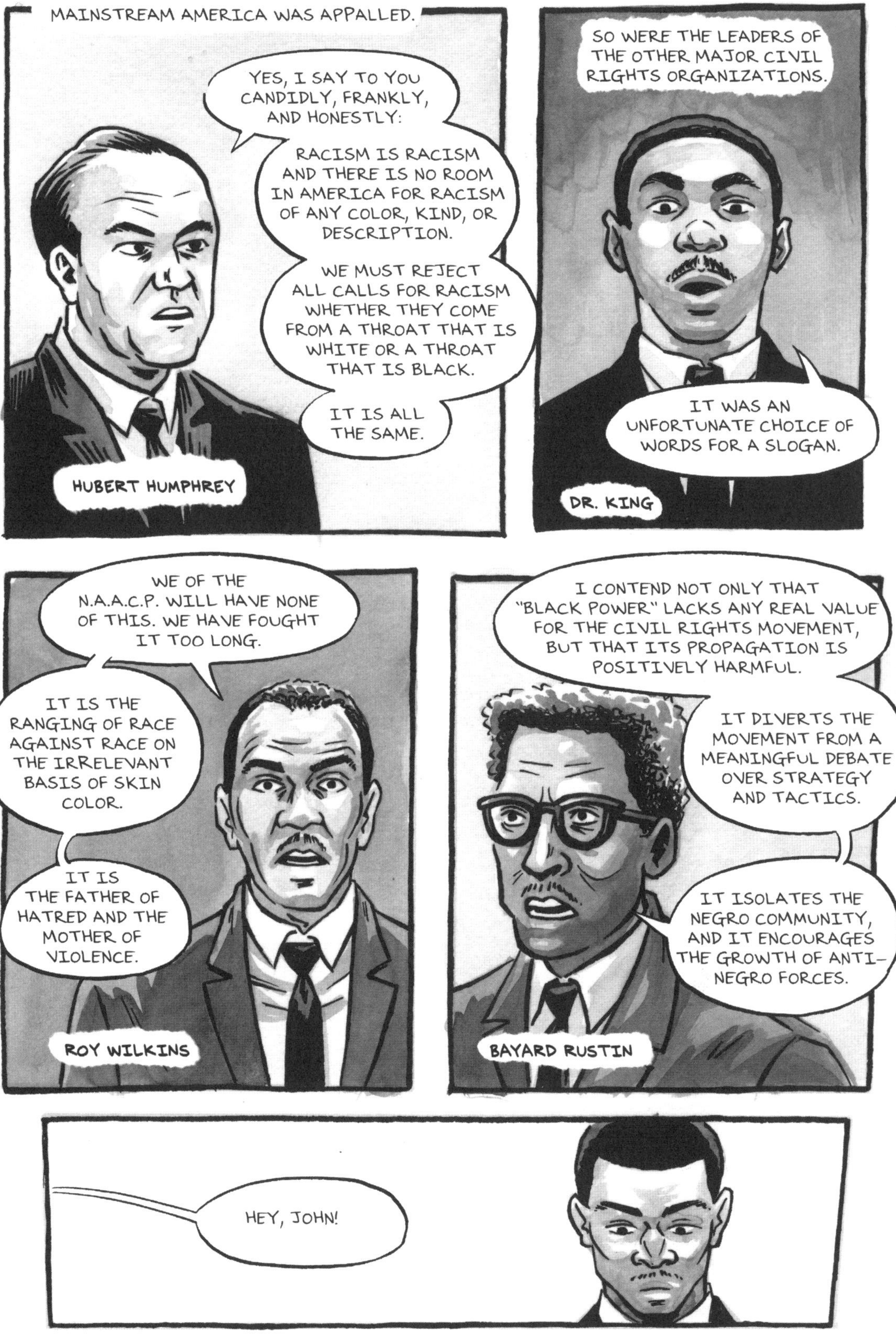
MAINSTREAM AMERICA WAS APPALLED.
YES, I SAY TO YOU CANDIDLY, FRANKLY, AND HONESTLY:
RACISM IS RACISM AND THERE IS NO ROOM IN AMERICA FOR RACISM OF ANY COLOR, KIND, OR DESCRIPTION.
WE MUST REJECT ALL CALLS FOR RACISM WHETHER THEY COME FROM A THROAT THAT IS WHITE OR A THROAT THAT IS BLACK.
IT IS ALL THE SAME.
HUBERT HUMPHREY
SO WERE THE LEADERS OF THE OTHER MAJOR CIVIL RIGHTS ORGANIZATIONS.
IT WAS AN UNFORTUNATE CHOICE OF WORDS FOR A SLOGAN.
DR. KING
WE OF THE N.A.A.C.P. WILL HAVE NONE OF THIS. WE HAVE FOUGHT IT TOO LONG.
IT IS THE RANGING OF RACE AGAINST RACE ON THE IRRELEVANT BASIS OF SKIN COLOR.
IT IS THE FATHER OF HATRED AND THE MOTHER OF VIOLENCE.
ROY WILKINS
I CONTEND NOT ONLY THAT "BLACK POWER" LACKS ANY REAL VALUE FOR THE CIVIL RIGHTS MOVEMENT, BUT THAT ITS PROPAGATION IS POSITIVELY HARMFUL.
IT DIVERTS THE MOVEMENT FROM A MEANINGFUL DEBATE OVER STRATEGY AND TACTICS.
IT ISOLATES THE NEGRO COMMUNITY, AND IT ENCOURAGES THE GROWTH OF ANTI-NEGRO FORCES.
BAYARD RUSTIN
HEY, JOHN!

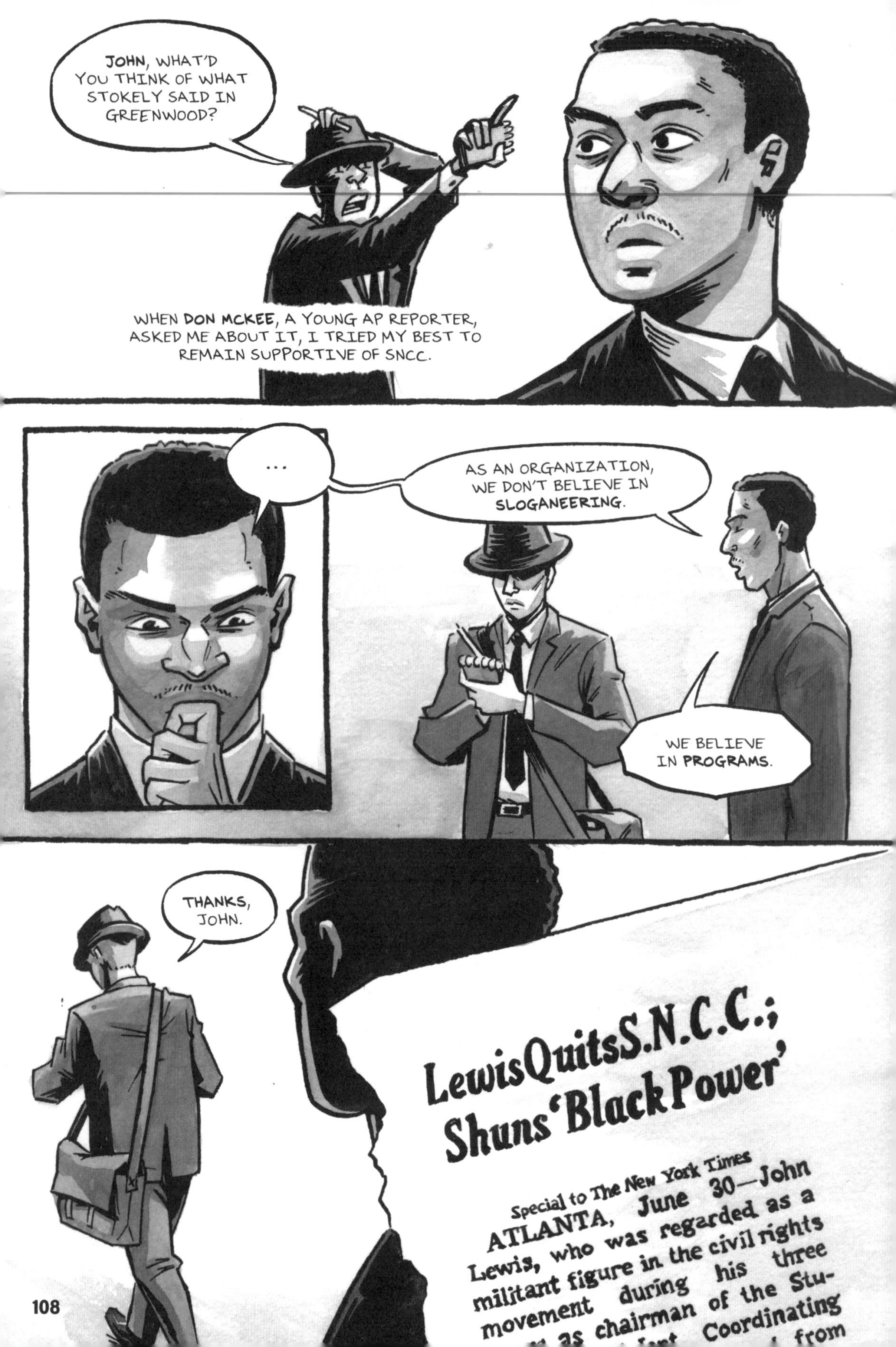
JOHN, WHAT'D YOU THINK OF WHAT STOKELY SAID IN GREENWOOD?
WHEN DON MCKEE, A YOUNG AP REPORTER, ASKED ME ABOUT IT, I TRIED MY BEST TO REMAIN SUPPORTIVE OF SNCC.
...
AS AN ORGANIZATION, WE DON'T BELIEVE IN SLOGANEERING.
WE BELIEVE IN PROGRAMS.
THANKS, JOHN.
Lewis Quits S.N.C.C.; Shuns 'Black Power'
Special to The New York Times
ATLANTA, June 30—John Lewis, who was regarded as a militant figure in the civil rights movement during his three
as chairman of the Stu-
Coordinating
from

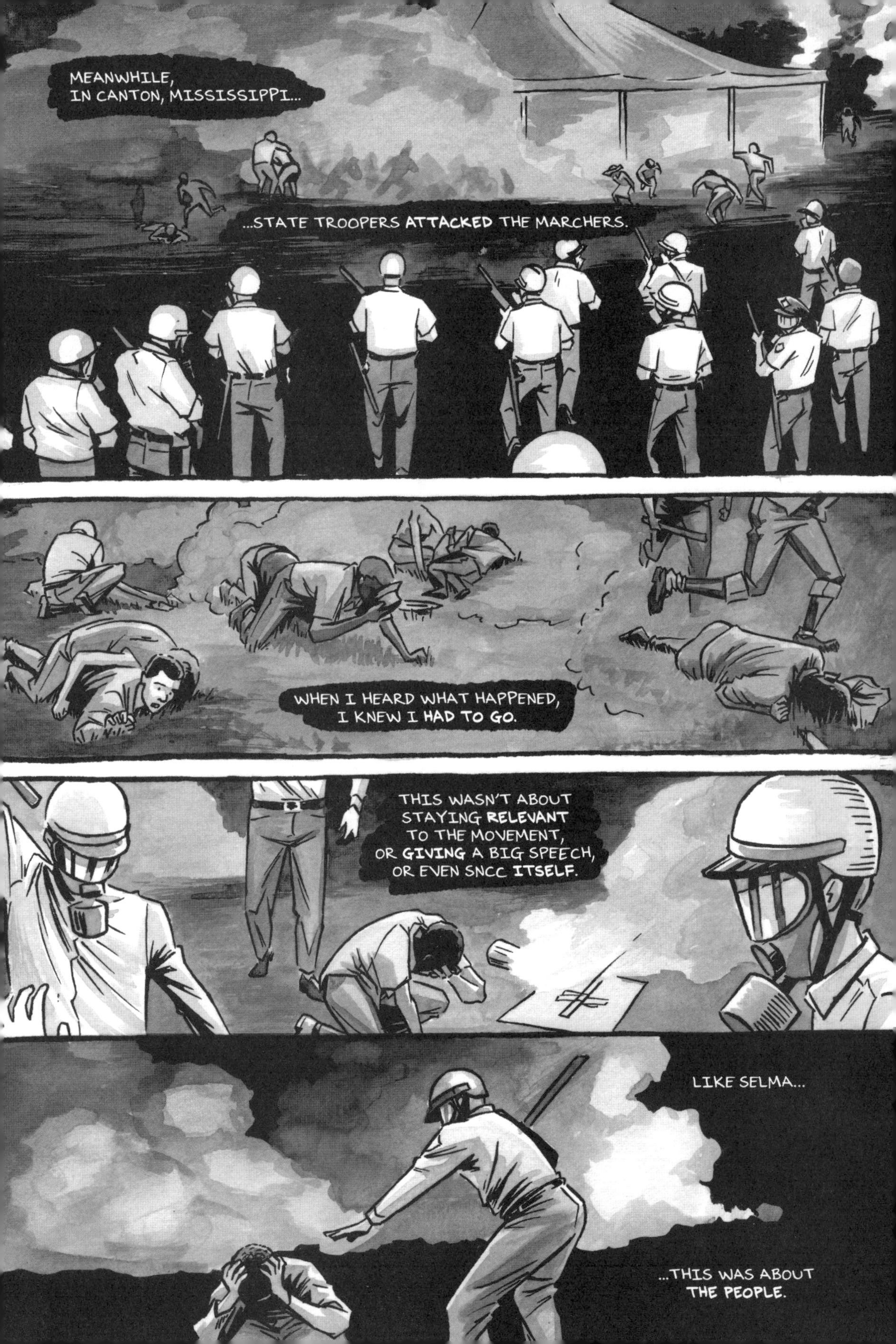
MEANWHILE, IN CANTON, MISSISSIPPI...
...STATE TROOPERS ATTACKED THE MARCHERS.
WHEN I HEARD WHAT HAPPENED, I KNEW I HAD TO GO.
THIS WASN'T ABOUT STAYING RELEVANT TO THE MOVEMENT, OR GIVING A BIG SPEECH, OR EVEN SNCC ITSELF.
LIKE SELMA...
...THIS WAS ABOUT THE PEOPLE.

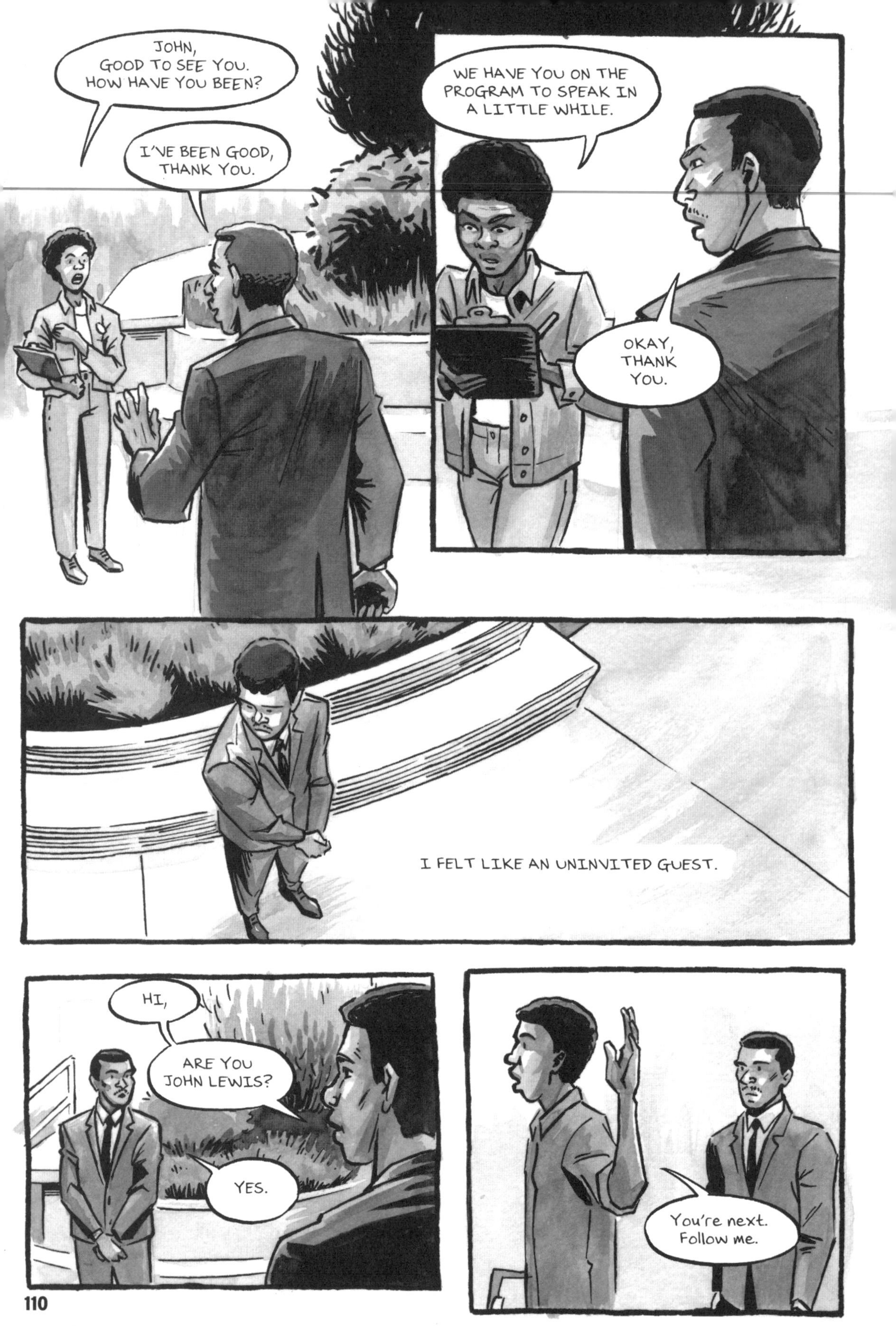
JOHN, GOOD TO SEE YOU. HOW HAVE YOU BEEN?
I'VE BEEN GOOD, THANK YOU.
WE HAVE YOU ON THE PROGRAM TO SPEAK IN A LITTLE WHILE.
OKAY, THANK YOU.
I FELT LIKE AN UNINVITED GUEST.
HI,
ARE YOU JOHN LEWIS?
YES.
You're next. Follow me.

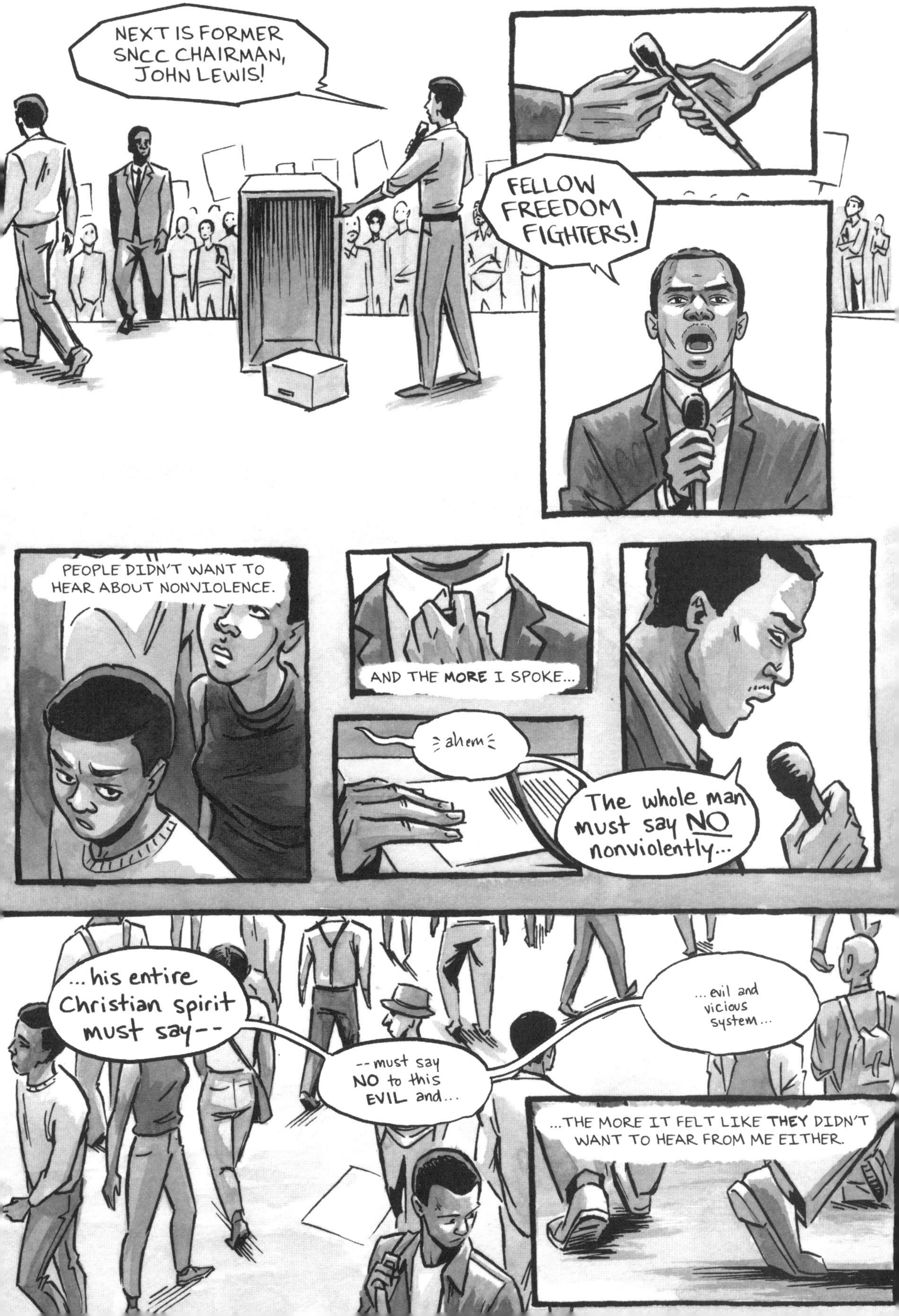
NEXT IS FORMER SNCC CHAIRMAN, JOHN LEWIS!
FELLOW FREEDOM FIGHTERS!
PEOPLE DIDN'T WANT TO HEAR ABOUT NONVIOLENCE.
AND THE MORE I SPOKE...
ahem
The whole man must say NO nonviolently...
...his entire Christian spirit must say--
--must say NO to this EVIL and...
...evil and vicious system...
...THE MORE IT FELT LIKE THEY DIDN'T WANT TO HEAR FROM ME EITHER.

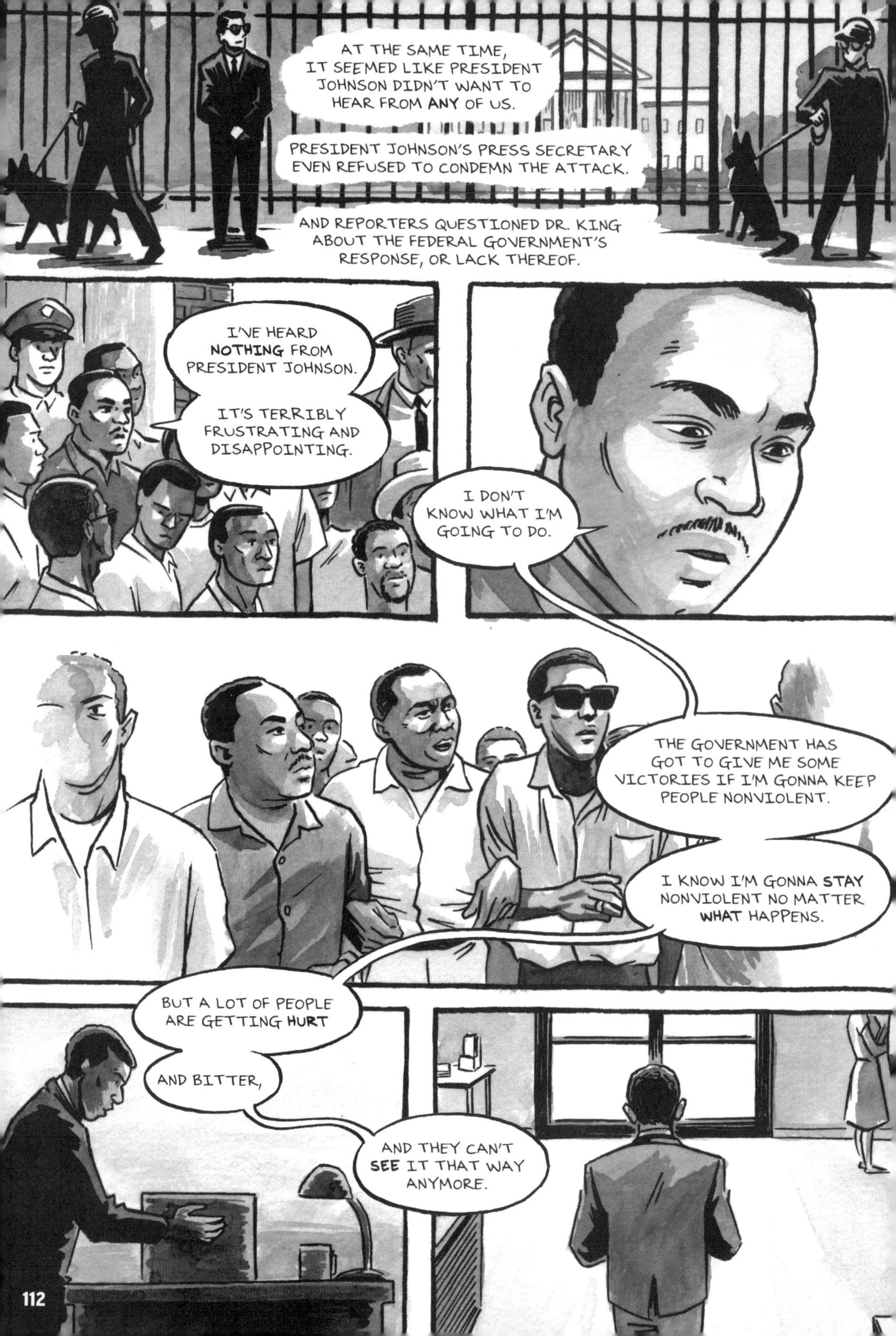
AT THE SAME TIME, IT SEEMED LIKE PRESIDENT JOHNSON DIDN'T WANT TO HEAR FROM ANY OF US.
PRESIDENT JOHNSON'S PRESS SECRETARY EVEN REFUSED TO CONDEMN THE ATTACK.
AND REPORTERS QUESTIONED DR. KING ABOUT THE FEDERAL GOVERNMENT'S RESPONSE, OR LACK THEREOF.
I'VE HEARD NOTHING FROM PRESIDENT JOHNSON.
IT'S TERRIBLY FRUSTRATING AND DISAPPOINTING.
I DON'T KNOW WHAT I'M GOING TO DO.
THE GOVERNMENT HAS GOT TO GIVE ME SOME VICTORIES IF I'M GONNA KEEP PEOPLE NONVIOLENT.
I KNOW I'M GONNA STAY NONVIOLENT NO MATTER WHAT HAPPENS.
BUT A LOT OF PEOPLE ARE GETTING HURT
AND BITTER,
AND THEY CAN'T SEE IT THAT WAY ANYMORE.

"A RIOT IS THE LANGUAGE OF THE UNHEARD," DR. KING WOULD SAY.
"WHAT IS IT THAT AMERICA HAS FAILED TO HEAR?"

AND AS DR. KING FELT THE MOVEMENT SLIPPING AWAY,
MY LIFE AS I KNEW IT WAS **OVER**.

AND I COULD FEEL **EVERYTHING** SLIPPING AWAY...

I WAS TWENTY-SIX YEARS OLD...

I WAS **BROKE**...

I HAD NO **JOB**...

FOR MY ENTIRE ADULT LIFE, THE MOVEMENT HAD BEEN MY **FAMILY**.

I HAD NO **WIFE**...

NO **CHILDREN**...

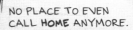

NO PLACE TO EVEN
CALL **HOME** ANYMORE.

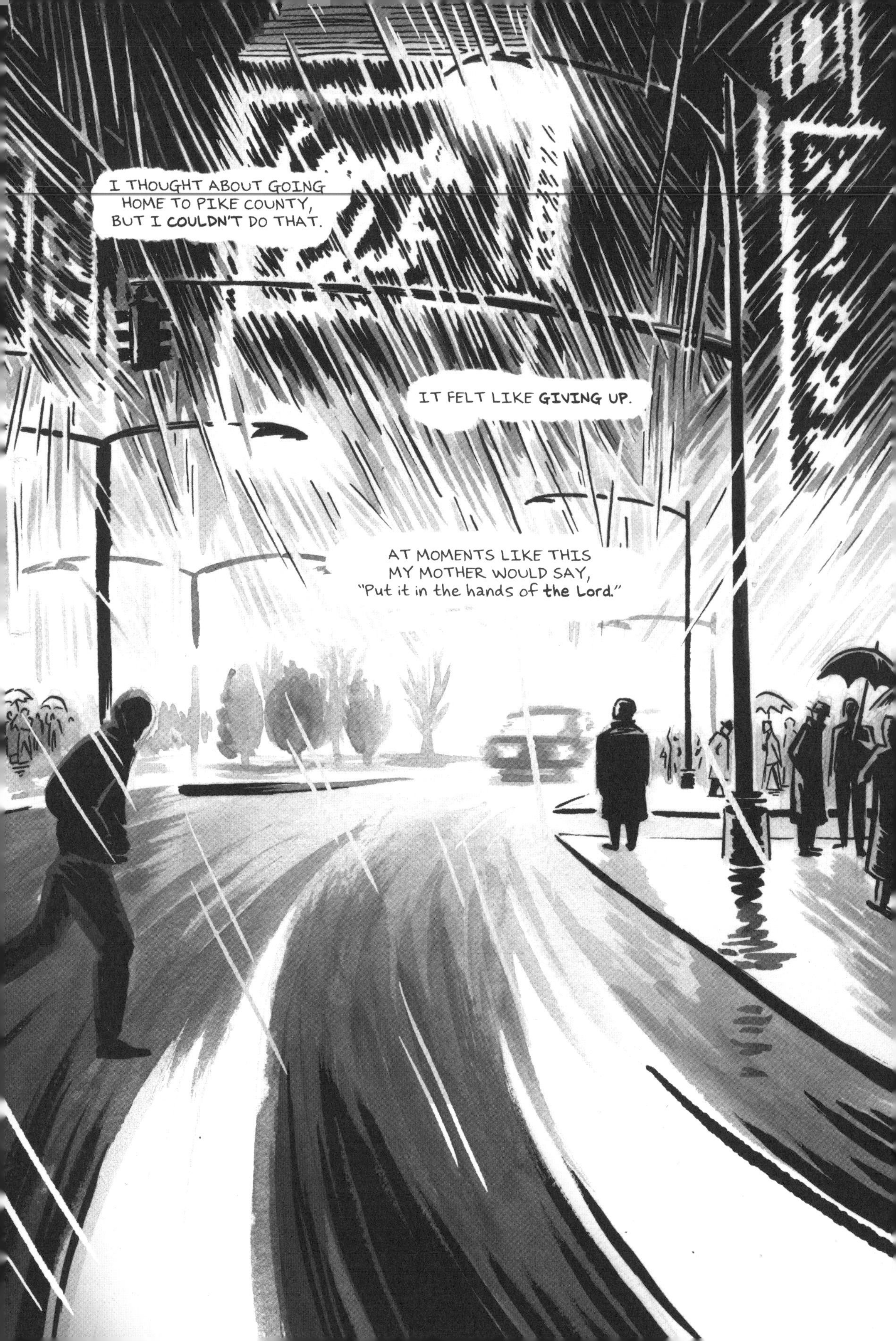
I THOUGHT ABOUT GOING HOME TO PIKE COUNTY, BUT I **COULDN'T** DO THAT.
IT FELT LIKE **GIVING UP**.
AT MOMENTS LIKE THIS MY MOTHER WOULD SAY, "Put it in the hands of **the Lord**."

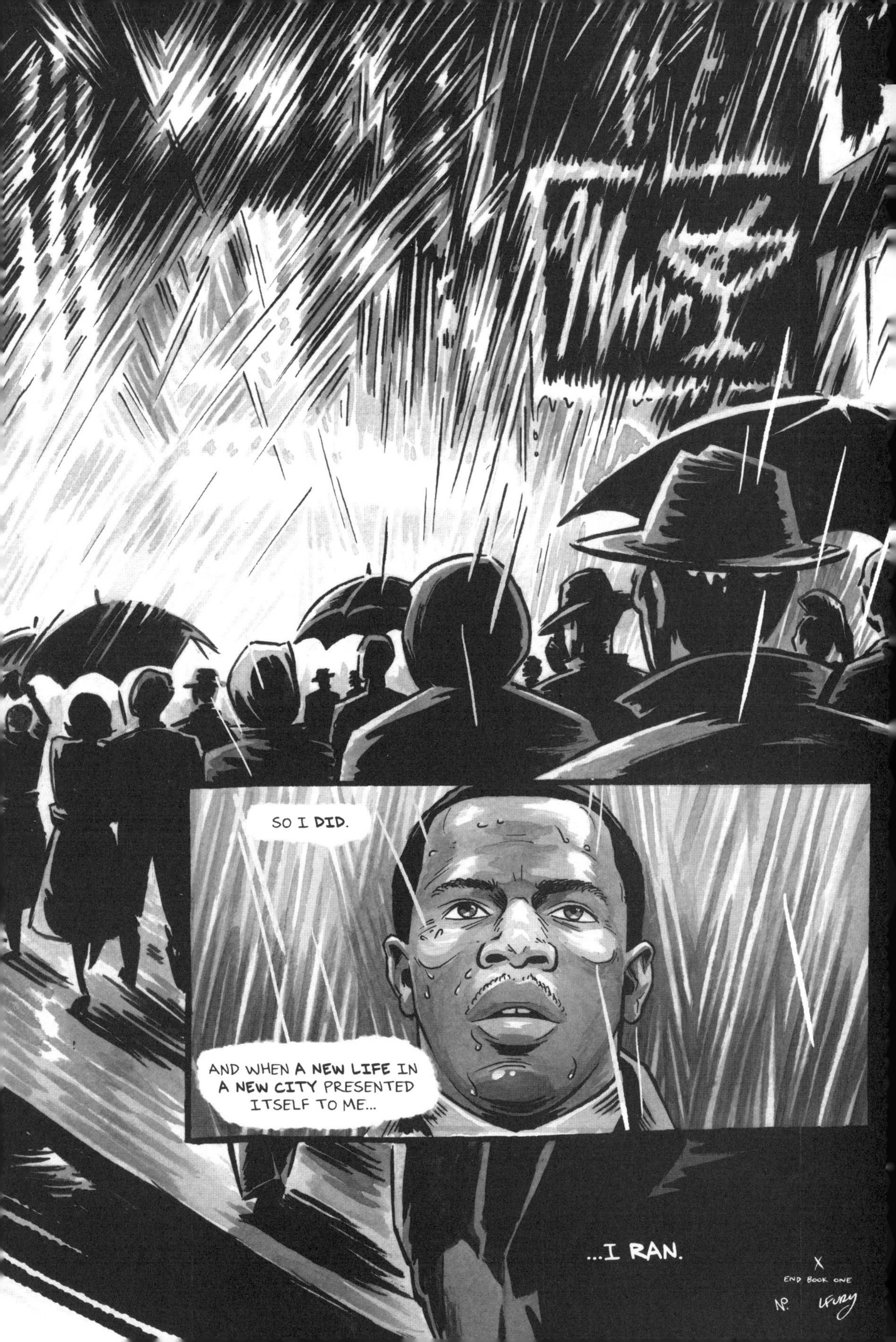
SO I DID.
AND WHEN A NEW LIFE IN A NEW CITY PRESENTED ITSELF TO ME...
...I RAN.
X
END BOOK ONE

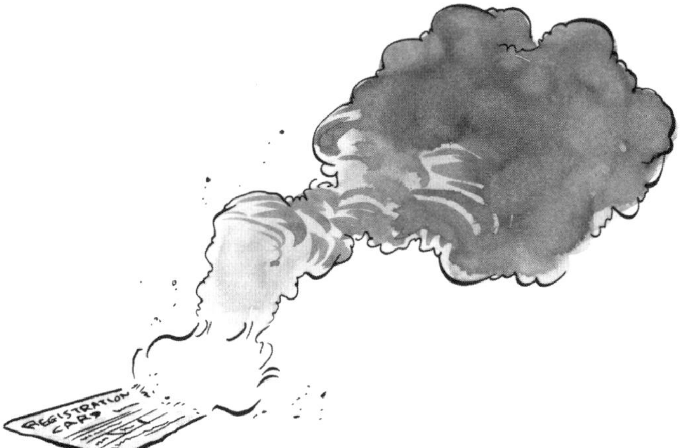
REGISTRATION CARD

BIOGRAPHIES OF THE MOVEMENT

JOYCE BAILEY (b. unknown–d. unknown) was a nineteen-year-old Student Nonviolent Coordinating Committee (SNCC) worker when she attempted to patronize Varner's Cash Store in Hayneville, Alabama, on August 20, 1965. She and sixteen others had just been released from jail after protesting in her hometown of Fort Deposit, Alabama. Following the incident in Hayneville, Bailey toured the nation detailing her ordeal.

MARION BARRY (1936–2014) was trained in nonviolent direct action by the Reverend Jim Lawson, participating in nonviolence workshops alongside Diane Nash, John Lewis, Bernard Lafayette, James Bevel, and others in the early days of the Nashville Student Movement. Barry was elected SNCC's first chairman in April 1960. In September 1960, Barry stepped down as chair to return to school, but remained with SNCC organizing in Mississippi and elsewhere in the South. In 1964, Barry joined SNCC's New York City office where he worked until 1965, when he moved to Washington, DC, to launch a SNCC chapter in the nation's capital. Barry became deeply involved in local DC politics, and was elected to the board of education, city council, and as mayor.

PENNY BARTLETT (1940–d. unknown) became a SNCC staff member in 1963. Bartlett wrote a memo dated December 11, 1965, on John Lewis's physical exhaustion after driving him to a series of events in the San Francisco Bay Area. She noted that Lewis "discharged his responsibilities with an unusual amount of care, concern, and regard for the movement he represents and for the people with whom he came in contact," but "John Robert Lewis is *tired* (me, too) and that he needs a Rest. I had the illusion most of the time that I was driving a hearse, because the person contained therein resembled a corpse more than any other thing."

MIKE BAYER (b. unknown–d. unknown) was a member of the SNCC research department in 1965 and 1966. His purview was Georgia.

HARRY BELAFONTE (b. 1927) is an award-winning musician, actor, and civil rights activist. Belafonte helped organize the 1963 March on Washington and provided important financial support for SNCC.

FAY BELLAMY (1938–2013) served in the U.S. Air Force before joining SNCC in 1965. Bellamy led the SNCC office in Selma, and eventually worked in the SNCC headquarters in Atlanta.

JAMES BEVEL (1936–2008) was trained in nonviolent direct action by the Reverend Jim Lawson, participating in nonviolence workshops alongside Diane Nash, John Lewis, Bernard Lafayette, Marion Barry, and others in the early days of the Nashville Student Movement. Bevel became a key figure first in SNCC, and then in Southern Christian Leadership Conference (SCLC) for his role in the Mississippi Nonviolent Movement, the Children's Crusade in Birmingham, and the Selma-to-Montgomery marches. Bevel ran for Congress in Illinois in 1984.

HORACE MANN BOND (1904–1972) was a noted African American university administrator, serving as president of Fort Valley State College and Lincoln University, where he graduated and was the school's first African American president. He is the father of Julian Bond.

JULIAN BOND (1940–2015) was born in Nashville to parents Julia Agnes Washington and Horace Mann Bond. As a student at Morehouse College in Atlanta, Bond became the coordinator and spokesman for civil rights demonstrations as part of the sit-in movement. Based on that work, Bond was invited to attend the April 1960 meeting at Shaw University in Raleigh, North Carolina, organized by SCLC secretary Ella Baker and the Reverend Jim Lawson, among others. At the conference, Bond became a founding member of SNCC. Bond fought for civil rights throughout his career as president of the NAACP, founder of the Southern Poverty Law Center, SNCC spokesperson, and as a national media figure. At the Democratic National Convention in 1968, Bond became the first African American to be nominated for the vice presidency. Bond died at the age of seventy-five. President Barack Obama hailed him as "a hero."

BARBARA BRANDT (b. 1943) was a white staff member in the Atlanta SNCC office. She ran the Wide Area Telephone Service, which helped spread on-the-ground information quickly between SNCC members. She lives in Somerville, Massachusetts.

PAT BROWN (1905–1996) served as governor of California from 1959 to 1967. He led the state during the Watts Riots, which took place August 11–16, 1965.

STOKELY CARMICHAEL (1941–1998) was born in Trinidad and Tobago, moving to the United States at age eleven. While a Howard University student, Carmichael was inspired to join the civil rights movement by images of the sit-ins at segregated lunch counters in 1960. He quickly rose through the ranks, marching alongside John Lewis and Dr. Martin Luther King, Jr., numerous times. Carmichael became embittered with the philosophy of nonviolence and, in 1966, led a "coup" against Lewis for the chairmanship of SNCC. Carmichael pushed for more radical approaches to combating racial oppression and helped popularize the Black Power slogan. SNCC disavowed Carmichael in 1969. He later moved to Africa, where he promoted Pan-Africanism and scientific socialism. He eventually changed his name to Kwame Ture and in 1998 died of prostate cancer in Conakry, Guinea.

JAMES CHANEY (1943–1964) was assassinated in June 1964 by Ku Klux Klan members in Philadelphia, Mississippi, at the age of twenty-one. Seven men were eventually convicted of killing Chaney and two other civil rights workers, Andrew Goodman and Mickey Schwerner. A federal trial in 2005 convicted Edgar Ray Killen of manslaughter—he had been acquitted in a trial in 1965.

JIM CLARK (1922–2007) served as Dallas County sheriff from 1955 to 1966. Clark ordered the assault and arrest of peaceful protesters on the Edmund Pettus Bridge on March 7, 1965, which became known as Bloody Sunday. "Basically, I'd do the same thing today if I had to do it all over again," Clark said in a 2006 interview.

CHARLIE COBB (b. 1943) participated in the sit-in movement as a student at Howard University. Cobb joined SNCC as a field secretary from 1961 to 1967 and authored the paper proposing "Freedom Schools" as a component of the 1964 Mississippi Summer Project. Cobb became a journalist, co-founding the National Association of Black Journalists, and authoring *This Nonviolent Stuff'll Get You Killed: How Guns Made the Civil Rights Movement Possible* in 2014.

TOM COLEMAN (1910–1997) shot at seventeen-year-old civil rights worker Ruby Sales as she tried to shop at Varner's Cash Store in Hayneville, Alabama, on August 20, 1965. Instead, Coleman killed Jonathan Myrick Daniels, a twenty-six-year-old seminarian who protected Sales from the gunshot, and wounded former Catholic priest Richard Morrisroe. Coleman boasted about his violence, was acquitted by an all-white jury, and told an interviewer if given the opportunity again he would respond "in exactly the same way."

THEOPHILUS EUGENE (BULL) CONNOR (1897–1973) early on gained notoriety as a baseball radio announcer, which he parlayed into elected office, winning a seat in the Alabama legislature in 1934 and launching his career in government. As commissioner of public safety for Birmingham, Alabama, Connor became a well-known face of segregation in the South by allowing and directing gruesome attacks on civil rights activists during the 1961 Freedom Rides and the 1963 Children's Crusade. Forced from office when a mayor council form of government replaced the commissioner format, Connor became president of the Alabama Public Service Commission in 1964, where he served until 1973 when he was defeated for reelection.

COURTLAND COX (b. 1941) helped establish the Lowndes County Freedom Organization, a new party organized under the auspices of SNCC to empower African American voters shut out from the local Democratic Party. In an effort to strengthen voter literacy, Cox helped create and distribute a series of comic books. He also helped popularize the Black Panther icon. Following his SNCC days, Cox promoted Pan-Africanism and eventually rose to the position of director of the Minority Business Development Agency under President Bill Clinton. Cox serves as president of the SNCC Legacy Project.

CALVIN F. CRAIG (1934–1998) twice joined then left the Ku Klux Klan to fight for equality. A series of conversations with civil rights icon Xernona Clayton prompted Craig to abandon the title of Grand Dragon of the Georgia chapter of the KKK in 1968. He then toured the nation with Clayton, calling for racial harmony. Craig became disillusioned with that cause and rejoined the KKK in 1975, only to renounce his membership again in 1984, and, seemingly, the cause of white supremacy.

VERNON DAHMER (1908–1966) was a wealthy businessman from Hattiesburg, Mississippi. On January 9, 1966, Dahmer's house was firebombed by members of the Mississippi White Knights of the Ku Klux Klan. He died after protecting his wife and ten-year-old daughter. Dahmer was light-skinned enough to pass as white but chose not to. He served as president of the Forrest County chapter of the NAACP and said he would pay poll taxes for poor Black citizens who could not afford them—prompting the KKK assault on his home. Dahmer was born in Mississippi's Kelly Settlement.

JONATHAN MYRICK DANIELS (1939–1965) gave his life protecting fellow activist Ruby Sales. Daniels was a twenty-six-year-old Episcopal seminarian who went with Sales and several others to Varner's Cash Store in Hayneville, Alabama, on August 20, 1965. Daniels was shot by Tom Coleman, who was working at the store. In 1994, the Episcopal Convention dedicated the August 14 liturgy of the Book of Common Prayer to "Jonathan Myrick Daniels, Seminarian and Martyr."

JOHN DOAR (1921–2014) was the chief attorney in the Department of Justice's civil rights division. John Lewis said of Doar: "Throughout that period people would say, 'Call John Doar if anything happens.' Many of us had his personal telephone number. If it hadn't been for him, I don't know what would have happened to many of us." President Barack Obama awarded Doar the Presidential Medal of Freedom in 2012.

IVANHOE DONALDSON (1941–2016) was the director of SNCC's New York office and a field secretary in Mississippi and Virginia. Donaldson became a powerful figure in elected politics, helping elect Julian Bond to the Georgia General Assembly in 1965; Richard Hatcher mayor of Gary, Indiana, in 1967; and managing the successful campaigns of former SNCC chairman Marion Barry for city council in 1974 and his upset primary victory for mayor of Washington, DC, in 1978.

JAMES FARMER (1920–1999) founded the Congress of Racial Equality (CORE). Farmer was a key organizer and participant in the Freedom Rides of 1961, successfully challenging segregation on interstate busways. He worked for President Richard Nixon as assistant secretary in the Department of Health, Education, and Welfare. President Bill Clinton awarded Farmer the Presidential Medal of Freedom in 1998.

RICHMOND FLOWERS (1918–2007) was the attorney general of Alabama from 1963 to 1967. He campaigned "unalterably for segregation," but while in office became a fierce prosecutor against segregationists. Flowers first gained attention as attorney general prosecuting the killers of Viola Liuzzo. Flowers ran for governor against Lurleen Wallace, wife of the term-limited Governor George Wallace.

JAMES (JIM) FORMAN (1928–2005) was one of the original Freedom Riders and served as executive secretary of SNCC from 1961 until his resignation from the post in 1966. Following his departure from SNCC, Forman worked with the Black Panther Party. He wrote the "Black Manifesto," which demanded reparations from white religious groups. Forman continued to organize and write about social justice causes until his death in 2005.

MILDRED FORMAN PAGE (1934–2018) came to the Atlanta SNCC office with her husband James Forman and worked as a SNCC field secretary. One of her duties was managing the SNCC Freedom Singers. Later, she returned to Chicago, remarried, and raised three children. She was active with the Chicago Friends of SNCC and the Chicago SNCC History Project, of which she was a founding member.

MARQUETTE FRYE (1944–1986) was arrested in Los Angeles on August 11, 1965, by a white police officer who believed Frye to be driving under the influence. Frye's arrest, under questionable circumstances, prompted the Watts Riots that left thirty-five people dead and caused an estimated $200 million in damages. The riots were a touchstone moment in the civil rights movement. Frye continued to speak out against injustices, but his influence was short-lived, and his life quickly spiraled out of control. He died in his hometown of Los Angeles in 1986 at age forty-two.

RONALD FRYE (c. 1943–d. unknown) was a passenger when his stepbrother, Marquette, was pulled over and arrested in Los Angeles on August 11, 1965—an event that prompted the Watts Riots.

BETTY GARMAN ROBINSON (b. 1939) came to the Atlanta SNCC office from Berkeley and worked for SNCC from 1962 to 1966. She managed the Friends of SNCC operation, and also served in Mississippi and the DC office. She lives in Baltimore.

ANDREW GOODMAN (1944–1964) was one of the three civil rights workers, along with James Chaney and Mickey Schwerner, who were assassinated by Ku Klux Klan members in Philadelphia, Mississippi, in June 1964. Goodman and Schwerner were both Jewish; Chaney was Black.

DAVID GORDON (b. unknown–d. unknown) was a reporter for *Life* magazine. He was attacked while covering protests in Lowndes County with Sanford Ungar.

MOLLY HAGAN (b. unknown–d. unknown) was a secretary in the SNCC research department.

WILLIAM (BILL) HALL (1936–2013) was a SNCC staff member in New York City, his hometown, and in Alabama.

FANNIE LOU HAMER (1917–1977) was raised in Sunflower County, Mississippi. Hamer dropped out of school at age twelve to work in the fields picking cotton. In 1961, Hamer was forcibly sterilized when she went to a Sunflower County hospital for minor surgery to remove a tumor. The forced sterilization propelled Hamer to activism, and in 1962, she attempted to register to vote at the Indianola courthouse. In retaliation, Hamer was arrested, fired from her job, and evicted from her home. Undeterred, she became a legendary activist in Mississippi, cofounding the Mississippi Freedom Democratic Party (MFDP), and testifying on behalf of the MFDP's challenge to the segregationist Mississippi delegation at the 1964 Democratic National Convention in Atlantic City, New Jersey.

WILLIAM (BILL) HANSEN (b. 1936) worked with SNCC as director of the Arkansas SNCC Project. He is currently a professor at the American University of Nigeria.

CASEY HAYDEN (b. 1937) was a white SNCC staffer in the Atlanta office. She wrote a paper along with Mary King titled "Position of Women in SNCC," highlighting gender inequities within the organization. Hayden lives in Tucson, Arizona.

H. K. HENDERSON (b. unknown–d. unknown) lived in Americus, Georgia, where he was the city's fire chief. In 1965, he blocked civil rights protesters, including John Lewis, from entering First Baptist Church in Americus before having them arrested while they attempted to pray on the church's steps.

FRANK HOLLOWAY (b. unknown–2018) was one of the original Freedom Riders. He worked in the Atlanta SNCC office and the SNCC Atlanta Project in Vine City as an assistant office manager and occasionally in the print shop.

RUTH HOWARD CHAMBERS (b. unknown) held many positions within SNCC, most notably in the communications department with Julian Bond. Howard helped design the Black Panther logo after originally suggesting a dove for the Lowndes County Freedom Organization. She lives in North Carolina.

HUBERT HUMPHREY (1911–1978) was vice president of the United States, serving under Lyndon B. Johnson from 1965 until 1969. An advocate for civil rights, Humphrey was born in Wallace, South Dakota, and died in Waverly, Minnesota in 1978.

JOE JACKSON (b. unknown–d. unknown) was a deputy sheriff in Fort Deposit, Alabama.

SHERRON JACKSON (1948–2011) worked as a field secretary for SNCC in Harlem and Greenwood, Mississippi.

LUX JOHNSON (b. unknown–d. unknown) was a deputy sheriff in Fort Deposit, Alabama.

LYNDON B. JOHNSON (1908–1973) became the thirty-sixth president of the United States after the assassination of John F. Kennedy, serving from 1963 until 1969. Johnson's presidency was tumultuous, but included the signing of two vital civil rights bills: the 1964 Civil Rights Act and the 1965 Voting Rights Act. Despite this, advocates for equality contended that LBJ could have gone further and acted swifter to advance the cause of justice. Johnson died in his hometown of Stonewall, Texas in 1973.

SHESLONIA JOHNSON (1937–1995) was SNCC's treasurer and head of bookkeeping. She was ousted from her position when Stokely Carmichael was elected chairman in 1966.

MARY ELIZABETH KING (b. 1941) was a white staffer in the SNCC communications department. King wrote a paper along with Casey Hayden titled "Position of Women in SNCC," highlighting gender inequities within the organization. She lives in Virginia.

MARTIN LUTHER KING, JR. (1929–1968) was the leader of the civil rights movement. Born in Atlanta, Dr. King became pastor of Dexter Avenue Baptist Church in Montgomery, where he was selected to head the Montgomery Improvement Association in 1955 and spearhead the Montgomery Bus Boycotts. In 1957, King cofounded the Southern Christian Leadership Conference (SCLC), serving as president of the organization until his assassination in Memphis on April 4, 1968.

BERNARD LAFAYETTE (b. 1940) was trained in nonviolent direct action by the Reverend Jim Lawson, participating in nonviolence workshops alongside Diane Nash, John Lewis, James Bevel, Marion Barry, and others in the early days of the Nashville Student Movement. Lafayette participated in the 1961 Freedom Rides, and led SNCC's Alabama voter registration project. Lafayette was severely beaten in Selma in 1963. He eventually left SNCC to work for SCLC as national program administrator but returned to Selma during the 1965 Selma voting rights campaign. Today, Lafayette is a leading authority on strategies for nonviolent social change and nonviolent direct action.

REVEREND JAMES (JIM) LAWSON (b. 1928) was a Methodist minister and devout pacifist who became a field secretary for the Fellowship of Reconciliation, before moving to Nashville to pursue graduate studies in divinity at Vanderbilt University. In Nashville, Lawson led nonviolent workshops that trained many prominent leaders of the movement including John Lewis, Diane Nash, Bernard Lafayette, and others. Lawson was expelled from Vanderbilt University in 1960 for his role in training student activists to participate in sit-ins and direct-action campaigns.

He joined the Freedom Rides in 1961 and was incarcerated at Parchman Farm in Sunflower County, Mississippi, before moving to Memphis, Tennessee, to serve as a pastor. In 2006, Lawson was invited to return to Vanderbilt as a visiting professor.

JENNIFER LAWSON (b. 1946) worked as a field secretary for SNCC after participating in the Children's March in Birmingham in May 1963. Later that year, Lawson joined SNCC as a student at Tuskegee University. In an effort to strengthen voter literacy, she illustrated a series of comic books with Courtland Cox. Lawson went on to a successful career in film and television. In 1990, *Entertainment Weekly* recognized her as one of the "101 Most Influential People in Entertainment," and in 1994 the *Hollywood Reporter* named her to the "Power 50," or the fifty most influential women in entertainment. In 2011, Lawson became senior vice president for television and digital video content at the Corporation for Public Broadcasting.

STANLEY LEVISON (1912–1979), an attorney from New York City, was Dr. King's confidant, attorney, lawyer, and occasional ghostwriter. Levison also helped raise money for civil rights causes.

WORTH (WILLY) LONG (b. 1932) was born in Durham, North Carolina, and joined SNCC in 1962 while a student in Arkansas. In 1963, Long replaced Bernard and Colia Lafayette as SNCC field secretary in Selma, Alabama. In 1966, Long challenged the results of John Lewis's reelection at SNCC's annual conference in Holly Springs, Mississippi. The challenge allowed for Stokely Carmichael to become chairman. After leaving SNCC, Long became noted for his work as a folklorist. He was honored by the Smithsonian Institute in 2012 for his work documenting and preserving African American folklore.

DANNY LYON (b. 1942) was hired by Jim Forman as SNCC's first staff photographer. He was one of several white staff members who left following Stokely Carmichael's election as SNCC chairman.

BOB MANTS (1943–2011) was a friend of John Lewis and in the second row of protesters on Bloody Sunday. Mants died in Lowndes County, Alabama, in 2011.

DON MCKEE (b. unknown) covered civil rights for the Associated Press. He lives in Cobb County, Georgia.

FLOYD MCKISSICK (1922–1991) was the first African American student at the University of North Carolina School of Law. McKissick was elected director of the Congress of Racial Equality (CORE) in 1966. He won the election after promising to move CORE in a more militant direction.

JAMES MEREDITH (b. 1933) was the first African American student to graduate from the University of Mississippi, earning a history degree in 1966. Born in Kosciusko, Mississippi, Meredith was a key figure in the civil rights movement, but disavowed any formal association. He initiated a one-man "March Against Fear" in 1966 to embolden African Americans in Mississippi. Meredith was shot on day two of the 250-mile march, prompting Martin Luther King, Jr., and other civil rights leaders to continue the journey into Jackson, Mississippi, along with some fifteen thousand activists. Meredith had a long career in public service, running for office as a Republican in New York City and in Mississippi. He worked for former segregationist senator Jesse Helms of North Carolina.

LEE MINIKUS (1934–2013) was the white California Highway Patrol officer who arrested Marquette Frye. The arrest sparked the Watts Riots. In 1990, Minikus said: "I caught up with Marquette a few times after the riots, and we would talk. I liked him, and I think he liked me. He would tell me about the pressure that he felt the Black community was putting on him. It was a lot for him to deal with."

JACK MINNIS (1926–2005) was a white lawyer who was invited by Jim Forman in 1963 to start and lead SNCC's research department. In 1965, Minnis circulated a weekly mimeographed newspaper called *Life with Lyndon in the Great Society*, which connected the Johnson administration with corporate interests. One of his major projects was documenting attacks against civil rights workers in Mississippi. Minnis was the last remaining white SNCC staffer.

RICHARD MORRISROE (b. 1940), a former Catholic priest, joined the civil rights movement after John Lewis spoke at his church in Chicago. Morrisroe and Episcopal seminarian Jonathan Myrick Daniels were shot on August 20, 1965, protecting seventeen-year-old Ruby Sales. Daniels gave his life to save Sales. Born in Chicago, Morrisroe is now a professor, attorney, and city planner in East Chicago. He lobbied the Episcopal Convention to honor Daniels in the church's *Book of Common Prayer*. In 1994, the convention dedicated the August 14 liturgy to "Jonathan Myrick Daniels, Seminarian and Martyr." Morrisroe named his son Jonathan to honor Daniels.

DIANE NASH (b. 1938) was trained in nonviolent direct action by the Reverend Jim Lawson, participating in nonviolence workshops alongside John Lewis, Bernard Lafayette, James Bevel, Marion Barry, and others in the early days of the Nashville Student Movement. Nash is a cofounder of SNCC and helped lead the Nashville sit-in movement, the 1961 Freedom Rides, and the Selma voting rights campaign. Nash settled in Chicago following her involvement with the movement and continues to advocate for civil rights and nonviolence.

LAVERN LILLY NEBLETT (b. unknown–d. unknown) worked as a bookkeeper in SNCC headquarters.

MARTHA PRESCOD NORMAN NOONAN (b. 1943) served in several capacities in SNCC and its auxiliary organizations. Prescod left SNCC following the election of Stokely Carmichael as Chair in 1966. She lives in Baltimore.

GWEN PATTON (1943–2017), the first chair of the SNCC women's commission, was a leading critic of the Vietnam War within SNCC. Patton came up with the term "scholar-activist" to describe herself and, while student body president at the Tuskegee Institute, she led a march to the Alabama state capitol—defying threats of expulsion. Patton was an archivist at H. Councill Trenholm State Technical College, later H. Councill Trenholm State Community College, in Montgomery, where a collection is maintained on civil rights leaders.

JOHN PERDEW (1941–2014) joined SNCC in 1963, working in the southwest Georgia division. He also worked in the SNCC research department. Originally from Denver, Perdew helped establish the Americus Civil Rights Institute and Interpretive Center.

SIDNEY POITIER (b. 1927) became the first African American to win an Academy Award for Best Actor. Poitier provided financial and celebrity backing to the civil rights movement.

ADAM CLAYTON POWELL (1908–1972) represented Harlem in the United States Congress from 1945 to 1971. He was the first African American elected to Congress from the state of New York.

RENA PRICE (1916–2013) was the mother of Marquette Frye, whose arrest sparked the Watts Riots. While the exact details of the arrest are unclear, Price arrived at the scene, scolded her son, and somehow acted in a manner to spark unrest with the crowd of bystanders. Price was arrested for interfering with a police officer. She continued to live in Los Angeles, where she was a longtime community activist.

A. PHILIP RANDOLPH (1889–1979) founded the International Brotherhood of Sleeping Car Porters, the first trade union intended primarily for African Americans. Randolph served as chairman of the 1963 March on Washington organizing committee. Dr. King called Randolph "truly the Dean of Negro leaders."

REVEREND JAMES REEB (1927–1965) heeded Martin Luther King, Jr.'s call to clergy to join the civil rights movement. He went to Selma, where he was beaten and later died from his injuries.

JUDY RICHARDSON (b. 1944) worked at SNCC headquarters in several positions including as secretary to James Forman. She was part of the voter-registration drive in Lowndes County, Alabama, in 1965. She lives in Silver Spring, Maryland.

WILLIE RICKS (b. 1943) began protesting discrimination during the sit-in movement of 1960. He eventually joined SNCC in 1963, working as a field secretary throughout the Southeast. Ricks was known as a fiery orator and was a more militant voice in the movement. In 1966, he helped coin the phrase Black Power, and his actions played a role in the splintering of SNCC. Ricks eventually left SNCC and became active with the Black Panther Party. Born in Chattanooga, Ricks continues to advocate for Pan-African socialism.

PAUL ROBESON (1898–1976) was a well-known recording artist who lent his celebrity to advance civil rights causes. He also used the phrase Black Power in response to the crisis over the Little Rock Nine in 1957.

RUBY DORIS SMITH ROBINSON (1942–1967) was elected executive secretary of SNCC in 1966, replacing Jim Forman, who was retiring. Prior to her election, Smith was administrative secretary of the organization, running the secretarial pool, and participated in numerous marches. She served forty-five days in prison for her involvement with the Freedom Rides. Smith's headstone reads, "If you think you are free, you are free."

JAMES (JIMMY) ROGERS (b. unknown) served as SNCC field secretary in Lowndes County, Alabama, in 1965. He oversaw the effort to register Black voters in the county. He lives in Oakland, California.

BAYARD RUSTIN (1912–1987) organized the March on Washington in 1963. In addition to his work for racial harmony, Rustin was a trailblazer for gay rights as an openly homosexual man. Rustin was one of the original members of the Congress for Racial Equality in 1942. He also helped organize the Southern Christian Leadership Conference and is said to have introduced Dr. Martin Luther King, Jr., to the work of Mahatma Gandhi.

RUBY SALES (b. 1948) nearly died at age seventeen attempting to shop at Varner's Cash Store in Hayneville, Alabama, on August 20, 1965. The owner, Tom Coleman, opened fire on Sales, Richard Morrisroe, and Jonathan Myrick Daniels. Sales recalled hearing Coleman saying, "Bitch, I'll blow your brains out." Sales continued to participate in SNCC marches, including the Selma-to-Montgomery marches. Born in Jemison, Alabama, and raised in Columbus, Georgia, Sales continues to be a civil rights movement leader. She founded the SpiritHouse Project in Atlanta in 2000, where she still serves as director. The SpiritHouse Project is a national civil rights movement based on interfaith theological doctrines. Among some of its projects are exposing the extrajudicial murders of African Americans by white vigilantes and police. Sales continues to preach and speak about social justice issues.

MICHAEL (MICKEY) SCHWERNER (1940–1964) was one of the three civil rights workers, along with James Chaney and Andrew Goodman, who were assassinated by Ku Klux Klan members in Philadelphia, Mississippi, in June 1964. Goodman and Schwerner were both Jewish; Chaney was Black.

MARVIN SEGREST (1897–1986) shot and killed Sammy Younge in 1966. Younge had asked Segrest, the night bathroom attendant at the Standard Oil station in Tuskegee, Alabama, to use the bathroom. Younge was Black and Segrest was white. The two had an altercation and Younge later returned to the scene, where Segrest shot him. Segrest told authorities he mistook a golf club in Younge's hand for a gun. Segrest was acquitted by an all-white jury. In 2008, the FBI opened an investigation into the shooting and closed the case in 2011 on the grounds that Segrest was deceased and "no other persons were directly involved."

CLEVELAND (CLEVE) SELLERS (b. 1944) was elected program director for SNCC in 1965, after he spearheaded African American voter registration drives in Mississippi. Known as "Cleve," Sellers marched across Mississippi in 1966 and was shot in the 1968 Orangeburg Massacre. He was the only person charged for inciting violence and served seven months in prison. In 1993, Sellers was pardoned. He has had a long career in politics and academia following his release, serving as the head of the University of South Carolina's African American Studies Department and president of the historically Black Voorhees College in his hometown of Denmark, South Carolina, from 2008 to 2016.

CHARLES SHERROD (b. 1937) participated in SNCC's founding conference and was the first SNCC field secretary for southwest Georgia. Sherrod helped pioneer the "Jail, No Bail" strategy during the sit-in movement, and became a legendary figure in the Albany, Georgia, movement. Sherrod resigned when SNCC decided to expel its white members from decision making, saying, "I didn't leave SNCC, SNCC left me." He lives in Albany, Georgia.

SAM SHIRAH (1943-1980) was a white SNCC staffer who participated in multiple campaigns throughout the South, including the White Folks Project, which attempted to organize poor whites in Mississippi alongside the 1964 Summer Project to create an "interracial movement of the poor."

SCOTT B. SMITH JR. (b. unknown–d. unknown) helped popularize the use of the Black Panther logo in Lowndes County. He was a SNCC member from 1965 to 1967.

SANDRA STOVALL (b. unknown–d. unknown) was the receptionist in the SNCC Atlanta office and secretary to John Lewis.

STROM THURMOND (1902–2003) holds records for being the oldest-serving U.S. senator at age one hundred, the longest-serving senator at forty-eight years, and for giving the longest individual speech on the Senate floor when he filibustered the 1957 Civil Rights Act for twenty-four hours and eighteen minutes. In 1925, Thurmond fathered an African American daughter out of wedlock, despite being an avowed segregationist. Thurmond denied being a racist, insisting, "We've looked out for the state and everything that was honorable to get, we got it."

VIRGINIA (GINNY) TIEGER (b. unknown–d. unknown) was a member of the SNCC research department who conducted research on Arkansas.

SANFORD UNGAR (b. unknown–d. unknown) was a correspondent for *Life* magazine. He was attacked while covering protests in Lowndes County in 1965 with David Gordon.

BRENDA USHER (b. unknown–d. unknown) was a general secretary in the SNCC research department.

WILLIE VAUGHN (b. unknown–d. unknown) played a major role in registering new voters during the Lowndes County voter registration efforts.

GEORGE WALLACE (1919–1998) is perhaps the most well-known governor of Alabama, declaring in 1963 he believed in "segregation forever." Wallace was governor on three different occasions, serving four terms total.

LURLEEN WALLACE (1926–1968) succeeded her term-limited husband George as governor of Alabama. She served two years before dying in office.

WILLIAM (BILL) WARE (1935–2014) wrote the "Black Power Position Paper" in 1966, along with two other SNCC members. The paper called for African Americans to assume control of Black organizations without assistance from sympathetic whites.

TOM WATSON (1856–1922) enjoyed a lengthy career in elected service for Georgia, holding offices at the local, state, and federal levels. A staunch segregationist, Watson's statue stood in front of the main entrance of the Georgia state capitol until its removal in 2013.

JEAN WILEY (1942–2019) joined SNCC while in college at Morgan State University and was a reporter for the group's *Student Voice* publication. In addition to reporting on SNCC's activities, Wiley would relay information to local offices for rapid responses, whether it be arrests of members or attacks on demonstrators. Wiley was raised in Baltimore and worked for SNCC from 1960 to 1967. She became an expert in education following her civil rights work.

ROY WILKINS (1901–1981) became chairman of the NAACP in 1955. Wilkins created the Leadership Conference on Civil Rights—a multireligious and multiethnic civil rights organization. He also participated in the March on Washington in 1963, the Selma-to-Montgomery marches in 1965, and the March Against Fear in 1966. Wilkins was awarded the Presidential Medal of Freedom by Lyndon Johnson in 1967. Wilkins led the NAACP until his retirement in 1977.

HOSEA WILLIAMS (1926–2000) was a veteran civil rights leader who, at the urging of Dr. Martin Luther King, Jr., helped organize the first march from Selma to Montgomery, co-led with John Lewis, on March 7, 1965. Williams joined the Southern Christian Leadership Conference in 1963 and held several leadership positions including two periods as executive director. Williams ran for and held numerous elected positions in Atlanta, and founded the Hosea Feed the Hungry and Homeless program in Atlanta.

GERALDINE WILLIAMSON (b. unknown–d. unknown) worked in the SNCC research department in Atlanta and was responsible for typing and computational bookkeeping.

MYRNA WOOD (b. unknown–d. unknown) was an Atlanta headquarters SNCC employee, coordinating the libraries and helping in the research department.

ROB WOOD (b. unknown–d. unknown) was a member of the SNCC communications department, responsible for writing articles and printing posters.

RICHARD WRIGHT (1908–1960) is a celebrated author, most notably for his novel *Native Son* (1940) and his memoir *Black Boy* (1945). Wright is recognized for one of the first documented uses of the Black Power phrase, using it as the title for his 1954 memoir of his travels in Africa.

WHITNEY YOUNG (1921–1971) was appointed executive director of the National Urban League in 1961, and led the organization to greater participation in the civil rights movement. Young was viewed as a critical link between the civil rights movement and the business community. He was a close adviser to Lyndon B. Johnson, and became known for the Domestic Marshall Plan, which helped shape President Johnson's domestic policy agenda. Johnson awarded Young the Presidential Medal of Freedom in 1968. Young's 1971 drowning death in Lagos, Nigeria, aroused suspicion after the initial autopsy performed in Lagos suggested Young died of a "subarachnoid hemorrhage." The results of a later autopsy performed in the United States and released in a report by the National Urban League attempted to confirm the cause of death as drowning.

SAMUEL (SAMMY) YOUNGE JR. (1944–1966) served in the United States Navy before joining SNCC. He was shot and killed by attendant Marvin Segrest after asking to use the bathroom and purchasing items at the Standard Oil station in Tuskegee, Alabama. Younge was Black and Segrest was white. Three days after Younge's murder, SNCC announced its opposition to the Vietnam War.

ROBERT (BOB) ZELLNER (b. 1939) was born in Alabama, and both his father and grandfather were members of the Ku Klux Klan. Zellner became SNCC's first white field secretary and faced violence many times, including being beaten unconscious in McComb, Mississippi, in 1961. Zellner left SNCC along with other white staff members in 1966, joining the Southern Conference Education Fund, which worked closely with SNCC and funded many nonviolent projects in the South during the movement.

NOTES

Over the four-and-a-half years spent creating this book, more than three dozen historical texts, four hundred newspaper and magazine articles, seventy hours of archival and documentary footage, and one thousand pages of primary documents were reviewed. More than a half-dozen former Student Nonviolent Coordinating Committee (SNCC) staffers were interviewed or consulted, and countless more friendships were forged. This process has raised many questions, and, in some cases, managed to provide answers. But, through it all, the goal remained the same: Tell the story, the whole story, and make it plain for people to see.

Research for nonfiction graphic narratives often seeks different truths than writing for other media. We have to re-create the narrative *and* the visual, blending the two in a hopefully successful marriage that builds understanding neither element could create alone. The process can seem strange to even a seasoned academic. A well-known story can appear to be easily retold in comics with little new scholarship, but accurately re-creating the time and place in a three-dimensional print representation takes a different *kind* of scholarship. Well-wrought story details such as a location or dialogue have to be studied with greater depth when building them into comics form.

And the process itself is also more complex. There are more people involved. There are the writers, editors, and researchers, of course, but first and foremost there is the artist in addition to the letterer and the designer, all of whom have to be rowing in the same direction, and each have their own particular reference needs. Hours of work are devoted to tracking down more complete quotes to understand not just what was said, but how and where it was said. And once you lay out the script, questions emerge, such as, what clothes were they wearing or what season of the year was it? Would they be wearing coats? What kind of cars were they driving? Not just what did that year's model look like, but what was the actual age of the cars they were driving? Or road signs: How have they changed over the years and what did the signs on that particular stretch of road look like at the time? Or, perhaps most vexing, what happens when two participants or historical texts offer differing accounts? Dig down into the primary documents and see what's there. Conduct interviews. Verify. Verify. *Verify.*

To that end, the glue that holds this work together is the efforts of numerous librarians and archivists who aided us along the way, particularly Bruce Hartford and other volunteers at the Civil Rights Movement Archive. Because of Bruce and his colleagues' archival efforts, we have been able to use meeting minutes, after-action reports, press releases, newsletters, internal correspondence, and other SNCC records to re-create as accurately as possible the events we depict without the filter of history or memory. But we must remember, this is John Lewis's story, told from his perspective, and it reflects his memories as well as his point of view.

Run: Book One also relies heavily on scholarly works including Hasan Kwame Jeffries' *Bloody Lowndes*, Taylor Branch's *At Canaan's Edge*, and Ari Berman's *Give Us the Ballot*, as well as memoirs by Congressman Lewis (*Walking with the Wind*) and Jim Forman (*The Making of Black Revolutionaries*).

In these notes, there are sources ranging from texts and interviews to primary documents, newspaper articles, and archival footage, as well as explanations of how those sources were used. In some places, additional quotes and context are provided for particular sources and scenes. Bolded names mark the first appearance of major figures within the narrative.

Pages 1–9:

The confrontation between protesters and the Klan in front of First Baptist Church is a clear-cut example of how the forces of segregation and white supremacy immediately went to work attacking and undermining the new law, using the tactics developed by the movement to fight back against it. The immediate pushback should dispel any notion that the great victories of the movement, or any movement, are allowed to stand unchallenged, even for the briefest amount of time. In Americus, Georgia, the counterattack began immediately with Klan hoods and robes in an orderly march, eerily similar to those led by SNCC, Southern Christian Leadership Council (SCLC), Congress of Racial Equality (CORE), and others. Lewis,[1] Branch,[2] and Berman[3] discuss these events in their books, but contemporaneous news coverage provided the compelling quotes and details.

Visual references for the scenes in Americus come from news footage from a young Tom Brokaw, who was covering the demonstrations for WSB-TV.[4]

A deacon at First Baptist, **H. K. Henderson** also served as Americus's fire chief. Just a week earlier he had similarly turned away Black protestors trying to enter the church. Henderson's warning is sourced from an article in the *Atlanta Constitution,* which reported him saying: "This is not an integrated church. The Federal Government doesn't have one five-cent piece in it. This is the third time you have come here and disturbed our worship. Now git or I'll have you arrested."[5]

Grand Dragon Calvin Craig's speech to the marching Klansmen is sourced from a front-page article in the *Hartford Courant*.[6] Following the rallies in 1965, KKK Grand Dragon Calvin Craig took a twisting path away from racial hatred. Throughout the sixties he was a white-robe racist activist against desegregation, but in April 1968, shortly after the death of Martin Luther King, Jr., Craig held a press conference and announced he had resigned from the KKK and would work for a nation where "Black men and white men can stand shoulder to shoulder in a united America." He stated that civil rights activist Xernona Clayton influenced his change of heart. However, in the mid-seventies, Craig rejoined the Klan, only to quit again later in the mid-eighties.[7]

Pages 10-17:

The questioning of **Marquette Frye** by California Highway Patrol Officer **Lee Minikus** comes from a 1990 article looking back at how the legacy of the Watts Riot ruined Frye's life.[8]

Although hailed by many as a hero, Frye never accepted the label. To distance himself from the tragedy, he changed his last name but was unable to shake off the tragic consequences of his arrest. "It just happened to me, and there's nothing I can do about it," Frye said.

His attorney for the arrest, and later California superior court judge, Stanley Malone, said he was "a perfect example of a young Black man who has been done in by society…[W]hatever possibility Marquette had of rising above his situation was beaten out of him."

Frye said the police beat and maced him while in custody. Arrested twenty-eight times in total over the years, Frye ended up on state disability, lost a son, and attempted suicide. He died of pneumonia when he was only forty-two.[9]

Pages 18–22:

The pointed statement from SNCC responding to the civil unrest in Los Angeles and Chicago has been reproduced in full in the text.[10]

The SNCC founding document was adopted at Shaw University in Raleigh, North Carolina, in April 1960.[11]

The names and responsibilities of the SNCC staff come from a memo titled "Who Does What in Atlanta," which is historically notable both for the detail it provides in understanding the organizational structure of SNCC at the time, but also as a reminder that SNCC was struggling to maintain order within its own ranks. Of additional interest is the fact that it was prepared by the northern staff, showing the growing influence and drive for control of the "northern faction" within SNCC, and the distance from the central office in Atlanta felt by field staffers. The memo opens: "Because of the lack of information about each person's responsibility in the Atlanta offices towards the field staff and Friends of SNCC groups, the NORTHERN COORDINATION office has compiled a list describing the functions of each office, and the person's responsibility within the offices for use of all staff people and Friends of SNCC groups." (The emphasis on "Northern Coordination" office is in the original memo text.)[12]

Pages 23–36:

Details and dialogue from the Fort Deposit episode come from several sources, including contemporary and eyewitness accounts.

SNCC reports from August 1965 note that shooter **Tom Coleman**'s sister was the superintendent of schools in Lowndes County, his son was a highway patrolman, and his brother was chairman of the Montgomery City Water Works. Coleman, who was also assistant deputy sheriff of Lowndes County (a part-time deputy), said the SNCC staff members were picketing the store and he was acting in his "official" capacity with the sheriff's office when he shot **Jonathan Daniels** and the **Reverend Richard Morrisroe**. Coleman also claimed self-defense and stated that Daniels had a knife when he entered the store. These SNCC reports also offer a more complete accounting of the timeline of events pertaining to the SNCC members' release from jail and subsequent encounter with Tom Coleman.[13]

Ruby Sales described the scene during a 2005 interview with SNCC staff members **Jean Wiley** and Bruce Hartford.[14] *At Canaan's Edge* provides **Stokely Carmichael**'s words and other details.[15] Additional dialogue is derived from a 2015 panel discussion at Stanford featuring **Jimmy Rogers** and other SNCC members[16] as well as from the book *Bloody Lowndes*.[17]

Pages 37–44:

Some reference material and context were sourced from the "Segregation in America" report by the Equal Justice Initiative.[18]

The quote from South Carolina senator **Strom Thurmond** is from a Senate floor speech debating the Civil Rights Act of 1964.[19]

Fanny Lou Hamer, depicted on the television testifying at the Democratic National Convention in 1964, was elected as vice-chair of the Mississippi Freedom Democratic Party (MFDP). The party demanded representation at the Democratic Convention because the Mississippi Democratic Party remained segregated. Hamer testified on national television for inclusion of the MFDP, and President Johnson, so alarmed by Hamer's powerful message, hosted an impromptu press conference to distract from her messaging.[20] This episode is depicted at greater length in *March: Book Three*.[21]

Pages 45–53:

The staff meeting depiction utilizes unaltered quotes condensed from portions of the meeting minutes kept during the November 24–29, 1966 SNCC staff conference.[22] These meeting notes stretch more than twenty pages and offer a wide-ranging view of the decision-making process. The SNCC debates were free-flowing and complicated. New ideas were introduced and discarded rapidly while moving toward

a more broad-based group consensus. A direct action campaign against the United Nations was considered, as well as years-long commitments to voter education and empowerment programs. The decision-making process allowed for the consideration of bold ideas that the group could weigh and build into manageable (or sometimes unmanageable) programs. The meeting minutes show how SNCC used a form of parliamentary procedure to come to an agreement, offering motions that sometimes found seconds, and sometimes did not. Proposals lived and died on votes held by the members that were present and were subject to a majority rule.

The comics created for the Lowndes County Freedom Organization (LCFO) are part of the long history of comics in the civil rights movement including, as referenced in *March: Book One*, the sixteen-page illustrated comic *Martin Luther King and the Montgomery Story*. That comic was published in December 1957 and discussed the Montgomery Bus Boycott, Dr. Martin Luther King, Jr., and Gandhian nonviolence.[23]

A 2014 interview with **Courtland Cox** by Andrew Aydin revealed Cox's work writing these comics for the Lowndes County Freedom Organization in 1966, with **Jennifer Lawson** as illustrator. These comics were aimed at first-time African American voters to help explain the roles of various elected officials. *The Political Education Primer*, published in 1966, featured a black panther on the cover and separate comics discussing the role of the sheriff, tax collector, tax assessor, board of education, and coroner. A longer-form comic called *Us Colored People* was also created by Cox and Lawson as part of the same initiative.[24]

Cox and Lawson describe the goal of the LCFO comics and SNCC's involvement: "Because the Lowndes County Freedom Organization wanted to move beyond just registering people to vote to taking responsibility for governance in Lowndes County, the SNCC field staff had to develop a way of communicating complex responsibilities of each office for governance and to help create a sense of consciousness so that those who had not voted over the years would feel empowered to not only vote, but vote for members of their community for public office."[25]

The image of the black panther versus the rooster, a symbol of the all-white Democratic Party, was featured in a 1966 pamphlet from the Lowndes County Freedom Organization.[26]

Pages 54–59:
The timeline of events leading to Sammy Younge's murder is based on eyewitness accounts of the incident documented in court affidavits.[27] [28] Younge was trying to buy a pack of cigarettes and use the restroom. For that, he was chased out of the gas station and into the bus station parking lot next-door, where he was shot in the head.

A 2011 U.S. Department of Justice report outlined the facts of the case and stated it should be closed because the shooter, Marvin Segrest, had died.[29] According to this report, the trial of Segrest was moved from Macon County to Lee County because the trial judge determined that the accused could not receive a fair trial in Macon County, where the African American population was twice the white population. In Lee County, where the jury was all white, Segrest was found not guilty after a deliberation of only seventy-one minutes.

The killing set off weeks of protests and marches by thousands of students and faculty from the Tuskegee Institute (now Tuskegee University) as well as local Black citizens. Student body president Gwendolyn Patton warned at the time, "The students at Tuskegee will tear this town to bits if justice is not sought. If any people out there wish to take us on, we welcome you."[30]

Pages 60–69:

The statement John Lewis delivered at the press conference was read as prepared, and widely disseminated, running in many papers.[31] However, it was not reprinted in SNCC's own paper, *The Student Voice*, since it had ceased production with the December 20, 1965, issue likely due to Julian Bond's election to the Georgia General Assembly.

African Americans made up a disproportionate percentage of Vietnam draftees. According to historian James Westheider, "Between 1965 and 1970, the height of American involvement in Vietnam, Blacks constituted slightly over 11 percent of the draft-eligible population…but represented 14.3 percent of all draftees. During the 382,000-man draft of 1966, over 47,500, or 13.4 percent of the inductees were African Americans. The following year, 37,000 Blacks were drafted, representing over 16 percent of the total."[32]

Making up 31 percent of the combat infantry, African American soldiers in Vietnam were also much more likely than white soldiers to be killed in action. Westheider notes: "African Americans suffered casualties far exceeding their percentage of American military forces in Southeast Asia. Between 1961 and the end of 1965, the death rate for African Americans in the army was 18.3 percent. In 1965, one out of every four American soldiers killed or wounded was Black. By late 1966, basically the first full year of U.S. combat, African Americans accounted for 22 percent of all American casualties. In 1967, Black Americans still comprised over 14 percent of American deaths in Vietnam."[33]

Roy Wilkins, executive director of the NAACP, responded forcefully to SNCC's statement on Vietnam: "The public must be careful to recognize that this statement is one by [...] only one of the many civil rights groups, and is not the statement of other groups or of what is loosely called the civil rights movement."[34] Wilkins then published an op-ed under the headline: "SNCC Speaks Only For SNCC." Wilkins wrote that the statement is:

> [H]ardly the official sentiment of 20 million Negro Americans or of the many organized bodies through which they express their group opinions…In the first years, in its

enthusiasm and naivete, SNCC was contemptuous of all others, black and white, who did not fit a doctrinaire formula of thinking and acting…Obviously, SNCC has considered the possible consequences of the harsh wording of its Vietnam resolution. It has decided that its objectives, stated and implied, are worth the turbulence. But it is important that Americans remember that this document, while an expression of but the smallest of the civil rights groups, is, in some substantial measure, the product of the snail's pace of racial justice in the United States. Intemperate statements on racial matters are shaped, not around conference tables by 23 persons, but by the stubborn hostility of crude or subtle white supremacists.[35]

Julian Bond's words in support of SNCC's position on Vietnam are sourced from his statement to a local radio station, which was included in the Supreme Court decision that allowed Bond to be seated in the Georgia House of Representatives.[36] Below is his statement as it appears in that decision:

Why, I endorse it, first, because I like to think of myself as a pacifist, and one who opposes that war and any other war, and eager and anxious to encourage people not to participate in it for any reason that they choose, and secondly, I agree with this statement because of the reason set forth in it—because I think it is sorta hypocritical for us to maintain that we are fighting for liberty in other places and we are not guaranteeing liberty to citizens inside the continental United States. […]

Well, I think that the fact that the United States Government fights a war in Viet Nam, I don't think that I, as a second-class citizen of the United States, have a requirement to support that war. I think my responsibility is to oppose things that I think are wrong if they are in Viet Nam or New York, or Chicago, or Atlanta, or wherever.

When the interviewer suggested that our involvement in Vietnam was because "if we do not stop Communism there, that it is just a question of where will we stop it next," Bond replied:

Oh, no, I'm not taking a stand against stopping World Communism, and I'm not taking a stand in favor of the Viet Cong. What I'm saying that is, first, that I don't believe in that war. That particular war. I'm against all war. I'm against that war in particular, and I don't think people ought to participate in it. Because I'm against war, I'm against the draft. I think that other countries in the World get along without a draft—England is one—and I don't see why we couldn't, too. […]

…I'm not about to justify that war, because it's stopping International Communism, or whatever— you know, I just happen to have a basic disagreement with wars for whatever reason they are fought… fought to stop International Communism, to promote International Communism, or for whatever reason. I oppose the Viet Cong fighting in Viet Nam as much as I oppose the United States fighting in Viet Nam. I happen to live in the United States. If I lived in North Viet Nam, I might not have the same sort of freedom of expression, but it happens that I live here—not there.

The interviewer also asked Bond if he felt he could take the oath of office required by the Georgia Constitution, and Bond responded that he saw nothing inconsistent between his statements and the oath. Bond was also asked whether he would adhere to his statements if war were declared on North Vietnam and if his statements might become treasonous. He replied that he did not know "if I'm strong enough to place myself in a position where I'd be guilty of treason."

The Supreme Court reversed the lower court's decision saying that "while the State has an interest in requiring its legislators to swear to a belief in constitutional processes of government, surely the oath gives it no interest in limiting its legislators' capacity to discuss their views of local and national policy." The decision was an endorsement that legislators' political speech is protected by the First Amendment.

John Lewis's words lamenting other civil rights organizations' lack of a position on the Vietnam War are sourced from his memoir.[37] **Martin Luther King, Jr.**'s statement on Bond is from *At Canaan's Edge*,[38] and the statements made by representatives in the Georgia General Assembly were sourced from the legislative record of the proceedings.[39]

Pages 70–73:
Images of the march and quotes from Dr. King's speech are based on archived news footage from WSB-TV.[40] The Tom Watson statue was removed from its prominent location at the Georgia State Capitol in 2013. However, the statue was not destroyed; instead, it was moved across the street to a park area known as Talmadge Plaza.[41]

Pages 74–76:
Lewis's comments about America's role as the world's cop and its wartime economy are sourced from a radio interview at that time and included in his memoir.[42] Bond's quote about running again is from his obituary in the *Washington Post*.[43]

Pages 77–84:
The phrases "extremism for the sake for extremism" and "destructive mischief-making" are taken from a *New York Times* editorial titled "Sabotage in Alabama" which stated, "the Student Nonviolent Coordinating Committee's call for Negro voters to boycott the primary is destructive mischief-making. It derives from the same attitude of extremism for the sake of extremism … in the refusal of the Mississippi Freedom Democrats to accept a generous compromise worked out in their behalf at the 1964 Democratic National Convention."[44]

Dr. King's response to Lurleen Wallace's victory is sourced from a *Jet* magazine article that begins: "The Alabama Negro 'laid low his burden' the day of the Democratic primary election and ushered in the most vital phase of the Second Reconstruction. But he awoke the next morning to find that strange and perplexing political entrapments had corroded his vote."[45]

Stokely Carmichael's response to the large turnout in Lowndes County and what it meant for Black separatism is sourced from *At Canaan's Edge*.[46]

Pages 85–97:

Stokely Carmichael was particularly frustrated that John Lewis campaigned for **Richmond Flowers** instead of the LCFO ticket, and **Jack Minnis** "lobbied quietly" for Stokely to run to unseat Lewis.[47]

Bill Ware, a Mississippi native who joined SNCC after spending much of 1964 in Ghana, popularized the idea of Black-only organizations within SNCC. Ware became director of SNCC's Atlanta project when, in January 1966, around the same time SNCC released its statement opposing the Vietnam War, Ware published a paper with input from several Spelman College students arguing that Black people needed all-Black organizations to establish their own identities and directions. Ware's leadership of the Atlanta Project saw success organizing urban areas with Black-only involvement.[48]

Worth "Willy" Long's protest against the reelection of John Lewis as SNCC chairman is based on Lewis's memory of Long "emerging from the darkness," his descriptions of the episode in *Walking with the Wind*, and a 2015 interview with Long. In that interview, Long says:

> I voted for, along with everybody else, by acclamation, John Lewis, for chairman. And everybody felt good because they had been in discussion and some people had gone home to go to sleep because they had been in the SNCC-like discussion which [laughs] is a lifetime. [Laughter] So after the election, I thought that there was a contradiction that existed. One of the contradictions was that people had not talked about what they, what was their platform, what they were going to do. There was an election but there was no discussion about what they were going to do, and even the people who were elected, they were not asked to tell, to commit to doing what people had discussed to do. So basically, I did what the Ms. Hamer and Guyot and people in the Freedom Democratic Party would probably hope that I would do. I said, "I rise as the local people" [laughs] because I was not on paid staff at that time. I was not on paid staff. I thought I had a voice based on my history, and I said, "I rise as the local people" and then I said that I was probably, want to challenge the election… And people voted to do it, to have a discussion of the issues, and in discussing the issues, both Stokely, who was a candidate who had not won, and Lewis, who had won by acclamation [sic], had a discussion. They kind of looked at their discussion, people looked at their discussion as it related to the issues that they faced. The solutions that people proposed, they voted for on the next round based on not who they thought would solve the solution, but what ideas and proposals they thought, within the platforms, would help solve the situation.[49]

Worth's version of the vote differs from the account presented in Branch's *At Canaan's Edge*, where Worth is portrayed as being surprised by the vote and reacting with racial overtones to white staffer Jack Minnis. Branch writes:

> Worth Long of Arkansas, having arrived late from Mississippi with Julius Lester, a quick-witted SNCC worker from Fisk University, gained the floor to ask what just happened, and his awed response silenced the hall. "John Lewis?" Long frowned. "How'd y'all do that? You can't do that." Jack Minnis, who seldom spoke in meetings, vented his frustration that the candid objection came too late to do any good. "Sorry 'bout that, white boss," retorted Long, who jumped from exposed personal ground to a procedural outburst: "I challenge this election!" He accused Forman of allowing the vote to proceed on sentimental regard for Lewis once half the staff members had slipped off to bed. In pandemonium, while some rushed to summon absentees and others fumbled for the bylaws…[50]

Pages 98–108:

The text of the May 16, 1966, SNCC press release regarding its newly elected leadership is available in full at the Civil Rights Movement Archive.[51]

   Floyd McKissick's quotes about nonviolence are found in Lewis Perry's book *Civil Disobedience: An American Tradition.*[52]

   Lewis's overhearing of Sellers's conversation to hijack the Meredith March and Willie Ricks's quote "Black Power for Black people," including the history of the phrase "Black Power," are also from *Walking with the Wind.*[53]

   Stokely Carmichael's speech about Black Power is sourced from a *New York Times* article,[54] and the dialogue is a composite from that article, *At Canaan's Edge*,[55] and *Walking With the Wind.*[56]

   Vice President **Hubert Humphrey**'s reaction comes from a speech he made at the 1966 NAACP national convention.[57]

   Martin Luther King, Jr.'s full quote follows: "[Black Power] had a ready appeal. Immediately, however, I had reservations about its use. I had the deep feeling that it was an unfortunate choice of words for a slogan."[58]

   Roy Wilkins's quote comes from his 1966 keynote address to the NAACP's annual convention,[59] and **Bayard Rustin**'s quote comes from an essay he published in *Commentary* that year.[60]

   In the fall of 1966, after four months as chairman of SNCC, Stokely Carmichael published a wide-ranging article in the *New York Review of Books* titled "What We Want,"[61] in which he describes, among other things, how he believed the use of nonviolent tactics led to the riots in Watts and elsewhere. Carmichael wrote:

> One of the tragedies of the struggle against racism is that up to now there has been no national organization which could speak to the growing militancy of young Black people in the urban ghetto. There has been only a civil rights movement, whose tone of voice was adapted to an audience of liberal whites. It served as a sort of buffer zone between them and angry young Blacks. None of its so-called leaders could go into a rioting community and be listened to. In a sense, I blame ourselves—together with the mass media—for what has happened in Watts, Harlem, Chicago, Cleveland, Omaha. Each time the people in those cities saw Martin Luther King get slapped, they became angry; when they saw four little Black girls bombed to death, they were angrier; and when nothing happened, they were steaming. We had nothing to offer that they could see, except to go out and be beaten again. We helped to build their frustration.

Pages 109–115:

John Lewis's quotes from the rally in Canton, Mississippi are from *Walking with the Wind.*[62]

   Martin Luther King, Jr.'s frustrated comments about President Johnson are sourced from an interview with journalist Paul Good in Canton.[63] Protestors had recently been gassed with tear gas, and the White House press secretary refused to condemn the police attack.

SOURCES

1 John Lewis, *Walking with the Wind: A Memoir of the Movement* (New York: Simon & Schuster, 1998), 368.

2 Taylor Branch, *At Canaan's Edge: America in the King Years, 1965–68* (New York: Simon & Schuster, 2006), 272–73.

3 Ari Berman, *Give Us the Ballot: The Model Struggle for Voting Rights in America* (New York: Farrar, Straus and Giroux, 2015), 37.

4 Tom Brokaw, various newsfilm clips, WSB-TV, Atlanta, GA, July–August, 1965, Walter J. Brown Media Archives and Peabody Awards Collection, University of Georgia Libraries.

5 Bill Shipp, "Klan Leader Suggests Biracial Council Settle Protests at Americus, 700 Pay Tribute to Slain Boy," *Atlanta Constitution*, August 9, 1965.

6 Associated Press, "Negroes, Klansmen in Marches: 22 Arrested in Americus," *Hartford Courant*, August 9, 1965.

7 Robert Mcg. Thomas Jr., "Calvin F. Craig, 64, Enigma In Klan and Civil Rights Work," *New York Times*, April 24, 1998, nytimes.com/1998/04/24/us/calvin-f-craig-64-enigma-in-klan-and-civil-rights-work.html.

8 Michael Szymanski, "How Legacy of the Watts Riot Consumed, Ruined Man's Life," *Orlando Sentinel*, August 5, 1990, orlandosentinel.com/news/os-xpm-1990-08-05-9008031131-story.html.

9 Burt A. Folkart, "Marquette Frye, Whose Arrest Ignited the Watts Riots in 1965, Dies at Age 42," *Los Angeles Times*, December 25, 1986.

10 John Lewis, "Statement by John Lewis on Los Angeles and Chicago" (Atlanta: Student Nonviolent Coordinating Committee, August 16, 1965), content.wisconsinhistory.org/digital/collection/p15932coll2/id/68190.

11 Student Nonviolent Coordinating Committee, "Founding Statement" (Raleigh, NC: Student Nonviolent Coordinating Committee, April 15–17, 1960), crmvet.org/docs/sncc1.htm.

12 Student Nonviolent Coordinating Committee, "Who Does What in Atlanta," internal staff memo, n.d., library.duke.edu/digitalcollections/snccdigitalgateway/sncc_atlanta_ofc.pdf.

13 Student Nonviolent Coordinating Committee, "First Report on Shooting from Lowndes County," internal reports, August 20, 1965, crmvet.org/docs/650820_sncc_daniels.pdf.

14 Ruby Sales, interview by Jean Wiley and Bruce Hartford, September 2005, crmvet.org/nars/rubysale.htm#rubyjonathan.

15 Branch, *At Canaan's Edge,* 291, 303–4.

16 Jimmy Rogers et al., "Fear, Courage, and Commitment in the Freedom Movement" (panel discussion at *Past and Present: A Gathering with Freedom Movement Veterans* at Stanford University, Stanford, California, April 11, 2015), crmvet.org/disc/1504_fcc.htm).

17 Hasan Kwame Jeffries, *Bloody Lowndes: Civil Rights and Black Power in Alabama's Black Belt* (New York: NYU Press, 2010), 81–82.

18 Equal Justice Initiative, "Segregation in America," 2018, segregationinamerica.eji.org.

19 Strom Thurmond (SC). "Civil Rights Act of 1964," Congressional Record 110 (June 18, 1964), 14–311.

20 Bruce Hartford, "Civil Rights Movement History Mississippi Freedom Summer Events," Civil Rights Movement Archive, crmvet.org/tim/tim64b.htm#1964atlantic.

21 John Lewis and Andrew Aydin, *March: Book Three* (Marietta, GA: Top Shelf, 2016), 106–113.

22 Student Nonviolent Coordinating Committee, staff meeting minutes, November 24-29, 1966, crmvet.org/docs/6511_sncc_staff_min.pdf.

23 Alfred Hassler and Benton Resnik, *Martin Luther King and the Montgomery Story* (Nyack, NY: Fellowship of Reconciliation, 1957), rmvet.org/docs/ms_for_comic.pdf.

24 Courtland Cox and Jennifer Lawson, *Political Education Primer* (Lowndes County Freedom Organization, 1966), crmvet.org/docs/lcfo-pe.htm.

25 Courtland Cox and Jennifer Lawson, "The Reason for the Lowndes County Comics" (forthcoming).

26 Lowndes County Freedom Organization, pamphlet, 1966, docspopuli.org/articles/Yuen/BPP_logo.html.

27 James Forman, *Sammy Younge, Jr.: The First Black College Student to Die in the Black Liberation Movement* (New York: Grove Press, 1968).

28 Bruce Hartford, "The Murder of Sammy Younge (Jan)," Civil Rights Movement Archive, crmvet.org/tim/timhis66.htm#1966younge.

29 U.S. Department of Justice Civil Rights Division, "Notice to Close File No. 144-2-1431" (Washington, DC: U.S. Department of Justice, 2011), justice.gov/crt/case-document/marvin-l-segrest-samuel-l-younge-jr-notice-close-file.

30 Mary Ellen Gale, "Killing of Rights Worker Jolts Tuskegee Students," *Southern Courier,* January 8–9, 1966, southerncourier.org/standard/Vol2_No02_1966_01_08.pdf.

31 Student Nonviolent Coordinating Committee, "Statement on Vietnam," (Atlanta, GA: Student Nonviolent Coordinating Committee, January 6, 1966), snccdigital.org/inside-sncc/policy-statements/vietnam.

32 James Westheider, *Fighting on Two Fronts, African Americans and the Vietnam War* (New York University Press, 1997), 20.

33 James Westheider, *The African American Experience in Vietnam: Brothers in Arms* (Lanham, MD.: Rowman & Littlefield Publishers, 2008), 47–48.

34 Associated Press, "NAACP Disagrees on Vietnam: Disclaims SNCC Blast," *Lincoln Journal Star,* January 8, 1966.

35 Roy Wilkins, "SNCC Speaks Only For SNCC," *Journal Herald* (Dayton, OH), January 15, 1966.

36 *Bond v. Floyd*, 385 U.S. 116 (1966).

37 Lewis, *Walking with the Wind*, 376.

38 Branch, *At Canaan's Edge*, 409.

39 *Georgia General Assembly House of Representatives Journal,* January 10, 1966.

40 Martin Luther King, Jr., newsfilm clip, WSB-TV, Atlanta, GA, January 14, 1966, Civil Rights Digital Library (clip: 49971), University of Georgia.

41 Kristina Torres, "Tom Watson statue removed from Georgia's Capitol steps," *Atlanta Journal-Constitution*, November 30, 2013, ajc.com/news/tom-watson-statue-removed-from-georgia-capitol-steps/lXsGyKnHtKqWHvabgEzNVP.

42 Lewis, *Walking with the Wind*, 380.

43 Matt Schudel and Victoria St. Martin, "Julian Bond, charismatic civil rights figure, dies at 75," *Washington Post*, August 16, 2015, washingtonpost.com/national/julian-bond-charismatic-civil-rights-figure-and-naacp-leader-dies-at-75/2015/08/16/8c7eebaa-4424-11e5-846d-02792f854297_story.html.

44 "Sabotage in Alabama," *New York Times*, April 21, 1966.

45 Chester Higgins, "Ala. Negro Vote 'Strange,' " *Jet*, May 19, 1966.

46 Branch, *At Canaan's Edge*, 464.

47 Branch, *At Canaan's Edge*, 465.

48 Bill Ware, "Black Power" (Atlanta, GA: SNCC Vine City Project, 1966), wcadatadashboard.iac.gatech.edu/library/files/original/2d33e635abe2e20e614ff8ef077ec05b.pdf.

49 Worth Long, interview by Emilye Crosby, December 6, 2015, Civil Rights History Project, Southern Oral History Program, Smithsonian Institution's National Museum of African American History and Culture and the Library of Congress, tile.loc.gov/storage-services/service/afc/afc2010039/afc2010039_crhp0122/afc2010039_crhp0122_ms01.pdf.

50 Branch, *At Canaan's Edge*, 466.

51 Student Nonviolent Coordinating Committee, press release regarding spring conference and leadership election (May 16, 1966), crmvet.org/docs/pr/660516_sncc_pr_stokely.pdf.

52 Lewis Perry, *Civil Disobedience: An American Tradition* (New Haven, CT: Yale University Press, 2013), 243.

53 Lewis, *Walking with the Wind*, 388.

54 Gene Roberts, "Mississippi Reduces Police Protection for Marchers," *New York Times*, June 17, 1966.

55 Branch, *At Canaan's Edge*, 486–87.

56 Lewis, *Walking with the Wind*, 388.

57 Hubert Humphrey, "Speech at the NAACP National Convention," (Los Angeles, CA, July 6, 1966), efootage.com/videos/71346/hubert-humphrey-racism.

58 Martin Luther King, Jr., *The Martin Luther King, Jr. Companion: Quotations from the Speeches, Essays, and Books of Martin Luther King, Jr.* (New York: St. Martin's Press, 1998), 77.

59 John Hollitz, *Contending Voices, Volume II: Since 1865* (Belmont, CA: Wadsworth Publishing, 2010), 217.

60 Bayard Rustin, "Black Power and Coalition Politics," *Commentary*, September 1966.

61 Stokely Carmichael. "What We Want," *New York Review of Books*, September 22, 1966, nybooks.com/articles/1966/09/22/what-we-want.

62 Lewis, *Walking with the Wind*, 390.

63 John Dittmer. *Local People: The Struggle for Civil Rights in Mississippi* (Champaign, IL: University of Illinois Press, 1995), 401.

FROM THE ARTIST

Working on a nonfiction story, particularly one with such weighty subject matter as *Run*, presented unique challenges. The task of keeping things historically accurate led to late nights combing through online listings of items such as period-appropriate typewriters, searching for a photo at just the right angle. It raised many questions, some as trivial as *when were Post-it notes invented?* and other questions to which the answers were not so straightforward: *How do we sufficiently convey the horror of these events while maintaining journalistic integrity?*

Very early on, I worried that any amount of artistic interpretation would invalidate the reality of the events portrayed. I soon found that the goals of portraying these events as accurately as possible, and capturing the horrors undergone by so many, were one and the same.

Thanks to the tremendous efforts to record and preserve the history of the Movement by numerous sources such as crmvet.org, the SNCC Digital Gateway, and others, there are thousands of photos, videos, and other documentation available to help us create as complete a picture as possible. Creative license was used sparingly, and only after having consulted research materials for historical representation. No exaggeration was needed to convey the emotional impact of these scenes, the best direction coming from the very images of the Movement itself.

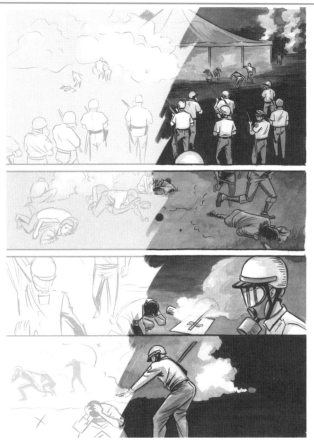

Panels 1–2 are referenced from photos of the June 23, 1966, events in Canton, Mississippi, while panel 3 was constructed from compiled accounts. The final panel is a visual homage to footage of John Lewis from "Bloody Sunday" in Selma, Alabama, on March 7, 1965. I set up the page to show the original layout on the left side and the final inks on the right (page 109).

This drawing is based on photos from John Lewis's office (page 97).

SETTING THE SCENE

Fashion is not static. It is constantly evolving, so it was important to consider not just the trends of the 1960s but the staples carried over from decades prior. Age, occupation, socioeconomic status, and more were taken into consideration when deciding how to dress the people on the page. Young people, especially college students, would likely embrace newer trends, while older generations might opt for a more established look.

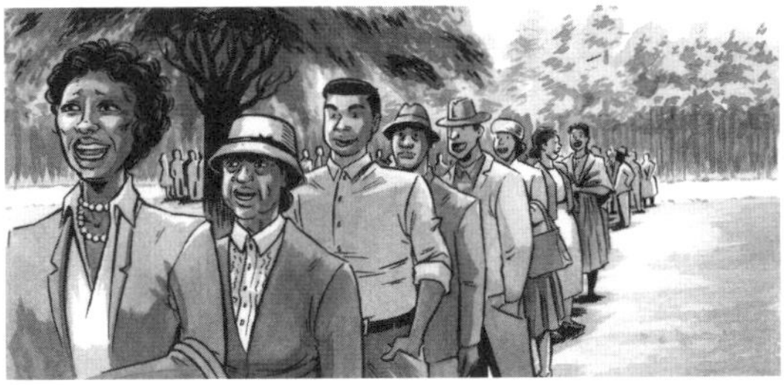

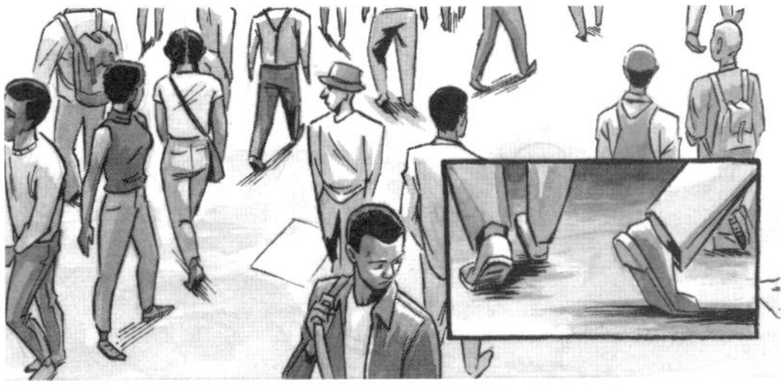

(ABOVE LEFT) This panel features examples of clothing and hairstyles on older voters waiting at a rural polling place (page 83). (ABOVE RIGHT) When John Lewis spoke to a crowd of disillusioned young activists, I had them wearing more casual clothing and natural hair. As this takes place later in the book, I wanted the more "modern" fashion to serve as a visual representation of the evolution of the movement (page 111).

Socioeconomic status had to be taken into account as well, and one method was through the cars featured. For the SNCC conference in Tennessee, since many attendees were students, older car models from the 1950s or even earlier were referenced (page 96).

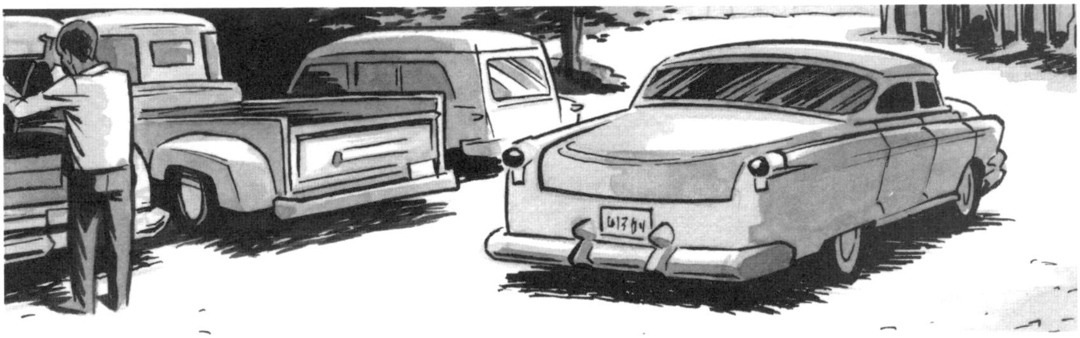

(RIGHT) The cars often featured wear and tear to further signal the lived events of the vehicles and their drivers (page 10).

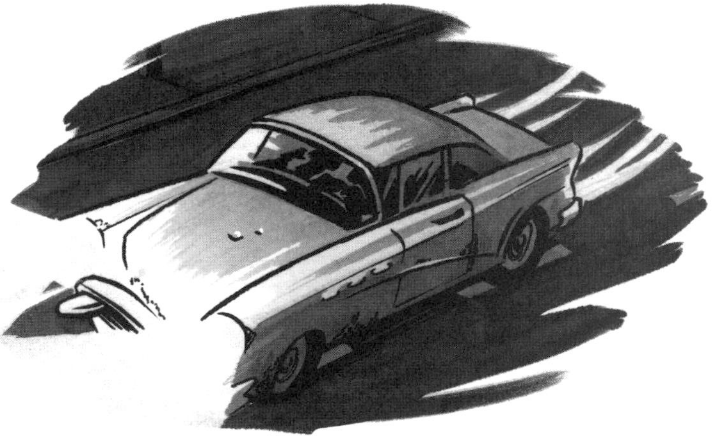

LIFE INTO ART

Because it can be so comfortable to only view the world via our own biases, it was crucial for me to check in with my references regularly and, where possible, the actual persons whose stories I was illustrating.

With the first sketch at right, I had been working from a single photo of Jennifer Lawson and my own flawed presumption of what the LCFO headquarters might have looked like. After generous guidance and additional reference from Ms. Lawson herself, the updated panel was far more reflective of her actual experience.

In retrospect, it is easy to forget how young many of these activists were, knowing the lasting impact they have had. This assumption is what led to my giving her professional equipment, at first, neglecting that many in the Movement were still students.

The comics that came out of the LCFO, created by Courtland Cox and Jennifer Lawson, were a testament to the power graphic storytelling had in the Movement—power that is still felt today.

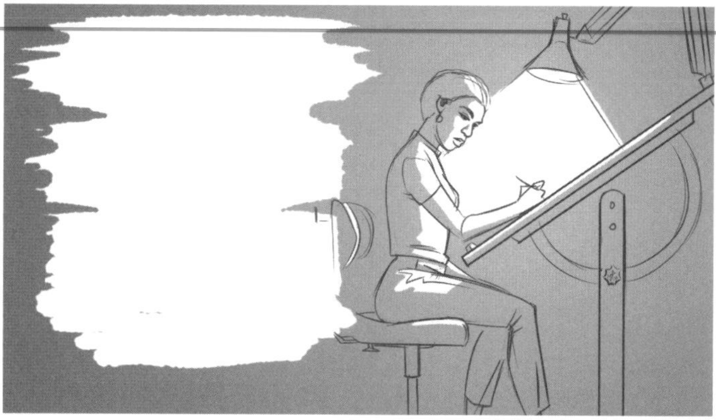

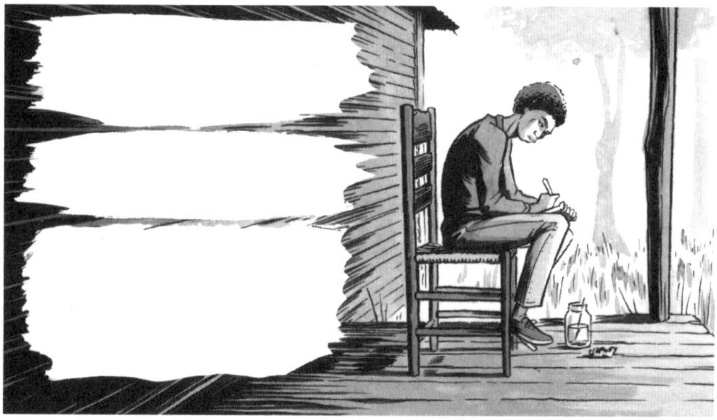

(TOP) The original layout: a sterile and overly formal environment (page 46).
(BOTTOM) Final art (page 46).

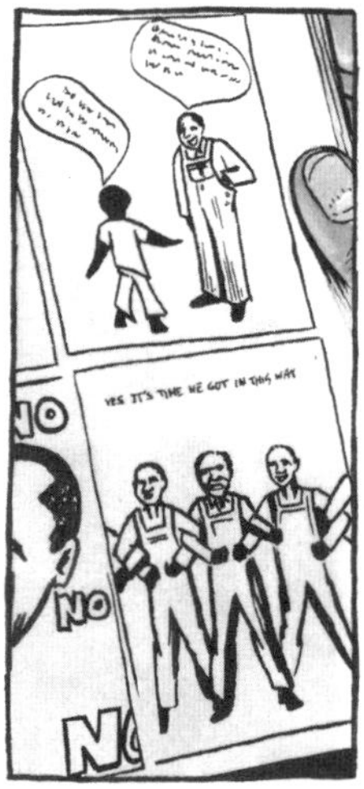
YES IT'S TIME WE GOT IN THIS WAY
NO
NO

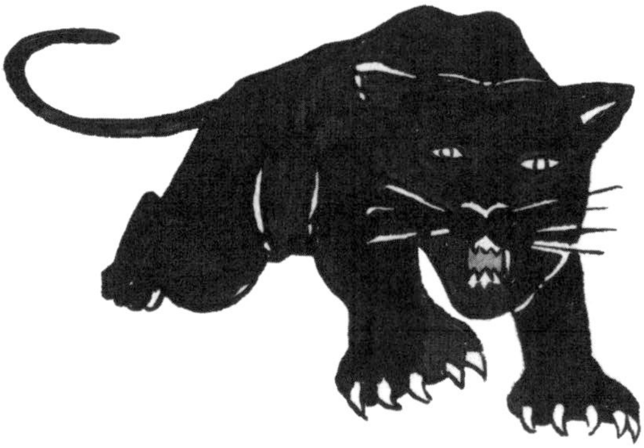

Re-created art from the LCFO comics, including the Black Panther logo used by the organization (page 82).

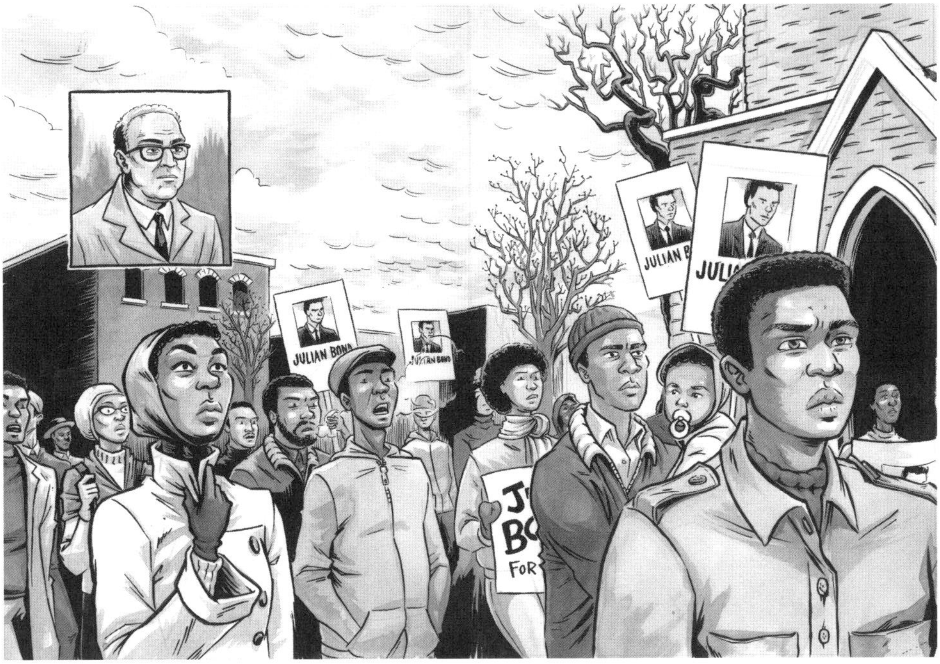

Wherever possible, I wanted to draw upon the likenesses of people in the reference photos and footage we had, both to keep the scene as realistic as possible, and as a way to honor the countless persons involved in the Movement. The task of drawing a realistic likeness and the task of creating a comic book character from scratch are two very different processes producing very different results. I greatly underestimated the challenge of combining the two! Photos from this time period tended to be face shots, front and center, so I sometimes had to imagine a person's face from an angle I did not have direct reference for. For John Lewis, I wanted to strike a delicate balance between Nate Powell's style and my own, while still capturing Lewis's likeness.

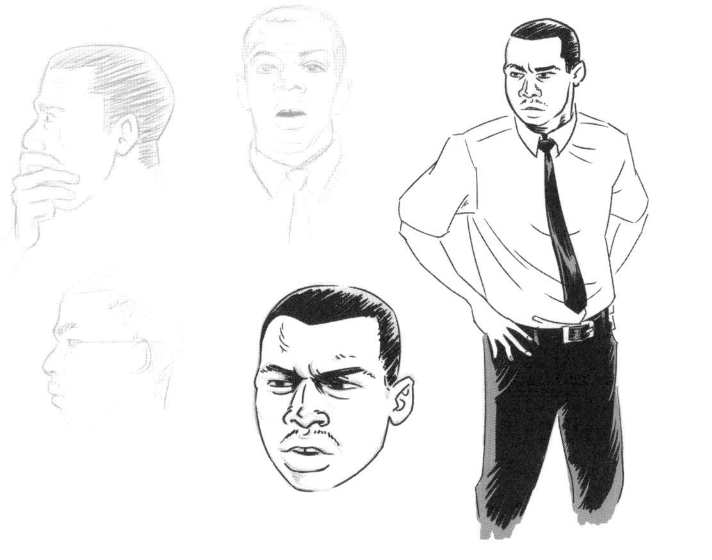

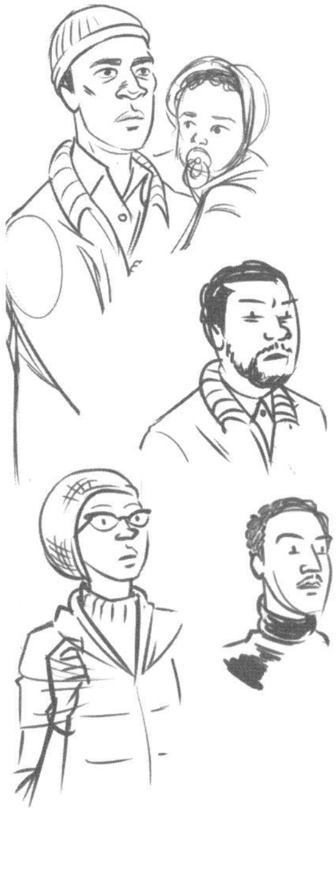

(ABOVE) Early character studies of John Lewis. (RIGHT) The persons depicted in the spread at top are inspired by footage of actual marchers at the event. (TOP) The original version of the spread detailing the march for Julian Bond in Atlanta, Georgia, on January 14, 1966 (pages 70–71).

ACKNOWLEDGMENTS

This book is framed by, and consumed by, loss. The lives lost through senseless racist violence, the battles lost by John Lewis and his colleagues in their struggle for systemic change, and, in the immediate sense of my own life, the losses of those I hold most dear. In the course of writing this book, my mother, my grandmother, and Congressman Lewis all passed away. I never could have imagined so much of my world could simply disappear in such a short time.

But in that loss, I think I have begun to understand Congressman Lewis's strength more clearly. To keep going after losing the chairmanship of SNCC, to keep going after the loss of Dr. King and Robert Kennedy, to keep going when it seemed like no matter what he accomplished in the past, the future held only tragedy and struggle—that is the immeasurable courage that we all must find.

As the congressman would say, our struggle is not the struggle of a day, a week, a month, or a year, it is the struggle of a lifetime. For every moment I witnessed the congressman receive public adulation, I witnessed countless more of him doing the hard, necessary work to create the climate and the environment for change. And through this book, and others, we carry on the work of bearing witness, of sensitizing ever-younger generations to the oppressive legacy of American bigotry and racism so that we may one day see emerge the "Beloved Community" that John Lewis fought and bled for. But we must have the courage to keep going.

I am grateful to L. Fury, Nate Powell, Lauren Sankovitch, Chris Ross, Vaughn Shinall, Kelly Sue DeConnick, Matt Fraction, Valentine De Landro, and Turner Lobey for the countless hours of work and support you put into making this important book, as well as the emotional support to carry me through it, no matter how bleak the world seemed. I cannot begin to say how proud I am of this team and all that we have to look forward to from them in the future.

Thank you to Jeffrey Posternak, Mia Vitale, and the Wylie Agency for your hard work, kindness, and for always having my back. Thank you to Andrew Smith, Charlie Kochman, Charlotte Greenbaum, and everyone at Abrams ComicArts for giving us a new home that is unafraid to embrace bold and innovative ideas. Thank you, Tom Spurgeon.

Thank you to Congressman Lewis for all you've done for the world. You were many things to many people, but as for me, I am most thankful for your mentorship, your kindness, for being the closest thing I ever had to a father, and for taking the leap with me into this wild comics world.

And thank you, Mama. None of this would have been possible without you.

Andrew Aydin

I will forever be grateful to Congressman John Lewis, Andrew Aydin, and everyone at Good Trouble for taking a chance on me and giving me a sense of purpose in a world I often feel powerless to change. A special thanks to Lauren Sankovitch for her guidance and cheerleading. To Nate Powell: Thank you for your inspiring work on the *March* series, and for your generosity and moral support during the making of *Run*. You're a tough act to follow, but I wouldn't have it any other way.

Thank you to my parents for a lifetime of love, encouragement, humor, and hard work; to my sister, for her company during the late-night grinds; and to Jesse, for wading through the sludge with me. This would not have happened without you.

To everyone doing the difficult, vulnerable work of sharing their experiences and opening hearts and minds, and the people quietly doing that work inside themselves: Thank you.

L. Fury

I'm so thankful for the friendship and inspiration of Congressman Lewis and his lifelong efforts toward a more just, humane society, and for his trust in this creative team's work bringing these experiences—this shared history—back into the light with new urgency. Thanks to my collaborators Andrew Aydin, L. Fury, and Chris Ross; the editorial and publishing wizards at Good Trouble and Abrams ComicArts: Lauren Sankovitch, Charlie Kochman, Kelly Sue DeConnick, and Matt Fraction; Leigh Walton, Top Shelf/IDW, and Charlie Olsen. My work couldn't be done without the support and inspiration of Rachel, Harper, and Everly. This is dedicated to all who actively work against the forces of white supremacy, and to the unrecognized, everyday foot soldiers of organized, nonviolent protest movements across the globe.

Nate Powell

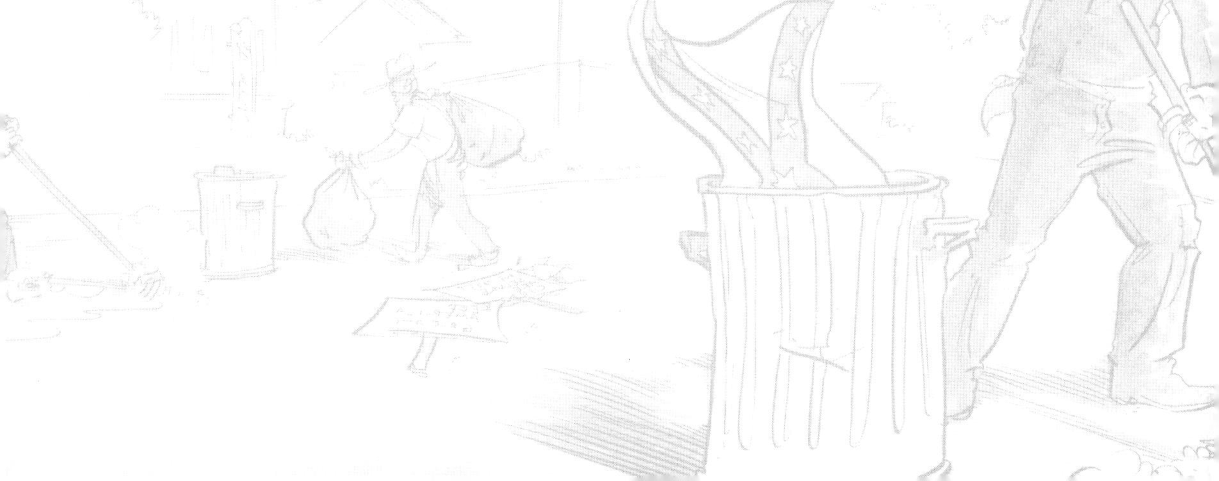

ABOUT THE AUTHORS

JOHN LEWIS (1940–2020) served as the U.S. Representative for Georgia's fifth congressional district from 1987 until his passing in 2020 and was an American icon widely known for his role in the civil rights movement.

The 1Point8

As a student at American Baptist Theological Seminary in 1959, Lewis organized sit-in demonstrations at segregated lunch counters in Nashville, Tennessee. In 1961, he volunteered to participate in the Freedom Rides, which challenged segregation at interstate bus terminals across the South. He was beaten severely by angry mobs and arrested by police for challenging the injustice of Jim Crow segregation in the South.

From 1963 to 1966, Lewis was Chairman of the Student Nonviolent Coordinating Committee (SNCC). As head of SNCC, Lewis became a nationally recognized figure, dubbed one of the "Big Six" leaders of the civil rights movement. At the age of twenty-three, he was an architect of and a keynote speaker at the historic March on Washington in August 1963.

In 1964, John Lewis coordinated SNCC efforts to organize voter registration drives and community action programs during the Mississippi Freedom Summer. The following year, Lewis helped spearhead one of the most seminal moments of the civil rights movement. Together with Hosea Williams, another notable civil rights leader, John Lewis led over six hundred peaceful, orderly protesters across the Edmund Pettus Bridge in Selma, Alabama, on March 7, 1965. They intended to march from Selma to Montgomery to demonstrate the need for voting rights in the state. The marchers were attacked by Alabama state troopers in a brutal confrontation that became known as "Bloody Sunday." News broadcasts and photographs revealing the senseless cruelty of the segregated South helped hasten the passage of the Voting Rights Act of 1965.

Despite enduring physical attacks, serious injuries, and more than forty arrests, John Lewis remained a devoted advocate of the philosophy of nonviolence. After leaving SNCC in 1966, he continued to work for civil rights, first as associate director of the Field Foundation, then with the Southern Regional Council, where he became executive director of the Voter Education Project (VEP). In 1977, Lewis was appointed by President Jimmy Carter to direct more than 250,000 volunteers of ACTION, the federal volunteer agency. In 1981, Lewis was elected to the Atlanta City Council. He was elected to the U.S. House of Representatives in November 1986 and represented Georgia's fifth district until his passing in 2020.

In 2011, Lewis was awarded the Medal of Freedom by President Barack Obama. Lewis's 1998 memoir, *Walking with the Wind: A Memoir of the Movement*, won numerous honors, including the Robert F. Kennedy, Lillian Smith, and Anisfield-Wolf Book Awards. His subsequent book, *Across That Bridge: Life Lessons and a Vision for Change* (2012), won the NAACP Image Award. *March*, a graphic novel series co-written with Andrew Aydin and illustrated by Nate Powell, chronicles Lewis's civil rights work and received numerous awards including the National Book Award—a first for both comics and a congressperson.

Lewis passed away on July 17, 2020, at his home in Atlanta. He is survived by his son, John Miles.

ANDREW AYDIN, an Atlanta native, served for more than thirteen years on the staff of Congressman John Lewis, predominantly serving as digital director and policy advisor. In 2008, after learning that his boss had been inspired as a young man by the 1957 comic book *Martin Luther King and The Montgomery Story,* Aydin conceived the *March* trilogy and began collaborating with Rep. Lewis to write it, while also composing a master's thesis on the history and impact of *Martin Luther King and The Montgomery Story.* Additionally, Aydin served as communications director and press secretary during Rep. Lewis's 2008 and 2010 re-election campaigns, as district aide to Rep. John Larson (D-CT), and as special assistant to Connecticut Lt. Governor Kevin Sullivan. Today, Aydin continues to write comics and lecture about nonviolent civil disobedience and the history of comics in the civil rights movement. Aydin is a graduate of the Lovett School in Atlanta, Trinity College in Hartford, and Georgetown University in Washington, DC.

The 1Point8

Visit andrewaydin.com for more information.

A lifelong resident of Houston, Texas, **L. FURY**'s interest in visual storytelling blossomed in high school. She received her BFA in Animation from Sam Houston State University in 2010. After a stint in the gaming industry and then marketing, Fury dove into comics full time in 2015 with humor webcomic *Bastard Comics*, self-publishing several longer comics including *Etiquette for the Modern Lady* and *Another F★cking Stan Lee Cameo*, and contributing to the *Launch Party* anthology. She then shifted her sights to long-form comics, illustrating the unreleased *Double Barrel Shogun. Run: Book One* is Fury's first graphic novel.

Visit L-Fury.com for more information.

Christopher Lee

NATE POWELL is the first cartoonist ever to win the National Book Award. His work includes *Save It For Later,* the *March* trilogy, *Come Again,* viral comic essay *About Face, Two Dead, Any Empire, Swallow Me Whole,* and *The Silence of Our Friends.* Powell's work has also received the Robert F. Kennedy Book Award, three Eisner Awards, two Ignatz Awards, the Michael L. Printz Award, and the Comic-Con International Inkpot Award. He has discussed his work at the United Nations, on MSNBC's *The Rachel Maddow Show,* PBS, CNN, and Free Speech TV. Powell lives in Bloomington, Indiana.

Visit seemybrotherdance.org for more information.

Ben Rains

CONGRESSMAN JOHN LEWIS was my friend, my boss, my coauthor, and my mentor. He was my hero and my leader. Knowing him changed my life, as it did for so many of us. His words and actions changed our nation and made it a better, fairer, and more just place for all who have been left out and left behind. And he was never afraid to take risks for the causes he believed in. He often said, "Once you lose your sense of fear, only then are you truly free."

It was his mission to tell the story of the civil rights movement and to serve as a living reminder of all those who gave the last full measure of devotion to this country so that we may one day redeem the soul of America and build the "Beloved Community." In service to that mission, Congressman Lewis took a chance on a young man with a big idea—that he should write a comic book about the movement. That idea—*March*—took on a life of its own, and Congressman Lewis embraced it wholeheartedly. Together with artist Nate Powell, we barnstormed across America, speaking at schools, libraries, comic conventions—anywhere we could go to spread our message. Congressman Lewis cosplayed—as himself—and we led dozens of children on marches at the San Diego Comic-Con. He crowd-surfed on *The Late Show with Stephen Colbert*. And, ultimately, he prevailed. In 2016, *March: Book Three* became the first graphic novel to win the National Book Award, and the books are now some of the most widely taught graphic novels in America.

But the question of how to explain what happened after Selma always nagged at us. It made sense to end the *March* series there. But it did not make sense to stop telling the story through comics. So in 2017 we set out to make *Run*. The idea was simple: First you *March*, then you *Run*—just as John Lewis had in his own life. He felt—and *we* felt—that we had to keep going. We had to keep telling the story. We had to explain what happened next. Progress never moves in a straight line. Too many people did not understand the forces that gathered to attack and weaken the Voting Rights Act almost immediately after its passage. And today the attacks on voting rights continue and bear an all-too-familiar pedigree, like those Congressman Lewis faced in Alabama, Mississippi, Georgia, and elsewhere during the early days of the civil rights movement.

So, we kept going. We went back to work. And we wrote more comics together. With each new page he saw, the congressman became more and more excited to get back out on the road, to go back to Comic-Con, and to visit his beloved librarians. When I asked him if he worried how some people might react to these books—some parts remain controversial to this day—he said simply, "No, not at all. It's what happened. We have to tell the story."

But the Lord Almighty or the Spirit of History had other plans for us.

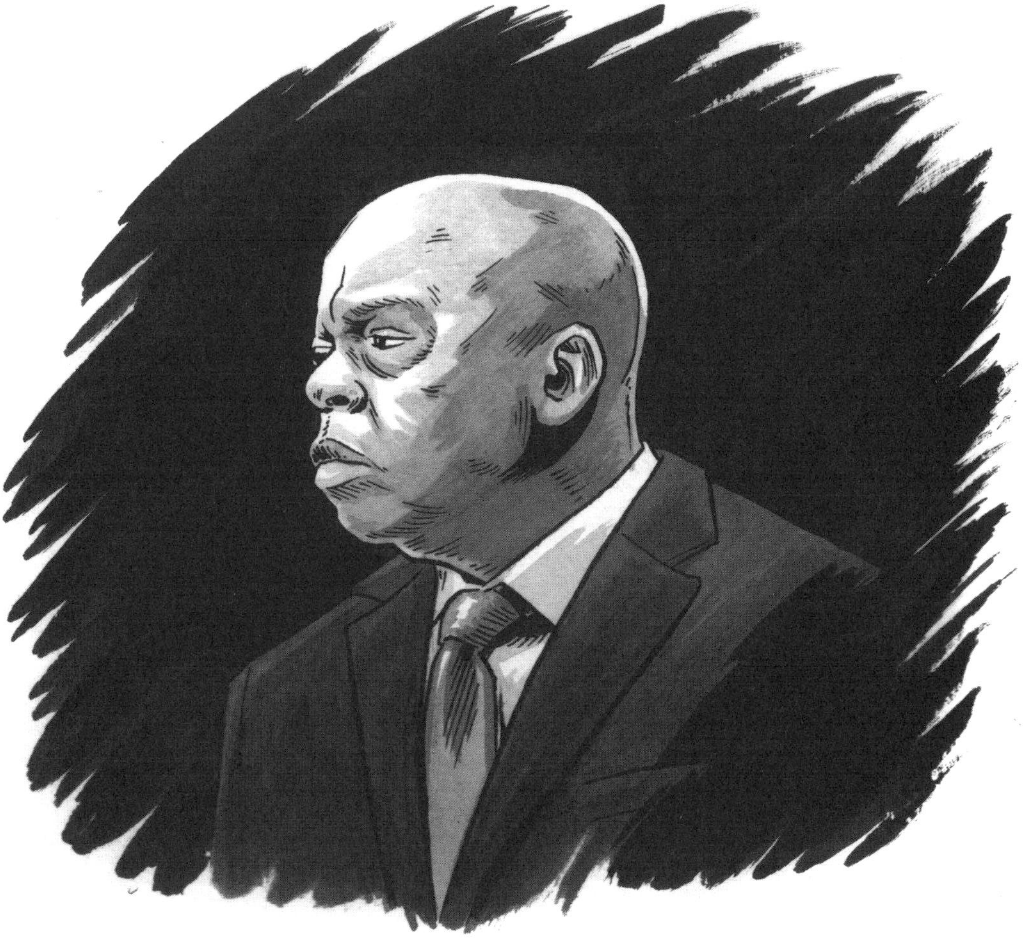

Not a day goes by where I don't think of him or hear his voice in my mind. And I know what he would tell us to do. Keep going. Keep pushing. Keep pulling. Keep speaking up and speaking out. Tell the story. Tell the whole story. Make it plain. Make it real. Our struggle is not the struggle of a day, a week, a month, or a year.

It is the struggle of a lifetime.

Now it is our turn to carry the unbelievable weight he bore on his shoulders for so long. It is our turn to use our bodies to hold up this house—the American house—that he loved so deeply. We must be unafraid. We must have courage—raw courage. And we must carry on his work to build the Beloved Community.

Andrew Aydin
November 2020
Washington, DC

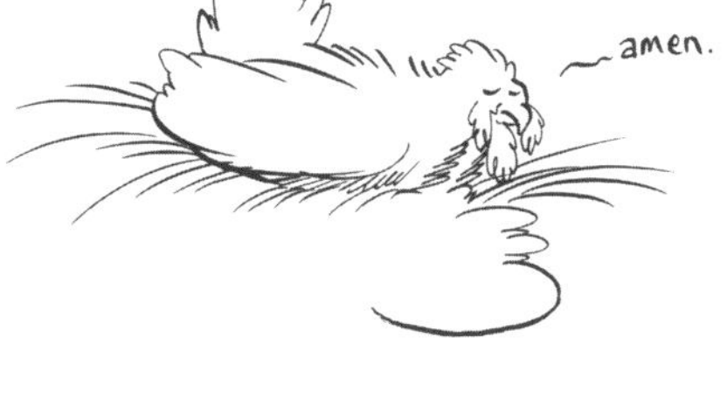
~amen.

PRAISE FOR THE *MARCH* TRILOGY

March: Book One	*March: Book Two*	*March: Book Three*	*March* (Trilogy Slipcase Set)
128 pages, $14.95 (US)	192 pages, $19.95 (US)	256 pages, $19.99 (US)	Three volumes, $49.99 (US)
ISBN: 978-1-60309-300-2	ISBN: 978-1-60309-400-9	ISBN: 978-1-60309-402-3	ISBN: 978-1-60309-395-8

#1 *New York Times* and *Washington Post* Bestseller
National Book Award
Coretta Scott King Book Award
Michael L. Printz Award
Will Eisner Comic Industry Award
Robert F. Kennedy Book Award—Special Recognition
Robert F. Sibert Informational Book Medal
YALSA Nonfiction Award
Walter Dean Myers Award
Flora Stieglitz Straus Award
YALSA's Outstanding Books for the College Bound
***Reader's Digest*'s Graphic Novels Every Grown-Up Should Read**
Added to New York City Schools curriculum and taught in over 40 states
Selected for college and university reading programs across America

"Congressman John Lewis has been a resounding moral voice in the quest for equality for more than 50 years, and I'm so pleased that he is sharing his memories of the civil rights movement with America's young leaders. In *March*, he brings a whole new generation with him across the Edmund Pettus Bridge, from a past of clenched fists into a future of outstretched hands."

—President Bill Clinton

"With *March*, Congressman John Lewis takes us behind the scenes of some of the most pivotal moments of the civil rights movement. In graphic novel form, his first-hand account makes these historic events both accessible and relevant to an entire new generation of Americans."

—LeVar Burton

"*March* is one of the most important graphic novels ever created—an extraordinary presentation of an extraordinary life, and proof that young people can change the world. I'm stunned by the power of these comics, and grateful that Congressman Lewis's story will enlighten and inspire future generations of readers and leaders." **—Raina Telgemeier**

"Powell captures the danger and tension in stunning cinematic spreads, which dramatically complement Lewis's powerful story…The story of the civil rights movement is a triumphant one, but Lewis's account is full of nuance and personal struggle, both of which impart an empowering human element to an often mythologized period of history…this is a must-read."

—*Booklist*, starred review

"A powerful tale of courage and principle igniting sweeping social change, told by a strong-minded, uniquely qualified eyewitness…The heroism of those who sat and marched…comes through with vivid, inspiring clarity." —***Kirkus Reviews***, starred review

"Lewis's remarkable life has been skillfully translated into graphics…Segregation's insult to personhood comes across here with a visual, visceral punch. This version of Lewis's life story belongs in libraries to teach readers about the heroes of America." —***Library Journal***, starred review

"Superbly told history." —***Publishers Weekly***, starred review

"This memoir puts a human face on a struggle that many students will primarily know from textbooks…Visually stunning, the black-and-white illustrations convey the emotions of this turbulent time…This insider's view of the civil rights movement should be required reading for young and old; not to be missed." —***School Library Journal***, starred review

"*March* provides a potent reminder that the sit-ins, far from being casually assembled, were well-coordinated, disciplined events informed by a rigorous philosophy…Likely to prove inspirational to readers for years to come." —***Barnes and Noble Review***

"When a graphic novel tries to interest young readers in an important topic, it often feels forced. Not so with the exhilarating *March*…Powerful words and pictures." —***Boston Globe***

"The civil rights movement can seem to some like a distant memory…John Lewis refreshes our memories in dramatic fashion." —***Chicago Tribune***

"*March* offers a poignant portrait of an iconic figure that both entertains and edifies, and deserves to be placed alongside other historical graphic memoirs like *Persepolis* and *Maus*." —***Entertainment Weekly***

"In a new graphic memoir, the civil rights leader shows youth how to get in trouble—good trouble." —***In These Times***

"An astonishingly accomplished graphic memoir that brings to life a vivid portrait of the civil rights era, Lewis's extraordinary history and accomplishments, and the movement he helped lead…Its power, accessibility and artistry destine it for awards, and a well-deserved place at the pinnacle of the comics canon." —**NPR**

"Emphasizing disruption, decentralization and cooperation over the mythic ascent of heroic leaders, this graphic novel's presentation of civil rights is startlingly contemporary." —***New York Times***

"A riveting chronicle of Lewis's extraordinary life…it powerfully illustrates how much perseverance is needed to achieve fundamental social change." —***O, The Oprah Magazine***

"Powell's drawings in *March* combine the epic sweep of history with the intimate personal details of memoir, and bring Lewis's story to life in a way that feels entirely unfamiliar. *March* is shaping up to be a major work of history and graphic literature." —***Slate***

"Essential reading…*March* is a moving and important achievement…the story of a true American superhero." —***USA Today***

"There is perhaps no more important modern book to be stocked in American school libraries than *March*." —***Washington Post***

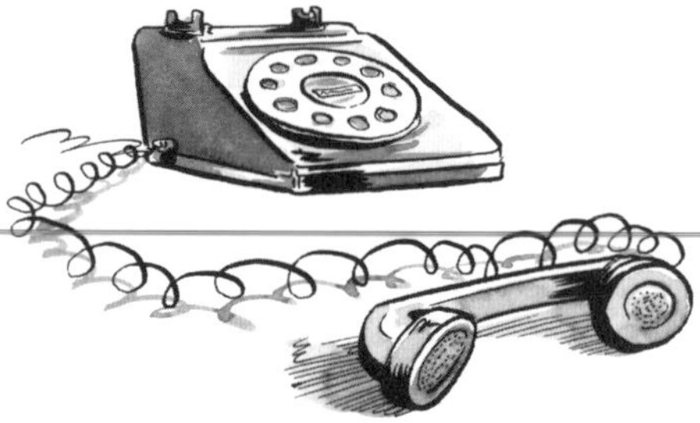

Good Trouble Productions
Principals: Andrew Aydin, Kelly Sue DeConnick, Valentine De Landro, Matt Fraction, and Vaughn Shinall
Managing Editor: Lauren Sankovitch
Production and Design: Chris Ross
Research: Joshua Rogin, Ed Hula, Olivia Blackwood, Vaughn Shinall, Turner Lobey, and Andrew Aydin
Art Consultant: Laurenn McCubbin

Abrams ComicArts
Editors: Charles Kochman and Charlotte Greenbaum
Art Director: Pamela Notarantonio
Managing Editors: Mary O'Mara and Amy Vreeland
Production Manager: Alison Gervais

Cataloging-in-Publication Data has been applied for and may be obtained from the Library of Congress.

ISBN 978-1-4197-3069-6
B&N ISBN 978-1-4197-5961-1

Written by John Lewis and Andrew Aydin
Art by L. Fury with Nate Powell
Lettering by Chris Ross and Nate Powell

Printed and bound in U.S.A.

10 9 8 7 6 5 4 3 2

ABRAMS The Art of Books
195 Broadway, New York, NY 10007
abramsbooks.com

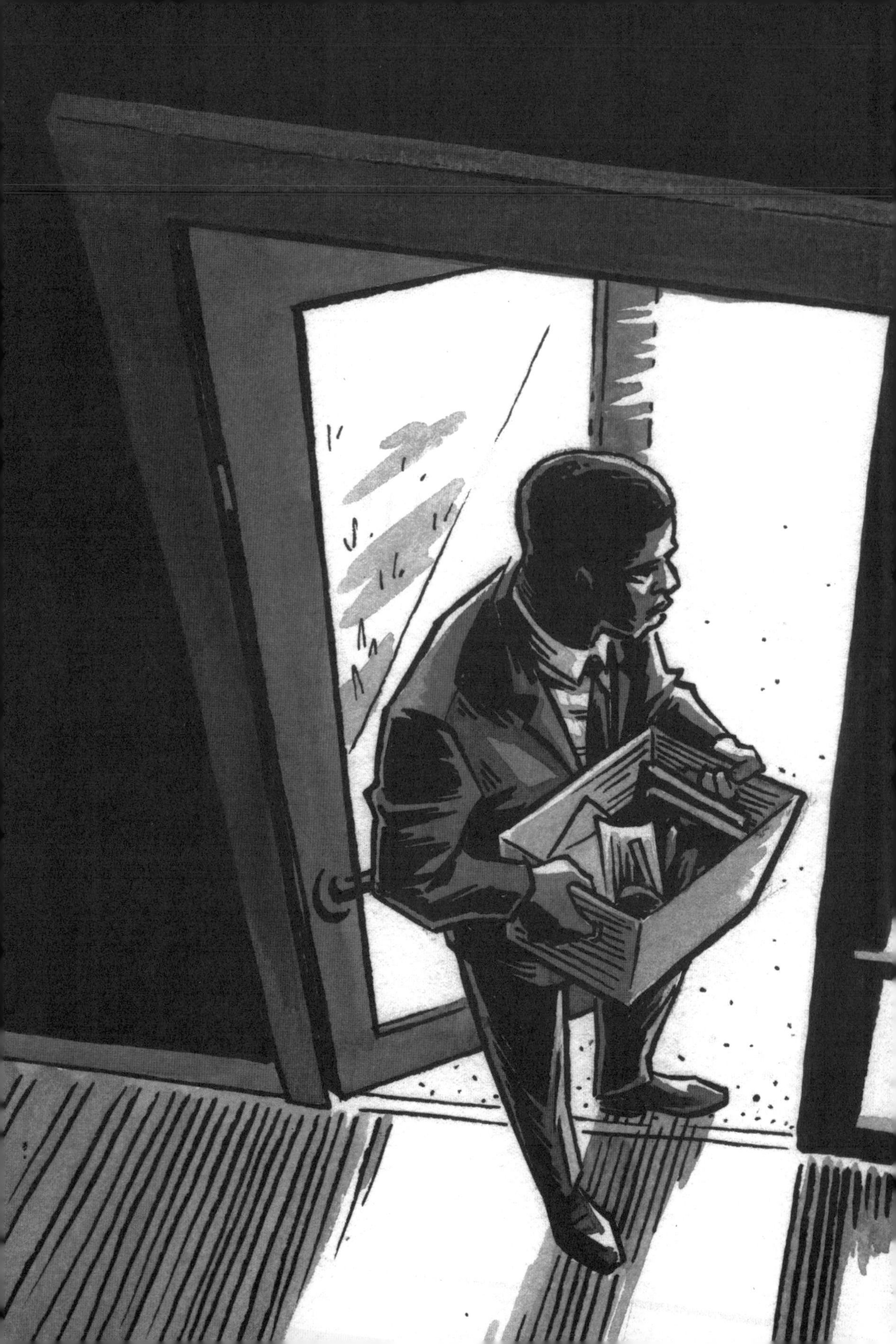